D1416741

communication
FOR
families
IN
CRISIS

PETER LANG
New York • Washington, D.C./Baltimore • Bern
Frankfurt • Berlin • Brussels • Vienna • Oxford

communication
FOR
families
IN
CRISIS

theories, research, strategies

EDITED BY

Fran C. Dickson and Lynne M. Webb

PETER LANG
New York • Washington, D.C./Baltimore • Bern
Frankfurt • Berlin • Brussels • Vienna • Oxford

Library of Congress Cataloging-in-Publication Data

Communication for families in crisis: theories, research, strategies / edited
by Fran C. Dickson, Lynne M. Webb.
p. cm.
Includes bibliographical references and index.
1. Communication in families. 2. Emergency management. 3. Communication
in families. I. Dickson, Fran C. II. Webb, Lynne M.
HQ734.C642   646.7'8—dc23   2011037900
ISBN 978-1-4331-1101-3 (hardcover)
ISBN 978-1-4331-1102-0 (paperback)
ISBN 978-1-4539-0522-7 (e-book)

Bibliographic information published by **Die Deutsche Nationalbibliothek**.
Die Deutsche Nationalbibliothek lists this publication in the "Deutsche
Nationalbibliografie"; detailed bibliographic data is available
on the Internet at http://dnb.d-nb.de/.

The paper in this book meets the guidelines for permanence and durability
of the Committee on Production Guidelines for Book Longevity
of the Council of Library Resources.

From Fran C. Dickson:

To my mother, Marion Ruth Dickson,
who taught me how to navigate life's crises with
strength and dignity.

From Lynne M. Webb:

To the ones I loved and lost, to my angels,
and the generations of wisdom I inherited from them:
My son, Reed J. Moberly
My brother, Charles G. McGovern
My father, Charles R. McGovern
My aunts, Gerry McGovern and Margaret Harris Knapp
My maternal grandparents, George and Beulah May Hefner Harris
My fraternal grandparents, James and Mary Madeline Zimmerman
McGovern

Table of Contents

Foreword

Families in Crucibles: Toward a Communication Perspective on Helping Families in Crises

John P. Caughlin

In the first chapter of this volume, Webb and Dickson suggest that the publication of this book demonstrates that scholarship on family communication has achieved an important level of maturity. I concur. Just a few decades ago, researchers interested in family communication had to argue for the importance of family communication as a distinct research context. Now Webb and Dickson are able to start with the presumption that communication researchers understand that families and family communication are important. Consequently, this volume can immediately begin with the substantive issue at hand: What is the role of communication in helping families manage crises? As Webb and Dickson point out, the production of volumes focusing on specialized topics (as this book does) demonstrates that scholarship by family communication scholars has become diverse and rich.

Yet, the emergence of this volume represents more than the increasing richness of the literature in general; it also reflects an important addition to the main agenda of family communication scholarship. Traditionally, most family communication research fits with a statement in Vangelisti's (2004) preface to the *Handbook of Family Communication*: "the family is the crucible of society" (p. ix). This broad statement reflects the myriad ways families affect their members and vice versa. Thinking about the family as the crucible of society is reflected in most extant research by family communication scholars, which focuses on questions like how marital communication influences partners' satisfaction, how parenting helps socialize new family members, how family members make sense of their lives, how particular family relations or forms influence family communication and family members, and so forth.

As this volume demonstrates, there recently has been a noticeable increase in family communication research examining what happens when a family confronts crisis. It has become routine, for example, for the program at the National Communication Association convention to include multiple papers (and sometimes multiple panels) on how family members cope with various health crises. Such scholarship indicates that family communication researchers are intent on putting a new twist on Vangelisti's statement: Although families remain a crucible of society, the current volume easily could have been called "families in society's crucibles." Communication scholars undoubtedly will continue to be interested in overall connections between family communication and family well-being, but there is now a distinct additional focus on understanding what happens to families when they encounter extremely difficult circumstances.

I applaud the editors of this book for bringing these chapters together and the authors of these chapters for engaging in research that seeks to understand real problems that real families encounter. I also was impressed that the editors asked the authors of each chapter to explicitly discuss applied implications of their research, describing the "best practices" for communication during these crises. This move toward direct applications of family communication scholarship is an exciting development.

Because the current volume is likely to portend increased interest in researching families communicating during crises, it is useful to consider the challenges that scholars may encounter as research in this area becomes more common and prominent. It is impossible to predict all the potential pitfalls, but based on scholarship in the larger discipline, it is possible to foresee some potential challenges. I discuss three such challenges here.

Understanding Specific Crises without Becoming Too Theoretically Narrow

The research in this volume examines a number of specific crises, ranging from the death of a child (Johnson & Webb), to a family member being deployed for war (Maguire & Sahlstein), to various health crises and economic crises. Collectively, these crises pose very heterogeneous difficulties for families. Given such heterogeneity, knowing what communication challenges confront families in a given crisis often will tell us little about what a family will encounter in a different crisis.

Research on how couples manage one partner's illness makes this point clearly. Goldsmith, Lindholm, and Bute (2006), for example, studied how couples cope with one partner having a serious cardiac event. One communicative challenge that the patients' partners faced was how to encourage the medically recommended dietary changes without coming across as too controlling or nagging. This challenge is linked to the specifics of the disease and treatment; that is, the same issue would probably not be relevant in most other circumstances involving a patient and a partner. For example, a partner encouraging a breast cancer patient to continue with her recommended treatment would not be viewed as nagging, at least not in the same way that a partner of a heart disease patient may be viewed when telling his or her partner to order fish instead of a cheeseburger at a restaurant. Health crises, and the best communicative practices for coping with them, need to be understood in situ.

The need to understand crises in situ, however, does not mean that communication scholars should come to each circumstance as if we know nothing about communication generally. Ideally, scholars would be able to examine the specifics of a crisis while still being able to draw upon existing knowledge, and they would to be able say something that has theoretical value beyond the particular context. This is difficult. Research that does an excellent job of making concrete and applied differences is often subject to criticism that it is not theoretical enough. Conversely, scholars who attempt to examine an existing theory or model in a new context are sometimes accused of not knowing enough about the context to understand what is really important.

The challenges of understanding a context and also contributing broadly to theory are both practical and theoretical. On the practical side, no one scholar is likely to be fully trained to do both. This means that collaboration is probably essential to fulfill the long-term promise implied by this volume. I was therefore very pleased to see that several of the chapters used multidisciplinary teams, bringing clinical and nursing perspectives to the analysis. The theoretical problem is more vexing because most communication theories have focused more on generalizable principles than on understanding the nuances of a particular context. The few theories that focus on specific contexts tend to shy away from making broad statements about how communication operates.

There are, of course, some productive ways to deal with this problem, and I discuss two here. First, scholars can put the understanding of a specific socially important problem in the foreground and then draw upon existing theories to help inform how we should go about trying to understand and address that problem. This strategy typically involves borrowing useful ideas and concepts from more than one broad theory or literature and then making a more specific argument about the problem at hand. Sometimes readers of this type of research mistakenly think that it is not theoretical because it does not begin with a summary of some single theoretical framework that drives the entire study. This is an unfortunate misconception of what it means to be theoretical. Indeed, I would argue that in many cases the ability to integrate theoretical ideas from several sources is more impressive (and often more useful) than rote application of a single theory. The Maguire and Sahlstein chapter is a great example of this type of theoretical work addressing a specific problem. Their chapter uses the literature on stress and stressors as well as research on communal coping to provide a general understanding of coping processes. Then Maguire and Sahlstein use the existing literature to make an argument for which specific features of the military context are likely to be most important for understanding stress and coping. This is a theoretical argument about how to usefully understand the specific problem at hand, and it provides an example of how family communication researchers can connect specific applied problems to broader theoretical ideas and understandings.

Another strategy for addressing the need to be both theoretically broad yet pertinent to specific applied problems is to use theories that provide us with a general mechanism for thinking about specific situations. One theory that is exceptional in this regard is Goldsmith's (2004) rhetorical/normative model. Her model is specific in the sense that it focuses attention on the communicative challenges of particular types of circumstances. It is also general in the way it makes a theoretical argument for what counts as best practices in communication: Sophisticated communication involves enacting the acts and strategies that best manage the multiple (and often competing) communicative challenges in a particular situation. Goldsmith's model provides a general theoretical mechanism for thinking about particular circumstances, and it also highlights the need to understand the specifics. Even if Goldsmith's model itself is not adopted widely, the way that it addresses both the general and the specific illustrates that scholars do not need to choose between understanding a context and being theoretical.

Retaining Unique Communication Perspective

When communication scholars first began to study family communication, there were already substantial bodies of research on family interaction in other disciplines (Caughlin, Koerner, Schrodt, & Fitzpatrick, 2011). Over time, communication scholars brought a distinct perspective to family interaction. Although they used many different theories and methods, family communication scholars shared certain research foci, like being interested in features of messages and the meaning of these messages in particular contexts. The interest in messages and meaning is in contrast with most scholarship about family interaction from disciplines like psychology, family studies, and sociology (Caughlin, 2010).

Although family communication scholars have articulated their own perspective, there is a danger in moving into research areas that previously have been dominated by scholars from other disciplines. The impact of crises on families has been a major topic of research among family studies scholars and family sociologists. It is natural to look to this existing research to help understand family crises, but family communication scholars should be wary of being too influenced by the conceptualizations and measures of communication that exist outside the field. There are certainly exceptions, but scholars from outside the discipline of communication frequently have an impoverished view of communication. Often they summarize family interaction as a single variable representing either frequency or affect.

There are reasons to worry that interacting with other fields can lead communication researchers to forget their unique perspective.

For example, some of the more advanced techniques for analyzing data, such as structural equations models (SEM), are becoming more common among interpersonal and family communication scholars. Yet, these techniques do not lend themselves well to the kinds of thinking that has distinguished communication scholars. Using SEM, for example, pushes one toward thinking in terms of dimensions of communication and tends to make it difficult to think in terms such as those implied by Goldsmith's (2004) model, which points out that the effectiveness of a message depends on how well it is adapted to the particular demands of a given communicative circumstance. Outside influences explain why it is becoming more common to see communication researchers reduce communication constructs into a small number of variables (or latent constructs) and sometimes even into a single variable like frequency (e.g., frequency of online communication). It is good to borrow any methods or concepts from other fields that are useful, but as a discipline we must retain our comparatively nuanced way of thinking about communication, taking into account specific features of messages as well as the aspects of context that influence meaning.

Fortunately, the current book gives us some great examples that demonstrate why it is so important to conceptualize communication in nuanced ways. Amason and her colleagues, for example, make a distinction between feeling supported and actually receiving "any particular type of support." The supportive communication that was really helpful was that which enabled "the person to better understand the crisis, accept the cause of the crisis, and ultimately make decisions to move beyond the crisis in a positive direction." Amason et al.'s argument implies that it is not the frequency of support that matters; instead what matters most is the extent to which the support elicits more positive framing. The chapter by Amason and colleagues, as well as the collection of chapters in this volume as a whole, should serve as evidence of the value of thinking about nuances in communication.

Avoiding Overly Simplistic Advice

The authors of the chapters were asked to provide practical advice about "best practices." This is an exciting development, but there is a difficulty in offering concrete advice: The more one makes specific advice that is easy to follow, the more likely it is to oversimplify communication. The literature from clinical scholars and therapists is full of straightforward advice like "seven secrets" to more successful family communication. Much of this advice makes sense at first glance; for example, one of the most common advisements in books about relationships and families is the seemingly reasonable suggestion of having open communication.

One admirable attribute of the current volume is that its advice is not so simplistic. In their introductory chapter, for example, Webb and Dickson note that many of the chapters discussed the importance of open communication in certain circumstances, but that does not mean family members should talk about absolutely everything. Instead, it means that there are certain crises that can be best coped with through expanded disclosure about particular kinds of issues, thoughts, and feelings.

The advice implied by Webb and Dickson is more complex than the usual "seven steps" type of advice, and it is more congruent with what we know about family communication. Consider, for example, Buzzanell and Turner's chapter on family narratives about job loss. Buzzanell and Turner saw cases in which families effectively coped with the job loss through talking about the situation, but they also recognized that there were some benefits of not talking. Sometimes there are both positive and negative effects of either discussing or not discussing a particular aspect of a crisis, which makes deciding whether it is a good idea to discuss a particular issue extraordinarily complex. Buzzanell and Turner noted that Brad was so good at shielding his family from the details of the financial situation that it seemed successful at lessening their feelings of stress. This is clearly a benefit to the other family members (at least in the short term), but it might come at a cost to Brad and might not be sustainable if the unemployment continued indefinitely. Clearly, not talking openly has both potential costs and benefits to Brad's family. Of course, as Buzzanell and Turner's chapter implies, the effects of expanded (or decreased) disclosure do not only depend on how much information is discussed: Exactly how a situation is discussed also matters. There are more and less functional ways to frame a situation, and people's ability to construct a positive narrative may be more important than the absolute amount of information exchanged.

On a related note, Webb and Dickson's critical discussion of what is meant by openness should be helpful to our field as we move forward. Family studies scholars often discuss openness as if its meaning were obvious, but it has various meanings. Openness does not have to mean actually talking frequently about a topic. Galvin, Grill, Arntson, and Kinahan's chapter provides a good example of this. They interviewed adult survivors of pediatric cancer (and one of the survivor's parents), and found that these families do not discuss the cancer experience frequently anymore. They do, however, sometimes discuss is when there is a current health issue that triggers the conversation. This suggests that "being open" in these families may mean willingness to talk when necessary rather than actually talking frequently.

There are other possible meanings of being open. For example, one study about how parents and adolescents discuss sex demonstrated that when family members say they are completely open, they rarely mean actually talking about sex frequently or in detail (Kirkman, Rosenthal, & Feldman, 2005). For some family members, openness means being willing to talk with adolescents if they have questions (and they often do not); for others it means that parents should be honest if asked direct questions, but the family should not focus on the topic; for still others openness means talking about issues unless they elicit embarrassment.

The nuances of what openness can mean provide just one example of the complexities of family communication. These complexities imply that what counts as good advice about communication is inherently situational. The scholars in this volume were wise to focus on particular situations because specific types of situations have specific kinds of communication challenges. Even within a particular kind of crisis, each family may face unique communication challenges, meaning there is a danger in making broad recommendations. Even advice that is usually good may be a bad idea in a particular crisis for a particular family. Given this, the ideal strategy may be to teach people how to think about the difficulties in a particular situation and how to consider the implications of different communicative acts. This is a difficult task, but it is one that communication scholars like the authors of this book are in the best position to accomplish.

Conclusion

The contributors to this volume are on the leading edge of an exciting development in family communication: research that begins to systematically understand how families cope with various crises. Clearly, no single volume will be able to answer every question about such a complex subject, but these chapters are an excellent beginning. They advance our theoretical focus, and they also provide useful advice for families experiencing crises.

This book is also an important part of a larger trend that is seeing family communication scholars beginning to address real problems faced by families. There is still much work to be done, and scholars addressing such issues should be mindful of the kinds of challenges and pitfalls I mentioned above. Addressing such research challenges will not be easy, but there is reason for optimism. The current volume illustrates and advances the distinct perspective of family communication scholars, and if we continue to focus on our unique expertise, we can make important differences for families.

References

Caughlin, J. P. (2010). A multiple goals theory of personal relationships: Conceptual integration and program overview. *Journal of Social and Personal Relationships, 27,* 824–848.

Caughlin, J. P., Koerner, A. F., Schrodt, P., & Fitzpatrick, M. A. (2011). Interpersonal communication in family relationships. In M. L. Knapp & J. A. Daly (Eds.), *Handbook of interpersonal communication* (4th ed.). Thousand Oaks, CA: Sage.

Goldsmith, D. J. (2004). *Communicating social support.* New York: Cambridge University Press.

Goldsmith, D. J., Lindholm, K. A., & Bute, J. J. (2006). Dilemmas of talk about lifestyle changes among couples coping with a cardiac event. *Social Science and Medicine, 63,* 2079–2090.

Kirkman, M., Rosenthal, D. A., & Feldman, S. S. (2005). Being open with your mouth shut: The meaning of "openness" in family communication about sexuality. *Sex Education, 5,* 49–66.

Parks, M. R. (1982). Ideology in interpersonal communication: Off the couch and into the world. In M. Burgoon (Ed.), *Communication yearbook 6* (pp. 79–107). Beverly Hills, CA: Sage.

Vangelisti, A. L. (2004). *Handbook of family communication.* Mahwah, NJ: Erlbaum.

Chapter 1

Effective Family Communication for Coping with Crises

Lynne M. Webb and Fran C. Dickson

Families inevitably experience crises. Recent events including the Gulf Oil Spill, Hurricane Katrina, and the Iraq War demonstrate how trouble simply "happens." Internal events such as divorce, death, and illness also can strike unexpectedly and threaten the well-being of the family. While people typically cannot control nor prevent negative events, they often turn to their families for support as they attempt to manage the aftermath of such crises. Effective management of unexpected negative events necessarily involves effective crisis communication within families. This book provides a collection of carefully selected essays describing how families effectively communicate during crises.

For purposes of this book, we adopted Baxter and Braithwaite's (2006) definition of family as "a social group of two or more persons characterized by ongoing interdependence with long-term commitments that stem from blood, law, or affection" (p. 3) and their definition of communication as "symbol use between persons through verbal and nonverbal means" (p. 3). We conceptualized a crisis as an unexpected, negative event that does not allow the family to continue functioning in their usual manner; further, we note that most families are unprepared for crises and find addressing such circumstances both challenging and stressful.

This chapter introduces the book via five major sections. First, we describe the development of the scholarly specialty area of family communication to provide an understanding of the intellectual development that lead to this book. Second, we describe the book as a whole—its development, goals, and contributions. Third, we advise scholars, teachers, and practitioners on how to use this book. Fourth, we preview the individual chapters. Finally, we describe effective coping strategies for families in crisis.

A History of the Development of the Specialty Area of Family Communication

Most communication scholars link the specialized area of scholarship known today as family communication to the development of the more general research area of interpersonal communication. Webb and Thompson-Hayes (2002) as well as Whitchurch and Dickson (1999) dated the intellectual development of interpersonal communication, as a distinct area of study, to the publication of Watzlawick, Beavin, and Jackson's 1967 treatise *Pragmatics of Human Communication*, a theoretical commentary focused on marital and family communication. Galvin (2001) noted that in the 1960s interpersonal communication scholarship began to focus on long-term relationships, including marriage. Family communication as a specialty distinct from interpersonal communication gained formal recognition in the mid-1970s with the appearance of two essays: Bochner's "Family Communication Research" (1974) and "Conceptual Frontiers in the Study of Communication in Families" (1976). These essays articulated a distinct identity for the specialty.

In the mid-1970s, articles on family communication began to appear regularly in communication journals (e.g., Allen & Chaffee, 1977; Leckenby, 1977; Sheinkopf, 1973; Walters & Stone, 1971) and on conference programs in the academic discipline of communication (e.g., Chaffee, 1978; Fontes et al., 1973; Moore & Moschis, 1978; Sheinkopf, 1971; Sheinkopf & Atkins, 1972). Barnes (1977) edited the first special issue of a communication journal on family communication. In the late 1970s and early 1980s, the *Journal of Communication* published relevant symposia on marital communication (i.e., Beier & Sternberg, 1977; Sternberg & Beier, 1977; Young, Korner, Gill, & Beier, 1977) and on family communication (Bavelas & Segal, 1982; Canter & Reilly, 1982; Steier, Stanton, & Todd, 1982). In 1984, the National Communication Association (NCA) Research Board and the Northwestern University School of Speech cosponsored a summer conference titled "The Family Communication Research Conference" (Yerby, 1985).

Scholarship in family communication facilitated the development of a distinct organizational unit on family communication within the National Communication Association; sponsored programs first appeared at the 1989 meeting. In 1995, the *Journal of Applied Communication Research* published the first special issue on family communication in a *national* communication journal (Whitchurch & Webb, 1995). During the same time period, specialty books on family communication began to appear on the market (e.g., Socha & Stamp's (1995) *Parents, Children, and Communication*). Essays such as Socha, Sanchez-Hucles, Bromley, and Kelly's (1995) "Invisible Parents and Children: Exploring African-American Parent-Child Communication" as well as books such as Socha and Diggs' (1999) *Communication, Race, and Family* brought issues of diversity and family communication into sharp focus. By the mid-1990, "family communication in the communication discipline encompassed scholarship on family units and various subunits" (Whitchurch & Webb, 1995, p. 239). Finally, a distinct journal on the subject, the *Journal of Family Communication*, published its premier issue in the fall of 2001.

Courses in family communication began appearing in college curricula across the country during the 1970s and early 1980s (Whitchurch & Dickson, 1999). Galvin (2001) credited Communication faculty at Michigan State University, Temple University, University of Denver, Cleveland State University, University of Wisconsin at Madison, and Northwestern University with pioneering the pedagogy of this specialized area. Because there were no textbooks on family communication per se, instructors assembled readings from various disciplines, including communication, psychology, family therapy, and sociology. Early classics in family studies, such as Christensen's *Handbook of Marriage and the Family* (1964) also served as assigned texts (Whitchurch, 1992).

Paralleling the intellectual development of the family communication area, and the introduction of family communication courses, a body of scholarship developed in family communication pedagogy. Goldberg and Goldberg (1976) articulated the first published curriculum structure for a course in family communication. Other essays on the pedagogy of family communication soon followed (Galvin, 1979, 1985; Glaser & Glaser, 1977; Goldberg, 1978; Gonzalez, 1991; Kramer, Arbuthnot, Gordon, Rousis, & Hoza, 1998; Long & Grant, 1992; Vangelisti, 1991; Whitchurch, 1992, 1993).

Despite research and pedagogical interest through the 1970s, the first collegiate textbook that focused solely on the topic of family communication was not published until 1982 (i.e., Galvin & Brommel, 1982). Subsequent decades witnessed the publication of multiple competitors as well as reviews of these texts. In a traditional book-review essay, Whitchurch (1992) reviewed the four undergraduate textbooks in family communication available during the early 1990s (i.e., Beebe & Masterson, 1986; Galvin & Brommel, 1991; Pearson, 1989; Yerby, Buerkel-Rothfus, & Bochner, 1990). A decade later, Amason (2002) replicated and extended Whitchurch's 1992 work, again providing a comprehensive book-review essay of the four undergraduate textbooks in family communication available at the dawn of the 21st century (i.e., Galvin & Brommel, 2000; Noller & Fitzpatrick, 1993; Turner & West, 1998; Yerby, Buerkel-Rothfus, & Bochner, 1995). Two years later, Webb, Bourgerie, Schaper, Johnson, Dubbs, Mountain et al. (2004) provided a content analysis of the latest versions of the same set of four books (i.e., Galvin & Brommel, 2000; Noller & Fitzpatrick, 1993; Turner & West, 2002; Yerby, Buerkel-Rothfus, & Bochner, 1995), describing coverage of gender and diversity issues. As we begin the second decade of the 21st century, five undergraduate textbooks are available in family communication (Arnold, 2007; Floyd & Morman, 2006; Galvin, Byland, & Brommel, 2007; Le Poire, 2005; Segrin & Flora, 2011; Turner & West, 2006).

We believed that the communication discipline did not need another generalized textbook on family communication, given the many wonderful textbooks currently available (Arnold, 2007; Floyd & Morman, 2006; Galvin, Byland, & Brommel, 2007; Le Poire, 2005; Turner & West, 2006). Instead, we desired to develop a specialty book that provided a narrower consideration of family communication. We wanted to develop a book for the sophisticated reader—for scholars, graduate students, and professional social service providers. We wanted a collection of chapters that were theory-based, but ultimately practical in that they provided research-based advice on how families might communicate most effectively in the face of crises.

The Book: History, Development, and Contributions
History of the Project and Development of the Book

This book began during a casual conversation in a hotel room at an NCA (National Communication Association) convention. If you were to develop a book for a graduate course in family communication, what would be the topic of the book? Our answers were identical: We wanted to gather essays for a book about the saving grace and healing power of communication within families as they faced a myriad of crises. Worth noting, a few sentences into the conversation, we simply began tossing around titles, because we were on the very same page about content and form.

We almost immediately wrote our call for chapter proposals and quickly posted it far and wide. We also wrote to a few prolific family communication scholars with a history of producing applied scholarship about family communication during crises. We received 26 proposals. That summer, we met in Boulder, Colorado, and collaboratively selected the chapters. We organized a tentative Table of Contents that never changed from that moment to this. Within a week, we drafted our book proposal.

Our Vision for the Book

From the beginning, we imagined an edited volume of original, cutting-edge research focusing on applied communication. We wanted accurate information about how communication enables families to beat the odds, to survive, and to thrive, despite the worst life could throw at them: loss of homes, jobs, spouses, children, even identity. We proposed an edited volume that covered the intellectual ground at the intersection of two important bodies of scholarship–family communication and crisis communication.

Focus. This book provides a theoretically rich, image of how families use communication to cope effectively with unexpected crises. The book offers an expansive approach to its succinct topic via this overview chapter followed by 14 research reports that have never previously been published. Each of the next chapters presents a competitively-selected report of original research, that describes a distinct crisis (e.g., pediatric cancer, job loss, infidelity), articulates a distinct theoretical approach (e.g., narrative theory, dialectical theory), and identifies communication strategies (i.e., best practices) that enable families to cope effectively with crisis. All chapters were written specifically for this book.

Scholarly contribution. The body of research in family communication has grown by leaps and bounds such that a sufficient body of scholarship exists to warrant an edited volume of essays on a specialized topic within the broader knowledge base on family communication. Our book adds to the literature of the discipline by bringing together multiple ideas, topics, theories, and authors addressing effective family communication during crises. We hope our book inspires and facilitates further growth of the family communication area of the discipline of communication.

Specialized seminars in family communication with specific content focus have become increasingly common. The number of positions available for recent PhD graduates who specialize in family communication is increasing–thus augmenting pressure for multiple seminars in the area of family communication. Professors teaching specialized seminars in family communication must select books and readings that reasonably represent the diversity of scholarship in family communication in terms of theory, methodology, and relational focus, while maintaining unity in subject matter. Our book accomplishes that task by offering a text with an appropriately narrow focus containing 14 reports of original research from a diversity of methodological and theoretical approaches as well as relational foci.

First of its kind. We wanted this book to be a first of its kind in multiple ways. We reasoned that because scholarship in family communication was growing at such a rapid rate, it was only a matter of time before specialty books and courses began appearing in multiple narrower subject areas within the broad family communication area. Only a few specialized books have been published: Socha and Diggs (1999) treatise on issues of race and family communication (Socha & Diggs, 1999) as well as four books on communication with children (Meyer, 2003; Socha & Stamp, 1995, 2009; Socha & Yingling, 2010). We wanted a book in our interest area, family communication during crises, to be next to appear on the scene. We believed that if we could develop a readable book, accessible to graduate students, professors, and practitioners serving families during difficult times, that the book would encourage the development of graduate courses in family communication area beyond simply the "general course" in family communication as well as encourage further research about effective family communication during crises. Thus, our goals were twofold: (1) to inspire further research and teaching on the subject and (2) to inform scholars and practitioners unfamiliar with this body of research about its existence as well as its enormous potential to assist us in understanding effective family communication in the 21st century.

Debunk the myths. The popular press emphasizes negative aspects of family communication during crises (e.g., child abuse, families separated after tsunamis). However, we believed such a depiction is misleading as it fails to describe how the vast majority of families employ effective communication to recognize and address difficulties as well as to develop, maintain and reconfigure family relationships. We wanted our book to be among the first to contradict these negative, popular notions, not once or twice, but systematically, with chapter after chapter examining diverse bodies of research during a wide variety of crises.

Theory-based chapters. We wanted to develop, for the first time, an edited volume of research reports on family communication from a multi-theoretical perspective. Essays in this book are draw from diverse theoretical perspectives including adult development theory, attribution theory, communal coping theory, dialectical theory, family stress models, the theory of family communication environments, narrative theory, social constructionism, structurating activity theory, symbolic interactionism, system theory, and uncertainty reduction theory. A special issue of the *Journal of Family Communication* (2004) focused on theory and Baxter and Braithwaite published *Engaging Theories in Family Communication: Multiple Perspectives* in 2006. However, we could locate no previously published collection of research reports on family communication, based on a diversity of theories. Our book provides multiple, in-depth discussions of communication theory vis-à-vis empirical findings. Indeed, we designed our book to integrate theory with recent research findings in applied lines of research (e.g., loss of a child, military deployment).

Represent the diversity of the research. We wanted each chapter to describe relevant theory and research regarding *one distinct crisis* and the successful family communication that can surround coping with such crises (e.g., homelessness). For this reason, we selected chapters that (1) examine a diverse array of crises (children with disabilities, death of a child, homelessness, infertility, infidelity, job loss, mothers with breast cancer, parental deployment, pediatric cancer, post-hurricane survival) that (2) analyzed interactions at a wide variety of communicative levels (words, language, interacts, transactions, relational stages, communication patterns across relationships and groups of relationships), and that (3) examined messages communicated in a wide variety of family relationships (e.g., marital partners, parent-child, sibling-sibling). Additionally, the selected essays report on research from a variety of sources including grant-supported research, scholar's independent research, as well as thesis and dissertation research. The collection as a whole addresses the communication behavior of family members across the life span from toddlers to frail elders. The chapters represent a plurality of theoretical orientations and research methods. In sum, we elected to examine the phenomenon under study in its complexity. Indeed, at every turn, we embraced opportunities to expand rather than limit our examination of successful family communication during crises.

Organizing the diversity. We settled on an organizational scheme for the chapters that we believe provides a fair representation of the diversity of existing approaches to the study of family communication during crises. The chapters address three types of crises: (1) *relational crises* (infidelity, infertility, parental deployment, death of a child), (2) *health crises* (mothers with breast cancer, children with disabilities, pediatric cancer), and (3) *economic crises* (job loss, homelessness, post-hurricane survival). These chapters are united by a common perspective–the perspective of the applied communication scholar.

How to Use This Book

A Word to Scholars about This Volume

Our book adds to the literature of the discipline by offering the first collection of essays on crisis communication in the family. Given that families almost inevitably experience crises, it benefits researchers, practitioners, and humanity to discover how families might communicate most effectively in such situations.

A Word about Using This Volume as a Textbook

Previous family communication books were innovative at the time of their publication and do an outstanding job covering the breadth of family theory, research, and praxis. In contrast to a typical family communication textbook, this book offers a specialized, in-depth look at one focused area of study—family communication during crises.

Our volume is appropriate for courses in two subject areas: (a) family communication and (b) family studies. In family studies, the textbooks tend to assume an intervention perspective for coping with stress and crises, offering family therapists strategies for helping families navigate these crises. The family communication books focus on the communicative and/or interactional processes. The book you hold in your hand fits into *both* of these descriptive categories.

To Graduate Instructors in Communication. The idea for the book arose from one of the coeditor's difficulties locating readings for a graduate seminar on family communication in non-typical situations, such as unexpected crises. While an instructor can pull together a collection of readings on topics such as homelessness, military deployment, and families facing medical dilemmas, our book serves as the perfect textbook for such a class.

In multiple ways, our book will assist professors of graduate seminars to cope with the large body of scholarship published in family communication:

1. Our book provides focus (i.e., how families effectively communicate to manage crises) for a narrowly drawn family communication seminar.

2. Our book would be an obvious choice of textbook for a course on Applied Family Communication, perhaps supplemented by a readings list of additional research reports.

3. Our book suggests multiple frameworks (e.g., normal development versus unexpected changes in the family) for a broader seminar in family communication. In this scenario, our book could be used as the text for a significant segment of the class.

4. When an instructor desires to teach a "broad sweep" seminar in family communication that offers a sampling of the theory, research methods, and relational foci (marital dyad, sibling interactions, parent-child interactions), our book could serve as one of multiple texts.

In sum, our proposed volume is designed to function as the core text for a specialized graduate seminar in family communication and as a supplemental text for (a) broad-based graduate seminars in family communication and (b) advanced undergraduate classes and honors seminars in family communication.

To Graduate Instructors in Family Studies. Professors of family studies seminars on change and stress may find our book a useful supplement, as it expands their traditional subject matter by focusing on how families cope successfully with crises through effective communication among family members. Family psychology seminars may find our book a useful addition in expanding their traditional focus on dysfunction and intervention to include functional, communicative coping mechanisms as well as an examination of internal family dynamics.

To Undergraduate Instructors in Communication. Our book could be used as a supplemental text with a traditional undergraduate textbook in an undergraduate senior-level class or honors seminar in family communication, when the instructor would like students to read interesting and well-written examples of original research.

Selecting the Chapters

We selected chapters from submissions in response to an open call for chapter proposals; the selected essays were written by prominent family communication scholars presenting their most recent research.

The call was submitted to multiple venues (websites, listservs, news-letters) of five professional associations of communication scholars at the international, national, and regional levels. Additionally, we invited five scholars who write extensively about family communica-tion to submit chapter proposals; three accepted our invitation. Each of the coeditors proposed a chapter. In sum, we received and re-viewed 26 submissions. Based on our previous extensive experience as reviewers for journals, editors of special issues, and authors of multiple book chapters in edited volumes, we selected 14 of the submissions for inclusion in our volume based on the following criteria:

- Focus on the topic at hand.
- Quality of the described execution of the project's research methodology.
- Quality of the writing in the proposal and in the authors' ex-emplary previous publications.
- Credible explanation of effective family communication to ad-dress the examined crisis successfully.
- Quality of the tentative bibliographies for the chapters.
- Authors' experience as scholars, judged by the submitters' vi-tae.

Our Author List

The authors of the selected chapters are the best family scholars writing about crisis communication today. They includes new, "rising stars" in the scholarly world of family communication as well as a sampling of the best established family communication scholars. Together they comprise an eclectic mix of communication scholars who vary in age, sex, geographic location, and type of affiliated institution (public versus private). In addition, they represent diverse career stages from graduate student to tenured full professors. Our author list includes former and/or present provosts, deans, associate deans, department chairs, and directors of schools of communication as well as full, associate, and assistant professors—and their graduate students. This diversity benefits our edited volume as the authors provide diverse viewpoints that we believe will appeal to readers desiring multiple perspectives.

Previewing the Book: Abstracts and Descriptions of Chapters

Ultimately, it matters little what we set out to do or how we came to our decisions. What will matter is the opinion of the readers and users of this edited volume. We hope that users of this book find the chapters useful in augmenting their understanding of how family members communicate effectively during crises. Here is our synopsis of the chapters that we found so compelling:

1. *Effective Family Communication for Coping with Crises*. Lynne M. Webb and Fran C. Dickson. This chapter explains the book's origins, chapter selection process, organizational schema, and summarizes the "best practices" sections of subsequent chapters, identifying effective family communication practices during crises.

Section One: Relational Crises

This section highlights relational crises (e.g., infidelity, infertility, and deployment) that often result in the re-definition of family relationships through communication.

2. *Family Communication and Effectively Addressing Infertility*. Patricia Amason, Megan L. Wilson, and Justin T. Rusinowski. The chapter reports on the thematic analysis of interviews with 25 infertile informants. Using uncertainty reduction theory, the chapter describes informants' choices of information sources and sources of emotional support.

3. *Parental Infidelity: Adult Children's Attributions for Parents' Extramarital Relationships*. Allison R. Thorson. This chapter reports on interviews with 38 adults who knew about their parent's/parents' infidelity. Using attribution theory, the author identifies six attributions for the infidelity: dysfunction/deficiencies; justifications/excuses; restoring credibility/character; "offending" parent blame; "faithful" parent blame, and denial of parent involvement.

4. *And Then He Was a She: Communication Following a Gender-Identity Shift*. Christine Aramburu Alegría and Deborah Ballard-

Reisch. Grounded in symbolic interactionism, schema theory, and exchange theory, this chapter examines the relationship maintenance activities of married couples experiencing the disclosure of transsexualism. Seventeen couples with one natal female partner and one male-to-female transsexual partner completed questionnaires and participated in individual interviews.

5. *In the Line of Fire: Family Management of Acute Stress during Wartime Deployment*. Katheryn Maguire and Erin Sahlstein. The chapter examines the narratives of 41 military wives with husbands deployed in Afghanistan or Iraq between 2003 and 2005. Using a communication-based model of communal coping, the chapter describes how the families communicated effectively to manage both chronic and acute stress before, during, and after the deployment.

6. *Death of a Child: Mothers' Accounts of Interactions with Surviving Children*. Kayla B. Johnson and Lynne M. Webb. The chapter reports on the thematic analysis of interviews with 20 mothers about communication with their surviving children after the death of a child. Using dialectical theory, the chapter describes the multiple ways mothers' communication is rich with both contrasting to and consistent with their families' past parent-to-child communication practices.

Section Two: Health Crises

This section highlights the communication surrounding health crises in the nuclear family, such as mothers with breast cancer, children with disabilities, and pediatric cancer.

7. *Children with Invisible Disabilities: Communicating to Manage Family Contradictions*. Heather E. Canary. Analysis of interviews with 21 families as well as transcripts of 18 parent-professional meetings reveals the role of contradictions during crises (early stages of recognizing "something is wrong") and coping (incorporating disability and ability into everyday life). Structurating activity theory explains how contradictions serve as generative mechanisms for family system development during crises surrounding a child with invisible disabilities.

8. *"Linked Lives": Mother-Adult Daughter Communication after a Breast Cancer Diagnosis*. Carla L. Fisher and Jon F. Nussbaum. The chapter examines how mothers and daughters communicate follow-

ing the mothers' diagnosis of breast cancer. The chapter employs adult development theory to interpret a turning-points analysis of in-depth, individual interviews with 38 mother-daughter pairs.

9. *Women Coping with Cancer: Family Communication, Conflict, and Support.* Jennifer A. Samp and Tara J. Abbot. Data from a quantitative survey of 49 females with cancer are interpreted via theory on family communication environments.

10. *Beyond the Crisis: Communication between Parents and Children Who Survived Cancer.* Kathleen M. Galvin, Lauren H. Grill, Paul H. Arnston, and Karen E. Kinahan. The chapter examines the long-range impact of childhood cancer on parent-child interactions. Data from interviews with 53 adult survivors and 42 parents conducted an average of 16 years past initial treatment reveal communication patterns ranging from comfortable to avoidant.

11. *Mom Is No Longer My Mom: Adult Children Discuss Their Parents' Acute Health Events.* Kandi L. Walker, Joy L. Hart, Lindsay Della, Mary Z. Ashlock, and Anita Hoag. Using social constructionism, the chapter discusses emergent themes in 16 interviews with adult children who recently managed aging parents' health crises. This chapter examines adult children's relational entailments and the familial implications of their stories.

Section Three: Economic Crises

This section highlights family communication to manage eco-nomic crises, such as job loss, unplanned single-parenthood, and homelessness.

12. *Effective Family Communication and Job Loss: Crafting the Narra-tive for Family Crisis.* Patrice Buzzanell and Lynn H. Turner. Using narrative theory, this chapter analyzes data from seven families who experienced job loss of the primary wage earner. Analysis reveals families' narrative techniques for successfully managing the crisis.

13. *Sibling Alliances in Family Crises: Communication Surrounding Redefinitions of Family.* John H. Nicholson and Steve Duck. This chapter examines the relating practices of siblings and the larger family as they encounter and adapt to parental divorce and widow-hood as well as the economic pressures that often accompany these events. Siblings collectively co-construct, shape, and interpret their

experiences to make sense of parental messages in the wake of significant economic change in the family.

14. *Communicative Challenges of Parenting in Homeless Families*. Fran C. Dickson, Justin Borowsky, Daniel Johnson, Jennifer K. Corti, Kathryn Tiffiani Baldwin, Lucie Lawrence, and Joseph Velasco. Using dialectic theory, the chapter reports on the thematic analysis of 44 semi-structured interviews with homeless parents to discover the parenting strategies they employ and the kinds of conversations they have with their children about their homelessness.

15. *Family Communication Surrounding Emotional Trauma: The Aftermath of Hurricanes*. James M. Honeycutt and Christopher M. Mapp. The chapter reports on interviews with individuals from five families coping with trauma created by recent hurricanes. Using family stress models as interpretive lens, the chapter identifies effective patterns of family communication in the aftermath of the storms.

Effective Coping Strategies for Families in Crisis

We asked each chapter author(s) to end their research report with practical advice for families on how they might communicate effectively in the face of the particular crisis they investigated. We called these sections "Best Practices" and noted that commonalities began to appear across the sections. To investigate the perceived commonalities as well as deduce universal principles of effective crisis communication in families, independent of the specific crisis, we undertook a thematic analysis of the Best Practices sections of our fourteen chapters. In employing thematic analysis, we attempted to identify participants' "recurring similar assertions" (Reinard, 1998, p. 182). Below we describe our methodology as well as our findings.

Methods

The second editor cut and pasted the Best Practices sections from twelve of the fourteen chapters into one large document. The twelve selected chapters were the first twelve revised chapters received by the editors. Next, she read and reread this document three times to discover common themes across the sections. Using a grounded theory approach (Berger & Luckmann, 1967; La Rossa, 2005; Owen, 1984; Strauss & Corbin, 1990), themes emerged from the text rather than imposing category systems on the authors' suggestions. A theme was defined as any idea that appeared in three of more of the sections. The coder marked potential themes in the text during each reading, noting a tentative name for each theme and the relevant lines of text that exemplified the theme. Using a dynamic analysis process, insights from later readings influenced themes and, occasionally, prompted the reinterpretation and revision of themes identified in earlier readings (Charmaz, 1983). Fourteen themes emerged after three careful readings of the document. She then reread the document, noting all incidences of the fourteen themes as well as checking for any additional themes. No additional themes emerged.

Next, the coder wrote the name of each theme on an index card and attempted to categorize the cards in multiple ways, including as steps in a developmental model of coping and as the object of crisis management (i.e., the crisis, the family, the communication). While no clear organization system emerged that readily accounted for the 14 themes, the 14 themes collapsed into 12 themes that eliminated some conceptual overlap. Next, she attempted to arrange the 12 themes in a path model. The model of effective coping depicted in Figure 1.1 readily emerged. Finally, the Best Practices sections from the remaining two chapters were cut and pasted into a document and examined for evidence of the 12 emergent themes. The coder found evidence of ten of the twelve themes in the document, thus providing evidence of the validity of the themes' existence and their ability to provide an model for effective family communication during times of crisis.

Results

Whenever a family faces a crisis, they have the fundamental choice of three responses: ignore the crisis, flee the crisis, or cope with the crisis. All of our authors recommended coping with the crisis. Coping seems the most rational course of action, given that families typically face crises that are not avoidable. Virtually all our chapters mentioned the word "coping" in describing communicative best practices. Thus, it seemed rational to place coping at the top of our model and to acknowledge that the emergent model was a model of effective family coping with unavoidable, negative crises.

Our authors discussed effective coping with family crises as driven by three primary impulses: (1) the need to make sense of challenging situations (2) through the use of expanded disclosure (3) while remaining positive about the family's ultimate survival and perhaps specific outcomes. Making sense, expanded disclosure, and remaining positive emerge as the three primary pillars of coping. That is, a family must engage in all three of these activities to cope effectively. Expanded disclosure through interpersonal communication among family members emerges as the key coping skill as communication is necessary to the co-construction of a rational explanation for events (i.e., sense-making) as well as the co-construction of a positive view of the ultimate outcomes of the crisis. Given its centrality in the model, a more explanation of the term expanded disclosure may be warranted here.

While multiple chapter authors used the term "open communication," a close read of their data and interpretations reveals that their participants used "expanded disclosure" of topics not previously discussed in the family to cope effectively with crises. The open communication here described was *not* unfettered revelation of any and all information, but rather strategic, expanded disclosure. For example, families may need to make an evacuation plan in the face of eminent danger, such as a hurricane. They do this through discourse. They may need to assign a meeting place and a designated relative to take over child care duties, if needed, in the face of war, homelessness, and/or job loss. They do this through communication within the family and sometimes outside the family–communication that necessitates expanded disclosure. These are not conversations families typically have or topics they discuss often. Such instrumental communication may only appear on a perceived need-to-know basis. Nonetheless, to cope effectively with crises, these unusual topics must be broached; these challenging and sometimes difficult conversations must take place.

In addition to such necessary instrumental information exchange, families experience a compelling need to disclose feelings that may have previously been unvoiced—even in families that do not usually talk about feelings. For example, parents who reported "losing" a child to their surviving children thought they were protecting the surviving siblings from further pain and grief. In reality, many of these survivors experienced increased fear that their parents would "lose" them too. They feared walking home from school alone and physically clung to their parents. Further, they were confused about why their parents did not launch a search for the "lost" sibling. As the survivors attempted to process and address this new situation, they experienced increased emotional distance from their parents, leading to nightmares, bed-wetting, etc. If the parents simply asked the children what they were feeling and openly discussed their own grief, they would have quickly learned that their surviving children experienced curiosity more than sadness and wanted the details of how their sibling died—not the cover-up of a "lost" child. When disclosure, the details surrounding the death prevented the survivors from developing fear, as they typically saw such situations as unique to the deceased ("He was born with a heart defect and I was not"). Thus, the expanded disclosure allowed healthy coping.

In sum, we argue effective family coping with crisis involves expanded disclosure of two types: instrumental communication to address the crisis itself and communication of emotion related to the crisis. We acknowledge that such expanded disclosure may occur on a contingency basis with families only increasing disclosure when they deem it necessary. We also acknowledge that the specific kind of instrument and/or emotional disclosure will differ from crisis to crisis. Certainly, homelessness will call for differing types of specific disclosures than job loss. A diagnosis of infertility will call for different kinds of specific disclosures than the diagnosis of pediatric cancer. Nonetheless, we assert that effective coping with crisis in the family necessitates expanded disclosure. The fourteen chapters that follow identified the specific disclosures that best assist in coping with the particular crisis discussed in each chapter, although we encourage further research on these 14 and other types of crisis so that communication scholars might more definitively identify the specific expanded disclosures that are essential for families to effective cope with each specific crisis.

When families cope in this manner (make sense of challenging situations through expanded disclosure while remaining positive about the family's ultimate survival), two outcomes result. They enact the necessary change and transformation to adjust to the crisis, while retaining a sense of normalcy—indeed, often by developing a new normal. In other words, through effective expanded disclosure, remaining positive, and sense-making, the families can effectively manage the dialectic of change and consistency—even in the face of crises. We note with interest the emergence of "normalcy" as a theme, an important element in Buzzanell's (2010) theory of resilience.

Six themes emerged that appear to offer insights into specific ways and means of managing the dialect of change while maintaining normalcy. These six themes seem to function as dialects themselves and thus form three pairs of opposing objectives that are accomplished via communication. They include the following:

- Obtaining the training and education to enact necessary change while maintaining essential family routines that provide a sense of normalcy.
- Coping effectively with outsiders and service providers who assist in the necessary change and transformation while maintaining family cohesion and togetherness that provides a sense of normalcy.
- Attending to the needs and interests of individual family members so that they might effectively enact change and transformation while also maintaining family relationships and involvement that provides an ongoing sense of normalcy.

It is interesting to note that these dialectics appear to answer the question of who does what to whom to achieve the dialectical goals of enacting change while maintaining normalcy. Indeed, the two columns depicted in Figure 1.1 seem to provide two distinct answers: To enact change and transformation, family members address their individual needs and interests with outsiders, including service providers, to gain the training and education they need to cope with the crisis. Simultaneously, to achieve family normalcy, family members maintain their family cohesion and togetherness by maintaining their family routines via enacting their family relationships and involvement. What would this look like?

We can envision, for example, both parents accompanying a newly diagnosed child to doctor appointments. At these appointments, the parents and child learn about the "new normal" diet and exercise routines they will be enacting to cope with the diagnosis. We imagine the family using their typical forms of dialog to reassure each other that the child will be fine in the end because they are a strong family and can make these simple changes to obtain the positive outcome. In this example, the family copes by making sense of the situation by seeking medical assistance and advice through expanded disclosure with healthcare providers and each other. They remain positive by focusing on the potential positive outcome for the child as well as the positive belief that the family "can do this!" They maintain normalcy by employing regular interaction routines, by attending appointments together, and by staying involved in the coping process through their discourse with each other. Simultaneously, they change and transform their exercise and diet routines as needed by learning form health-care professionals how to cope with their individual child's needs and by doing what is necessary to address those needs. This is indeed a picture of effective coping.

While the proposed model may seem complex, the families described in this book are coping with complex situations and attempting to achieve complex goals. The model has 12 elements, more than many models of coping, but its descriptions seem rational and helpful. Further, we believe this model places effective family communication at the center of the effective coping. The model describes what families must do to cope with crisis: The must enact expanded disclosure as the essential coping activity.

Figure 1.1

How Families Communicate Effectively to Cope Successfully with Crises

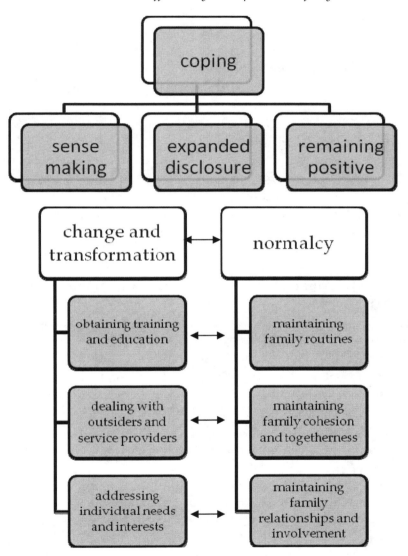

References

Allen, R. L., & Chaffee, S. H. (1977). Racial differences in family communication patterns. *Journalism Quarterly, 54*, 8–13, 57.

Amason, P. (2002). Choosing an undergraduate text from limited options: A review essay of family communication textbooks. *Journal of Family Communication, 2*, 41–56.

Arnold, L. B. (2007). *Family communication: Theory and research.* Boston, MA: Allyn & Bacon.

Barnes, R. E. (Ed.). (1977). Focus on family communication [Special issue]. *Journal of the Wisconsin Communication Association, 7* (2).

Bavelas, J. B., & Segal, L. (1982). Family systems theory: Background and implications. *Journal of Communication, 32* (3), 99–107.

Baxter, L. A., & Braithwaite, D. O. (Eds.). (2006). *Engaging theories in family communication: Multiple perspectives.* Thousand Oaks, CA: Sage.

Beebe, S. A., & Masterson, J. T. (1986). *Family talk: Interpersonal communication in the family.* New York: McGraw-Hill.

Beier, E. G., & Sternberg, D. P. (1977). Marital communication: Subtle cues between newlyweds. *Journal of Communication, 27* (3), 92–96.

Berger, P. L., & Luckmann, T. (1967). *The social construction of reality: A treatise in the sociology of knowledge.* Garden City, NY: Anchor.

Bochner, A. (1974, November). *Family communication research: A critical review of approaches, methodologies, and substantial findings.* Paper presented at the annual meeting of the Speech Communication Association, Chicago, IL.

Bochner, A. (1976). Conceptual frontiers in the study of communication in families: An introduction to the literature. *Human Communication Research, 2*, 381–397.

Buzzanell, P. M. (2010). Resilience: Talking, resisting, and imagining new normalcies into being. *Journal of Communication, 60*, 1–14.

Cantor, J., & Reilly, S. (1982). Adolescents' fright reactions to television and films. *Journal of Communication, 32* (3), 87–99.

Chaffee, S. H. (1978, November). *Communication patterns in the family: Implications for adaptability and change.* Paper presented at the annual meeting of the Speech Communication Association, Minneapolis, MN. (ERIC Document Reproduction No. ED 170 792).

Floyd, K., & Morman, M. T. (Eds.). (2006). *Widening the family circle: New research on family communication.* Thousand Oaks, CA: Sage.

Fontes, N., et al. (1973, April). *An application of force aggregate theory in family communication networks.* Paper presented at the annual meeting of the International Communication Association, Montreal, Canada. (ERIC Document Reproduction No. ED 077 059)

Galvin, K. M. (1979). Social stimulation in the family communication course. *Communication Education, 28,* 68–72.

Galvin, K. M. (1985). *Workshops on family communication.* Annandale, VA: Speech Communication Association. (Booklet in series titled TRIP: Theory and Research into Practice) (ERIC Reproduction Service No. ED 255 968)

Galvin, K. M. (2001). Family communication instruction: A brief history and call. *Journal of Family Communication, 1,* 15–20.

Galvin, K. M., & Brommel, B. J. (1982). *Family communication: Cohesion and change.* Belmont, CA: Wadsworth.

Galvin, K. M., & Brommel, B. J. (1991). *Family communication: Cohesion and change* (3rd ed.). New York: HarperCollins.

Galvin, K. M., & Brommel, B. J. (2000). *Family communication: Cohesion and change* (5th ed.). New York: Longman.

Galvin, K. M., Bylund, C. L., & Brommel, B. J. (2007). *Family communication: Cohesion and change* (7th ed.). Boston, MA: Allyn & Bacon.

Glaser. P. A., & Glaser, S. R. (1977, November). *Marital communication: An addition to the interpersonal communication curriculum.* Paper presented at the annual meeting of the Speech Communication Association, Washington, D.C. (ERIC Document Reproduction No. ED 150 666)

Goldberg, J. (1978, November). *Family communication: Insideness and outsideness.* Paper presented at the annual meeting of the Speech Communication Association, Minneapolis. (ERIC Reproduction Service No. ED 168 094).

Goldberg, J., & Goldberg, A. (1976). Family communication. *Western Speech Communication Journal, 40,* 104–110.

Gonzalez, M. C. (1991, May). *Familia or family? A demonstration of the inability to generalize cross-culturally present research and pedagogy on family and interpersonal relationships.* Paper presented at the annual meeting of the International Communication Association, Chicago, IL. (ERIC Document Reproduction Service No. ED 335 724)

Kramer, K. M., Arbuthnot, J., Gordon, D. A., Rousis, N. J., & Hoza, J. (1998). Effects of skill-based versus information-based divorce education programs on domestic violence and parental communication. *Family and Conciliation Courts Review, 36,* 9–31.

La Rossa, R. (2005). Grounded theory methods and qualitative family research. *Journal of Marriage and Family, 67,* 837–857.

Leckenby, J. D. (1977). Attribution of dogmatism to TV characters. *Journalism Quarterly, 54,* 14–19.

Le Poire, B. A. (2005). *Family communication: Nurturing and control in a changing world.* Thousand Oaks, CA: Sage.

Long, B. W., & Grant II, C. H. (1992). The "surprising range of the possible": Families communicating in fiction. *Communication Education, 41,* 89–107.

Meyer, J. (2003). *Kids talking: Learning relationships and culture with children.* Lanham, MD: Rowman & Littlefield.

Moore, R. L., & Moschis, G. P. (1978, August). *Family communication patterns and consumer socialization.* Paper presented at the annual meeting of the Association for Education in Journalism, Seattle, WA. (ERIC Document Reproduction No. ED 163 459)

Noller, P., & Fitzpatrick, M. A. (1993). *Communication in family relationships.* Englewood Cliffs, NJ: Prentice Hall.

Owen, W. F. (1984). Interpretive themes in relational communication. *Quarterly Journal of Speech, 70,* 274–287.

Pearson, J. C. (1989). *Communication in the family: Seeking satisfaction in changing times.* New York: HarperCollins.

Reinard, J. (1998). *Introduction to communication research.* San Francisco: McGraw-Hill.

Segrin, C., & Flora, J. (2011). *Family communication* (2nd ed.). Retrieved from www.ebookstore.tandf.co.uk/html/index.asp.

Sheinkopf, K. G. (1971, August). *Family communication environment and citizenship norm acquisition.* Paper presented at the annual meeting of the Association for Education in Journalism, Columbia, SC. (ERIC Document Reproduction No. ED 055 953)

Sheinkopf, K. G. (1973). Family communication patterns and anticipatory socialization. *Journalism Quarterly, 50,* 24–30, 133.

Sheinkopf, K. G., & Atkin, C. K. (1972, April). *Communication and learning: Teaching future citizenship norms via family communication patterns.* Paper presented at the annual meeting of the International Communication Association, Chicago, IL. (ERIC Document Reproduction No. ED 063 751)

Socha, T. J., & Diggs, R. C. (1999). *Communication, race, and family: Exploring communication in Black, White and bi-racial families.* Mahwah, NJ: Erlbaum.

Socha, T. J., Sanchez-Hucles, J., Bromley, J., & Kelly, B. (1995). Invisible parents and children: Exploring African-American parent-child communication. In T. J. Socha & G. H. Stamp (Eds.), *Parents, children, and communication: Frontiers of theory and research* (pp. 127–145). Hillsdale, NJ: Erlbaum.

Socha, T. J., & Stamp, G. H. (Eds.). (1995). *Parents, children, and communication: Frontiers of Theory and Research.* Mahwah, NJ: Erlbaum.

Socha, T. J., & Stamp, G. H. (Eds.). (2009). *Parents and children communicating with society: Managing relationships outside of the home.* New York: Routledge.

Socha, T., & Yingling, J. (2010). *Families communicating with children.* Cambridge, UK: Polity.

Steier, F., Stanton, M. D., & Todd, T. C. (1982). Patterns of turn-taking and alliance formation in family communication. *Journal of Communication, 32* (3), 148–160.

Sternberg, D. P., & Beier, E. G. (1977). Marital communication: Changing patterns of conflict. *Journal of Communication, 27* (3), 97–99.

Strauss, A., & Corbin, J. (1990). *Basics of qualitative research: Grounded theory procedure and techniques.* Newbury Park, CA: Sage.

Turner, L. H., & West, R. (1998). *Perspectives on family communication.* Mountain View, CA: Mayfield.

Turner, L. H., & West, R. (2002). *Perspectives on family communication* (2nd ed.). Mountain View, CA: Mayfield.

Turner, L. H., & West, E. (Eds.). (2006). *The family communication sourcebook.* Thousand Oaks, CA: Sage.

Vangelisti, A. L. (1991). The pedagogical use of family measures: "My how you've grown!" *Communication Education, 40,* 187–201.

Walters, J. K., & Stone, V. A. (1971). Television and family communication. *Journal of Broadcasting, 15,* 409–414.

Watzlawick, P., Beavin, J. H. & Jackson, D. D. (1967). *Pragmatics of human communication: A study of interactional patterns, pathologies, and paradoxes.* New York: Norton.

Webb, L. M., Bourgerie, A. J., Shaper, M. W., Johnson, K. B., Dubbs, K. L., Mountain, K. N., Harp, K. K., & Walker, A. M. (2004). Gender and diversity in family communication: A content analysis of the four undergraduate textbooks. *Journal of Family Communication, 4,* 35–52.

Webb, L. M., & Thompson-Hayes, M. E. (2002). Do popular communication textbooks in interpersonal communication reflect a common theory base? A telling content analysis. *Communication Education, 51,* 210–224.

Whitchurch, G. G. (1992). Communication in marriages and families: A review essay of family communication textbooks. *Communication Education, 41,* 337–343.

Whitchurch, G. G. (1993). Designing a course in family communication. *Communication Education, 42,* 255–267.

Whitchurch, G. G., & Dickson, F. C. (1999). A communication perspective on families. In M. B. Sussman, S. K. Steinmetz, & G. Peterson (Eds.), *Handbook of marriage and the family* (2nd ed.) (pp. 687–704). New York: Springer/ Plenum Press.

Whitchurch, G. G., & Webb, L. M. (1995). Applied family communication research: Casting light upon the demon. *Journal of Applied Communication Research, 23,* 239–246.

Yerby, J. (Ed.). (1985). *Research directions in family communication: Proceedings of the family communication research conference.* Annandale, VA: Speech Communication Association.

Yerby, J., Buerkel-Rothfuss, N., & Bochner, A. P. (1990). *Understanding family communication.* Scottsdale, AZ: Gorsuch Scarisbrick.

Yerby, J., Buerkel-Rothfuss, N., & Bochner, A. P. (1995). *Understanding family communication* (2nd ed.). Scottsdale, AZ: Gorsuch Scarisbrick.

Young, D. M., Korner, K. M., Gill, J. D., & Beier, E. G. (1977). Marital communication: "Beneficial" aggression. *Journal of Communication, 27* (3), 100–103.

Section One:

Relational Crises

Chapter 2

Family Communication and Effectively Addressing Infertility

Patricia Amason, Megan L. Wilson, and Justin T. Rusinowski

Much research has examined stress and coping efforts occurring with the diagnosis and treatment of infertility and during and after the adoption process, no research has explored ways in which adoptive parents communicate with potential sources of support in the effort to reduce and manage the associated uncertainties of infertility and adoption. In the present study parents who chose to adopt as a result of infertility issues were interviewed about their perceptions of their communication with their partners, family and social network members, and involved professionals (i.e., social workers, physicians, attorneys) in their efforts to reduce and manage the uncertainties and ultimately cope with the stress associated with infertility issues and their eventual decisions to adopt. Adoptive parents relied heavily on support sources, particularly spouses, family and social network members in their efforts to cope with the crisis of infertility diagnoses, through efforts to conceive using medical intervention, and throughout the process of adopting.

> . . .you're like God totally hates me, you know, because this is something every other human being on the planet gets to experience, only not me and why doesn't He want to trust me with kids. . . . It's not just depressing . . .it is literally soul-killing because you do feel so abandoned by God . . . this is just one of the kind of basic, fundamental human things that you as a human being . . . you feel utterly abandoned by God . . .you just think I can't deal with this anymore. ("Penelope")

A significant number of people hold the major life goal of creating a family with children as parenthood typically is connected to a strong sense of self (Brodzinsky & Huffman, 1988; Busfield & Paddon, 1977; Rapoport, Raporport, & Strelitz, 1977). Indeed, most married couples plan to have children together (Woollett, 1985). Unfortunately, the desire to create a family with children comes with seemingly insurmountable obstacles for many couples often the result of infertility issues. Infertility is diagnosed when unprotected inter-course for a minimum of one year fails to result in conception (Jordan & Revenson, 1999). The crisis of infertility compromises family life plans and a sense of control. Ways in which couples communicate with one another and with family and social network members may affect their perceptions of their coping with this family crisis. We explore how persons facing the crisis of infertility describe their communication with their spouses, members of their social networks, and health care professionals as they attempted to cope with, reduce and manage their uncertainties associated with their infertility crisis and ultimately their creation of their families as those with adopted children.

Family Crises

Families experience trials and hassles on a daily basis. They em-ploy coping methods developed over time and familiar to them as they deal with these everyday stresses and strains. However, often families face unforeseen setbacks forcing them to find new strategies for managing particular stressors from which they are in crisis. Families go into crisis mode when they or others perceive the stressor as highly unusual requiring atypical or yet unidentified coping mechanisms, or they lack the necessary physical, emotional, and/or psychological means for coping with the stressor (McCubbin & Patterson, 1982). Therefore, the higher the degree of life change or adjustment necessary and the fewer the resources available for coping the more likely the family will consider the event to be a crisis. Crises also contribute to great degrees of uncertainty as well as loss of self-esteem, self-denigration, and/or a sense of loss of control (McCubbin, Joy, Cauble, Comeau, Patterson, & Needle, 1980). The diagnosis of infertility is viewed by many couples as a crisis.

The Crisis of Infertility

The number of infertile couples is significantly rising and is at-tributed to such factors as delaying childbearing until later years, the effects of an increased number of sexually transmitted infections such as the human papillomavirus, and the earlier use of invasive means of contraception such as intrauterine devices (Jordan & Revenson, 1999).

Infertility may be attributed to problems associated with females in 34% of the cases, 35% with the male, with both partners in 20% of the cases while 10% of the cases go undiagnosed (Leibman, 1997). In the year 2002, approximately 2% of women of reproductive age sought some form of medical treatment for a problem identified as infertility-related. An additional 2.1 million (7%) married women of reproductive age indicated they had not conceived although they were not using contraception for at least 12 months (2002 National Survey of Family Growth). The rate of infertile women is projected to rise to as high as 7.7 million by 2025 (Stephen & Chandra, 1998).

Societal and cultural expectations about family permeate person's own self-expectations as they begin visualizing and even fantasizing about "family" and their "future family" during the role-play of children in their pre-school years (Brodzinsky & Huffman, 1988). As persons enter into adolescence and young adulthood, they develop expectations of conceiving children at the time of their choosing, typically with little thought of experiencing difficulty in doing so. However, the crisis of infertility confronts 10–15% of adults in child-bearing years (see Brodzinsky & Huffman). The diagnosis of infertility may seem as a "death sentence" for persons' fantasies and hopes of producing children as these desires are compromised or even eliminated. This loss of idealized children is much like the ambiguous loss experienced by persons whose loved ones are lost at war or other unforeseen circumstances, whose children mysteriously disappear, or the psychological loss experienced when persons' loved ones succumb to dementia and other mental disabilities (Boss, 1999). Different phrases used to describe these feelings show the devastating loss associated with infertility such as "childlessness," "empty arms," "empty cradle," and "empty womb." Kossmann (2007) refers to her own personal infertility experience as resulting in her feeling "different than other women: I won't hold a child that looks like my husband and me" (p. 76). She identifies herself as "barren . . . I'd always have a weed-filled field, scrub trees, and emptiness. Here in this infertile place, I kept the grief about 'Pea' and the other lost embryos, along with the fantasies about what might have been" (p. 77).

Couples facing the life crisis of infertility experience stress in their personal relationship as well as their relationships with their families and in their social networks (Pook, Krause, & Rohrle, 1999). These stressors affect persons' sense of self and their personal boundaries, often resulting in depression, anxiety, and guilt increasing the need for support. Thus, these personal traumas greatly impact how the couple communicate with one another and with family and friends and their overall relational satisfaction (*c.f.* Edelmann & Connolly, 1986; Jordan & Revenson, 1999; Kraft, Palumbo, Mitchell, Dean, Meyers, & Schmidt, 1980; Lemmens, Vervaeke, Enzlin, Bakelants, Vanderschueren, Hooge, et al., 2004, Levy-Shiff, Bar, & Har-Even, 1990; and Matthews & Matthews, 1986 for complete reviews of this literature). In addition to stress, couples facing infertility report a great sense of loss regarding the actual childbearing experience and their perception of themselves as normal, fertile persons, resulting in sadness and grief. Accompanying the remorse, infertile couples indicate feelings of fear, anger, shock, being different from others, and perceiving a lack of fairness (Conway & Valentine, 1988; Kossman, 2007). Moreover, infertility often results in threats to persons' masculinity and femininity (Sherwin, Smith, & Cueman, 1984).

Couples remaining childless not by choice must deal with the devastating effects of infertility problems while confronting relational and personal stress largely placed on them by society (Seibel & Taymor, 1982). In North American culture, for example, the expectation is that married people produce children such that remaining childless is stigmatized and is considered by many as an act of deviance (Veevers, 1980). Therefore, because of the stigma towards childlessness, couples who wish to create a family with children but are unable to reproduce are in crisis. Seibel and Taymor summarize literature indicating that infertile women, as compared to those who are fertile, have increased levels of dependency, neuroses, and anxiety. Daniluk and Hurtig-Mitchell (2003) interviewed infertile women who expressed concern for lack of social support for their childlessness. One woman stated, "It's like a deprogramming process. We could probably fill this room with books on how to parent, but where do you find books on how to be childless and happy" (p. 393).

The strain that infertility puts on the couple's personal relationship creates additional challenges. The couple must negotiate the most appropriate way to proceed if they still want to attempt having biological children. Decisions must be made about whether to seek medical intervention, support from family and personal networks as well as mental health professionals. It also takes a toll on intimacy. In writing about her own infertility experiences, Kossman (2007) writes:

"How can I explain what the infertility journey does to a sex life? First, there's the fun, the joy of trying to make something. Then, there's the fear of making something you will lose. Then, there's the stress of having to make something on a schedule and the fact that hoping at all becomes so painful. The pain is like a small, deep cut that won't heal." (p. 76)

Many couples facing the infertility crisis consider medical intervention in assisting them in conceiving a child. This decision is not an easy one. Intervention methods come with negative side-effects such as possible perforations in the uterus, abdominal distension, nausea, infections, painful injections, and complications from anesthesia (Witte & Zmuidzinas, 1992). These physical side-effects are accompanied by emotional and psychological side-effects including mood swings, grief when attempts to intervene medically fail, fear, and a sense of hopelessness. Each failed attempt may result in an ever increasing sense of loss, an ambiguous loss—like losing the dream of having a child over and over.

Boss and others (1984; 1990; 1999) explain that ambiguous loss creates a unique type of stress often described as "torturing…the most devastating because it remains unclear, indeterminate" (Boss, 1999, pp. 5–6) leaving persons with a reduced sense of control and abilities to cope with their loss. In coping with such loss the couple must find new ways of constructing their reality of "family." For couples experiencing ambiguous loss associated with infertility, they must confront their reproductive difficulties by seeking information and support about their particular circumstance and come to some form of reconciliation about their future. Some couples reconcile their situation by choosing to remain childless and create a new reality of their family as one without children. Others pursue their dream of having children by medical intervention in order to increase their chances in creating a child such as through surrogacy. However, this method comes at high emotional and financial risk.

Others persons elect to use Assisted Reproductive Technology (ART) such as using fertility drugs, undergoing surgical procedures or attempting in vitro fertilization. Inherent risks are associated with ART, as well, such as side-effects from the medication, surgical complications, and the small success rate of in vitro procedures. Moreover, these choices are emotionally and financially expensive and rarely covered by insurance.

Whatever choice the couple makes about whether to seek alternative means of creating a family with children or not the decision-making process compounds the stress of coping with the crisis of infertility and coming to terms with its inevitability. The result is a period of grief much like that experienced following the death of a loved one. Thus, the couple has to confront the failure to biologically conceive a child of their own and experience a grieving period for the loss of their potential offspring. Grieving also occurs once couples decide to end unsuccessful ART attempts.

In understanding the decision to end IVF treatments after unsuccessful attempts, Peddie, Teijlingen, and Bhattacharya (2005) interviewed 25 women. These women reported experiencing difficulty in accepting their infertility and were over-optimistic about their potential to conceive through IVF. They indicated they often relied on friends, family, and information obtained from the media in the effort to decide whether to continue IVF treatments. Their decisions to end the treatments left them with issues to confront such as the inevitability of their infertility. Some indicated they were relieved to end the emotional shifting from high to low with each unsuccessful attempt (see also Daniluk, 2001, for similar results). Rather than enduring the emotional and financial strains of surrogacy or the use of ART, or after failed attempts to conceive through ART many couples elect to adopt. Adoption was found to be the choice of 10% of couples surveyed following unsuccessful ART attempts (Kupka, Dorn, Richter, Schmutzler, van der Ven, & Kulczycki, 2003).

Adoption

Adoption often is seen as a "backup plan" if infertility treatments were not elected or were unsuccessful. Kossmann (2007) compares adoption to a "fantasy, a way to imagine a life that ran parallel to this (an infertile) one, in some other universe" (p. 77). While reconciling their infertility adoptive parents tend to reframe their views of childlessness and see adoption in a new light as a result of "a process of resocialization during which they shifted their identity from seeing themselves as biological parents to seeing themselves as adoptive parents" (Daniluk & Hurtig-Mitchell, 2003, p. 393).

Although many infertile couples select adoption in managing this particular family crisis, the decision presents a host of new stressors making communication with family and members of social networks crucial in coping with the transition from attempting to conceive to attempting to adopt. Once the decision is made to pursue adoption, the grieving period from the loss of the biological child creates a transition to a period of hope with the outcome being the accomplishment of the dream to create a family by adoption (Hajal & Rosenberg, 1991). Therefore, it becomes necessary for persons to cope with myriad stressors. These stressors include experiencing uncertainty about becoming a parent (Mercer, 2004), facing potential stigma attached to adoption as a means of creating a family with children (Wegar, 2000), having concerns about the ability to love a non-biological child as much as a biological child, questioning whether possible physical problems with the child can be accepted, fearing the birth mother will attempt to reclaim the child, worrying about whether the child would later reject the adoptive parents, feeling a lack of control while in the adoption process, making the necessary time and financial commitments, managing the constant scrutiny of the couple's personal lives, and perceiving the need to justify to others their decision to adopt (Daniluk & Hurtig-Mitchell, 2003).

The same sense of powerless experienced in confronting the diagnosis of infertility and undergoing infertility treatments also occurs in the lengthy adoption process requiring couples to seek social support as a means of coping. Coping strategies such as setting distinct boundaries between themselves and the adoption process, focusing on other aspects of their lives, relying on friends and family and attending to the positive aspects of their personal relationships were the most commonly identified coping strategies by persons who resolved their sense of powerlessness while in the adoption process (Daniluk & Hurtig-Mitchell, 2003). Adoptive parents in Daniluk and

Hurtig-Mitchell's study saw the trials of the adoption process as manageable because sharing this experience with their partners created a common bond. One participant offered, "Through this process, we certainly learned who our support people were . . .and that's each other" (p. 395). The conclusion that may be drawn from the literature, however, is that all of these fears and concerns were worth the pursuit, as having children was a necessary component of adoptive parents' perceptions of "family" and of life fulfillment.

When faced with infertility issues, much uncertainty ensues such as what are the most reliable sources of information about the condition and treatment options, who to seek for support, the unknown about success rates for various treatment methods, and alternative means of creating a family such as adoption. With the decision to adopt, much uncertainty follows such as the unknown about the potential success of the process—if a placement will be made, if the birth parents will hold their commitment to the placement, the unknown about the child's genetic and medical history, and concern for later resentment or abandonment by the child. These uncertainties and ambiguities create tremendous stress for the persons experiencing the crisis of infertility and the decision to adopt. The management of these uncertainties and ambiguities through communication with family, social network members and professionals may aid in helping persons who choose to adopt make the transition from grief to hope.

Uncertainty Reduction and Management

Persons facing uncertainties about their circumstances and life choices typically seek out others in their efforts to achieve affiliation and clarity as a means by which to reduce those uncertainties and better understand the unknown (Albrecht & Adelman, 1987). Thus, interaction serves to help those encountering stressful situations identify ways to interpret the stressor and determine the most effective means for coping. Uncertainty reduction thus results in a dual outcome by creating a sense of control or mastery over the stressor and strengthening the relational bond between the interactants (Albrecht & Adelman, 1987; Berger & Calabrese, 1975; Parks & Adelman, 1983). Uncertainty reduction theory (URT) provides an explanation of the communication process occurring in situations where clarity is sought with the ultimate goal of eventual coping with the stressor creating the uncertainty (Baxter & Braithwaite, 2008; Berger & Bradac, 1982; Berger & Calabrese, 1975; Berger & Gudykunst, 1991). Persons encountering stressful situations leading to uncertainty respond to the stressor and resulting uncertainty cognitively by a lack of understanding of the stressor itself or the reason in which the stressor occurred (Albrecht & Adelman, 1987). Persons facing the crisis of infertility often wonder "why is this happening?" or "why is this happening to me?" Questions such as these continue throughout the process of coming to terms with the inevitability of infertility. Kossman (2007) writes, "How long does it take to give birth to oneself as a childless woman?" (p. 77).

Uncertainty occurs again while making the decision to adopt and throughout the adoption process. It becomes difficult to decide how to act in order to achieve positive outcomes. Albrecht and Adelman (1987) argue that supportive communication functions to reduce anxiety and stress and provides for an increased sense of perceived control over the stressful circumstances. Moreover, supportive communication empowers individuals to have a "personal impact on their situations." (Albrecht & Adelman, p. 26) a key factor in coping (c.f. Lazarus, 1974; 1975; McFarlane, Norman, Streiner, Roy, 1983). When faced with uncertainties regarding matters of health, persons confront degrees of ambiguity (where they assign meaning to the situation in a number of ways); complexity in regard to how they manage or cope with the uncertainty often resulting in the inability to adequately process all of the information; and limited information about how to proceed with the future (Albrecht & Adelman, 1987; Mischel, 1984; 1985).

Building on the notion of social support as aiding in uncertainty reduction, Babrow and others offer the perspective that social support not only aids in uncertainty reduction, but also in uncertainty management or the action people take when faced with the stressor. This premise is based on the assumptions offered by Parkes (1971) that the management of uncertainties is crucial in circumstances where persons must make transitions from one world view to another— described by Ford, Babrow, and Stohl (1996) as "psychosocial transitions." Building on previous work on coping (Cohen, 1993; Elliott &

Eisdorfer, 1982; Lazarus & Folkman, 1984; Pearlin, 1985; Roth & Cohen, 1986), it is argued that an individual facing uncertainties process through "repeated cycles of encounter, retreat, acknowledgement, and adaptation as one reassesses previous points in the sequence and/or as new stressors emerge"(Ford et al., p. 191). As persons achieve a greater understanding of their situation and of coping mechanisms, they gain a sense of empowerment as they come to an understanding of the stressor yet leading to a sense of incapacity often leading them to ask, "Given these circumstances, how do I proceed from here?" Once infertile persons realize the inevitability of their diagnosis and they come to terms with it they have achieved uncertainty reduction. Infertile couples then must choose whether to redefine their family as one without children, seek medical intervention, or elect to adopt ultimately resulting in some degree of management of their crisis. Additional uncertainties then will arise depending on their decision.

Solchany (1998) indicates that putting the decision to adopt into action aids to establish a sense of control. In the effort to cope with the stress and fears associated with infertility issues and the decision to adopt, persons must find ways to reconcile these associated uncertainties. Persons must use communication in order to reduce these uncertainties and stressors (Powell & Afifi, 2005). However, even attempting to identify the most reliable persons with whom to communicate may result in more stress, feelings of uncertainty, and a lack of control (Levy-Shiff, Bar, & Har-Even, 1990; Lobar & Phillips, 1996; Solchany, 1998).

Rationale for the Study

While much research has been published examining stress and coping efforts occurring with the diagnosis and treatment of infertility, as well as those experienced during and after the adoption process, no research was found exploring ways in which adoptive parents communicate with potential sources of support in the effort to reduce and manage the associated uncertainties of infertility and adoption. In the present study, we interviewed parents who chose to adopt as a result of infertility issues about their perceptions of their communication with their partners, family and social network members, and involved professionals (i.e., social workers, physicians, attorneys) in their efforts to reduce and manage the uncertainties and ultimately cope with the stress associated with infertility issues and their eventual decisions to adopt. Thus, we sought to identify how communication facilitated the stages in the transition from grief to hope. We offer the following research questions in regard to parents who chose to adopt because of infertility issues:

RQ1: How do these parents perceive their communication with their relational partners, members of their families, and persons in their social networks in their efforts to cope with the crisis of infertility and their decisions to adopt?

RQ2: What attempts were made by these parents to reduce and manage uncertainties about infertility issues through their communication with their relational partners, members of their families, and persons in their social networks?

RQ3: What were the perceptions of the adoptive parents' conversations with relational partners, family members, or other social network members in their attempts to reduce and manage their uncertainties of their infertility issues and their decisions to adopt?

RQ4: Who provided the most assistance in reducing and managing the uncertainties associated with their infertility issues and their decision to adopt?

Method

Sample

Following the University's Institutional Review Board's approval, participants were recruited using a snowball sampling technique beginning with personal contacts of the authors along with offering students in undergraduate communication classes extra credit in exchange for the recruitment of an adoptive parent to participate in the interview process. Anonymity was guaranteed in informed consent forms which assured participants that names were gathered only for extra credit purposes.

Semi-structured interviews were conducted by the second author. Interviews were conducted with three participants not included in the final interviews to gauge the usefulness of both the demographic questionnaire and the interview protocol. These participants were recruited using the same protocol outlined above. These initial participants were afforded the opportunity to offer suggestions for changes to either the demographic questionnaire or the interview protocol. After each of these interviews, the interview protocol was altered to reflect the suggestions offered by participants. The preliminary interviews concluded once the apparent need for clarification ceased and/or the participant offered no new suggestions for changes to the interview protocol or demographics questionnaire.

Procedures

Interviews were conducted via telephone. Telephone interviews allowed for more flexibility in terms of both time and geographical distance. Once the interview was scheduled, participants were emailed or mailed (participant's choice) the demographic questionnaire as well as informed consent forms. These questionnaires were administered prior to the interview *in every other case*; in the alternative cases, the questionnaires were administered immediately following the interview to ameliorate order effects. During the conduct of the interviews, the researcher wrote down the comments provided by the participants and the interviews were digitally recorded.

Also, the researcher provided contact information for a national family counseling service hotline for all participants. Hotline information included a short explanation that some interviews may prompt thoughts or emotions in participants about which they may choose to discuss with a professional.

Participants

Overall participants ranged in age from 26-68 years with a mean age of 49 years. Most of the participants were female (N=13), though two adoptive fathers were interviewed. The participants lived in states in the southern and midwestern regions of the US. Nine participants had seen previous adoptions within either their immediate or their extended families.

The number of adopted children in these families ranged from one to three. A total number of thirty-nine children were adopted into these families with 20 of the adoptions occurring domestically while 19 were international adoptions. Ethnicities of the adopted children included Caucasian (14), Asian (seven), blended (five), and His-panic/Latino (five).

Data Analysis

Upon completion, the recorded interviews were transcribed and notations from the field notes were added during occasions where the recording was difficult to understand. Transcripts were numbered and subjected to thematic analysis using the grounded theory ap-proach. The grounded theory approach, first developed by Glaser and Strauss (1967), is seen as a highly effective approach for exploring communication within families (LaRossa, 2005; Strauss & Corbin, 1998). Anonymity in reporting the results of the interviews was guaranteed as pseudonyms were assigned to each participant. Gener-ally, the data are reported in the aggregate rather than by individual participants however, specific comments are provided in the results section to instantiate the various themes identified. The authors individually read the transcripts. The second and third authors searched for themes associated with each research question and then met to discuss those themes. Once a consensus was reached on themes, these authors met with the first author to discuss these themes further.

Results

In answering the first research question we searched for themes that particularly dealt with communication between the adoptive parents and their relational partners, members of their families, or members of their own social networks in their efforts to cope with their infertility crises. Specifically, we were looking to gauge our participants' perceptions of their communication with others regard-ing the crisis of infertility and their decision to adopt.

Participants described these interactions in both positive and neg-ative terms. In the descriptions indicating that communication was positive, three themes emerged. First, several indicated that they sought assistance from persons who shared similar experiences. "Joslin" stated:

> My best friend had been in my shoes . . . so she knew the questions in my
> head, often before I would ever come out and ask them. So I knew I could
> talk to her about anything dealing with this issue and we would be able to
> talk it out.

"Grace" shared similar feelings: "my closest friends that knew about it were very, very supportive, and a lot of them were going through it, too."

The second theme emerged with persons stating they received support from other members of their families and found comfort in being able to share their situation with these others. This theme best was described by "Susan":

> You got your family, your husband, your parents, your sister, you know, all
> of those people who were instrumental in keeping you kind of grounded
> and reminding you that, you know what, it's not really that bad . . . just be-
> cause you can't have a child doesn't mean that the end of the world is near .
> . . it could be worse, it could be you're sick . . . so not being able to have a
> child is not that big of a deal.

Social networks members also were an important source of support. "Kariann" stated:

> My friends often took me out to get my mind off things. We would go to a
> movie or go hiking somewhere beautiful. Or, at one time, one of my closest
> friends came over with a big envelope in her hand and she had booked three
> flights for herself, me, and another one of our close friends to fly to Hawaii
> for a weekend just to leave the troubles behind us.

"Grace" concurred: "I talked to people, friends of my parents."

The third theme that emerged was the sharing of participants' personal stories in an attempt to actually convey social support *to* others experiencing a similar crisis. This may have occurred as the participants attempted to achieve reciprocated social support by reassuring themselves as well as others going through the *shared* experience of reconciling the infertility crisis and that the process can be survived with the support of others. Moreover, adoption was seen as a viable alternative for creating a family with children. "Claire" put it this way:

> We were more comfortable around others. We love talking about adoption to other people and usually a lot of people will ask us about our kids because we're such a standout family.

Some of the participants indicated that not all interactions were positive as members of their network provided little to no support. Therefore, they avoided situations in which such conversations might occur as is indicated by "Claire's" comments: "it's pretty much all people wanted to talk about . . . and I just didn't want all that talk anymore. It seemed so depressing." "Jacob" also avoided including family:

> Oh, I didn't tell (my family) anything . . . it wouldn't have done any good. There were times that I didn't want to talk about this stuff anymore and they (my friends) usually wanted to ask questions about how things were going, have you tried this treatment option yet, did that work for you? And sometimes I didn't want to talk about that anymore, I knew they were only asking because they were concerned about me and cared for me.

"Claire" indicated she avoided situations involving pregnant friends and opportunities where she was expected to share in the joy of their impending motherhood:

> There were lots of baby showers. . . . I never went to a baby shower, never, never. Couldn't do it . . . but I found on my online support groups that people talked about that a lot—about not going to baby showers.

"Maria" described feeling separated from the fertile world: "There were times where it did isolate you from the standpoint of you didn't want to talk about it . . . you just clammed up."

Participants also described situations in which others did not seem to try to understand their situation. "Claire" recalled conversations with friends who joked about their own unplanned pregnancies:

> And their little story was 'that contraceptive wasn't effective' he he he. And I just wanted to smack them. . . . I think I had a great deal of resentment and hostility towards people who . . .didn't appreciate their children.

"Penelope" experienced a lack of support from her mother-in-law:

> She's very, very, very proud of her sons and I don't think she can ever truly wrap her head around that. Hence the frequent suggestion that I just need to take more of whatever vitamin supplement or eat chili peppers, whatever…

Several participants indicated they avoided disclosing much information about their situations with members of their families. "Claire" stated: "my folks probably *would have been supportive* but, I guess I really didn't talk with them a whole lot about it."

Similar feelings were shared by "Joslin":

> I talked to my mother a few times right after I was diagnosed about what I would do if I ever wanted to have children of my own someday but once I moved off that boat, we never really revisited it again.

"Rebekah" concurred:

> My daddy would have just been very uncomfortable talking about anything along those lines, so I left him out of the loop of conversation until we were actually in the middle of going through the process of adoption . . . he was one of those people you only told on a need to know basis.

To answer Research Question two the researchers searched for themes specifically dealing with how adoptive parents attempted to reduce and manage their uncertainties about their infertility issues and decisions to adopt through communication with their relational partners, members of their family, or other members of their social networks.

Many participants commented they relied most often on medical professionals such as family physicians, obstetricians, and reproductive endocrinologists. Others talked to friends with similar experiences such as indicated in "Joslin's" remark: "Well I always valued my friend's opinion on the matter because I knew she lived through and walked out the other side."Other persons stated they relied on sources that had not experienced the loss and pain of infertility or had not made the decision to adopt such as family members and close friends. For example, when asked about what types of coping mechanisms were used to manage the infertility crisis and the ultimate decision to adopt, "Lisa" stated:

Well I had some friends that I talked to throughout the process, each step along the way . . . nearly daily, about what I was dealing with medically and what I was feeling emotionally. They were a big support to me throughout the whole process and sometimes just getting to tell them what I was going through was a huge help to me.

A commonly reoccurring theme was that participants sought counsel and solace from persons sharing similar experiences they encountered through online resources. "Maria" indicated:

We tried to support each other as best as we could, but we were scattered across the country and so this was all done over email but we sort of checked in on each other and asked each other how things were going and kept up with what treatments folks were going to try next.

"Claire" stated that she

blogged my ass off. I wrote every day, sometimes multiple times a day. . . . I read other people's blogs . . . who were going through the same thing . . . emailed back and forth.

Online support groups also were mentioned:

I actually found an online support group for women facing infertility. It was not only encouraging, but various members helped point me in the right direction as far as what medical paths to take next and finally when to consider adoption was another option. ("Rebekah")

"Claire" stated that she "formed my own support group . . . that was the biggest source of support."

To answer Research Question three the researchers explored themes that dealt with specific perceptions the adoptive parents' had of their conversations with relational partners, family members, or other social network members in their attempts to reduce their uncertainties of their infertility issues and their decisions to adopt.

Participants stated both positive and negative reactions to their attempts to reduce and manage uncertainty about their situations with family, friends, and health care providers. Some indicated a satisfaction with their communication with friends, particularly those who were sharing similar circumstances and feelings. For example, "Joslin" shared:

> . . . my friend who also has PCOS, I could go into a little more detail with her just because I knew that she understood every detail with grave clarity.

Others found their communication to cause them more harm than good such as "Claire" who indicated that she

> . . . just didn't want all that talk anymore. It seemed so depressing. . . . I just wanted to be away from that. . . . I didn't want to wallow in grief anymore. I was done grieving.

Many participants described how they relied on their spouse for support in dealing with the infertility issues they were facing and their ultimate decision to adopt. For example, "Joslin" provided that her

> . . . husband has always been an amazing supporter and cheerleader for me in everything I've done and so I would talk to him a lot, just knowing how positive he would always be.

"Susan" agreed and referred to her husband as her "coping mechanism." Further, "Jaime" stated that she

> . . . would talk to (husband) about it and he really was the biggest help to me because sometimes I just could not, you know, as much as I wanted to not catastrophize and not have that all or none thinking, it kept happening. And he would be like honey, you know, let's just see about this.

Additionally, "Maria" added:

> . . . my biggest one was really talking to my husband about it. He and I really made a decision that we were going to walk down this road together, no matter how many bumps and bruises came along the way. . . . If there was something I was struggling a lot with, all I would have to do is come to him and share this with him and he would somehow feel the pain with me. It was always very comforting to know that I had a partner through this whole process and no matter how much I may not always have a whole lot of friends who understood me or my situation, I was never alone in this struggle.

To answer the fourth research question the researchers sought to identify which persons in the participants' social networks provided the most assistance in reducing and managing their uncertainties when dealing with their infertility and the decision to adopt. Participants listed their spouses as a significant source of assistance as well as family members and close friends. These sources offered emotional, financial, and instrumental support. Additionally, some of the participants indicated receiving assistance from fertility clinics in the form of support groups or individual counseling.

Discussion

Overall, participants indicated experiencing anguish over the crisis of their infertility diagnosis. Infertility is viewed as a family crisis—there is a piece missing in the puzzle of how these persons envisioned "family." The diagnosis of infertility—the inability to conceive or the inability to conceive without risky medical intervention renders these persons with the belief that a part of their identity is missing. This rang clear in the comments of many of the participants:

If you're going through infertility, going through daily life is sheer hell, because you go to the bank, you go to the grocery store, whatever, there are millions of people with small adorable children or pregnant women. . . . I just could not be around people with children. ("Penelope")

I went through a grieving time then, right after I was diagnosed. I had seen what my best friend had gone through and the fertility treatments that she had tried and had to stop and realize that being a mother, being pregnant, and having a baby were all things that I had fantasized about since I was very young, and now I had to stop and think about the fact that this was not a very high possibility anymore. ("Joslin")

I felt like it was really unfair. I felt like maybe, I don't know, God was punishing me. I went through this whole kind of existential kind of, oh, what have I done wrong, Lord, process. ("Jaime")

When I was going through all of the fertility treatments to try and get pregnant, it all seemed very, um, almost like I was subhuman or something like

that, and I don't mean to sound dramatic, but there were many times when I
simply wondered what on earth was wrong with only me that nothing that
we ever tried seemed to work. ("Kariann")

The participants indicated they all imagined having children. Children enabled them to move from seeing themselves as a couple to
seeing themselves as a family. That image was shattered with the
infertility diagnosis. The anguish continued until their uncertainties
were managed and inevitability of the diagnosis was realized and
they came to terms with their situation as "Claire" stated: "You know,
you don't find happy infertiles until that person has gotten past the
grief ."

Once the grief stage is reconciled, the participants indicated that
they were able to move forward with options. The anguish was
relieved and managed once clarity occurred and the missing piece for
their "family" puzzle was realized. This realization led them to the
transition of viewing conceiving a child to create their family with
children to realizing that adoption was a viable option to building
their family as one with children. The next step was then deciding to
adopt and ultimately proceeding with adoption. Therefore, adoption
offered the participants a way to gain the family with children that
they had been dreaming of most of their lives.

The participants indicated that their interactions with their spouses, family and social network members helped them grieve over then
come to terms with their diagnoses, work through their grief, and
ultimately make the decision to adopt. Thus, they went from a state of
uncertainty about their inability to conceive a child to uncertainty
reduction.

it was a very, very, very dark time . . . and then I had friends I could talk to
about it who had gone through it before or had adopted . . . but there is just
no good way to cope with it. ("Penelope")

Once the decision to adopt was made, the participants indicated
they did not want to dwell on the negatives associated with infertility
and the dreams shattered by that diagnosis. They wanted to move
forward, think about the positive, and the ways in which they were
able to reconstruct their shattered dream of a family by adopting a

child. They wanted to pursue communication with persons who were in support of that decision and of the need to focus on the future rather than dwell on the sadness of what was not meant to be. Thus, these persons had attained management of the stressors causing the uncertainty.

Participants sought assistance from key sources in their efforts to reduce the uncertainties they faced with their diagnoses and their later decisions to adopt. They stated they turned to others when particular information was needed concerning treatment options and the specifics of the adoption process were needed in order to reduce and ultimately manage their uncertainties. As "Kariann" expressed:

> I think just that I realized at the end of this whole process the importance of family and friends and the support that they can provide.

Overall, however, they indicated that knowing that the support was available was of greater value than any particular *type* of support they received. Many participants offered they found solace in the communication of social support in gaining support from and giving support to others experiencing the same family crises as Albrecht and Adelman (1987) describe as "a reciprocal process" (p. 19) involving strong ties with spouses, social network members and family as well as weak ties such as with health professionals, among members of online support groups and among other relationships derived through mediated channels. When confronting emotional uncertainties, participants relied most on their social networks. Additionally, similar to findings reported by Daniluk and Hurtig-Mitchell (2003), spousal support was crucial to coping. Our participants revealed that the quality of their relationship with their spouse impacted their abilities to work through the crisis collaboratively.

Communication with significant sources of support is crucial to surviving life's stresses and strains. When faced with family crises, communication is a vital aspect to coping by enabling the person to better understand the crisis, accept the cause of the crisis, and ultimately make decisions to move beyond the crisis in a positive direction. Persons seeking supportive communication gain help in facing the crisis of infertility ultimately freeing them to make decisions of how to reframe their dreams of creating a family by choosing to remain childless, or in the case of our participants, by electing to create their vision of family as one with children through the joys of adoption. The participants revealed a common sentiment, "Kariann" seemed to state it the most succinctly:

> it's more than just getting through, it's about thriving more than just surviving and I wish I had realized that I needed to stay in touch with the people around me who cared about me and wanted to see me get through this too and wanted me to have a happy family as much as I did.

References

Albrecht, T. L., & Adelman, M. B. (1987). Communicating social support: A theoretical perspective. In T. L. Albrecht & M. B. Adelman (Eds.), *Communicating social support* (pp. 18–39). Beverly Hills, CA: Sage.

Berger, C. R. (1997). Producing messages under uncertainty. In J. O. Greene (Ed.), *Message production: Advances in communication theory* (pp. 221–244). Mahwah, NJ: Erlbaum.

Berger, C. R., & Bradac, J. J. (1982). *Language and social knowledge: Uncertainty in interpersonal relationships.* London: Edward Arnold.

Berger, C. R., & Calabrese, R. J. (1975). Some explorations in initial interaction and beyond: Toward a developmental theory of interpersonal communication. *Human Communication Research, 1,* 99–112.

Berger, C. R., & Gudykunst, W. B. (1991). Uncertainty and communication. In B. Dervin & M. J. Voight (Eds.), *Progress in communication sciences, Vol. 10* (pp. 21–66). Norwood, NJ: Ablex.

Boss, P. (1999). *Ambiguous loss: Learning to live with unresolved grief.* Cambridge, MA: Harvard University Press.

Boss, P., Caron, W., Horbal, J., & Mortimer, J. (1990). Predictors of depression in caregivers of dementia patients: Boundary ambiguity and mastery. *Family Process, 29,* 245–254.

Boss, P., & Greenberg, J. (1984). Family boundary ambiguity: A new variable in family stress theory. *Family Process, 23,* 535–546.

Brodzinsky, D. M., & Huffman, L. (1988). Transition to adoptive parenthood. *Marriage and Family Review, 12,* 267–286.

Cohen, M. H. (1993). The unknown and the unknowable: Managing sustained uncertainty. *Western Journal of Nursing Research, 15,* 77–95.

Conway, P., & Valentine, D. (1988). Reproductive losses and grieving. *Journal of Social Work and Human Sexuality, 6,* 43–64.

Daniluk, J. C. (2001). Reconstructing their lives: A longitudinal, qualitative analysis of the transition to biological childlessness for infertile couples. *Journal of Counseling and Development, 79,* 441–449.

Daniluk, J. C., & Hurtig-Mitchell, J. (2003). Themes of hopes and healing: Infertile couples' experiences of adoption. *Journal of Counseling and Development, 81,* 389–399.

Edelmann, R. J., & Connolly, K. J. (1986). Psychological aspects of infertility. *British Journal of Medical Psychology, 59,* 209–219.

Elliott, G. R., & Eisdorfer, C. (1982). *Stress and human health: Analysis and implications of human research.* New York: Springer-Verlag.

Fontenot, H. B. (2007). Transition and adaptation to adoptive motherhood. *Journal of Obstetric, Gynecologic, and Neonatal Nursing, 36,* 175–182.

Ford, L. A., Babrow, A. S., & Stohl, C. (1996). Social support messages and the management of uncertainty in the experience of breast cancer: An application of problematic integration theory. *Communication Monographs, 63,* 189–207.

Grotevant, H. D., Dunbar, N., Kohler, J. K., & Esau, A. M. L. (2000). Adoptive identity: How contexts within and beyond the family shape developmental pathways. *Family Relations, 49,* 379–387.

Hajal, F., & Rosenberg, E. B. (1991). The family life cycle in adoptive families. *American Journal of Orthopsychiatry, 61,* 78–85.

Knobloch, L. K. (2008). Uncertainty reduction theory: Communicating under conditions of ambiguity. In L. A. Baxter & D. O. Braithwaite (Eds.), *Engaging theories in interpersonal communication: Multiple perspectives* (pp. 133–148). Thousand Oaks, CA: Sage.

Kossmann, D. D. (2007). Barren: Coming to terms with a lost dream. In *Annual editions: The family* (pp. 74–77). Dubuque, IA: McGraw-Hill.

Kraft, A. D., Palombo, J., Mitchell, D., Dean, C., Meyers, A., & Schmidt, A. W. (1980). Psychological dimensions of infertility. *American Journal of Orthopsychiatry, 50,* 618–628.

LaRossa, R. (2005). Grounded theory methods and qualitative family research. *Journal of Marriage and Family, 67,* 837–857.

Lazarus, R. (1974). Psychological stress and coping in adaptation and illness. *International Journal of Psychiatry in Medicine, 5,* 321–333.

Lazarus, R. (1975). The self-regulation of emotion. In L. Levi (Ed.), *Emotions, their parameters and measurement* (pp. 47–67). New York: Raven.

Lazarus R., & Folkman, S. (1984). Coping and adaptation. In W. D. Gentry (Ed.), *The handbook of behavioral medicine* (pp. 282–385). New York: Guilford.

Levy-Shiff, R., Bar, O., & Har-Even, D. (1990). Psychological adjustment of adoptive parents-to-be. *American Journal of Orthopsychiatry, 60,* 258–267.

Matthews, A. M., & Matthews, R. (1986). Perspective on the social psychology of infertility and involuntary childlessness. *Family Relations, 35,* 479–487.

McFarlane, A. H., Norman, G. R., Streiner, D. L., & Roy, R. G. (1983). The process of social stress: Stable, reciprocal and mediating relationships. *Journal of Health and Social Behavior, 24,* 160–173.

Parks, M. R., & Adelman, M. B. (1983). Communication networks and the development of romantic relationships: An expansion of uncertainty reduction theory. *Human Communication Research, 10,* 55–79.

Pearlin, I. I. (1985). Social structure and processes of social support. In S. Cohen & L. Syme (Eds.), *Social support and health* (pp. 43–60). Orlando, FL: Academic Press.

Peddie, V. L., van Teijlingen, E., & Bhattacharya, S. (2005). A qualitative study of women's decision-making at the end of IVF treatment. *Human Reproduction, 20,* 1944–1951.

Powell, K. A., & Afifi, T. S. (2005). Uncertainty management and adoptees' ambiguous loss of their birth parents. *Journal of Social and Personal Relationships, 22,* 129–151.

Roth, S., & Cohen, L. (1986). Approach, avoidance, and coping with stress. *American Psychologist, 41,* 173–186.

Seibel, M. M., & Taymor, M. L. (1982). Emotional aspects of infertility. *Fertility and Sterility, 37,* 137–145.

Sherwin, L. N., Smith, D. W., & Cueman, M. A. (1984). Common concerns of adoptive mothers. *Pediatric Nursing, 10,* 127–130.

Sobol, M. P., Delaney, S., & Earn, B. M. (1994). Adoptees' portrayal of the development of family structure. *Journal of Youth and Adolescence, 23,* 385–401.

Stephen, E. H., & Chandra, A. (1998). Updated projections of infertility in the United States: 1195–2025. *Fertility and Sterility, 70,* 30–34.

Toller, P. W. (2005). Negotiation of dialectical contradictions by parents who have experienced the death of a child. *Journal of Applied Communication Research, 33*, 46–66.

Witte, K., & Zmuidzinas, M. (1992). The impact of relational dimensions of risk communication on infertility patients' risk perceptions. *The Southern Journal of Communication, 57*, 308–317.

Wrobel, G. M., Kohler, J. K., Grotevant, H. D., & McRoy, R. G. (2003). The family adoption communication (FAC) model: Identifying pathways of adoption-related communication. *Adoption Quarterly, 7*, 53–84.

Chapter 3

Parental Infidelity: Adult Children's Attributions for Parents' Extramarital Relationships

Allison R. Thorson

This chapter briefly summarizes the prevalence of infidelity, theorizing on accounts and attributions, and provides an example of a study which was conducted to better understand the ways adult children make sense of the infidelities which occur in their parents' relationship. In order to uncover the accounts and attributions adult children make for a parent's infidelity, 38 in-depth semi-structured interviews with individuals whose parents' relationship involved infidelity were conducted. Results indicate that children's accounts can be clustered into five broad categories: dysfunction and deficiency; justifications and excuses; restoring credibility and character; blame; and denial of parent involvement. In addition, each of these accounts is classified according to its underlying dimensions of attributions: causal locus, stability, and controllability. Overall, these findings shed light on the ways children talk about their parents' infidelity in their attempt to make sense of these events.

Research suggests that following a negative family event, such as divorce, children spend a great deal of time trying to understand the reasons why their parents' relationship deteriorated and they often remain conflicted about the affairs that they believe may lie at the heart of their parents' conflicts (Duncombe & Marsden, 2004). The accounts children make and the attributional processes they experience are instrumental in shaping family communication following these events.

One particular family crisis in which children's experiences are often overlooked is parental infidelity. This taboo family crisis regularly threatens communication within the family system and occurs both separate from and/or intertwined with children's experiences of divorce. In an effort to demonstrate the importance of children's sense-making processes following the discovery of a parent's infidelity, I developed the following chapter to highlight the accounts children make for a parent's infidelity: *dysfunction/deficiency; justifica-*

tions/excuses; restoring credibility/character; blame; and *denial of parent involvement*–and to suggest how the underlying attributions reflected in these accounts may play an important role in reflecting past relationships and shaping future family interactions.

Prevalence of Parental Infidelity

A 1994 study conducted by Laumann, Gagnon, Michael, and Michaels, found that approximately 25% of married men and 15% of married women admit to having had sex with someone other than their husband or wife while married. This finding is alarming considering that sexual infidelity is the most commonly stated reason for divorce cross-culturally (Betzig, 1989). Although the above statistics are limited to sexual infidelity, Thompson (1984) suggests that if emotional infidelities are taken into consideration, rates of infidelity could increase to as high as 42% for women and 45% for men. Considering that roughly half of first marriages end in divorce, that slightly more than half of all divorces involve children under the age of 18 (Cherlin, 1992), and that infidelity is cited between 25% and 50% of the time as the primary cause for divorce (Kelly & Conley, 1987), these findings cannot be ignored.

Despite its prevalence, it is unclear how many children know about the infidelities which occur in their parents' relationships. Aside from a recent study which asserts that children know much more about their parents' relationship than they are given credit (Thorson, 2009), too often children's experiences with parental infidelity are studied via their parents' interpretation rather than learning about the experience from children themselves (Duncombe & Marsden, 2004). This finding signals that researcher must examine the first hand accounts and attributions children make for these events in order to better understand its greater impact on communication within the family system.

Accounts and Attributions

Accounts are the narratives individuals create to explain events (Manusov, 2006). They refer to the communicative process of describing and answering the question "Why?" Whereas accounts are the stories individuals form to explain events, attributions are the underlying cognitive meanings to which individuals refer when making sense of an event (Manusov, 2006). Hence, attributions, as they are conceptualized in the current chapter, do not refer to the predictive behaviors or characteristics of infidelity, but to the cognitive inferences which inform the account that a child provides for his or her parent's extramarital behavior.

Among the three dimensions often underlying attributions are: locus of control, stability, and controllability (Weiner, 1986, 2004). Locus of control, as defined by Russell (1982), relates to an individuals' assessment of whether or not a cause of a behavior is something internal or external to the transgressor. As such, if a son, when explaining his parent's infidelity, says, "this was my parent's fault—it had nothing to do with anyone or anything else. This is just who he is," the locus of control to which he is referring is classified as internal. Stability, according to Russell, concerns whether or not a cause is stable/constant or variable/unstable over time. For example, if a daughter shares, "She did this all the time—it was anything but a one night stand," her account is considered a stable attribution. Last, controllability refers to whether or not a cause could be changed or affected by the transgressor. To illustrate, if a son comments, "she could have stopped it–she just chose not to," this account would be classified as a controllable attribution.

Researchers argue that the accounts and attributions individuals make for hurtful events are shaped by the event-specific communication surrounding the incident (e.g., Canary, Cody, & Manusov, 2003; Rusbult, Hannon, Stocker, & Finkel, 2005). Thus, one way to better understand family communication surrounding parental infidelity is to examine the accounts children make for their parents' behavior. In turn, the underlying attributional dimensions or attributional valence of an account can signal important information about the parent-child relationship. Specifically, Vangelisti (2006) and Vangelisti and Young (2000) report that satisfied individuals judge, or attribute, the intentionality of an individuals' hurtful behavior as having less importance than those who are dissatisfied. Gottman (1994) also reports that individuals in happy relationships tend to believe that negativity is unstable and uncontrollable, whereas those in an unhappy relationship believe that negativity is stable and controllable. Likewise, Mills,

Mills, Nazar, and Farrell (2002), in their study on parent-child hurtful interactions, report that, among parents and children in close relationships, a positivity bias protected partners from making "extremely negative interpretations about one another's interactions" (p. 748). Hence, it is likely that the interactions leading up to individuals' accounts and attributional episodes surrounding parental infidelity shape these interpretations.

Given its utility, it is not surprising that theorizing on accounts and attributions is regularly applied to studies examining how individuals make sense of hurtful relationship and family events (e.g., Heider, 1958; Manusov, 2006; Manusov & Spitzberg, 2008). Specifically, in their studies on dyadic infidelity, Mongeau and his colleagues (Mongeau, Hale, & Alles, 1994; Mongeau & Schulz, 1997) employ theorizing on accounts and attributions to examine how individuals might verbally respond to and make sense of hypothetical sexual infidelities. Their findings suggest that differences in a hypothetical partner's infidelity influence the accounts and attributions offended partners use to explain these infidelities (Mongeau et al., 1994) and that hypothetical offenders' accounts are much more prevalent and honest as their knowledge of the infidelity increases (Mongeau & Schulz, 1997). Although these findings inform the current chapter, they are limited in that they focus on hypothetical dyadic infidelity. Thus, this chapter strives to paint a more complete picture of the communication surrounding this regularly experienced family crisis by examining the accounts and attributions which other family members (i.e., adult children) make for non-hypothetical infidelities.

A Study of Adult Children's Attributions for Parental Infidelity

Of the literature focusing on children, researchers report that children often experience stress upon becoming aware of their parents' infidelity (Saffer, Sansone, & Gentry, 1979). Thorson (2009) argues that adult children form communicative rules in order to protect and manage the information of their parents' infidelity, while Platt, Nalbone, Casanova, and Wetchler (2008) report that parental infidelity negatively impacts an adult child's view of the self and other. Still, there is a general lack of research on the specific types of accounts and attributions children use to make sense of a parent's infidelity. Thus, a qualitative study was conducted to answer the following research question:

RQ: What common accounts and attributions do adult children make for their unfaithful parents' motivations for infidelity?

Recruitment and Participants

In order to participate in this study, participants were required to meet the three following criteria: indicate that their parents were married to each other at some point during their life; indicate that one or both their parents (currently married, separated, or divorced) engaged in infidelity at some point during their marriage; and be at least 19-years-old. All participation was voluntary and participants were recruited using snowball and purposeful convenience sampling (Teddlie & Yu, 2007). More specifically, a recruitment email was sent to individuals in the researcher's social network and instructors at three Midwest universities shared information about this study with their students by posting research announcement on course and departmental web sites. In addition, the researcher personally an-nounced the study in 13 sections of introductory and upper-level communication courses at a large Midwestern university. Interviews were continued until saturation evident.

Of the 38 individuals, 16 (42.1%) men and 22 (57.9%) women, who volunteered to participate, 13 (34%) reported that their parents were currently married to each other, 1 (2.6%) separated, and 24 (63.2%) divorced. Participants ranged in age from 19 to 50 ($M = 23.95$, $SD = 7.31$) and reported finding out about their parents' infidelity from age 6 to 19 ($M = 11.84$, $SD = 4.04$). Participants were predominately White (32, 84.2%). Other ethnicities represented were Hispanic (4, 10.5%), Black and Asian/Hispanic (1, 2.6% each). In relation to the reported parent's extramarital relationship, 26 (71.1%) indicated that their father, nine (21.0%) indicated that their mother, and three (7.9%) indicated that both parents engaged in an extramarital relationship, for a total of 41 infidelities. Among those interviewed, many indi-viduals reported that their family experienced various structural changes following a parent's infidelity. Specifically, five (13.2%) participants indicated that a new sibling was born as a result of a parent's infidelity and 12 (31.6%) indicated that the person their parent had an extramarital affair with later became their stepparent.

Procedures

Upon volunteering for the study, participants were interviewed at a location in which they felt comfortable. Thus, interviews were conducted at a number of sites: 28 (73.7%) in an office or a reserved location on a university campus; six (15.8%) on the phone; three (7.9%) at a private residence; and one (2.6%) at a coffee shop. In order to answer the research question, a semi-structured interview protocol was developed and used as a guide for all interviews. At the completion of each interview participants were asked to answer a number of general demographic questions. Each interview lasted approximately 45 minutes. To ensure the accuracy of each participant's responses, interviews were audio recorded and then transcribed. Before any data were analyzed, each recording was compared to its transcription to ensure accuracy and verify that all special emphasis was correctly noted.

Throughout the recruitment, interview, and data collection process, many safeguards were put in place to minimize field issues. To ensure anonymity, participants' names were changed to pseudonyms immediately following each interview and participants were informed that their actual names would not be used. Participants were also provided contact information to the university psychological consultation center. No participant reported any risks upon participating in this study.

Data analysis

Data was analyzed using a phenomenological approach and Van Kaam's procedures, as suggested by Moustakas (1994). In addition to this process, further methodological rigor was attained through the application of validation techniques. This was accomplished by employing procedures suggested by Creswell (2007) and Baxter and Babbie (2004), such as peer briefing sessions, data conferences, and member checking. Before the start of the nine-month-long data collection process, a peer was enlisted to serve in the role of consult-ant throughout the research design, collection procedure, analysis, and results process. In addition, two additional researchers trained in qualitative methods were enlisted to participate in a data conference. In this data conference, the scholars reviewed and critiqued the analysis, refined categories, and validated the themes identified in the current study. Last, three interview participants conducted member checks as a way to confirm that the interpretations and findings were similar to their views.

Results

After analysis of the data was complete, five specific categories of accounts emerged: *dysfunction/deficiency*; *justifications/excuses*; *restoring credibility/character*; *blame*; and *denial of parent involvement*. The follow-ing provides a discussion of each account category, its corresponding underlying attributional dimension(s), and interview excerpts sup-porting each of the identified categories.

Dysfunction/deficiency. Participants describing the cause of their parents' infidelity as a *dysfunction* and/or *deficiency* indicated that his or her parent engaged in infidelity as a result of a socially learned pattern or a lack of communication skills collectively possessed by their parents. Specifically, participants whose accounts fell into this category described the cause of their parents' infidelity as a product of the deficiencies and dysfunction within their parents' marriage. For instance, one participant, Rob, described his family and his parents, stating:

> They both come from dysfunctional families. And, I don't know how far back the cycle goes. But, I noticed that in both of their families, they come from very dominant men that like to control everything... [These men] were basically searching for a co-dependent woman that would put up with their, put up with their infidelity and their abuse. And these women were subcon-sciously searching for men that would treat them bad. (lines 624–631)

Throughout his account, Rob described how his parents' learned patterns of behavior (e.g., patterns of infidelity and a lack of conflict resolution skills) played a role in his parent's infidelity.

As participants continued to make accounts for their parents' infidelities, Jared echoed the response of many others when suggesting: "the dynamics of their relationship, it was set up for something like this to happen" (272–273).

In relation to the underlying dimensions of controllability and stability attributions, the *dysfunction/deficiency* account described above is indicative of an uncontrollable, yet stable attribution. However, the locus of control highlighted within this account category is dialectical in nature. Meaning, participants referred to both internal and external underlying dimensions of locus of control for a parent's infidelity. Specifically, participants making dysfunction/deficiency accounts blamed their parent's infidelity on the combined nature of their parents' relationship—not one specific parent or the other. Participants believed the infidelity in their parents' relationship occurred because of something internal to their 'offending' parent. However, given that their 'faithful' parent was unable to break the pre-established patterns of infidelity that had been passed down from generation to generation, it is also important to simultaneously recognize the external locus of control attributional valence evidenced in this account category.

Justifications/excuses. Aside from the *dysfunction/deficiency* accounts identified above, many adult children spent a great deal of time making *justifications* and *excuses* for their parents' behavior. This was especially prevalent among those individuals whose parents' remained married to each other following the discovery of an infidelity. Specifically, participants often described the situation and early age at which their parents' married as being a cause of infidelity.

To illustrate, Katie, a participant whose father had engaged in infidelity, described her parents as immature when they got married, sarcastically sharing: "they got married right out of high school" (355). Brian, a participant whose father had engaged in infidelity, explained: "In my honest opinion, they were married way too young. He got involved way over his head. . . . He knocked her up. He had to get married. That was the policy of the sixties. That's what you do" (557–560). Others, such as Darren commented: "[My father] was a young guy in his mid-twenties [at the time] and he wanted something to entertain him and keep things exciting, lively, and going" (663–665). Throughout their interviews, these individuals pointed to a specific reason their parent engaged in infidelity.

For each of these participants, the *justifications* and *excuses* accounts they shared described how their parents' infidelity was instable and uncontrollable. They suggested that, because of his or her parent's maturity level and age at the time this event occurred, the parent could not control what was happening; it was just a product of the age and the situation at hand. In relation to the underlying attributional dimension of locus of control, participants did not specifically indicate whether they believed that their parents' infidelity was caused by something internal or external to their parent. As such, this account is neither classified as having an internal nor external locus of control.

Restoring credibility/character. Much like *justifications/excuses*, *restoring credibility/character* was used to minimize a parent's infidelity, rather emphasizing the positive character of the 'offending' parent. Similar to *justifications/excuses*, the underlying dimensions of this attributional category was classified as uncontrollable and unstable. This account category was different from the previous group because participants, while sharing their experience, simultaneously emphasized the positive qualities of their parent and deemed it important to talk about the satisfying relationships that they still have with the parent who engaged in the infidelity.

To illustrate, when explaining why infidelity had occurred in her parents' relationship, Amy replied: "My dad's like a phenomenal guy. . . . I mean, he's so cool and he's just so, so, selfless. And, he's just so caring and it's just ya know, he just screwed up" (295–298). As she talked, it was clear that Amy wanted to communicate the positive feelings she had toward her father and referred to this event as a mistake.

Another way that participants restored the credibility and character of their parent was by highlighting their role as "a parent," rather than their parents' ability to be a faithful "husband" or "wife." This distinction was made clear by Jacob, a participant who indicated that both his mother and father engaged in infidelity, stating: "They were good parents; they just didn't care about each other" (368–369).

A third way adult children used accounts to restore the credibility and character of their parent was by focusing on the fact that things had changed since their parent engaged in infidelity. For example, Joe, a young man whose father engaged in infidelity, described his father's extramarital behavior, saying:

> The way I see my dad now, it's almost like, unbelievable to me that that would happen because I couldn't ever picture him being in that. . . . I couldn't even imagine that he would even think about that even, like now. But that's definitely something that I know did happen and definitely something I know won't happen again. (143–149)

As illustrated above, *restoring credibility/character* accounts are indicative of unstable and uncontrollable underlying attributional dimensions. In each example, participants highlighted the great qualities of their parent while still acknowledging that this event did occur in their parents' relationship.

Blame. In relation to the fourth account type, *blame*, many participants personally blamed either their offending or faithful/unoffending parent as causing an infidelity. Those accounts made by participants who blamed their offending parent for the infidelity were classified as having an internal causal locus, whereas those individuals who used accounts blaming the faithful/unoffending parent for this behavior were identified as having an external causal locus. As such, 'offending' parent blame and 'faithful' parent blame are subcategories of *blame*. Each subcategory and a description of its corresponding underlying attributional dimension are described below.

The subcategory of *blame* titled *'offending' parent blame* is characterized by participants' negative descriptions of their unfaithful parent. For instance, Shelly, a young woman whose father engaged in infidelity, described her dad's personality as she talked about his infidelity, stating: "It just stems back from that they [my dad and his new wife] just do whatever they want" (586–587) and "I just think he thinks it was right because it was what he wanted to do" (212–213). While Shelly described her father as being selfish, others shared that their 'offending' parent was a jerk or lacked morals. Specifically, Lindsay, a participant whose father slept with another woman during her mother's pregnancy, said: "I think it probably goes back to his lack of morals" (367) and "I just don't really agree with his lifestyle" (326).

These excerpts are different from the accounts mentioned previously because they point to negative personal characteristics of the 'offending' parent as the cause for infidelity. As such, they illustrate that the cause of a parent's infidelity is something internal to that offending parent.

'Faithful' parent blame, a second subcategory of *blame,* was developed to represent those situations in which participants described their faithful parent as driving their 'offending' parent to engage in infidelity. Because this account subcategory emphasizes something that is outside the 'offending' parent, it has an external locus of control as its underlying attributional dimension. Hence, the cause is something that is external to the actual transgressor. Also, while some participants described their faithful parents' behaviors as being stable and uncontrollable, this was not consistent among participants. Thus, these attributional dimensions are not classified as such.

Similar to the account subcategory *'offending' parent blame,* some participants described their 'faithful' parent as being a jerk, confrontational, or unavailable. Specifically, Bobbie, a participant who learned of his mother's infidelity years ago stated: "I just thought he [my dad] was always a prick to my mom" (81–82). In sum, Bobbie blamed his father's temperament for his mother's infidelity. Tim, a participant whose father had engaged in infidelity, said: "My mother was overly confrontational" (1197) as he described the reasons why his father looked outside the marriage. Furthermore, Gretchen, when articulating why she believed her father engaged in infidelity, stated: "The fact that my mom is not, like, overly affectionate…my dad like wanted to like get that from somewhere else" (924–926).

These accounts are unique because they point to characteristics of the 'faithful' parent as motivating the 'offending' parent to look outside the marriage. They illustrate that the cause of their parents' infidelity was something external to the 'offending' parent.

Denial of parent involvement. The fifth and final account category developed after analyzing these data was *denial of parent involvement.* This category was formed to describe those situations in which an adult child blamed something external to both of their parents for causing the infidelity. Among these external locus of control accounts were alcohol, a parent's occupation, or the person outside the marriage.

A common thread in many of the interviews was that alcohol was instrumental in leading someone to engage in infidelity. For instance, when describing his mother's infidelity, Matt stated: "I think it mostly was, well definitely was, probably the alcohol. She couldn't stop herself" (432–433). Randy added: "My mom was an alcoholic at the time . . . so that was a big part of it" (104–105).

Like alcohol, other individuals indicated that their parents' job drove a parent to be unfaithful. In particular, Lindsay, when discussing her father's infidelity, commented: "Both my parents being in the health care profession . . . there is a lot of inter-hospital dating and extramarital relationships. It's [infidelity and dating] pretty normal between doctors and nurses" (358-360); whereas, Alyssa, when describing her dad's infidelity, emphasized: "He [Dad] travels a lot" (403).

A final example of *denial of parent involvement* accounts included blaming the event on the 'outside' person or the extramarital partner. For instance, when Ashley discussed her father's mistress, she pointed out: "This woman was kind of 'the temptress' type of woman and I think that was part of it" (472–473). Another participant, Robyn, when describing her mother's extramarital relationship, stated:

> My mom got very close to a friend of the family after his . . . wife died. The man sort of needed a woman, I think, very quickly. He didn't want to wait for anybody and saw that my mom was sort of . . . in marital distress. . . . I don't think he meant to have it happen the way it did necessarily, but sort of, in some way knew how to make my mom, in a slight way, manipulate her into really feeling that she needed and wanted more than what she had. (54–60)

As illustrated in the account above, in addition to the external locus of control attributions of alcohol and occupations, participants often considered the role of the 'outside' person when assessing the cause of a parent's infidelity.

Thus, the category of *denial of parent involvement* is classified as having an underlying external locus of control. Similar to *'offending'* and *'faithful' parent blame*, the classifications of stable/unstable or controllable/uncontrollable is not applicable to this category.

Table 3.1 provides a summary of the account categories described above and sorts them according to their underlying attributional dimension(s).

Table 3.1: Account Categories and Related Attributions for Parental Infidelity

Account	Underlying Attributional Dimension(s)
Dysfunction/Deficiency	Internal & External locus of control, Stable, and Uncontrollable
Justifications/Excuses	Unstable and Uncontrollable
Restoring Credibility/ Character	Unstable and Uncontrollable
Blame	
'offending' parent blame	
'faithful' parent blame	Internal locus of control
	External locus of control
Denial of Parent Involvement	External locus of control

Discussion of Attributions for Parental Infidelity and Family Interaction

The goals of this brief study were to highlight the different ways an adult child makes sense of his or her parent's infidelity. The construction of the textural-structural descriptions extends the understanding of how adult children use accounts and attributions to describe a parent's infidelity and are likely applicable to children's sense-making process following other hurtful and/or unexpected family events.

Participants describing the cause of their parents' infidelity as a *dysfunction* or *deficiency* shared that their parents' infidelity was a product of their family of origin or their parents' relationship itself. These accounts were categorized as being stable and uncontrollable, and having both an internal and external causal locus. The second account type, *justifications and excuses*, was formed as a result of participants describing their parents' infidelity as a product of their parents' relationship, such that their parents grew apart or were not right for each other in the first place. These accounts were categorized as uncontrollable and unstable attributions. The category of *restoring credibility and character* was used to describe those accounts used to minimize the infidelity, calling it an uncontrollable or unique occurrence. Like *justifications and excuses,* these accounts were categorized as uncontrollable and unstable attributions. In relation to the fourth account category, *blame,* participants often blamed either their offending or faithful parent as the cause an infidelity. Those participants who made accounts blaming their offending parent for an infidelity were categorized as having an internal causal locus, whereas those who made accounts in which they blamed their unoffending parent for this behavior were categorized as having an external causal locus. *Denial of parent involvement* was the final account type shared by participants. Participants making these accounts often stated that alcohol or their parents' occupation, something separate from either parent, was to blame for these affairs. These accounts were categorized as having an external causal locus. Although accounts and attributions are not static and can change over time, these categories shed light on the ways children talked about their parents' infidelity in their attempt to make sense of these events.

As researchers continually work to understand the impact parental infidelity has on children and family communication, it is important to acknowledge that children's accounts and attributions for hurtful or unexpected events are often influenced by past interactions and play a key role in shaping future family communication. They are closely tied to other aspects of the parent-child relationship. As such, the following sections highlight some of the findings from the current study and make connections to research which supports the link between accounts and attributions to past and future family interaction.

Family Interactions Taking Place before Discovery

Researchers argue that the interactions leading up to individuals' accounts and attributional episodes surrounding a crisis help shape the interpretations of a hurtful event (Gottman, 1994; Mills et al., 2002; Vangelisti, 2006; Vangelisti & Young, 2000). As related to the current study, it is likely that the ways families communicated about infidelity prior to participants being interviewed (i.e., as influenced by satisfaction in the parent-child relationship, parent-child disclosures about a parent's infidelity, sibling conversations, overhearing information for which the adult child was not supposed to be privy, or even religion) affect the way that adult children made sense of his or her parent's infidelity. Consistent with theorizing on attributions, those participants making accounts which fit under the categories of *justifications/excuses* or *restoring credibility/character* which are evident of unstable and uncontrollable, positively valenced, attributions may have also had a positive relationship with their 'offending' parent prior to discovering the information of his or her infidelity. It may also be true for those individuals who made accounts which fit under the subcategory of *'faithful' parent blame* or the category of *denial of parent involvement* given that the underlying dimensions of these categories were external. Alternatively, is it likely that participants making *dysfunction/deficiency* accounts may also have less satisfying relationships with their parent prior to discovering the information of his or her infidelity given that stable attributions are often negatively valenced. This may also be true for those individuals who make accounts fitting under the *'offending' parent blame* subcategory given that the underlying attributional dimension of this category is internal. While these ideas are merely speculative, they have implications for how family interactions prior to the discovery of a parent's infidelity may shape the accounts an adult child makes for this event.

The study highlighted in this chapter examines the accounts adult children make for their parents' infidelity. While it adds to the body of literature on this topic, it does not examine children's satisfaction with his or her parent prior to the discovery of their infidelity using a method that could make accurate group comparisons, nor does it examine how families talk about infidelity in parent-child interactions and sibling conversations. Rather, it gives some preliminary insight into how the accounts individuals make for their parents' infidelity may be influenced by family interactions taking place before a child discovers that his or her parent has engaged in infidelity. In order to further explore this topic, future research must be conducted to examine how accounts are directly influenced by pre-discovery satisfaction in the parent-child relationship and communication about infidelity between parents, their children, and their siblings.

Family Interactions Taking Place after Discovery

Just as family interactions which take place before a hurtful event can influence individuals' attributions, so can family interactions following a hurtful event. A number of researchers suggest that positively biased attributions, (i.e., those which suggest that a negative event is caused by an external, unstable, and uncontrollable source) are also predictive of outcomes for the parent-child relationship such as satisfaction, support, and forgiveness (Boon & Sulsky, 1997; Weiner, Graham, Peter, & Zmuidinas, 1991). Thus, when examining the communication surrounding hurtful events such as parental infidelity, researchers must examine the communication which occurs between children, their parents, and other family members in order to understand how the relationship is repaired and maintained (Hall & Fincham, 2006). Understanding how support is given to a child, how forgiveness is sought by a parent (if at all) after engaging in infidelity, or how forgiveness is granted to a parent (if at all) by their child after this event is processed is an important aspect for future studies to address. In addition, it may be important for future researchers to examine how, if at all, attributions for a parent's infidelity might influence either constructive or destructive communicative episodes occurring among parents-children following a child's discovery of parental infidelity.

Best Practices

When individuals are unable to make sense of a negative or unexpected, hurtful event they often experience stress and continue to ruminate about these events long after they are discovered. Additionally, their inability to produce an account or attribution often stifles their ability to communicate about events. Thus, an individual's ability to form attributions for these events is instrumental in helping them make sense of their experiences and the world in which they live.

Second, as we find ourselves in a culture where "flip-flopping" is perceived as a negative characteristic, it is important for readers to understand that attributions can and do change over time. In fact, as individuals mature, learn more about their parents' relationship, communicate with their parents and others about this event, and experience relationships of their own, they often re-evaluate how to make sense family events. With this said, no matter how much an event is discussed, accounts and attributions cannot be forced upon individuals nor can they be evaluated as "correct" or "incorrect."

As individuals read this chapter, they may be relieved to learn that they are not alone or be reassured by having read that someone else has made sense of a parent's infidelity in the same way that they have. Others may read this chapter and think that these accounts do not make sense because they understand their parents' infidelity much differently. No matter the case, a more important practice to take from this chapter is that accounts, whether stemming from an internal, uncontrollable, or stable attributional dimensions, are instrumental in understanding one's life experiences. Thus, I hesitate to conclude this chapter with a prescriptive note; rather, I hope that readers leave this chapter having a better understanding of the importance attributions play in helping individuals rebuild their relationships following hurtful and unexpected negative life events.

Summary

This chapter explores the prevalence of infidelity, theorizing on accounts and attributions, and provides findings from a qualitative study which was conducted to explain the accounts and attributions adult children make for the infidelities of their parents. After interviewing 38 individuals who indicated that infidelity occurred in their parents' relationship, five specific account categories emerged—*dysfunction/deficiency; justifications/excuses; restoring credibility/character; blame;* and *denial of parent involvement*—and the underlying attributional dimensions of each were identified. The findings highlighted in

this chapter provide a better understanding of the ways adult children make sense of this often unexpected, negative event.

References

Baxter, L. A., & Babbie, E. (2004). *The basics of communication research.* Belmont, CA: Wadsworth.

Betzig, L. (1989). Causes of conjugal dissolution: A cross-cultural study. *Current Anthropology, 30,* 654–676.

Boon, S. D., & Sulsky, L. M. (1997). Attributions of blame and forgiveness: A policy-capturing study. *Journal of Social Behavior and Personality, 12,* 19–44.

Canary, D. J., Cody, M. J., & Manusov, V. (2003). *Interpersonal communication: A goals-based approach* (3rd ed.). New York: Bedford/St. Martin's Press.

Cherlin, A. J. (1992). *Marriage, divorce, remarriage.* Cambridge, MA: Harvard University Press.

Creswell, J. W. (2007). *Qualitative inquiry and research design: Choosing among five approaches* (2nd ed.). Thousand Oaks, CA: Sage.

Duncombe, J., & Marsden, D. (2004). Affairs and children. In J. Duncombe, K. Harrison, G. Allen, & D. Marsden (Eds.), *The State of Affairs: Explorations in Infidelity and Commitment.* Mahwah, NJ: Lawrence Erlbaum & Associates.

Gottman, J. M., & Noratis, C. I. (2000). Decade review: Observing martial interaction. *Journal of Marriage and the Family, 62,* 927–947.

Hall, J. H., & Fincham, F. D. (2006). Relationship dissolution following infidelity: The roles of attributions and forgiveness. *Journal of Social and Clinical Psychology, 25,* 508–522.

Heider, F. (1958). *The psychology of interpersonal relations.* New York: Wiley.

Kelly, E. L., & Conley, J. J. (1987). Personality and compatibility: A prospective analysis of marital stability and marital satisfaction. *Journal of Personality and Social Psychology, 52,* 27–40.

Laumann, E. O., Gagnon, J. H., Michael, R. T., & Michaels, S. (1994). *The social organization of sexuality: Sexual practices in the United States.* Chicago: University of Chicago Press.

Manusov, V. (2006). Attribution theories: Assessing causal and responsibility judgments in families. In D. O. Braithwaite & L. A. Baxter (Eds.), *Engaging theories in family communication: Multiple perspectives* (pp. 181–196). Thousand Oaks, CA: Sage.

Manusov, V., & Spitzberg, B. H. (2008). Attributes of attribution theory: Finding good cause in the search for theory. In D. O. Braithwaite & L. A. Baxter (Eds.), *Engaging theories in interpersonal communication: Multiple perspectives* (pp. 37–50). Thousand Oaks, CA: Sage.

Mills, R. S. L., Nazar, J., & Farrell, H. M. (2002). Child and parent perceptions of hurtful messages. *Journal of Social and Personal Relationships, 19,* 731–754.

Mongeau, P. A., Hale, J. L., & Alles, M. (1994). An experimental investigation of accounts and attributions following sexual infidelity. *Communication Monographs, 61,* 326–344.

Mongeau, P. A., & Schulz, B. E. (1997). What he doesn't know won't hurt him (or me): Verbal responses and attributions following sexual infidelity. *Communication Reports, 10,* 143–152.

Moustakas, C. (1994). *Phenomenological research methods.* Thousand Oaks, CA: Sage.

Platt, R. A. L., Nalbone, D. P., Casanova, G. M., & Wetchler, J. L. (2008). Parental conflict and infidelity as predictors of adult children's attachment style and infidelity. *The American Journal of Family Therapy, 36,* 149–161.

Rusbult, C. E., Hannon, P. A., Stocker, S. L., & Finkel, E. J. (2005). Forgiveness and relational repair. In E. L. Worthington, Jr. (Ed.), *Handbook of forgiveness* (pp. 185–205). New York: Brunner-Routledge.

Russell, D. (1982). The causal dimension scale: A measure of how individuals perceive causes. *Journal of Personality and Social Psychology, 42,* 1137–1145.

Saffer, J. B., Sansone, P., & Gentry, J. (1979). The awesome burden upon the child who must keep a family secret. *Child Psychiatry and Human Development, 10,* 35–40.

Teddlie C., & Yu, F. (2007). Mixed methods sampling: A typology with examples. *Journal of Mixed Methods Research, 1,* 77–100.

Thompson, A. P. (1984). Emotional and sexual components of extramarital relations. *Journal of Marriage* and *the Family, 46,* 35–42.

Thorson, A. R. (2009). Adult children's experiences with their parents' infidelity: Communicative protection and access rules in the absence of divorce. *Communication Studies, 60*(1), 32–48.

Vangelisti, A. L. (2006). Hurtful interactions and the dissolution of intimacy. In M. A. Fine & J. H. Harvey (Eds.), *Handbook of divorce and relationship dissolution* (pp. 133–151). Mahwah, NJ: Lawrence Erlbaum.

Vangelisti, A. L., & Young, S. L. (2000). When words hurt: The effects of perceived intentionality on interpersonal relationships. *Journal of Social and Personal Relationships, 17,* 393–424.

Weiner, B. (1986). *An attributional theory of motivation and emotion.* New York: Springer-Verlag.

Weiner, B. (2004). Attribution theory revisited: Transforming cultural plurality into theoretical unity. In D. M. McInerney & S. Van Etten (Eds.), *Big Theories Revisited* (pp. 13–30). Greenwich, CT: Information Age Publishing.

Weiner, B., Graham, S., Peter, O., & Zmuidinas, M. (1991). Public confession and forgiveness. *Journal of Personality, 59,* 281–312.

Chapter 4

And Then He Was a She: Communication Following a Gender-Identity Shift

Christine Aramburu Alegría and Deborah Ballard-Reisch

Crises for families come in many forms. For the couples described in this chapter, relational crises occurred within their established male-female relationships when the male partners disclosed their transsexual identities. Following the disclosure, communicative strategies allowed the partners to re-create their relationships while restoring equilibrium. The results of this study provide helpful guidelines for counselors, clinicians, and other caregivers working with couples and families facing similar crises.

When two people establish a close relationship, their ongoing interactions form the framework from which their relational expectations arise (Baldwin, 1992; Blumer, 1969). Through these communicative activities, partners jointly create and negotiate their relationships. Hence, as time goes on, expectations of self, partners, and relationships become established (Baldwin, 1992; Holmes, 2000).

Following the establishment of a relationship, couples employ maintenance strategies to prevent the relationship's decline or dissolution (Attridge, 1994; Canary, Stafford, & Semic, 2002; Duck, 1986). These relationship maintenance activities (RMA) include direct (e.g., face-to-face discussion) and indirect (e.g., running errands for the partner) forms of communication, as well as pro-relational cognitive activities (e.g., deliberate derogation of attractive alternative partners; Canary & Stafford, 1992; Johnson & Rusbult, 1989; Murray, 1999; Rusbult, Olsen, Davis, & Hannon, 2001). Thus, through the use of direct, indirect, and cognitive pro-relational activities, two processes occur within relationships: (a) relational norms and expectations become established, and (b) the relationship is maintained in an ongoing and interactive manner.

Though couples make efforts to establish and maintain their relationships at a level of equilibrium, unexpected events occur in all long-term relationship. Disruptive events can take many forms, including infidelity (e.g., Hall & Fincham, 2006), illness (e.g., Lavery & Clarke, 1999), economic hardship (e.g., Conger & Conger, 2002), and unexpected partner disclosures (e.g., Reynolds & Caron, 2000). When an unforeseen disruptive event occurs within a relationship, established relational norms may be disrupted, and the relationship at risk of crisis (e.g., Lavee, McCubbin, & Olson, 1987; McCubbin & Patterson, 1983). Previously established relational expectations may no longer provide an adequate framework for the relationship. Thus, to restore relational equilibrium, partners will undertake strategic communicative measures to renegotiate their relationship via the re-creation of relational norms and expectations.

Multiple studies have examined the effects of and responses to disruptive events on couples and families. For example, during economic hardship, families' communicative strategies include the provision of mutual support and problem-solving (Conger & Conger, 2002). In a study examining the relationships of couples in which one partner self-disclosed as homosexual, adaptive relational strategies included communication to renegotiate the relationship, counseling or therapy to make sense of the situation, and peer support (Buxton, 2001).

The present study examined the adaptive communicative strategies following a relational disruption in what has, thus far, been an under-examined population, couples which include male-to-female (MTF) transsexual individuals (i.e., natal male individuals who experience incongruence between their assigned gender as men and their gender identity as women; Vitale, 2001) and their natal female partners (i.e., female at birth; NF). Although transsexualism is gaining visibility, and furthermore, MTF individuals often marry and raise families, studies that examine relationships that include transsexual individuals and their partners are scarce (Gagné & Tewksbury, 1998; Tully, 1993; Vitale, 2001). The prevalence of MTF transsexualism is estimated to be 1 in 500, with approximately 1 in 2500 seeking sexual reassignment surgery (SRS) in the United States. These figures do not consider the number of MTF persons who seek SRS outside the United States, for example, Thailand (Conway, 2001). To date, the authors have been unable to find data on the number of close couple relationships that are affected by transsexualism—an indication that despite the increasing visibility and relatively high prevalence of transsexualism, the phenomenon remains under-examined. Specifically, the present study examined effective communication strategies in couples experiencing the disclosure of transsexualism by a relationship partner within an established relationship, and compared their strategic communication efforts with those of couples who have experienced other types of relationship crises.

Conceptual Framework

Grounded in symbolic interactionism (Blumer, 1969; Mead, 1934), exchange theory (Homans, 1950; Thibaut & Kelly, 1959), and schema theory (Baldwin, 1992; Holmes, 2000; Fiske & Taylor, 1991), this qualitative study examined the couples' investment of RMAs into their relationships as they renegotiated them, while re-creating relational norms and expectations (i.e., schema) following the disclosure.

Maintaining relationships at a stable and equitable level is a dynamic process, one that requires the partners' ongoing attention and investment of resources (Attridge, 1994). Adapting to relational disruptions is also a continual process, and is influenced by how situations are defined and perceived (Lavee et al., 1987; McCubbin & Patterson, 1983). These perceptions and interpretations (and consequent actions) are a function of the meanings individuals attach to situations and interactions, and are based on individuals' schemas, or expectations of themselves and their partners (Baldwin, 1992; Blumer, 1969; Holmes, 2000). In addition, the ability of a relationship to withstand and adapt to relational disruptions is affected by the strength of the relationship prior to the unexpected event and the resources available to the partners (McCubbin & Patterson, 1983).

Subsequent to the disruptive event, couples who continue their relationships will engage in activities to re-create relational stability, norms, and expectations and to maintain their relationships. Figure 4.1 illustrates the integration of the theories underlying this study. Specifically, the conceptual framework depicts the complex set of processes couples go through to renegotiate their relationships following a relational disruption within an already established relationship.

Figure 4.1: *Conceptual Framework Illustrating Relationship between Schema, Relationship Maintenance Activities (RMA), and Equity before and after Relational Crisis*

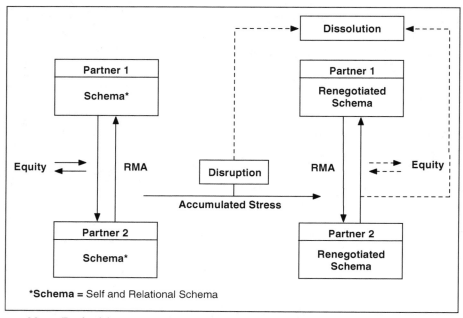

Note: Dashed lines indicate possible outcomes following relational disruption including dissolution, renegotiation leading to sustaining equity/equilibrium, or unsuccessful attempts at renegotiation leading to relationship dissolution.

The couples in the present study sustained a relational disruption when one partner disclosed a transsexual identity within a relationship that had been established based on the assumption that the female self-identified as a woman and the male self-identified as a man (i.e., non-transsexual). The initial reactions of wives to their husbands' disclosure of transsexualism often include feelings of betrayal, anger, and confusion, as well as the belief that the relationship continues to hold potential as a satisfying union (Gurvich, 1991). However, the manner in which partners effectively renegotiate their relationships following this type of relational disruption, and further, how the management of this type of disruption compares to other crises, has been scarce and unexamined. Thus, we posed two basic research questions:

RQ1. What communicative strategies (i.e., RMAs) do MTF-NF couples employ following the disclosure of transsexualism as they renegotiate their relationships, relational norms, and expectations?
RQ2. How do these communicative strategies compare to those employed by other couples and families who have sustained other types of relational crises?

Methods

Participants

Participants were recruited via internet forums and network sampling. A recruitment letter describing the study and inclusion criteria was posted on forums that address issues affecting transsexual individuals. Inclusion criteria specified that couples must include a partner who is a natal female and a partner who self-identifies as male-to-female transsexual, although identified as a natal male at birth. Criteria also included that the male-to-female transsexualism have been disclosed after the relationship was established, that the partners are in a committed relationship with each other, that the duration of the relationship was at least one year at the time of the study, and that both partners participate.

Seventeen MTF-NF couples, located throughout the western United States, were recruited through the forums and network sampling. Each participant attested to meeting the inclusion criteria. All participants described themselves as White/Caucasian. With the exception of one cohabitating and engaged couple, all of the couples were married and living together. The participants ranged in age from 30 to 69 (M = 51.6 years; SD = 8.71). Approximately three-fourths of the participants were between the ages of 50 and 69 (NF: n = 12; 70%; MTF: n = 13; 76.4%). More than one-half of the couples (n = 23; 67.6%) had a bachelor degree or a higher level of education.

The length of the couples' relationships ranged from three to 44 years (M = 21.8 years; SD = 11.19). Approximately one-third of the couples' relationships ranged from 20 to 29 years, and another one-third ranged in length from 10 to 19 years. At the time of the disclosure of transsexualism, the couples had been in their relationships from 1 ½ to 35 years (M = 16.2 years; SD = 9.76). The average length of time since the disclosure was approximately 5 years for the couples.

All MTFs self-identified as "female," "transsexual woman," or "trans-woman." Fourteen (82.3%) MTFs reported their sexual partner preference as women. Three MTFs (17.6%) reported an equal preference for men and women. Sixteen NFs (94.1%) reported their sexual partner preference as men; one NF (5.9%) reported equal preference for men and women.

The stage of transition among the MTF participants ranged from part-time *en femme* (i.e., as women), without body-altering proce-dures, to full-time *en femme* with sexual reassignment surgery. All MTF respondents reported the usage of feminization medications. More than three-fourths (n = 14; 82.4%) of the MTF respondents lived full-time *en femme*. Among those who are living full-time *en femme*, almost one-half have had sexual reassignment surgery (Table 4.1).

Table 4.1: *MTF Respondents Living En Femme*

MTF Transition N = 17		
MTF	%	n
Full-time, SRS	35.5	6
Full-time, Pre-op SRS	17.6	3
Full-time, No surgery	17.6	3
Full-time, Other surgery*	11.9	2
Part-time	17.6	3
Total	100	17

*Orchiectomy (i.e., removal of testicles), tracheal cartilage shave, vocal cord surgery.

Procedures and Instruments

The study involved two phases: (a) questionnaires and (b) indi-vidual, semi-structured interviews. The questionnaires elicited information on demographics, length of the relationship, feminizing behavior and relationship maintenance, providing an overview of and context for the relationship. The questionnaires and the informed consent information sheet were sent to participants via United States Postal Service. Two questionnaires were sent—one for each member of the couple. Participants were provided with individual envelopes—one for each member of the couple—in which to place their individual surveys. These individual envelopes were then placed in a large, self-addressed stamped envelope and returned to the first author. Contact information to set up the interviews was requested on the final page of the questionnaire. Thirty-four completed questionnaires were returned to the first author.

The interview schedule was developed by the researchers, and consisted of 25 open-ended questions grounded in relationship maintenance, identity, and transgenderism. These questions elicited information on partners' identity and relational renegotiation process. Examples of interview questions include "Are activities you use to maintain your relationship following the disclosure of transsexualism different from activities you used prior to the disclosure," and "Does transsexualism add any unique challenges and/or opportunities to your relationship?" The first author conducted, recorded, and transcribed verbatim all interviews. Interviews were conducted at participants' homes, and measures were taken to ensure each respondent's privacy during the interview. Each interview's duration was approximately one and one-half to two hours. Thirty-four interviews were completed, resulting in 60 hours of interview and 522 pages of transcription.

Data Analysis

Deductive and inductive methods were used in the analysis. Deductive analysis included the use of a typology of RMAs to identify the pro-relational activities of participants (Canary & Stafford, 1992; Dainton & Stafford, 1993; Haas & Stafford, 1998; Stafford & Canary, 1991). Inductive analysis included the use of the constant comparative method (i.e., an iterative process by which data is compared within and across subjects; Glaser & Strauss, 1967; Strauss & Corbin, 1998) to identify unique relationship maintenance activities not covered by the existing typology.

Intercoder reliability and member checks were employed to increase the credibility of the findings (Creswell, 1998; Lincoln & Guba,

1985; Miles & Huberman, 1994). The researcher and a second coder independently coded the surveys and the interviews for each partners' pro-relational activities that facilitated relational renegotiation post-disclosure. Additionally, to examine shared communication and the joint re-creation of relational norms and expectations, couple partners' data were compared to each other, and an activity was coded as being utilized by a couple if both partners reported it. For example, if both NF 1 and MTF 1 report using the activity, communication, Couple 1 is recorded as using communication. If NF 1 reports using communication but MTF 1 does not, communication is not reported as an activity for Couple 1. Thus, the units of analyses include NFs, MTFs, and couples.

The coders coded data from six couples (i.e., questionnaires and interviews), using the relationship maintenance typology (Canary & Stafford, 1992; Dainton & Stafford, 1993; Haas & Stafford, 1998; Stafford & Canary, 1991) adding categories as needed when the typology did not adequately categorize the present study's data. Upon completion of the independent codings, the researcher and the second coder met and reviewed the categories. Adjustments were made via consensus and a single modified typology was created for use in coding the remaining questionnaires and interviews. Each coder then proceeded to code the remaining data, collaborating as necessary on the development of categories. Consistent with the constant comparative method (Glaser & Strauss, 1967; Strauss & Corbin, 1998), categories from each data set were compared with other data sets throughout the process. Percent agreement was utilized to calculate intercoder reliability for the questionnaires (.94) and for the interviews (.92).

Member checks with participants allowed respondents to validate the researcher's interpretation of their experience. During the interviews, the researcher frequently repeated back to the respondents what they seemed to be reporting. This allowed the respondents to rectify and/or clarify the researcher's interpretation. Additionally, five couples (i.e., five MTFs and five NFs) participated in post-transcription member checks. All verified that the study findings described their experience.

Findings

Initial Reactions

Consistent with previous findings (Gurvich, 1991), the NFs in this study reacted to their partners' disclosure of transsexualism with feelings of confusion, shock, and betrayal. They also reported that their lack of knowledge about transsexualism prevented them from understanding what it meant in terms of their and their partners' identity, sexual orientation, and future. Further, without knowledge of similar others, the NFs perceived themselves as being isolated.

However, following these initial reactions to the disclosure, a process of restorative steps began as the couples made the decision to renegotiate and continue their relationships. Hence, they engaged in interactions to make sense of their situation, renegotiate their norms and expectations, and re-create their relationships in a mutually acceptable manner.

RQ 1. Relationship Maintenance Activities in MTF-NF Couples

The couples utilized a variety of direct and indirect communicative activities (i.e., RMAs) to restore relational equilibrium and re-create their relationship. Relationship maintenance activities that specifically facilitated relationship renegotiation following the disclosure of transsexualism include (a) positivity (e.g., positive interactions), (b) openness (e.g., self-disclosure, meta-relational communication, joint decision-making), (c) assurances, (d) social networking, (e) sharing tasks, (f) topic avoidance, (g) conflict management (i.e., compromise, limit-setting), (h) affection, (i) focusing on growth (e.g., counseling, education), (j) impression management in public, and (k) self-talk (e.g., framing, affirming, evaluating). These RMAs are described and their frequencies reported in Table 4.2 (for a detailed description of RMAs and the participants' use of them, the reader is referred to Aramburu Alegría, 2008). They are further illustrated in the following section.

Table 4.2: *Couple (N = 17), NF (N = 17), and MTF (N = 17)*
Use of Relationship Maintenance Activities

---

1. Positivity   13 (76.4)   15 (88.2)   14 (82.3)
("She smiles a lot more.")

2. Openness   17 (100)   17 (100)   17 (100)
("It's important to talk with your spouse.")

3. Assurances   15 (88.2)   16 (94.1)   16 (94.1)
("She stays home Fridays because I want her home then.")

4. Social networking   17 (100)   17 (100)   17 (100)
("We go out with other trans couples.")

5. Sharing tasks   6 (35.3)   8 (47.1)   9 (52.9)
("We divide chores more equitably now.")

6. Avoidance   10 (58.8)   11 (64.7)   12 (70.6)
("Sometimes I need to have [MTF] present as a man")

7. Conflict management   11 (64.7)   12 (70.6)   13 (76.4)
("She could dress like a woman only at certain times.")

8. Affection   14 (82.3)   16 (94.1)   14 (82.3)
("We still hug, kiss, and touch.")

9. Focus on growth /
Improvement   13 (76.5)   16 (94.1)   15 (88.2)
("I became a trans activist.")

10. Impression management   10 (58.8)   16 (94.1)   10 (58.8)

11. Self-talk   17 (100)   17 (100)
("I look at the positive qualities of the relationship.")

Note. Self-talk does not include couple frequency as it is an individual cognitive process, rather than an observable behavior of shared communication between partners. Rather than being directly interactional, self-talk reflects indirect pro-relational activity. All examples are taken from the present study's data.

RQ 2. Comparisons of the Activities of MTF-NF Couples to Other Relational Crises

In order to further contextualize the maintenance activities of couples who sustain a disclosure of transsexualism, the relational activities of MTF-NF couples were compared to the activities of couples who have sustained other types of relational crises. These crises include transgressions (e.g., an affair; Kelley & Waldron, 2005; Roloff, Soule, & Carey, 2001; Waldron & Kelley, 2005), a disclosure of homosexuality (Buxton, 2001; Oswald, 2002), a disclosure of cross-dressing (Reynolds & Caron, 2000), illness (Lavery & Clarke, 1999; McCubbin, McCubbin, Patterson, Cauble, Wilson, & Warwick, 1983; Skerrett, 1998; Wright & Aquilino, 1998), and economic hardship (Conger & Conger, 2002). In reviewing these studies on the activities of couples who have sustained crises, a comparison of activities suggests that MTF-NF and other couples use similar activities to maintain and rebuild their relationships following relational disruption. Table 4.3 summarizes the comparison of the activities of MTF-NF couples to other couples who have sustained relational disruptions.

Figure 4.3: *Summary of the Comparison of Relational Maintenance Activities of MTF-NF Couples to Other Couples Who Have Sustained Relational Crises*

| | Type of Crises | | | | |
| | Disclosure | | | Other Crises | |
MTF-NF	Transgression	Homosexuality	Cross-dress	Illness	Econ. Hardship
Positivity	Gift-giving Positive interactions			Maintain optimism	
Openness	Communication Discuss causes & motives Acknowledge impact Renegotiate covenant	Renegotiate relationship	Communication	Communication	Communication
Assurances	Problem-solve Assurances & promises Partner support			Joint approach Assurances Mutual support	Joint approach Assurances Mutual support
Social network	Social support	Social support		Social support	
Sharing tasks				Cooperation Maintain family unity	
Topic avoidance	Topic avoidance			Topic avoidance	

MTF-NF	Type of Crises				
	Disclosure			Other Crises	
	Transgression	Homosexuality	Cross-dress	Illness	Econ. Hardship
Conflict mgmt.	Compensating Limits on behavior	Limit-setting	Limit-setting		
Focus on growth	Education as resource Personal strength Counseling Family strength	Education	Education	Education Self-growth Promote independence	Self-determin.
Self-talk	Positive attributions Sense-making Frame event Minimize salience Interpret causes and motives	Positive attrib. Sense-making	Positive attrib.	Optimistic outlook Sense-making Affirming self-talk	Self-determin. Sense-making

Note: The sources for the comparison are as follows: Transgression (Kelley & Waldron, 2005; Roloff et al., 2001; Waldron & Kelley, 2005); Homosexuality (Buxton, 2001); Cross-dressing (Reynolds & Caron, 2000; Weinberg & Bullough, 1988); Illness (Lavery & Clarke, 1999; McCubbin et al., 1983; Skerrett, 1998; Wright & Aquilino, 1998); Economic hardship (Conger & Conger, 2002).

Disclosure. Unexpected disclosures, such as transgression, homo-sexuality, or cross-dressing can create relational crises, and couples that experience them generally require reconciliation before they can renegotiate their relationships (Buxton, 2001; Kelley & Waldron, 2005; Reynolds & Caron, 2000; Roloff et al., 2001). Following transgression, relational activities that enable couples a position to move forward from include: (a) acknowledging the emotional impact of the trans-gression, (b) sense-making of the situation, including its causes and motives, (c) communication, (d) renegotiating the relational covenant, (e) compensating, including placing conditions on behavior and increasing resources invested, and (f) providing assurances and promises (Kelley, 1998; Kelley & Waldron, 2005; Waldron & Kelley, 2005).

Examples of these activities are reflected in partners' statements such as, "I initiated discussion," "I gave him a hug," and "I said I would forgive only if things changed" (Waldron & Kelley, 2005, p. 732). These statements are indicative of efforts to open communica-tion and renegotiate relationship terms, and at the same time provide assurances that the relationship can continue. Sense-making of the situation also occurs, and involves reframing the situation, as illus-trated by the comment, "I know what occurred was not part of his normal character" (Kelley, 1998, p. 263).

MTF-NF couples in the present study reported similar activities to those described above, including: (a) openness, including self-disclosure, meta-relational communication, and joint decision-making; (b) assurances; (c) topic avoidance; (d) conflict management, including compensating, compromise, and limit-setting; (e) focus on growth; and (f) self-talk. For example, NF10's report that she fre-quently repeats "[her] approval of [her partner's] transition" similarly reflects communication and assurance that the relationship will continue. NF 5's statement that she examined and reflected upon the causes and motives of her partner's transition, finding that "MTF 5 has been this way all her life and she should [transition]," reflects her own efforts at self-education and self-talk as she made sense of why her partner had not disclosed the transsexualism prior to establishing the relationship with her and why her partner should now pursue her authentic self.

Minimization of disruptive events is also evident in studies of transgression (e.g., Kelley & Waldron, 2005; Roloff et al., 2001). For example, the statement, "I blew it off," suggests a minimization strategy (Waldron & Kelley, 2005, p. 734). In minimizing a situation, its importance or salience is consciously reduced–in essence, placing the situation into a more favorable perspective. In the present study, conceptually similar to minimization strategies was the activity, self-talk. Self-talk included, for example, reframing the perspective of the MTFs' transition, as illustrated in this statement by NF 8:

> In the grand scheme of things, [transsexualism] turned out not to be the biggest deal, as I first thought it might be. There are so many worse situations. Drug addiction, gambling, alcohol. This isn't like any of those.

A partner's disclosure of homosexuality or cross-dressing behavior after a couple's relationship has been established is another type of relational crisis (Buxton, 2001; Reynolds & Caron, 2000; Weinberg & Bullough, 1988). In studies examining the relationships of couples in which one partner has disclosed as homosexual (Buxton, 2001) or being engaged in cross-dressing activity (Weinberg & Bullough, 1988), restorative strategies included: (a) communication, (b) counseling to make sense of the situation, (c) peer support, and (d) limit-setting In the present study, similar activities included: (a) openness, (b) focus on growth through counseling, (c) use of social networks, and (d) conflict management, including limit-setting through compromise. In both situations–the disclosure of homosexuality and the disclosure of transsexualism–couple partners described the importance of having similar others to confide in, and of having counselors to assist with issues regarding deception and confusion, as well as with the continuation of relationships that society deems unconventional. Similar to couples in which one partner engages in cross-dressing, MTF-NF couples also addressed relational covenants and disagreements regarding *en femme* presentation by imposing limits. MTF 2 illustrated:

> As we began sorting through this process [of disclosure and transition], it was initially very tenuous. It has to be done together, and we needed to

communicate very honestly. There were limits on where and when I could dress [*en femme*]. Social gatherings, for example, I could not.

Other crises. Studies examining families' ability to cope with other types of stress and relational disruptions have resulted in findings similar to those of couples who experience unexpected disclosures (Hill, 1949; Lavee et al., 1987; McCubbin & Patterson, 1983; McCubbin, Joy, Cauble, Comeau, Patterson, & Needle, 1980). For example, similar to findings by Conger and Conger (2002) in their study of couples experiencing economic adversity, MTF-NF couples engaged in strategies such as assurances, meta-relational communication, transition decision-making, and self-disclosure in order to provide mutual support, control in the situation, and problem solving.

Similar activities are illustrated in a study by McCubbin and colleagues (1983) that examined coping patterns in families that have an ill child. Mechanisms by which the families coped included: (a) maintaining family integration, cooperation, and an optimistic definition of the situation; (b) utilizing social support; (c) maintaining self-esteem; and (d) educating themselves regarding the medical situation. For example, the activity, "Talking over personal feelings and concerns with spouse" (p. 364), is an example of using communication to maintain family integration and mutual support, similar to the present study's couples use of self-disclosure and meta-relational communication. In this example, MTF 1 described the thought process and communication that led to joint decision-making:

> At first it was my transition. Especially when so much of it was still in my head and not acted upon. Why would [my partner] need to hear about it or know about it or know what I am feeling? It was my deal, I thought. So I wasn't telling her stuff, and I realized that this was causing some problems for her and for us. We had words sometimes. And I came to the realization that she needed to know what's going on because this transition was really as much hers as mine. She was with me.

Similar to the sense-making found in studies on unexpected disclosures, the interpretation of a stressful event and the attributions partners make influence the ability to cope (Graham & Conoley, 2006; Hill, 1949; McCubbin & Patterson, 1983). Like couples in a study by McCubbin and colleagues (1983), MTFs and NFs used affirming and perspective-providing self-talk in order to maintain an optimistic outlook. Partners who make positive relational attributions are not as adversely affected by stressors as couples who make negative relational attributions. In the present study, partners engaged in positive self-talk. This self-talk included relational affirmations, such as in this example by NF 13:

> She really is very lovely, has grown into a lovely woman who now has more love to give. We are blessed, and things have turned out better than I ever could have imagined.

Processes similar to those described by couples coping with an ill child were also described by couples who were coping with the illness of one partner (Lavery & Clarke, 1999; Rolland, 1994; Skerrett, 1998; Wright & Aquilino, 1998). Couples coping with a partner's chronic illness described the following activities: (a) developing a positive attitude, (b) redirecting their thoughts away from illness, (c) avoiding or limiting the discussion of illness, (d) seeking information, (e) communication, (f) working as a team, (g) monitoring the health of the ill partner, and (h) seeking emotional support.

Maintenance activities similar to those described by the couples coping with an ill partner were reported by MTF-NF couples and included: (a) self-talk, (b) limit-setting, (c) focus on growth, (d) meta-relational communication and self-disclosure, (d) topic avoidance, (f) advice, and (g) assurances. For example, just as couples coping with breast cancer benefitted from education on the illness (Skerrett, 1998), MTF-NF couples were better able to communicate and gain perspective on transsexualism and options through education. For example, NF6 described how she and her partner read educational material together, stating, "She gave me a book written by an [MTF] and she said how it described her; that's who she was."

For both MTF-NF couples and couples experiencing the disability of one partner (Wright & Aquilino, 1998), social support, including emotional support from similar others, was reported as a resource that enhanced relationships. In the present study, NFs similarly described the need for support, as illustrated by NF14:

> Coping with partner's transsexual identity is a hard situation. I was too embarrassed to tell anyone, yet I needed to talk to someone who knew what I was going through. I'd go to support meetings with [MTF14] in case there might be another spouse there to talk to.

Distinct from couples who sustain disruptions in the form of unexpected disclosures, illness, or economic hardship, MTF-NF couples used impression management to manage their public image in response to perceived marginalization. These activities, including adopting a confident demeanor and carefully managing public displays of affection, were strategically executed in order to increase the couple's confidence in themselves and their place in the community as an MTF-NF couple. Further, couples reported that meeting acceptance from the public increased their confidence in their outings as MTF-NF couples. Consequently, more frequent social outings occurred, providing further reinforcement to their relationship. MTF13 described how exuding confidence has enabled others to feel more comfortable in her and her partner's presence:

> You feel that people are uncomfortable at first. Once you get over that as a couple, and you're just confident in yourself, it's easier. You exude self-confidence, and other people feel it. It seems as we became more confident in who we are, the other people around us did as well. And so, little by little, we were out and about more and more.

Discussion

Before further discussion regarding MTF-NF couples' communicative efforts to renegotiate their relationships is presented, an additional comment regarding the evolutionary nature of relationship maintenance and renegotiation processes is required. The respondents made it very clear during their interviews that interactions with their partners, and the renegotiation of their relationships, were very much evolutionary processes. A maintenance activity that may have been necessary during one period along the evolutionary trajectory of the partners' relational renegotiation may no longer have been necessary during subsequent periods of the partners' trajectories. One salient example includes the frequency of MTFs' en femme presentation. Specifically, limiting en femme behavior was an activity that was helpful at the initial phases of the renegotiation trajectory and less helpful at later phases as the relationship in its new form became established.

Thus, in accordance with the conceptual framework, what can be discerned is that (a) the study couples were maintaining their relationships prior to disclosure, and that relational norms and expectations were known; (b) their relationships were at a level of perceived equity and equilibrium such that they were not dissolving; and (c) following disclosure, the partners' assessment of their relationships and levels of accumulated stress did not lead to relationship dissolution. Following disclosure, couple partners began pro-relational communicative activities intended to make sense of their situation, find new ways of engaging with each other and their social world, and reform their relational norms and expectations.

In general, the relational activities utilized by the present study's MTF-NF couples post-disclosure are similar to the activities used by other couples following a crisis. These adaptive activities include interpreting the situation in the most positive way possible, enacting personal and family resources (e.g., education, social networks), and maintaining a sense of coherence and control within the situation. However, the couples in the present study also utilized a relational activity, impression management, that may be unique to couples who perceive marginalization. Engaging in impression management strategies such as effecting a positive affect or limiting displays of affection allowed the couples to partake of other pro-relational activities, such as dining out or taking a walk together. Further, as they met success (i.e., free of adverse events) as MTF-NF couples in public, their confidence and relational reformation advanced.

Best Practices

The findings from this study offer preliminary insights into an essentially unstudied population, MTF-NF couples. As such, one cannot generalize the findings from the present study to all MTF-NF couples. Nonetheless, the study findings can offer health care clinicians, marriage and family therapists, psychologists, and psychiatrists who work with the transsexual community an initial look into the relationship changes that occur in long-term couples who have been successfully renegotiating their relationship following a disclosure of transsexualism. Keeping in mind this caveat, the findings can provide useful information for those who provide care to MTF-NF couples.

Perhaps the most important strategy for couples who find themselves in this situation is effective communication. Without exception, communication must be open, authentic, frequent, and interactive. The couples in the present study were clear in their stance that dealing with one partner's transsexualism, as well as the male-to-female transition process, must be a joint venture. Indeed, many of the respondents referred to the MTF's transition as "our transition."

Further, for NFs, a healthy amount of "self-interest" is advisable. Most NFs described needing periods of time when their partners would not present *en femme*; they needed their partners to present as the men with whom they established relationships. These "respites" from transsexualism within their relationship allowed NFs time to assess, interpret, and make sense of their situation. Over time, these respites became less frequent and necessary. Thus, letting the NFs know that it is acceptable to put limits on *en femme* presentation, that it is acceptable to take "breathers" to recharge, that it is okay to say, "I cannot deal with *en femme* today," may enable the couples to successfully adapt to the situation in the long term. In short, a healthy self-interest should not be presented or viewed as a negative characteristic, but rather a pro-relational one.

In a similar vein, MTFs need to be aware that the need for periodic limitations on their male-to-female transition progress or *en femme* presentation do not mean that transition will not proceed. Rather, they need to recognize that patience and acceptance of a "two steps forward, one step back" approach may carry a positive long-term prognosis for relationships.

In addition, both partners may benefit from knowing that taking small steps as MTF-NF couples in public can be helpful. As successful outings occur and accumulate, confidence rises and outings become increasingly facile. Lastly, couples facing a disclosure of MTF transsexualism may also benefit from knowing that their situation involves strategies and changes similar to situations many other couples face in other forms of crises.

Limitations

Although measures to increase the credibility of the study were employed, as with any study, limitations exist. First, sample size and sampling bias limit the generalizability of the findings. For example, findings could be different for couples who are not "out." Second, the couples in the present study had been together a relatively long time at the time the disclosure occurred, and further, for most of the couples, more than three years had passed since the disclosure. The study findings could be different for couples who had not been together as long at the time of disclosure, or for couples who have not had as much time lapse since the disclosure. Issues such as race, educational level, and marital status may also affect outcomes.

Third, social desirability and the location of the interviews could have biased the interviews (Fontana & Frey, 2000). For example, respondents may have embellished their activities, or may have chosen not to reveal activities that they may feel are less socially desirable. Similarly, although measures to ensure privacy were employed, interviewing partners individually in their home could have biased the interviews as each partner knew the researcher would be speaking with the other partner.

Final Comment

The present study has provided insight into couple dynamics – how couples renegotiate their relationships using relationship maintenance activities following an unexpected disrupting event. Without exception, the couples reported that they hoped a greater understanding of transsexualism would result from the present study's findings. They wished for the deviancy and dysfunction that is typically associated with transsexualism to be refuted, and they hoped for a broader definition of what constitutes "normal." Indeed, the couples viewed themselves to be the same as others–just people, with many of the same trials and tribulations other families experience.

References

Aramburu Alegría, C. (2008). *Relational maintenance and schema renegotiation following disclosure of transsexualism: An examination of sustaining male-to-female transsexual and natal female couples.* Ph.D. dissertation, University of Nevada, Reno, United States—Nevada. Retrieved August 30, 2009, from Dissertations & Theses @ University of Nevada Reno. (Publication No. AAT 3316374).

Attridge, M. (1994). Barriers to the dissolution of romantic relationships. In D. J. Canary & L. Stafford (Eds.), *Communication and relational maintenance* (pp. 141–164). New York: Academic Press.

Baldwin, M. W. (1992). Relational schemas and the processing of social information. *Psychological Bulletin, 112,* 461–484.

Blumer, H. (1969). *Symbolic interactionism: Perspective and method.* Englewood Cliffs, NJ: Prentice-Hall.

Buxton, A. P. (2001). Writing our own script: How bisexual men and their heterosexual wives maintain their marriage after disclosure. *Journal of Bisexuality, 1,* 155–189.

Canary, D. J., & Stafford, L. (1992). Relational maintenance strategies and equity in marriage. *Communication Monographs, 59,* 243–267.

Canary, D. J., Stafford, L., & Semic, B. A. (2002). A panel study of the associations between maintenance strategies and relational characteristics. *Journal of Marriage and Family, 64,* 395–406.

Conger, R. D., & Conger, K. J. (2002). Resilience in midwestern families: Selected findings from the first decade of a prospective, longitudinal study. *Journal of Marriage and Family, 64,* 361–373.

Conway, L. (2001). How frequently does transsexualism occur? Retrieved June 10, 2010, from http://ai.eecs.umich.edu/people/conway/TS/TSprevalence.html#Article

Creswell, J. W. (1998). *Qualitative inquiry and research design.* Thousand Oaks, CA: Sage.

Dainton, M., & Stafford, L. (1993). Routine maintenance behaviors: A comparison of relationship type, partner similarity, and sex differences. *Journal of Social and Personal Relationships, 10,* 255–272.

Duck, S. (1986). *Human relationships.* Newbury Park, CA: Sage.

Fiske, S. T., & Taylor, S. E. (1991). *Social cognition.* New York: McGraw-Hill.

Fontana, A., & Frey, J. H. (2000). The interview: From structured questions to negotiated text. In N. K. Denzin & Y. S. Lincoln (Eds.), *Handbook of qualitative research* (pp. 645–672). Thousand Oaks, CA: Sage.

Gagné, P., & Tewksbury, R. (1998). Conformity pressures and gender resistance among transsexual individuals. *Social Problems, 45,* 81–101.

Glaser, B. G., & Strauss, A. L. (1967). *The discovery of grounded theory.* Chicago: Aldine.

Graham, J. M., & Conoley, C. W. (2006). The role of marital attributions in the relationship between life stressors and marital quality. *Personal Relationships, 13,* 231–241.

Gurvich, S. (1991). *The transsexual husband: The wife's experience.* Dissertation Abstracts International. (University Microfilms No. AAT 9203121)

Haas, S. M., & Stafford, L. (1998). An initial examination of maintenance behaviors in gay and lesbian relationships. *Journal of Social and Personal Relationships, 15,* 846–855.

Hall, J. H., & Fincham, F. D. (2006). Relationship dissolution following infidelity: The roles of attributions and forgiveness. *Journal of Social and Clinical Psychology, 25,* 508–522.

Hill, R. (1949). *Families under stress.* New York: Harper and Row.

Holmes, J. G. (2000). Social relationships: The nature and function of relational schemas. *European Journal of Social Psychology, 30,* 447–495.

Homans, G. C. (1950). *The human group.* New York: Harcourt, Brace, & World.

Johnson, D. J., & Rusbult, C. E. (1989). Resisting temptation: Devaluation of alternative partners as a means of maintaining commitment in close relationships. *Journal of Personality and Social Psychology, 57,* 967–980.

Kelley, D. (1998). The communication of forgiveness. *Communication Studies, 49,* 255–272.

Kelley, D. L., & Waldron, V. R. (2005). An investigation of forgiveness-seeking communication and relational outcomes. *Communication Quarterly, 53,* 339–358.

Lavee, Y., McCubbin, H. I., & Olson, D. H. (1987). The effect of stressful life events and transitions on family functioning and well-being. *Journal of Marriage and Family, 49,* 857–873.

Lavery, J. F., & Clarke, V. A. (1999). Prostate cancer: Patients' and spouses' coping and marital adjustment. *Psychology, Health, and Medicine, 4,* 289–302.

Lincoln, Y. S., & Guba, E. G. (1985). *Naturalistic inquiry.* Beverly Hills, CA: Sage.

McCubbin, H. I., Joy, C. B., Cauble, A. E., Comeau, J. K., Patterson, J. M., & Needle, R. H. (1980). Family stress and coping: A decade review. *Journal of Marriage and Family, 42,* 855–872.

McCubbin, H. I., McCubbin, M. A., Patterson, J. M., Cauble, A. E., Wilson, L. R., & Warwick, W. (1983). CHIP—Coping Health Inventory for Parents: An assessment of parental coping patterns in the care of the chronically ill child. *Journal of Marriage and Family, 45,* 359–370.

McCubbin, H. I., & Patterson, J. M. (1983). The family stress process: The double ABCX model of adjustment and adaptation. *Marriage and Family Review, 6,* 7–37.

Mead, G. H. (1934). *Mind, self and society from the standpoint of a social behaviorist.* Chicago: University of Chicago Press.

Miles, M. B., & Huberman, A. M. (1994). *Qualitative data analysis.* Thousand Oaks, CA: Sage.

Murray, S. L. (1999). The quest for conviction: Motivated cognition in romantic relationships. *Psychological Inquiry, 10,* 23–34.

Oswald, R. F. (2002). Resilience within the family networks of lesbians and gay men: Intentionality and redefinition. *Journal of Marriage and Family, 64,* 374–383.

Reynolds, A. L., & Caron, S. L. (2000). How intimate relationships are impacted when heterosexual men crossdress. *Journal of Psychology and Human Sexuality, 12,* 63–77.

Rolland, J. S. (1994). In sickness and in health: The impact of illness on couples' relationships. *Journal of Marital and Family Therapy, 20,* 327–348.

Roloff, M. E., Soule, K. P., & Carey, C. M. (2001). Reasons for remaining in a relationship and responses to relational transgressions. *Journal of Social and Personal Relationships, 18,* 362–385.

Rusbult, C. E., Olsen, N., Davis, J. L., & Hannon, P. A. (2001). Commitment and relationship maintenance mechanisms. In J. Harvey & A. Wenzel (Eds.), *Close romantic relationships* (pp. 87–113). Mahwah, NJ: Lawrence Erlbaum Associates.

Skerrett, K. (1998). Couple adjustment to the experience of breast cancer. *Families, Systems, and Health, 16,* 281–298.

Stafford, L., & Canary, D. J. (1991). Maintenance strategies and romantic relationship type, gender, and relational characteristics. *Journal of Social and Personal Relationships, 8,* 217–242.

Strauss, A., & Corbin, J. (1998). *Basics of qualitative research.* Thousand Oaks, CA: Sage.

Thibaut, J. W., & Kelly, H. H. (1959). *The social psychology of groups.* New York: Wiley.

Tully, B. (1993). Aspects of interpersonal relationships for people with gender dysphoria and associated paraphilias. *Sexual and Marital Therapy, 8,* 137–145.

Vitale, A. (2001). Implications of being gender dysphoric: A developmental review. *Gender and Psychoanalysis, 6,* 121–141.

Waldron, V. R., & Kelley, D. L. (2005). Forgiving communication as a response to relational transgressions. *Journal of Social and Personal Relationships, 22,* 723–742.

Weinberg, T. S., & Bullough, V. L. (1988). Alienation, self-image, and the importance of support groups for the wives of transvestites. *Journal of Sex Research, 24,* 262–268.

Wright, D. L., & Aquilino, W. S. (1998). Influence of emotional support exchange in marriage on caregiving wives' burden and marital satisfaction. *Family Relations, 47,* 195–204.

Chapter 5

In the Line of Fire: Family Management of Acute Stress during Wartime Deployment

Katheryn Maguire and Erin Sahlstein

Families under stress attempt to manage difficult situations to avoid negative mental or relational outcomes. Given that coping is best understood in a defined context, we examine how 41 Army wives, whose husbands deployed to Iraq or Afghanistan between 2003 and 2005, communicatively managed stress before, during, and after the deployment. Results indicate that the participants used seven different strategies: seeking social support, giving social support, focusing on the problem, focusing on the relationship, managing information, avoidance, and releasing emotions. There was little difference in the distribution of these strategies between wives at higher and lower risk of future negative outcomes. We conclude with practical and theoretical implications of our analysis for future research on military family stress and coping.

Family life is full of pitfalls and promises. For Army families coping with a wartime deployment, which Wiens and Boss (2006) describe as "defining experiences for military service members and their families" as well as "one of the most widely recognized and documented stressors for military families" (p. 12), it is easy to focus on the pitfalls. In addition to the chronic and acute stressors civilian families face (e.g., work-family balance), military families face unique stressors ranging from the mundane (e.g., preparing for the deployment) to the extreme (e.g., the potential capture and imprisonment of the service member). Furthermore, other major life events (MLEs), such as the death of a relative, personal injury, or dismissal from work also might occur (Holmes & Rahe, 1967), putting military family members at increased risk of negative outcomes and impairing their ability to successfully adjust to stress (Hobfoll et al., 1991). Whereas military families can emerge from such situations stronger and more resilient than before if they handle stress effectively (Black & Lobo, 2008), ineffective or inappropriate coping could lead to additional negative outcomes such as divorce or family violence (Malia, 2007; Wiens & Boss, 2006).

Coping is best understood in a narrowly defined context (Folkman & Lazarus, 1985); therefore, this chapter focuses on Army families who have experienced a wartime deployment. In support of similar work that identifies family interaction as a critical coping resource for families (Afifi, Hutchinson, & Krause, 2006), we believe that resilient families use communicative coping strategies to collaboratively cope with MLEs that occur during a wartime deployment. We also acknowledge that collaborative coping might have unintended consequences (e.g., emotional contagion) due to the interdependent nature of close committed relationships (Afifi et al., 2006; Coyne, Ellard, & Smith, 1990). Although it is important to use the family as the unit of analysis in studies of family stress, as opposed to using a single individual (Boss, 1992), in this chapter we report on a study that examined Army wives' communicative management of stress during a wartime deployment, as women head nearly ninety percent of military households during deployment (Norwood, Fullerton, & Hagen, 1996) and their ability to manage stress is linked to family adjustment during and after separation (Pittman, Kerpelman, & McFayden, 2004).

Literature Review

Stress and Stressors

In the family context, stress is often brought about by "disturbances in the steady state of the family" (Boss, 1992, p. 114). For the purposes of this investigation, the term *stressor* refers to "any environmental, social, or internal demand which requires the individual to readjust his/her usual behavior patterns" (Thoits, 1995, p. 54). In particular, discrete or acute stressors, also referred to as life events (Thoits, 1995), involve sudden changes within a short period of time that require readjustment. Rahe and colleagues (Holmes & Rahe, 1967; Miller & Rahe, 1997; Rahe, 1975) identified several of these life change events and scaled them according to the amount of adjustment that stressor would require (i.e., life change units, LCUs). At one end of the spectrum are MLEs that require substantial adjustment, such as the death of a spouse or birth of a child. At the other end of the scale are negative (e.g., trouble with in-laws) and positive (e.g., promotion at work) events that require less adjustment but are still considered MLEs (Miller & Rahe, 1997). Given that Rahe, Veach, Tolles, and Murakami (2000) found a positive correlation between the number and magnitude of recent life changes and participants' reporting of physical and psychological symptoms, we sought to determine the frequency and types of MLEs that Army wives may experience during a wartime deployment by posing the following question:

RQ1: What MLEs did the Army wives experience during the deployment process?

Communication and Coping

Although beneficial outcomes at the family level can occur as a result of a stressful encounter (e.g., greater cohesion; Boss, 1992), individual members will need to cope with any psychological distress that can occur when they appraise a stressful situation as harmful, threatening, or challenging, and exceeding their ability to manage the situation (Lazarus, 1999). An inability to effectively cope with psychological distress might lead family members to communicate with each other in hurtful ways, such as acting more punitively towards children (McKelvey et al., 2002), employing increased levels of emotional and/or confrontational behaviors during conflict (Sillars, Canary, & Tafoya, 2004), or displaying aggressive behaviors towards their loved ones (Frye & Karney, 2006).

Much of the work on family resiliency began with investigations of how families cope with wartime deployment (Hill, 1949; McCubbin & Patterson, 1983). According to McCubbin et al. (1980), families are able to meet obstacles when they have sufficient resources available to them and have "bonds of coherence" (e.g., share common interests, affection, and a sense of interdependence). Furthermore, successful adaptation to stress involves the development of a range of coping behaviors, from managing family stability and the anxiety of individual family members, to getting support from family, friends, and the community (McCubbin, 1979). In particular, family communication characterized by clarity, collaborative problem solving and open emotional expression, is one of the key attributes of healthy, resilient families that helps protect them from harm during crises (Black & Lobo, 2008).

One promising theoretical approach that addresses communication and coping in family relationships is communal coping, whereby multiple individuals impacted by the same stressor/event pool their resources and efforts to face adversity (Lyons et al., 1998). Communal coping rests on the belief that joining together to address the problem is beneficial. It is through interaction that interconnected individuals discuss their perceptions about the stressor and their ideas for coping with the situation (Afifi et al., 2006). According to Afifi et al., both the nature of the context in which a stressor takes place, as well as the type of stressor(s) that the family members face are critical for determining whether "a stressor should be owned and managed alone by certain individuals or collaboratively by the group" (p. 398). As such, stressors that involve multiple relationships and require other group members' participation will be managed differently than a stressor that is highly personal but might affect others in the family. Although the Afifi et al. (2006) model originated from a study of postdivorce families, we believe that it can be extended beyond divorce situations to the military family context.

To begin, Norwood et al. (1996) identified several unique aspects of the military context that are important to consider when examining stress and coping during a wartime deployment, such as frequent separations and reunions, regular relocations, the primary importance of the mission, regimentation and conformity to military life, threat of death, injury, or capture of a loved one, a structured and hierarchically organized social system, and separation from the nonmilitary community. Military families are also often separated from their extended family support network (Black, 1993). Given this isolation, military families may often feel estranged from civilian family and community members who are unable to empathize with their experiences, particularly during a wartime deployment (Bey & Lange, 1974). As a result, military families come to depend on each other like they would their own extended families.

Another important contextual factor to consider is the deployment process itself, as the service member's availability as a coping resource differs, depending the deployment phase. The predeployment phase is a busy time, where the soon-to-be-deployed family member is physically present but is becoming more psychologically absent as he or she prepares for the mission (Weins & Boss, 2006). In the deployment phase, although the deployed member is physically absent, the rest of the family attempts to maintain his/her psychological presence by staying connected and involving him/her in the family as much as possible. Finally, whereas the returned service member is physically present during the reunion phase, he or she might be psychologically absent as the service member begins to cope with his or her own wartime experiences (Weins & Boss). Given the variability in the service member's physical and/or psychological presence, they might not be available as a coping resource for the family.

Although spousal interaction is a common component of marital education programs offered to military families, Karney and Crown (2007) state that there has been little or no research on the interactions between military spouses to determine if the demands of military service inhibit effective marital communication. To begin to address this shortcoming, the present study examines one specific type of communal coping within the marital partnership, called *dyadic coping,* or "the interplay between the stress signals of one partner and the coping reactions of the other" (Revenson, Kayser, & Bodenmann, 2005, p. 4). Examples of dyadic coping strategies include positive dyadic coping (e.g., offers of support), common dyadic coping (e.g., joint problem solving), and negative dyadic coping (e.g., support accompanied by negative affect), all of which are communicative in nature (Bodenmann, 2005). At the same time, the service member might not be physically or emotionally present to help the family deal with stress; therefore, family members also must utilize individual coping efforts and depend on social support to cope. To determine the types of communicative coping strategies used by our participants, we posed the following research question:

RQ2: What communicative coping strategies do Army wives use to handle a wartime deployment?

Recognizing that stress affects families in different ways, we also wanted to compare military families who have experienced relatively few MLEs as well as those who have faced multiple MLEs. Given that individuals who face numerous MLEs might be at higher risk of future negative outcomes (e.g., illness, depression; Rahe et al., 2000), we wanted to determine whether there was a difference in the coping mechanisms utilized by Army wives who may be "higher risk" (i.e., they have experienced more MLEs that require significant life changes and therefore are more likely to experience negative outcomes) verses those who may be at "lower risk." Thus, we posed the following research question:

RQ3: Are there differences in the communicative coping strategies used by Army wives in higher verses lower risk categories?

Method

Participants

We recruited participants primarily through snowball sampling. An Army research team that supported the project introduced us to military chaplains and family readiness group (FRG) leaders, who then put us in contact with potential participants. We interviewed 41 women whose husbands had returned from their deployment. On average, the women were 30.53 years old (SD = 6.64), married for approximately seven years (M = 6.98, SD =6.08), and had 1.49 children (SD = 1.43) (13 participants did not have children). Their husbands were deployed to Iraq (n = 15) or Afghanistan (n = 26). The average number of months on which they reported was 19.85 months (SD = 2.95). Thirteen participants had experienced previous long-term deployments. We gave participants $20.00 to thank them for their time.

Interview procedures

Given that the deployment process generally begins at notification (Norwood et al., 1996), we examined stress and coping starting with the notification of the deployment, through the separation, and ending at the time of the interview. We used a modified version of the Retrospective Interview Technique (Huston, Surra, Fitzgerald, & Cate, 1981) in order to ask participants to recall the significant events, or turning points, during this entire deployment process. Participants graphed the significant events or turning points that happened to them and indicated their retrospective levels of both marital satisfaction and psychological stress at each turning point, and at the time of the interview, ranging from zero to 100%. Participants also reported how they maintained their marriage, their communication patterns with their husbands, the sources of stress that they experienced, and how they coped with their stress. Interviews lasted 90 minutes on average and the transcription of the 41 interviews produced over 1500 transcribed pages. We changed names and all identifying information in the transcripts to protect the identities of the participants and their families.

Classification of families

We used the Recent Life Changes Questionnaire (RLCQ) (Rahe, 1977) to identify and score life events that occurred during the full deployment period in order to classify the wives as either at higher risk or lower risk of future negative outcomes. Miller and Rahe (1997) created a more "modern day scaling" of the RLCQ that presented LCU scores for both males and females (p. 280). The RLCQ contained 74 events that ranged from the death of a child (135 LCUs) to taking a correspondence course (19 LCUs). Only those events that were above the midpoint event for females (i.e., marriage, 50 points) were coded, as we were interested in the major life events that the Army women in our study experienced, leaving 35 applicable MLEs. We each coded 75% of the transcripts with 25% (10 transcripts) overlapping between us. Intercoder reliability was acceptable (Cohen's kappa = .82). We discussed all disagreements and jointly decided the final coding. Once the transcripts were coded for the presence of these events, each participant was given a final LCU score. Based on previous research (e.g., Rahe et al., 2000), participants with LCU scores above 300 were identified as at higher risk for future negative outcomes; the remaining participants were considered to be in the lower risk category.

Coding of communicative coping strategies

To identify the different communicative coping strategies, we conducted data analysis in two stages. First, one of the researchers and a research assistant read 25% of the transcripts to identify the various coping strategies that the participants discussed using the constant comparison method of analysis (Lindlof, 1995), in which recurrent themes were "continually compared with ones that have already been grouped in the same category" to determine goodness of fit (p. 233). In particular, instances where the respondents directly answered inquiries regarding how they communicatively coped with stress in a given situation, as well as other descriptions of purposeful actions taken to manage their emotions, the problem, or their relationship as a result of a stressor, were coded as coping efforts. Second, both researchers and two research assistants coded the remainder of the transcripts based on the themes identified in the first stage. Intercoder reliability for the identified themes was acceptable (Cohen's κ = .74).

Results

RQ1.

The participants experienced a total of 202 MLEs, with an average of 4.93 (SD = 1.87) MLEs per person and a range from 1 to 10 (see Table 5.1). As would be expected, participants in the higher risk category (n = 23, M = 6.44, SD = 1.46) reported significantly more MLEs than those in the lower risk category [(n = 18, M = 3.74, SD = 1.17), F (1, 39) = 43.09, $p < .01$]. Furthermore, those in the higher risk category (M = 416.39, SD = 100.81) had significantly higher LCU scores than those in the lower risk category [(M = 232.96, SD = 57), F (1, 39) = 54.25, $p < .01$]. The most frequently noted MLE "separation from spouse" (n = 42, 20.8%) was due to the long-term deployment. Each participant experienced this MLE by default but one spouse went through two long-term deployments. The second most frequently reported MLE was "change in arguments with spouse" (n = 29, 14.4%), which included instances when the wife reported a pattern of conflict with her husband that was out of the ordinary (e.g., more frequent arguments). Third, several wives experienced job changes and/or took on FRG duties ("Change to different work", n = 26, 12.9%). The remaining categories each constituted less than ten percent of the total MLEs and are reported in the Table 5.1.

Table 5.1: *Major Life Events (MLEs) Experienced across Deployment Process (N = 190)*

	Life Event	*n*	% of sample	Description/explanation of Life Event from Participants.
1.	Separation from spouse.	42	20.80	Separation due to long-term deployment.
2.	Change in arguments with spouse.	29	14.40	Periods of increased fighting, for example.
3.	Change to different work.	26	12.90	Spouse acquired a new job or FRG duties.
4.	Move to different town.	18	8.90	Relation to a new city.
5.	Major illness or injury.	18	8.90	The spouse or anyone in her immediate family was diagnosed with a serious illness or was severely injured in an accident.
6.	Health change in family member.	18	8.90	This included any major health change in family members outside the immediate family as well as undiagnosed mental health issues of immediate family members.
7.	Major decision about the future.	17	8.40	Deciding to leave the military, for example.
8.	Separation due to work.	10	5.00	Training periods and short-term deployments.
9.	Pregnancy.	7	3.50	Spouse and her husband became pregnant.
10.	Birth of a child.	5	2.50	Child was born before, during, or after deployment.
11.	Death of close friend.	4	2.00	A soldier was killed in action.
12.	Death of a family member.	2	1.00	Death of an extended family member (e.g., cousin).
13.	Death of a parent.	1	0.01	Death of a mother or father.
14.	Relative moving in.	1	0.01	A mother, for example, moving in during the deployment.
15.	Miscarriage/ Abortion.	1	0.01	The spouse reported losing an unborn child.

16.	Separation for marital problems.	1	0.01	This occurred, for example, during post-deployment.
17.	Accident.	1	0.01	An immediate family was in an accident that did not result in major injuries.

RQ2.

Data analysis revealed 630 examples of communicative coping responses or tactics that were categorized into seven coping strategies (see Table 5.2). The most frequently identified coping strategy was *seeking support* (*n* = 197 tactics) from the husband, family members, friends and neighbors both inside and outside the military, and trained professionals. The second most common communication coping strategy was *focusing on problems* (*n* = 98 tactics), often with the husband, that resulted from logistical issues in preparing for the separation, as well as decisions about future plans for the deployment and behavioral or physical health changes in family members. The third communicative coping strategy to emerge from the analysis involved the *release of emotions* (*n* = 80 tactics), most often through crying but also via fights with their husbands. The fourth coping strategy was *communication geared at relational maintenance* (*n* = 78 tactics) and frequently took the form of spending quality time with the husband or the family. The fifth strategy involved the *management of information* (*n* = 68 tactics) via mass mediated channels (e.g., the news, the internet, the military). Sixth, several participants noted that *giving support* (*n* = 57 tactics) to family members, their spouse, other military wives, or other service members helped them handle their own stress. Finally, *avoidance* (*n* = 52 tactics) of individuals (including their husband) and/or topics of conversation was also mentioned as a coping strategy.

Table 5.2: *Communicative Coping Strategies for Stressors across Deployment* (N = 630)

	Strategy	N	% of sample	Description	Examples
1.	Seeking support	197	31.30	Soliciting support from family members, friends and neighbors both inside and outside the military, and trained professionals.	"I remember I couldn't stop crying and I called my parents for support and I'm like, 'I don't know what to do, this is so hard and I'm so upset.' I was really heart-broken" (participant 11e).
2.	Focusing on the problem.	98	15.60	Directly addressing problems in order to manage stress either through dyadic or individual coping.	"We got to the point in our relationship I said, 'Honey, I am so sick and tired of every time I have to do something I have to get a power of attorney.' I said, 'From now on everything is going to be in my name'" (participant 11a).
3.	Release of emotions	80	12.70	Expressing emotions privately or to others.	"When he left I was just like crying you know I just let it all out" (participant 16a).

4.	Communication geared at relational maintenance	78	12.40	Strengthening the relational bond.	"I just remember we tried to make the most of our time together, have as much fun as possible" (participant 3e).
5.	Management of information	68	10.80	Actively avoiding or pursuing information via the media or other information outlets (e.g., other military spouses or informational meetings provided through the military).	"I was hooked on the news a lot, just to see if I can see anything" (participant 22a).
6.	Giving support	57	9.00	Providing support to family members, their spouse, other military wives, or other service members.	"…our FRG we made goodie bags for our deployed soldiers and I sewed to be exact 456 goodie bags" (participant 1a).
7.	Avoidance	52	8.30	Avoiding topics, protectively buffering, and/or withdrawing from interactions with spouses, family members, friends, or other military spouses.	"I never talked about it, you know I'd tell people, 'Yeah yeah he's deployed,' but I never really let myself process that" (participant 5e).

RQ3.

To answer RQ3, a series of chi-square analyses were conducted to determine whether the number of tactics reported by participants in either the higher or lower risk groups was different than what would be expected. The participants used three of the seven coping strategies at different frequencies than was expected (i.e., in equitable amounts). First, the higher risk group used the tactic of *focusing on the problem* more than was expected, and the lower risk group used it less than was expected ($\chi^2_1 = 4.14$, $p < .05$). Second, the lower risk group used *seeking support* more than was expected, while the higher risk group sought support less than was expected ($\chi^2_1 = 4.04$, $p < .05$). Third, the lower risk group used *giving support* more, and the higher risk group used it less, than was expected ($\chi^2_1 = 7.13$, $p < .01$).

Discussion

The purpose of this study was to examine how Army wives communicatively coped with MLEs that occurred during the deployment process. Results of this investigation indicate that the participants experienced a number of different MLEs, many of which appeared to be closely aligned with the military context (e.g., separation from the spouse, change in argument patterns). To cope with these MLEs, the participants sought support from, and offered support to, their children, extended family members, other military wives or soldiers. In addition, the Army wives employed a number of dyadic strategies with their husbands, including seeking support from, or giving support to, their husbands, providing each other mutual emotional support, joint problem solving, focusing on the relationship, and releasing emotions by fighting with their spouses. Last, they used several individual coping strategies, such as the management of military-related information, individual problem-solving, release of emotions through crying, and avoidance. In the section below, we attempt to assess "fit" (Afifi et al., 2006), between the three most frequently reported MLEs with the communicative coping strategies identified in this study. In doing so, we hope to identify several options for military families who face a wartime deployment.

Communication, Coping, and the MLEs

Spousal separation. Separation from their spouse was the most commonly experienced MLE and the target for many of the coping efforts described by the women in our study. Indeed, spousal separation is a defining feature of the wartime deployment context and arguably one of the most stressful aspects of the situation (Norwood et al., 1996). Although the the stresses of military life have been found to impede wives' ability to maintain a healthy marriage (Karney & Crown, 2007), the participants in our study worked *with* their spouses to cope with separation by focusing on the relationship. Bodenmann (2005) describes relationship-focused coping as "efforts of one partner that are intended to reinforce or strengthen the psychological, physical, and social functioning of the other partner or to increase marital satisfaction" (p. 35). Although previously conceptualized as protective buffering (e.g., minimizing worries) or active engagement (e.g., talking with the partner about his/her emotions) (Coyne & Smith, 1991), the results of this study offer another way to conceptualize relationship-focused coping: as individual or joint efforts to maintain the relationship in the face of stress.

There is a very small but growing body of communication research that investigates the strategies individuals use to solidify relational bonds during times of stress (Merolla, 2010). Canary, Stafford, and Semic (2002) stated that relationship maintenance strategies are related to resilience in marriage in that they "allow partners to adapt in the face of change and re-achieve homeostasis in salient features, such as commitment to the union" (p. 396). The activities described in the present study mirror maintenance activities identified in this body of research, such as affectionate expression, positivity, openness, and mediated communication (Dainton & Stafford, 1993) and have been found in studies of spousal communication during wartime deployments (Maguire, 2007; Merolla, 2010). Given that previous research has linked relationship maintenance activities to improved marital satisfaction (Stafford & Canary, 1991) and decreased stress symptoms (Floyd et al., 2007), it is likely that maintenance strategies will play a critical role for military marriages in the wartime context. Results of the present investigation support the extension of relationship maintenance into the coping literature as another form of relationship-

focused coping and calls for more research to determine how relational maintenance strategies function in the coping process.

Military wives also coped with the separation from their spouse
by seeking support from family members, friends, other military
wives, trained professionals (e.g., military chaplains), and occasionally from their husbands. In particular, many of the participants identified fellow military wives as a critical coping resource, a result
supported in previous studies of wartime deployment (Faber, Willerton, Clymer, MacDermid, & Weiss, 2008). To help coordinate and facilitate communal coping efforts among military families, the Army
created Family Readiness Groups (FRGs), described as "a group of
family members, volunteers, soldiers, and civilian employees belonging to a unit/organization who together provide an avenue of mutual
support and assistance and a network of communication" among
military families, the Army, and community resources (Mancini, 2006,
p. 7). Whereas the FRG was a source of support for some wives, it was
a source of stress for others, particularly the FRG leaders. As one of
our participants stated, "Even though it was nice to help these ladies
out, that added so much more stress to the situation" (participant
11a). Harrell (2000) stated that the volunteer work of officer's wives,
who often lead FRGs, might be as time consuming as full-time employment. Although officers' spouses are expected to be involved in
the military culture (Knox & Price, 1999), and are considered to be the
ideal persons to lead an FRG as many of them have deployment experience (Black, 1993), such involvement could deplete their own coping resources, leaving them vulnerable to added stress.

Although several participants in this study also reported that they
would seek support from their spouse to cope with the emotions surrounding the impending separation, or frustrations they encountered
during or after the deployment, other participants refrained from
seeking such support. This conflict is evident in the research as well:
whereas some researchers recommend direct, open, and honest communication between spouses during a deployment to cope with the
situation and facilitate the deployed family member's reintegration
back into the family system (Drummet et al., 2003; Hill, 1949), other
research recommends that family members keep their communication
positive to avoid adding burdens on the service member (McNulty,

2005). The choice to avoid burdening one's partner with one's problems has consequences: not only does it remove a primary source of support during stressful times (Pistrang & Barker, 2005), it could also form a "closed communication climate" with one's partner that could last during the reunion phase (Faber et al., 2008).

In addition to seeking support from individuals inside and outside the family, participants enacted more individually oriented strategies (i.e., support provision, the management of information, and avoidance) to cope with separation-related stress, often in an attempt to handle their own emotions. Such emotion-focused coping efforts often help individuals manage self-distress, particularly when a situation is seen as as out of their control (Lazarus & Folkman, 1984). First, participants mentioned that offering support to others helped shift their focus away from their own situation. Aiding others has been linked to recovery from depression for bereaved individuals coping with the loss of a life partner (Brown, Brown, House, & Smith, 2008), and has been recommended (but not thoroughly studied) as a coping strategy for military wives (Hobfoll et al., 1991). Active coping strategies such as support provision may serve to protect the wives, and their families, from harm and help them, and others, be resilient in the face of adversity (Weins & Boss, 2006).

Second, several of the participants noted that they would either seek out information to help them decrease their uncertainty about the deployment, or avoid information from the news media to protect themselves from worry. For instance, to acquire information about the deployment as well as learn ways to adjust to the multiple phases of the deployment process, participants in this study attended FRG meetings or preparation classes to reduce their uncertainty and regain control over their situation. According to Drummet et al. (2003), the availability of adequate information from such sources is a critical component for the military family's successful adaptation to the deployment. The news media, however, was not a helpful information source for many of these women and ironically served to increase their stress as opposed to decrease it. According to Norwood et al. (1996), the "round the clock" news reporting of outlets like CNN during the first Gulf War created a "new set of stressors for Americans, who were bombarded by scenes reflecting the horror of war" (p. 176).

From an uncertainty management perspective (Bradac, 2001), then, individuals might attempt to maintain or increase their uncertainty, as opposed to lessen it, by avoiding the news, particularly when there is a high probability of an undesirable outcome (e.g., the death, capture, injury, or impairment of the deployed family member).

Third, a few participants avoided and/or withdrew from their partner in the period leading up to the deployment. Although psychic withdrawal from the partner is a common occurrence in the predeployment stage, particularly in the week before departure (Norwood et al., 1996), it can prevent the couple from enacting relationship-enhancing behaviors that might buffer the relationship from possible harm during the separation. Avoidance might be an appropriate coping choice, however, when used to preserve the relationship (e.g., withdrawal during a fight).

Changes. The second most frequently reported MLE was *change in argument patterns.* Often spouses recognized specific moments or periods of increased conflict expression with their husbands. This MLE was frequently associated with the release of emotions either through crying or quarrelling with their family members. Because military deployments are fraught with uncertainty and are out of the control of the military families (Sahlstein, Maguire, & Timmerman, 2009), the participants needed some sort of outlet to express their frustrations. Whereas cathartic behaviors such as crying can pave the way for more productive forms of coping (e.g., problem-focused or relationship-focused coping), lashing out at others is considered a negative coping pathway (Hobfoll et al., 1991) and might further diminish relationship satisfaction if the target is the spouse. Given the interdependent nature of family relationships, such cathartic actions might lead to greater stress for both the person venting as well as the family members on the receiving end of the catharsis (Afifi et al., 2006).

The third most common MLE was *changes in work duties.* This category included such changes as taking on new jobs or FRG duties. For some wives, their new responsibilities brought them added confidence and took them away from the worries of deployment, simultaneously making the MLE an outlet for coping with the deployment. Other women expressed frustration with their inability to balance their work and family. Leaders of FRGs frequently found themselves without adequate emotional support unless there were other wives around whose husbands held a similar rank. However, wives in this situation reported working with their husbands to fulfill their FRG duties, often referring to the "united front" and "teamwork" required to manage this MLE, a form of dyadic coping.

Differential uses of coping strategies

Although all the participants in our study used a broad range of coping strategies, our results indicated that the higher and lower risk families differed in their use of three communicative coping strategies. First, focusing on the problem was used more by higher risk than lower risk families. Given that the participants we classified as at higher risk for negative outcomes had faced more MLEs, and thus more problems, than those who theoretically faced lower risk of negative outcomes, it follows that more problem-focused coping efforts occurred in the higher risk group than would be expected in this group. Problem-focused coping refers to behaviors, cognitions or communication aimed at managing or altering the problem causing the distress and was most frequently enacted when conditions are appraised as amenable to change (Lazarus & Folkman, 1984). Research has shown that couples who work together to resolve conflict in mutually beneficial ways tend to have higher levels of satisfaction compared to those who resolve conflict in a competitive, win-lose manner (Bodenmann & Shantinath, 2004). Because of its importance to successful dyadic coping efforts (Widmer, Cina, Charvoz, Shantinath, & Bodenmann, 2005), joint problem solving is often included as part of marital intervention programs.

Second, the finding that the lower risk group sought more support and the higher risk group sought less support that would be expected was surprising; however, McKelvey et al. (2002) found a similar result in their investigation of family stress and mother-infant relationships. We imagine the lower risk group might feel that they are less of a burden on others while the higher risk group might decrease their support-seeking over time so as not to overburden their networks. Or, given that participants reported instances of unhelpful support, the wives at higher risk of negative outcomes might have learned to cope on their own. These are empirical questions worth asking in future studies. Third, and related to the previous finding, members of the lower risk group gave more support than the higher risk group. Families who experienced less stress likely had more support (i.e., social, instrumental, and financial) to offer others in their times of need. In contrast, higher risk families experienced more MLEs, thus taxing their abilities to extend their support to others.

Best practices

Based on the assessment of the "fit" between the coping responses employed by the military wives in this study and the specific qualities of the context and stressors examined, we offer some advice that might help other military families cope with wartime deployment. The first recommendation is for military families under stress to find active, pro-social outlets to cope with their emotions. In particular, we encourage the families to reach out to other individuals in crisis to refocus their energies in positive ways. One way for Army families to get involved is through their FRGs. Not only will these groups provide outreach opportunities for families to give back to others, but also will serve as an important coping resource for the families. To make these groups effective, however, and to support the FRG leaders who themselves also are coping with the same types of stressors, the military establishment should provide adequate training and support staff to assist the FRG leaders with the full-time job of running an FRG.

Second, we advise families to consider all their coping resources as they attempt to address stress throughout the deployment process. Research on Navy couples by Patterson and McCubbin (1984) suggests that utilizing multiple coping strategies allows for greater flexibility and more effective coping outcomes during long-term deployments. We strongly encourage military families to explore the many positive options for coping tactics at all levels of use (i.e., individual, dyadic, and communal). Furthermore, we support the recommendation of the wives in this study to spend more time together as a family to strengthen the relationship before separation. Such activities may serve to promote confidence in the relationship, increase marital satisfaction, and buffer the relationship from harm that results from separation (Karney & Crown, 2007). When possible, the families should also work together to solve or at least minimize controllable problems that may arise throughout the deployment process. Even if the deployed spouse is not physically present, involving him or her in problem-solving will help them feel connected with the family and prepare them for their return home (Black, 1993).

In conclusion, although the RIT allowed us to gather this data across phases, it is limited in that the accounts are retrospective and subject to reinterpretation as the participants reflected on their experiences. As such, the results reported in this chapter should be interpreted with caution. At the same time, they provide a preliminary indication that Army wives employ a variety of communicative coping strategies that address the context-specific life events experienced during long-term deployments. Communication scholars, in particular, should continue this work and include the perspective of the deployed spouse as well as their children. Future research also should assess the functioning of communicative coping strategies for martial satisfaction, stability, and family adjustment.

References

Afifi, T. D., Hutchinson, S., & Krouse, S. (2006). Toward a theoretical model of communal coping in postdivorce families and other naturally occurring groups. *Communication Theory, 16*, 378–409.

Bey, D., & Lange, J. (1974). Women under stress. *American Journal of Psychiatry, 131*, 283–286.

Black, K., & Lobo, M. (2008). A conceptual review of family resilience factors. *Journal of Family Nursing, 13*, 33–55.

Black, W. G. (1993). Military-induced family separation: A stress reduction intervention. *Social Work, 38*, 273–280.

Bodenmann, G. (2005). Dyadic coping and its significance for marital functioning. In T. Revenson, K. Kayser, & G. Bodenmann (Eds.), *Couples coping with stress: Emerging perspectives on dyadic coping* (pp. 33–50). Washington, DC: American Psychological Association.

Bodenmann, G., & Shantinath, S. D. (2004). The Couples Coping Enhancement Training (CCET): A new approach to prevention of marital distress based upon stress and coping. *Family Relations, 53*, 477–484.

Boss, P. (1992). Primacy of perception in family stress theory and measurement. *Journal of Family Psychology, 6*, 113–119.

Bradac, J. J. (2001). Theory comparison: Uncertainty reduction, problematic integration, uncertainty management, and other curious constructs. *Journal of Communication, 51*, 456–476.

Brown, S. L., Brown, R. M., House, J. S., & Smith, D. M. (2008). Coping with spousal loss: Potential buffering effects of self-reported helping behavior. *Personality and Social Psychology Bulletin, 34*, 849–861.

Canary, D. J., Stafford, L., & Semic, B. A. (2002). A panel study of the associations between maintenance strategies and relational characteristics. *Journal of Marriage and the Family, 64*, 395–406.

Coyne, J. C., Ellard, J. H., & Smith, D. A. F. (1990). Social support, interdependence, and the dilemmas of helping. In B. Sarason, I. Sarason, & G. Pierce (Eds.), *Social support: An interactional view* (pp. 129–149). New York: John Wiley.

Coyne, J. C., & Smith, D. A. F. (1991). Couples coping with a myocardial infarction: A contextual perspective on wives' distress. *Journal of Personality and Social Psychology, 61*, 404–412.

Dainton, M., & Stafford, L. (1993). Routine maintenance behaviors: A comparison of relationship type, partner similarity, and sex differences. *Journal of Social and Personal Relationships, 10*, 255–271.

Drummet, A. R., Coleman, M., & Cable, S. (2003). Military families under stress: Implications for family life education. *Family Relations, 52*, 279–287.

Faber, A. J., Willerton, E., Clymer, S. R., MacDermid, S. M., & Weiss, H. M. (2008). Ambiguous absence, ambiguous presence: A qualitative study of military reserve families in wartime. *Journal of Family Psychology, 22*, 222–230.

Floyd, K., Mikkelson, A. C., Tafoya, M. A., Farinelli, L., La Valley, A. G., Judd, J., et al. (2007). Human affection exchange XIII: Affectionate communication accelerates neuroendocrine stress recovery. *Health Communication, 22*, 123–132.

Folkman, S., & Lazarus, R. S. (1985). If it changes it must be a process: Study of emotion and coping during three stages of a college examination. *Journal of Personality and Social Psychology, 48*, 150–170.

Frye, N. E., & Karney, B. R. (2006). The context of aggressive behavior in marriage: A longitudinal study of newlyweds. *Journal of Family Psychology, 20*, 12–20.

Harrell, M. C. (2001). Army officers' spouses: Have the white gloves been mothballed? *Armed Forces and Society, 28*, 55–75.

Hill, R. (1949). *Families under stress: Adjustment to the crises of war separation and reunion.* New York: Harper.

Hobfoll, S. E., Spielberger, C. D., Breznitz, S., Figley, C., Folkman, S., Lepper-Green, B., et al. (1991). War-related stress: Addressing the stress of war and other traumatic events. *American Psychologist, 46*, 848–855.

Holmes, T. H., & Rahe, R. H. (1967). The social readjustment scale. *Journal of Psychosomatic Research, 11*, 213–218.

Huston, T. L., Surra, C. A., Fitzgerald, N. M., & Cate, R. M. (1981). From courtship to marriage: Mate selection as an interpersonal process. In S. Duck & R. Gilmour (Eds.), *Personal relationships 2: Developing personal relationships* (pp. 53–88). New York: Academic Press.

Insel, T. R. (2007, May 24). Post traumatic stress disorder research at the National Institute of Mental Health. Retrieved November 24,

2008, from http://www.hhs.gov/asl/testify/2007/05/t20070524a. html

Karney, B. R., & Crown, J. S. (2007). *An assessment of data, theory, and research on marriage and divorce in the military* (Rand Corporation MG-599-OSD). Retrieved November 26, 2008, from http://www.rand.org/pubs/monographs/MG599/

Knox, J., & Price, D. H. (1999). Total force and the new American military family: Implications for social work practice. *Families in Society: The Journal of Contemporary Human Services, 80,* 128–136.

Lazarus, R. S. (1999). *Stress and emotion: A new synthesis.* New York: Springer.

Lazarus, R. S., & Folkman, S. (1984). *Stress, appraisal, and coping.* New York: McGraw-Hill.

Lindlof, T. R. (1995). *Qualitative communication research methods.* Thousand Oaks, CA: Sage.

Lyons, R. F., Mickelson, K. D., Sullivan, M. J. L., & Coyne, J. C. (1998). Coping as a communal process. *Journal of Social and Personal Relationships, 15,* 579–605.

Maguire, K. (2007). Bridging the great divide: An examination of the relationship maintenance of couples separated during war. *Ohio Communication Journal, 45,* 131–158.

Malia, J. A. (2007). A reader's guide to family stress literature. *Journal of Loss and Trauma, 12,* 223–243.

Mancini, D. (2006). *U.S. Army FRG Leader's Handbook* (3rd ed.). Retrieved November 17, 2008, from http://www.armyfrg.org/skins/frg/display.aspx?moduleid=8cde2e88-3052-448c-893d-d0b4b14b31c4&CategoryID=1e9b3feb-985e-4dd2-b5b2-db37a8aa0d63&ObjectID=9f160323-3fb2-4097-9a64-da80876bedd5

McCubbin, H. I. (1979). Integrating coping behavior in family stress theory. *Journal of Marriage and the Family, 41,* 237–244.

McCubbin, H. I., Joy, C., Cauble, A., Comeau, J., Patterson, J., & Needle, R. (1980). Family stress and coping: A decade review. *Journal of Marriage and the Family, 42,* 855–871.

McCubbin, H. I., & Patterson, J. M. (1983). Family stress and adaptation to crisis: A double ABCX model of family behavior. In D. Olsen & B. Miller (Eds.), *Family studies review yearbook* (pp. 87–106). Beverly Hills, CA: Sage.

McKelvey, L. M., Fitzgerald, H. E., Schiffman, R. F., & Von Eye, A. (2002). Family stress and parent-infant interaction: The mediating role of coping. *Infant Mental Health Journal, 23,* 164–181.

McNulty, P. A. (2005). Reported stressors and health care needs of active duty Navy personnel during three phases of deployment in support of the war in Iraq. *Military Medicine, 170,* 530–535.

Merolla, A. J. (2010). Relational maintenance during military deployment: Perspectives of wives of deployed US soldiers. *Journal of Applied Communication Research, 38,* 4–26.

Miller, M. A., & Rahe, R. H. (1997). Life changes scaling for the 1990's. *Journal of Psychosomatic Research, 43,* 279–292.

Norwood, A. E., Fullerton, C. S., & Hagen, K. P. (1996). Those left behind: Military families. In R. J. Ursano & A. E. Norwood (Eds.), *Emotional aftermath of the Persian Gulf War: Veterans, families, communities, and nations* (pp. 163–197). Washington, DC: American Psychiatric Press.

Patterson, J. M., & McCubbin, H. I. (1984). Gender roles and coping. *Journal of Marriage and the Family, 46,* 95–104.

Pistrang, N., & Barker, C. (2005). How partners talk in times of stress: A process analysis approach. In T. A. Revenson, Tracey, K. Kayser, & G. Bodenmann (Eds.), *Couples coping with stress: Emerging perspectives on dyadic coping* (pp. 97–119). Washington, DC: American Psychological Association.

Pittman, J. F., Kerpelman, J. L., & McFadyen, J. M. (2004). Internal and external adaptation in army families: Lessons from Operations Desert Shield and Desert Storm. *Family Relations, 53,* 249–260.

Rahe, R. H. (1975). Epidemiological studies of life change and illness. In J. Lipowski, D. Lipsitt, & P. Whybrow (Eds.), *Psychosomatic medicine: Current trends and clinical applications* (pp. 421–434). New York: Oxford University Press.

Rahe, R. H., Veach, T. L., Tolles, R. T., & Murakami, K. (2000). The stress and coping inventory: An educational and research instrument. *Stress Medicine, 16,* 199–208.

Revenson, T. A., Kayser, K., & Bodenmann, G. (2005). Introduction. In T. Revenson, K. Kayser, & G. Bodenmann (Eds.), *Couples coping with stress: Emerging perspectives on dyadic coping* (pp. 3–10). Washington, DC: American Psychological Association.

Sahlstein, E., Maguire, K. C., & Timmerman, L. (2009). Contradictions and praxis contextualized by wartime deployment: Wives' perspectives revealed through relational dialectics. *Communication Monographs, 76*, 421–442.

Sillars, A. L., Canary, D., & Tafoya, M. (2004). Communication, conflict, and the quality of family relationships. *Handbook of family communication* (pp. 414–446). Mahwah, NJ: Erlbaum.

Stafford, L., & Canary, D. J. (1991). Maintenance strategies and romantic relationship type, gender and relational characteristics. *Journal of Social and Personal Relationships, 8*, 217–242.

Thoits, P. A. (1995). Stress, coping, and social support. Where are we? What is next? *Journal of Health and Social Behavior, (extra issue)*, 53–79.

Widmer, K., Cina, A., Charvoz, L., Shantinath, S., & Bodenmann, G. (2005). A model dyadic-coping intervention. In T. Revenson, K. Kayser, & G. Bodenmann (Eds.), *Couples coping with stress: Emerging perspectives on dyadic coping* (pp. 159–174). Washington, DC: American Psychological Association.

Wiens, T. W., & Boss, P. (2006). Maintaining family resiliency before, during and after military separation. In C. A. Castro, A. B. Adler, & T. W. Britt (Eds.), *Military life: The psychology of serving in peace and combat (Volume 3: The military family)* (pp. 12–38). Westport, CT: Praeger Security International.

Chapter 6

Death of a Child: Mothers' Accounts of Interactions with Surviving Children

Kayla B. Johnson and Lynne M. Webb

Approximately 42,000 infants and children die yearly in the U.S. (Fletcher, 2002). Such loss typically provokes a grief reaction in each family member. "Since parents usually bear primary responsibility for the care of their children, they are ordinarily expected to share their experience and insights with their children and to help children cope with death and loss" (Corr, 2006/2007, p. 237). The parent, then, is likely to consider surviving siblings' grief along with their own. As Fletcher (2002) noted, in such circumstances, parent-child communication may change in a number of ways including over-protectiveness of children, abandonment of children, or attempts to replace the deceased child with a surviving child. Further, "communication patterns within a family in part determine the ease or difficulty with which members are able to live with the death of a child" (Gibbons, 1992, p. 65). Multiple psychological researchers (Mahon & Page, 1995; Saldinger, Porterfield, & Cain, 2004) identified mothers as more helpful than fathers or siblings in assisting children to cope with the death of a sibling. While many lines of research have examined family life following the death of a child, few studies have addressed families' specific communicative responses to the death of a child. Therefore, our study explores parent-child communication by examining bereaved mothers' reports of their interactions with their surviving children following the death of a child.

Child Grief

"A child's death can have a profound and lasting effect on surviving siblings" (Walker, 1993, p. 325). However, until recently, sibling grief received little attention from clinicians or researchers (Davies, 1997). Some children conceal their feelings and avoid inquiries to protect their parents (Davies, 1997; Mahon & Page, 1995). Although

Mahon and Page identified sadness as "the most common reaction after sibling death" (1995, p. 15), a child's expression of grief may not be the same as adults' expression of grief. Clinicians note that children may appear perfectly happy and normal at times and then regress, often displaying anger rather than sadness; they also may go through phases of grieving, appear to have "gotten over it," and then suddenly begin asking questions or expressing sadness or fears (Stuber & Mesrkhani, 2001). Further, children may experience isolation as well as difficulties expressing their feelings and functioning at school (Rolls & Payne, 2007). Ultimately, children need permission to grieve and to discover meaningful ways to express their grief (Cornell, 2000).

Davies (1997) offered direct advice concerning parent-child communication during episodes of grief. Because some children react better to concrete messages, Davies suggested that parents employ open and direct communication to children about difficult family events. While she recommended that parents communicate simply and factually with children, the parents' encompassing grief can make such communication difficult or impossible. Further, "parents may want to shield their little ones from the sorrow and pain, [but] children do need some form of explanation" (Cornell, 2000, p. 80). Children may know consciously or unconsciously that the truth is being withheld, which in turn may erode their trust in their parents and emotional environment. Conversely, with open direct communication, each child's disposition can be addressed effectively in an age-appropriate manner (Goldman, 2004). While Davies' (1997) advice to communicate directly with children about the death of a sibling sounds reasonable, it is not based on research. Indeed, how parents and surviving siblings actually communicate following the death of a child remains unknown.

Parental Grief

Regardless of the deceased child's age or length of illness, parents consistently reported experiencing "a grief reaction characterized by an initial period of shock lasting hours to several weeks which evolved into a four- to six-month period of sadness/depression with somatic complaints, which slowly progressed to resolution through acceptance" (Henry & Taylor, 1982, p. 988). Hasui and Kitamura (2004) reported that in the year following the death of a child, most parents expressed aggression toward people around them. However, "bereaved parents differ in many regards depending upon factors such as the cause of death, the age of the child at the time of death, religious orientation before the loss, personality factors, differing perspectives on the role of talk in the recovery process, and differing strategies for coping with grief" (Hastings, 2000, p. 1). Parents who experience the death of a child at any age face the need to construct new realities and reconstruct old ones (Gibbons, 1992). "Previous research has suggested that grief following the death of a child is more severe, complex, protracted and traumatic than grief following any other death" (McLaren, 1999, p. 286). Thus, research, common sense, and life experiences indicate that loss of a child is possibly the most difficult of life's experiences. The subsequent grieving process, though intense, will differ from individual to individual.

Communication Research on Death and Dying

While scholars have researched the topic of communication surrounding death and dying for over two decades (e.g., Keeley, 2004, 2007; Morgan, 2004; Nimocks, Webb, & Connell, 1987), the studies typically address circumstances beyond the focus of the current study. Researchers have examined family communication about health issues (Bylund & Duck, 2004; Robinson & Turner, 2003), decisions surrounding palliative care (Ragan, Wittenberg, & Hall, 2003; Sorensen & Iedema, 2006), communication between health care providers and adults with terminal illnesses (Ayres & Hopf, 1995; Egbert & Parrott, 2003; Hines, Babrow, Badzek, & Moss, 2001; Kaplowitz, Campo, & Chiu, 2002; Miller & Knapp, 1986; O'Hair et al., 2003), and communication surrounding bereavement (Bergstrom & Holmes, 2000; Bosticco & Thompson, 2005; Capps & Bonanno, 2000; Cluck & Cline, 1986; Golish & Powell, 2003; Hastings, Musambira, & Hoover, 2007; Moore & Mae, 1987; Murray, 2002). Taken together, the results of these studies indicate that communication surrounding death can be complex and difficult. Accordingly, Logan and Murphy (2005/2006) call for "additional research measuring all bereaved family members' perception of their family functioning...to help clarify what represents optimal family cohesion and flexibility after the death of a child" (p. 305).

We located only three previously published studies that directly addressed family communication surrounding the loss of a child. Toller (2005) examined bereaved parents' communication experiences in their social networks. Her results indicated that parents experienced contradictions between the physical absence of and the continuing emotional bond with the deceased child. Additionally, parents experienced difficulty deciding whether to discuss the deceased child with others. In a second study, Toller (2008) explored changes in parents' identities following the loss of a child, analyzing two dialectic tensions that bereaved parents experience and that they resolve through talk with others: "(a) a parent without a child to a parent and (b) I'm an outsider—I'm an insider" (p. 306). The latter dialectic referenced identity as one of the select few who have experienced the loss of a child versus as one of the others who have not experienced such loss and thus cannot or will not acknowledge the parents' profound grief. In a third study, Toller and Braithwaite (2009) discuss dialectical tensions in marital communication following the death of a child, including the desire to grieve as a couple versus alone and the desire to be open versus closed when discussing their grief with one another.

While Toller's (2005, 2008, 2009) ground breaking studies focused attention on communication surrounding the loss of a child, they failed to address communication *within* the bereaved family, or specifically interactions between parents and their surviving children. Thus, our study represents a reasonable next step in continuing the line of research investigating communication surrounding death and dying as well as Toller's research on bereaved parents. Our study extends these lines of research to address maternal communication with surviving siblings following the death of a child. Thus, *the purpose of this exploratory study was to examine mothers' reports of their communication with their surviving children following the death of a child.* To this end, the following research questions were posed:

Research Question 1 (RQ1): Following the death of a child, what intentional and unintentional changes, if any, did mothers perceive in their communication with their surviving children?

Research Question 2 (RQ2): What communicative triggers or cues, if any, did mothers perceive in their conversations with their surviving children that led them to alter their communication patterns with these children?

Research Question 3 (RQ3): What communication strategies appeared to comfort surviving children?

Research Question 4 (RQ4): Did specific communication changes with surviving children remain consistent over time?

Methods

We elected to employ a qualitative methodology for four reasons: Qualitative methods (a) are appropriate for exploratory research (Cresswell, 1998), (b) provide maximum opportunity for the researcher to learn from the participant (Bouma & Ling, 2004), (c) "can give a fuller description of what is going on" (Bouma & Ling, 2004, p. 172), and (d) allow researchers to examine events "in their natural settings, attempting to make sense of, or interpret, phenomena in terms of the meanings people bring to them" (Denzin & Lincoln, 1994, p. 2).

We employed the specific qualitative methodology of interviewing for four reasons: (a) "At the root of in-depth interviewing is an interest in understanding the experience of other people and the meaning they make of that experience" (Seidman, 1998, p. 3). (b) Interviewing gains access to the individual's concrete experiences (Seidman, 1998) and (c) it allows access to the actor's perspective (Denzin & Lincoln, 1994). (d) Interviewing provides opportunity to "clarify ambiguous questions and probe for a detailed answer" (Ferman & Levin, 1975, p. 42).

Participants

Recruitment. We recruited participants using four methods: (a) We placed classified advertisements in two local newspapers approximately two months apart. (b) We posted notices with six groups on an international website for mothers *www.cafemom.com*. (c) We asked friends and family to recommend participants. (d) We asked each participant to recommend additional participants. Thus, we drew participants from four sources: newspaper advertisements ($n = 1$), *cafemom.com* ($n = 5$), friend and family connections ($n = 12$), snowball sampling ($n = 2$).

Description. Our convenience sample of 20 participants ranged in age from 24 to 88 years ($M = 47$, $SD = 16$). We reached saturation at the 17th interview but continued interviewing until we completed 20 interviews. All participants self-reported as Caucasian/European-American but they reported residency in eight U.S. states. The participants reported educational levels ranging from the seventh grade to post-graduate degrees, but the majority of the participants reported completing either high school (40%) or a bachelor's degree (30%). The majority of the participants (75%) reported being married; however, 15% reported being widowed, and 10% divorced. Only 20% of the married participants reported being married currently to a man who was *not* the father of the deceased child.

Participants reported the following details about their families: 45% had one surviving child at the time of loss, 45% had two surviving children, 5% had three, and 5% had five. All participants chose to report on communication with surviving biological children rather than surviving stepchildren. The majority (80%) of the surviving children were older siblings, 10% were younger siblings, and 10% were a twin or triplet of the deceased child. The surviving children ranged in age from 1 to 19 years ($M = 5$, $SD = 8.60$); fourteen participants (70%) reported about communication with male surviving children and six participants (30%) reported about communication with female surviving children.

The participants' deceased children ranged in age from nineteen weeks (gestational age) to nine years. Twelve (60%) were female and eight (40%) were male; all were Caucasian. The participants reported their children's causes of death as premature birth complications (20%), infant developmental disorders (15%), pregnancy complications (10%), pneumonia (10%), cancer (10%), accident (10%), diabetes with viral illness (5%), brain disorder (10%), S.I.D.S. (Sudden Infant Death Syndrome) (5%), and undiagnosed (5%).

Instruments

Each participant completed a short demographic questionnaire to facilitate sample description. Additionally, we developed an open-ended interview protocol to elicit communicative details about interactions with surviving siblings following the death of a child. The interviewer added probing questions as needed to facilitate specific answers to the protocol questions. If an interviewee seemed confused by the specific wording of an interview question, the interviewer restated the question in multiple ways until the participant indicated that she understood the query. If more than one sibling was living, participants reported conversations with one surviving sibling of their choice. Due to emotion distress, some participants appeared to experience occasional setbacks recalling conversations with the surviving sibling. However, the participants experienced no difficulty recalling several specific conversations, readily recalled their children's responses to the conversations, and often provided memorable quotations.

One female interviewer conducted the twenty interviews following the same interview protocol with each interviewee to minimize the introduction of bias. The interviewer pretested the protocol with two mothers recruited from the subject pool. After the pretests were administered successfully, and given that no changes to the interview protocol or procedures were necessary, the interviewer began conducting research interviews.

Procedure

Participants were provided the option of face-to-face interviews or telephone interviews. The majority (65%) elected face-to-face interviews. The interviewing process for the face-to-face interviews was divided into two parts: an initial contact, followed by the actual interviewing process. After receiving the participant's contact information, the interviewer contacted the mother and scheduled a time and place for the interview of the mother's choosing. Upon meeting, a consent form and a demographics form were presented to the mother. Upon completion of the forms, the interviewer requested permission to audio record the interview. All participants agreed to the audio recording. Next, the interview proceeded in a semi-structured manner providing consistency with flexibility for clarifying and follow-up questions, as needed.

The interviewing process for the telephone interviews was divided into three parts: initial contact, return of the signed consent form and demographics questionnaire, and then the actual interview. Following an initial contact by phone or e-mail, the interviewer either faxed or mailed the consent form and demographics questionnaire to perspective participants, depending on the participants' preference. After receiving completed forms, the interviewer called the participants and requested permission to audio record the interview. All participants agreed to the recording. After granting permission, the semi-structured interview proceeded. Following the interview, the interviewer offered all participants the option of receiving a summary of the finished project.

Analysis

The interviewer transcribed the recorded interviews, producing 61 typed, single spaced pages containing 2601 lines of data. To discover participants' recurring similar assertions, the interviewer conducted a thematic analysis using Owen's (1984) three criteria for identifying themes, i.e., repetition (relatively the same language to describe a phenomenon), recurrence (differing language but similar meanings for a phenomenon), and forcefulness (ideas strongly stressed verbally or nonverbally). Following Boyatzis (1998), themes emerged from the data rather than *a priori* categories imposed on the data. Similar to any analytic inductive technique based in grounded theory, the interviewer functioned as a textual critic interpreting language. "Thus, reliability [was] not established by intercoder agreement. Instead, integrity of the analysis [was] established through a constant comparison process" (Krusiewicz & Wood, 2001, p. 791). Insights from later responses influenced themes and, when appropriate, prompted the reinterpretations of previously reviewed responses and/or recorded themes (Charmaz, 1983).

The interviewer read each transcript three times, and during the third pass, underlined possible themes emerging from the data. During a fourth reading, she drafted charts, listing the answers to the interview questions and noting the interview sequence and participant number to identify examples and trace multiple occurrences of themes. During the fifth reading, she color-coded phrases based on the research questions. During the sixth and seventh readings, she developed charts of themes and frequencies based on the research questions.

Results

Thematic Findings on Communicative Changes

RQ1 queried the intentional and unintentional changes, if any, that mothers perceived in their communication with their surviving children. Analysis revealed three themes: *Changes in Tone* (maintained normal tone [same as before the death], negative changes, positive changes, softer tone), *Changes in Substance* (maintained normal substance, increased spiritual content, avoided talk about deceased sibling, focus on deceased sibling, age appropriate changes, expressed appreciation for surviving child), and *Changes in Frequency of Interactions* (maintained normal frequency, increased frequency, decreased frequency). Table 6.1 contains participants' illustrative quotations that exemplify each theme. Most participants reported maintaining normal tone and substance in their conversations with surviving children. However, participants were equally likely to increase, decrease, and maintain the same frequency of interaction with the surviving child.

Thematic Findings on Communicative Cues

RQ2 queried the communicative triggers or cues, if any, that mothers perceived in their conversations with their surviving children that led them to alter their communication patterns with these children. The analysis revealed three themes: *No Cues* (*n* = 6; no cues given, often due to the very young age of the surviving sibling), *Nonverbal Cues* (*n* = 8; neutral cues such as child crawling in bed with a well sibling and negative cues such as crying), and *Verbal Cues* (*n* = 6; questioning, negative comments).

Thematic Findings on Comforting Strategies

RQ3 queried mothers' reports of communication strategies they employed to comfort their surviving children effectively. The analysis revealed three themes: *Consistency* (*n* = 3; consistent behaviors), *Alternate Attention* (*n* = 16; open communication such as telling child s/he is special; non-verbal affection such as holding and rocking the child; a combination of verbal and non-verbal attention; and spiritual verbal attention such as saying the deceased child is safe in heaven), *Nothing* (*n* = 1; nothing due to young age of surviving child). Our participants' preferred form of comforting surviving children was to divert the child's attention to an alternative focus, such as praise and physical affection for the surviving child.

Thematic Findings on Changes in Communication over Time

RQ4 queried the specific communication changes that remained consistent across time. The participants reported following one of two practices regarding discussion of the deceased sibling with the surviving child: *Open Communication* about the deceased sibling and *Limited Mention* of the deceased sibling. Fifteen of the twenty participants reported having *open communication* (i.e., participants reported presently experiencing open and regular communication about deceased sibling). Conversely, five participants reported, at this time, no or minimal discussion of the deceased child with the surviving sibling (i.e., *Limited mention*).

Table 6.1: *Mother's Perceived Changes in Communication*

Category	Theme/Frequency of Ps	N	Illustrative Quote from Participant
Tone	Maintained normalcy	9	"I had to make it as normal as possible."
	Negative	5	"I don't feel like I treated him any different."
			"I became very distant for a while."
			"I was a little harsher."

	Positive	2	"I had a thankfulness in my heart."
	Softer	4	"I babied her more." "I became softer."
Substance	Maintained normalcy	8	"We just picked right up with our lives." "We continued to discuss everyday things."
	Spiritual	4	"We talked about heaven a lot more." "I bought more Bible story books."
	Avoidance	4	"It was like he didn't exist."
	Focus on sibling	2	"I kept getting questioned [about sibling]."
		1	"[Child] was moving toward toddler age."
		1	"I [started] appreciating my kids."
Frequ		7	"I went on like normal." "I wanted to decrease, but I didn't."
		7	"We probably talked about it more."
	Decreased	6	"I didn't communicate with anybody."

Note. Sample $N = 20$.

Discussion

Summary of Results

Each mother discussed how her communication with her surviving child changed or how she believed she should have changed in response to the death, as well as in response to interactional cues from the surviving sibling. As mothers enacted these changes, they struggled with the dilemma of wanting to return to former patterns of communication to restore a sense of normalcy versus the desire to address the crisis of the death in the family. Typically, the mothers reported solving this dilemma by keeping some aspects of communication the same (i.e., normal tone of voice and talking about everyday topics), while changing communication patterns to provide comfort to the surviving child (e.g., talking with the child more frequently; rocking the child more often). Either immediately following the death or later in the grieving process, virtually all mothers viewed open communication about the deceased child with the surviving siblings as part of an effective comforting strategy and response to the grieving process.

Interpretation of Results

Four overarching trends emerged, across the results.

1. *Dialectics of communicating with surviving children.* Consistent with Fletcher's (2002) observations that parent-child communication can change following the death of a sibling, very few of our participants reported that their mother-child communication patterns remained unaffected by the death. They described the changes they enacted as a resulting of balancing divergent and often opposite impulses to respond to their surviving child's needs versus their desire to restore "normal" family life.

Dialectical tensions typically occur as a result of the interplay of opposing and contradictory forces, such as the tensions that occur as a result of simultaneous needs for autonomy and connection, openness and closeness, or novelty and predictability (Baxter, 1988). Dialectical tensions are typically resolved through communication. For example, newlyweds may resolve their need to maintain autonomy by reserving one weekend a month to spend time with their individual friends, and maintain connectedness by spending the other weekends together. They resolve the dialectical tension through their communication during negotiation.

Multiple forms of dialectics exist, many specific to particular relationships and contexts. For example, Sahlstein (2006) described romance partners as negotiating certainty and uncertainty in long-distance relationships. Similarly, unique tensions may occur in mother-child communication as they mourn the death of a child. An examination of the identified themes as well as the transcripts reveals three recurring dialectics: (a) the desire to respond to their surviving child's needs and their desire to restore "normal" family life; (b) the desire to mourn the deceased child and the desire to continue to care effectively for the surviving children; as well as (c) their ability to express sadness surrounding the loss and the joy of knowing another child remains alive. Thus, like Toller (2005), we discovered preliminary dialectics in our participants' descriptions of the communication surrounding the death of their children.

   2. *Death per se prompted communicative changes.* Despite the various ways in which their children died, most participants (80%) in this study reported that it was the actual death of their child that prompted them to make communication changes with their surviving child, not diagnoses or illnesses. Soricelli and Utech (1985, p. 429) noted, "A child's death may follow quickly after the diagnosis of a fatal illness or a child's death may occur after many agonizing months and years." A child's death also may be sudden and research suggests "that it is harder to cope with the unexpectedness of losing a child through a sudden traumatic event" (Valios, 2005, p. 38). Eleven participants experienced the sudden and unexpected death of their child; logic as well as common sense dictates that they would report the death (per se) as the cause of changes in their communication with their surviving children. In contrast, however, five mothers in our sample endured the illness of their child; they also reported that it was the death itself that caused the communicative changes they described. Perhaps the hope for their ill child's recovery sustained these mothers and enabled them to communicate somewhat normally with their well children prior to the loss. Or perhaps their children's deaths necessitated an additional change separate from any change that accompanied the preceding illness.

   3. *Comforting is complex.* Despite the unique circumstances surrounding each tragedy, all but one of the interviewed mothers reported effectively comforting surviving children and all participants reported implementing *multiple strategies* to comfort their surviving children. Further, the reported comforting strategies *varied with the age of their surviving children.* In accordance with previous research documenting that understandings of death can vary with age (Finke, Birenbaum, & Chand, 1994; Webb, 2005), we categorized our partici-

pants' surviving children into Webb's (2005) three age divisions for thinking about death: (a) small children, ages 2–7 years old, do not tend to realize the finality of death, (b) elementary children, ages 7-11, usually show a clearer understanding of the finality of death, (c) secondary children, ages 9 years old through adolescence, exhibit a mature understanding of death.

In our sample, three surviving children were too young to be placed into Webb's (2005) age categories. Nonetheless, these mothers chose comforting strategies that appeared age appropriate. A fourteen month old surviving child was prematurely into her "terrible twos" and failed to respond to any forms of comfort that the mother employed, perhaps due to her confusion over the mother's constant crying and sadness. Eventually, the mother and her spouse intentionally spent one-on-one time with the surviving child and that seemed to comfort her. Also, due to her young age, an eighteen month old surviving child responded best to nonverbal affection that resembled the mother's behaviors prior to the tragedy.

Thirteen of the surviving children ranged in age from two to seven years old, the second category of children. Given that these children did not understand the finality of death, all but one of these mothers reported verbal communication to facilitate better understanding. Consistent with Davies' (1997) advice to parents to use open and direct communication with grieving children, most of these mothers chose to implement open communication, consisting largely of addressing questions raised by the surviving child about the death. These mothers openly expressed their feelings and allowed the surviving child to do so as well. Other mothers who had children in this category reported employing a combination of open communication and nonverbal affection to comfort their young surviving children. These mothers talked to their children, read books to them, held them, and rocked them. Four mothers talked about spiritual matters as a means of comforting their surviving children (e.g., explaining that the deceased sibling was happy in heaven with grandparents). One of these four mothers revealed that she maintained normalcy with her two-year-old for a month following the death, although she realized that he did not understand that his twin brother was actually dead. In retrospect, she reported that she should have simply told him that the deceased sibling was dead instead of allowing him to overhear her tell others that she had "lost" her son.

The two mothers with children ages seven to eleven realized that their children had a mature understanding of death and neither reported employing open communication as a comforting strategy. One mother reported knowing that the surviving child was aware of his brother's death; therefore, she did not see the need to discuss it and instead kept life as normal as possible. This strategy seemed to comfort the child. Another mother, who had difficulty discussing the tragedy due to its horror, found that her surviving child was comforted if she praised him for his good grades. She reported that grades were very important in their family, and when his hard work was recognized, he seemed to be comforted.

4. *Social Influence.* "The intensified search for meaning in mourning a child is...embedded in structural and cultural relations that both enable and constrain. Engagement by others can provide and possibly impose meaning; curiously this has been little researched" (Hass & Walter, 2007, p. 180). Each mother mentioned the influential factors of her situation and/or the influential individuals in her life. Thus, each mother discussed social influence.

Participants most frequently mentioned social influences in their discussion of changes in tone, frequency, and substance. Some participants reported being able to maintain a normal tone to cope sufficiently with their own grief and to help the surviving child cope with his/her own grief. Another mother reported acquiring a harsh tone toward her surviving child in reaction to her family's refusal to discuss the deceased sibling. She was frustrated by this, but other adults in the family persuaded her to move forward by acting as if the deceased child did not exist. She reported that if her family had reacted differently she would have taken an alternate communicative path, probably a more open and revealing path. Eventually (six months later), this mother chose more open communication with the surviving child. She reported that this change benefited her and the surviving child.

Participants frequently mentioned social influences when disclosing content of their mother-child interactions. For example, influenced by their religious environments, four mothers chose to speak more with their surviving children about spiritual matters. Another mother's surviving child influenced her to focus on the deceased sibling, because he asked repeated questions about the deceased sibling. Another mother reported spending countless hours discussing the ill sibling's sickness with the surviving sibling. Before the deceased sibling died, the surviving child wanted to know everything that was happening and everything that was going to happen. Her surviving child's desires influenced the communication choices which she made. In sum, each mother's situation involved a set of individuals with differing goals; therefore, each situation involved varied social influences. Nonetheless, each participant reported that their communication surrounding the loss of a child was influenced by others as well as by the mother's ability to accept or reject these influences.

From a systems theory perspective, "a system is a set of components" and the components or family members "interrelates with one another to form a whole. When individuals come together to form relationships, the result is larger and more complex than the sum of the individuals, or components" (Galvin, Dickson, & Marrow, 2006, p. 311–312). Following the death, the participants reported reformation of their family relationships. Of particular interest to this study, interdependence of systems often describes how a change in one part of the system can affect other parts or the entire system. When one family member is affected by a crisis, the entire family may change to adjust. Our participants were affected by the loss of their child, and their surviving children were affected by the grieving parent as well as by the absence of the deceased sibling. Although families had established communication patterns prior to the death, their communication patterns changed after the death. Indeed, the results of our study exemplified the principle of interdependence and demonstrated that subsequent communication patterns with surviving children can benefit from conscious reconstruction.

Best Practices

The results of this study indicate that the mother-child communication is likely to change following the death of the child's sibling. What kinds of changes in communication practices best serve the needs of the grieving mothers and their children? Reports from our participants lead to six central recommendations: (a) Mothers should be aware that the death of a child will prompt each mother to make important changes in their communication practices with their surviving children. (b) Surviving children will be most comfortable with and comforted by open communication about the deceased. (c) Children may display a variety of cues to indicate their need for comfort (e.g., child crawling in bed with a well sibling, crying, questioning, making negative comments); mothers should take note of these cues and respond with comforting. (d) Mothers can employ multiple comforting strategies (e.g., telling child s/he is special; nonverbal affection such as holding and rocking the child; a combination of verbal and non-verbal attention; spiritual verbal attention such as saying the deceased child is safe in heaven) to discover which strategies work most effectively with each individual child, as efficacy of any given strategy may vary with the age of the child, the norms of the family, and other factors. (e) Mothers can and should maintain normalcy by keeping select communicative patterns and practices consistent, even in the face of the death (e.g., praise for good grades), and also modify communication patterns and practices as appropriate to address the needs and desires of their children (e.g., rock a toddler more often).

Limitations and Suggestions for Future Research

Our exclusively Caucasian, convenience sample represents perhaps the greatest limitation to the generalizability of our results. A study replicating these results with a broader sample would test the general applicability of our findings. Further, while in-depth interviews with any small sample should reveal major concerns with minimal capital outlay, the samples are necessarily limited in size and scope, thus the generalizability of the findings also is limited. Future studies in this line of research could employ larger, more diverse samples.

While our data yielded consistent results across participants from eight states, our findings reflect conclusions about only *mother-child interactions*. Data from fathers or parental dyads may result in alternative findings. Gathering information from fathers may provide additional, helpful insights into effective communication with surviving children after the loss of a sibling. Further, future research could examine parent-child interactions at various points in the grieving process, as communication may differ in various stages of grief (Maciejewshi, Zhang, Block, & Prigerson, 2007). In addition, future research could examine how parents communicate with surviving children as the children pass through various developmental stages.

Conclusion

Despite these limitations, this study contributes to the discipline's knowledge base regarding mother-child communication. This study represents a necessary first-step, exploratory examination of mother-child interactions following the death of a child in the family. While the data are not generalizable to all mothers in such situations, nonetheless, the results offer insights into the patterns of communication that can occur following such a tragedy, including the dialectics that may be at play in interactions and lists of multiple, age-appropriate comforting strategies for grieving siblings. Further, these findings may aid in training counselors, physicians, and therapists to assist families who have lost a child. Finally, the study offered thoughtful suggestions for future research.

References

Ayres, J., & Hopf, T. (1995). An assessment of the role of communication apprehension in communicating with the terminally ill. *Communication Research Reports, 12,* 227–234.

Baxter, L. (1988). A dialectical perspective on communication strategies in relationship development. In S. W. Duck (Ed.), *A handbook of personal relationships* (pp. 257–273). New York: Wiley.

Bergstrom, M. J., & Holmes, M. E. (2000). Lay theories of successful aging after the death of a spouse: A network text analysis of bereavement advice. *Health Communication, 12,* 377–406.

Bosticco, C., & Thompson, T. (2005). The role of communication and story telling in the family grieving system. *Journal of Family Communication, 5,* 255–278.

Bouma, G. D., & Ling, R. (2004). *The research process.* South Melbourne, Australia: Oxford University Press.

Boyatzis, R. E. (1998). *Transforming qualitative information: Thematic analysis and code development.* Thousand Oaks, CA: Sage.

Bylund, C. L., & Duck, S. (2004). The everyday interplay between family relationships and family members' health. *Journal of Social and Personal Relationships, 21,* 5–7.

Capps, L., & Bonanno, G. A. (2000). Narrating bereavement: Thematic and grammatical predictors of adjustment to loss. *Discourse Processes, 30,* 1–25.

Charmaz, K. (1983). The grounded theory method: An explication and interpretation. In R. Emerson (Ed.), *Contemporary field research* (pp. 109–126). Boston: Little, Brown.

Cluck, G. G., & Cline, R. J. (1986). The circle of others: Self-help groups for the bereaved. *Communication Quarterly, 34,* 306–325.

Cornell, C. (2000). At a loss: Talking to kids about death. *Today's Parent, 17,* 80.

Corr, C. A. (2006/2007). Parents in death: Related literature for children. *Omega: Journal of Death and Dying, 54,* 237–254.

Cresswell, J. W. (1998). *Qualitative inquiry and research design: Choosing among five traditions.* Thousand Oaks, CA: Sage.

Davies, B. (1997). Commentary on Van Riper's article on sibling bereavement. *Pediatric Nursing, 23,* 594–595.

Denzin, N. K., & Lincoln, Y. S. (1994). *Handbook of qualitative research.* Thousand Oaks, CA: Sage.

Egbert, N., & Parrott, R. (2003). Empathy and social support for the terminally ill: Implications for recruiting and retaining hospice and hospital volunteers. *Communication Studies, 54,* 18–34.

Ferman, G. S., & Levin, J. (1975). *Social sciences research: A handbook for students.* New York: Schenkman.

Finke, L. M., Birenbaum, L. K., & Chand, N. (1994). Two weeks post-death report by parents of siblings' grief experience. *Child and Adolescent Psychiatric Nursing, 7*(4), 17–25.

Fletcher, P. N. (2002) Special issue: Bereavement in families and the community. *Family and Community Health, 25,* 57–71.

Galvin, K. M., Dickson, F. C., & Marrow, S. R. (2006). Systems theory: Patterns and (w)holes in family communication. In D. O. Braithwaite & L. A. Baxter (Eds.), *Engaging theories in family communication: Multiple perspectives* (pp. 309–324). Thousand Oaks, CA: Sage.

Gibbons, M. B. (1992). A child dies, a child survives: The impact of sibling loss. *Journal of Pediatric Health Care, 6*(2), 65–72.

Goldman, L. (2004). Counseling with children in contemporary society. *Journal of Mental Health Counseling, 26,* 168–187.

Golish, T. D., & Powell, K. A. (2003). "Ambiguous loss": Managing the dialectics of grief associated with premature birth. *Journal of Social and Personal Relationships, 20,* 309–334.

Hass, J., & Walter, T. (2007). Parental grief in three societies: Networks and religions social supports in mourning. *Omega: Journal of Death and Dying, 54,* 179–198.

Hastings, S. O. (2000). Self-disclosure and identity management by bereaved parents. *Communication Studies, 51,* 352–372.

Hastings, S. O., Musambira, G. W., & Hoover, J. D. (2007). Community as a key to healing after the death of a child. *Communication & Medicine, 4,* 153–163.

Hasui, C., & Kitamura, T. (2004). Aggression and guilt during mourning by parents who lost an infant. *Bulletin of the Menninger Clinic, 68,* 245–260.

Henry, G. W., & Taylor, C. A. (1982). Reactions of families to the death of a child with congenital heart disease. *Southern Medical Journal, 75,* 988–994.

Hines, S. C., Babrow, A. S., Badzek, L., & Moss, A. (2001). From coping with life to coping with death: Problematic integration for the seriously ill elderly. *Health Communication, 13,* 327–342.

Kaplowitz, S. A., Campo, S., & Chiu, W. T. (2002). Cancer patients' desires for communication of prognosis information. *Health Communication, 14,* 221–241.

Keeley, M. P. (2004). Final conversations: Survivors' memorable messages concerning religious faith and spirituality. *Health Communication, 16,* 87–104.

Keeley, M. P. (2007). "Turning toward death together": The functions of messages during final conversations in close relationships. *Journal of Social and Personal Relationships, 24,* 225–253.

Krusiewicz, E. S., & Wood, J. T. (2001). "He was our child from the moment we walked in that room": Entrance stories of adoptive parents. *Journal of Social and Personal Relationships, 18,* 785–803.

Leeds-Hurwitz, W. (2006). Social theories: Social construction and symbolic interactionism. In D. O. Braithwaite & L. A. Baxter (Eds.), *Engaging theories in family communication: Multiple perspectives* (pp. 229–242). Thousand Oaks, CA: Sage.

Lohan, J. A., & Murphy, S. A. (2005/2006). Mental distress and family functioning among married parents bereaved by a child's sudden death. *Journal of Death and Dying, 52,* 295–305.

Maciejewshi, P. K., Zhang, B., Block, S. D., & Prigerson, H. G. (2007). An empirical examination of the stage theory of grief. *JAMA: Journal of the American Medical Association, 297,* 716–723.

Mahon, M. M., & Page, M. L. (1995). Childhood bereavement after the death of a sibling. *Holistic Nursing Practice, 9*(3), 15–26.

McLaren, J. (1999). After the death of a child: Living with loss through the years. *British Journal of Guidance and Counseling, 27,* 286–288.

Miller, V. D., & Knapp, M. L. (1986). The post nuntio dilemma: Approaches to communicating with the dying. *Communication Yearbook, 9,* 723–738.

Moore, T. E., & Mae, R. (1987). Who dies and who cries: Death and bereavement in children's literature. *Journal of Communication, 37,* 52–64.

Morgan, S. E. (2004). The power of talk: African Americans' communication with family members about organ donation and its impact on the willingness to donate organs. *Journal of Social and Personal Relationships, 21,* 112–124.

Murray, C. I. (2002). Parental grief: Narratives of loss and relationship. *Journal of Family and Marriage, 64,* 276–278.

Nimocks, M. J. A., Webb, L., & Connell, J. R. (1987). Communication and the terminally ill: A theoretical model. *Death Studies, 11,* 323–344.

O'Hair, D., Villagran, M. M., Wittenberg, E., Brown, K., Ferguson, M., Hall, H. T., & Doty, T. (2003). Cancer survivorship and agency model: Implications for patient choice, decision making, and influence. *Health Communication, 15,* 193–202.

Owen, W. F. (1984). Interpretive themes in relational communication. *Quarterly Journal of Speech, 70,* 274–287.

Ragan, S. L., Wittenberg, E., & Hall, H. T. (2003). The communication of palliative care for the elderly cancer patient. *Health Communication, 15,* 219–226.

Robinson, J. D., & Turner, J. (2003). Impersonal, interpersonal, and hyperpersonal social support: Cancer and older adults. *Health Communication, 15,* 227–234.

Rolls, L., & Payne, S. A. (2007). Children and young people's experience of UK childhood bereavement services. *Mortality, 12,* 281–303.

Sahlstein, E. M. (2006). Praxis strategies for negotiating uncertainty-certainty in long-distance relationships. *Western Journal of Communication, 70,* 147–165.

Saldinger, A., Porterfield, K., & Cain, A. C. (2004). Meeting the needs of parentally bereaved children: A framework for child-centered parenting. *Psychiatry, 67,* 331–352.

Seidman, I. (1998). *Interviewing as qualitative research: A guide for researchers in education and social sciences* (2nd ed.). New York: Teachers College Press.

Sorensen, R., & Iedema, R. (2006). Integrating patients' nonmedical status in end-of-life decision-making: Structuring communication through "conferencing." *Communication & Medicine, 3,* 185–196.

Soricelli, B. A., & Utech, C. L. (1985). Mourning the death of a child: The family and group process. *Social Work, 30,* 429–434.

Stuber, M. L., & Mesrkhani, V. H. (2001). What do we tell the children? *Western Journal of Medicine, 174,* 187–192.

Toller, P. W. (2005). Negotiation of dialectical contradictions by parents who have experienced the death of a child. *Journal of Applied Communication Research, 33,* 46–66.

Toller, P. W. (2008). Bereaved parents' negotiation of identity following the death of a child. *Communication Studies, 59,* 306–321.

Toller, P. W., & Braithwaite, D. (2009). Grieving together and apart: Bereaved parents' contradictions of marital interaction. *Journal of Applied Communication Research, 37,* 257–277.

Valios, N. (2005). *Unthinkable...unbearable.* Retrieved October 18, 2007, from http://www.communitycare.co.uk/Article/2005/04/28/490831/unthinkable-unbearable.html

Walker, C. L. (1993). Sibling bereavement and grief response. *Journal of Pediatric Nursing, 8,* 325–334.

Webb, N. B. (2005). Groups for children traumatically bereaved by the attacks of September 11, 2001. *International Journal of Group Psychotherapy, 55,* 355–374.

Section Two:

Health Crises

Chapter 7

Children with Invisible Disabilities: Communicating to Manage Family Contradiction

Heather E. Canary

Families often experience a crisis period when child disability is diagnosed, followed by long-term coping. This chapter examines how contradictions serve as generative mechanisms for family system development for families of children with invisible disabilities. The chapter discusses how families communicatively manage contradictions during periods of crisis and in ongoing coping. Interviews with family members and educational professionals (N = 36) as well as transcripts from parent-professional meetings (N = 38) were analyzed using qualitative methods. Results indicate that several types of contradictions surface during the crisis and coping phases, and that family communicative responses range in effectiveness. Suggestions are offered for best practices for communicatively managing contradictions in crisis and coping phases.

Scholars across several disciplines, including communication, disability studies, education, and family studies, have acknowledged the potential impact of childhood disability on family life. They have responded with considerable research on families of children with various disabilities to better understand family processes in the context of disability (Canary, 2008a). Disabilities such as autism spectrum disorders, learning disabilities, speech and language impairments, mental retardation, and other conditions affect millions of children and their families (U.S. Department of Education, 2005). Many of these disabilities are "invisible" in that they are not immediately apparent to others (Matthews & Harrington, 2000). The hidden and often changing nature of these disabilities can make them difficult to recognize and to manage in everyday family living (Canary, 2008b). Communication among family members and between family members and professional support providers (e.g., educators, therapists, social workers, psychologists) is consequential for how family members cope with disability. Although significant multidisciplinary research has examined the nature and outcomes of support for these families, much remains to be explored regarding the communication processes people employ to meet the challenge of incorporating ability and disability into their family relationships.

Accordingly, the purpose of this chapter is to extend current understandings of communication in families of children with invisible disabilities by examining contexts of crisis and coping. The chapter concerns how *contradictions* serve as generative mechanisms for family system development when they are recognized and managed. Contradictions are inherent in social systems (Canary, 2010). As with all social systems, families are capable of developing or transforming by managing contradictions with changed processes, acquisition of resources, and via obtaining input from other systems. Yet, contradictions also can frustrate family interactions and dealings with outsiders, thereby hindering family transformations. This chapter begins with a review of research regarding interactions during crisis and coping for families of children with invisible disabilities. The brief literature review is followed by a description of the theoretical framework used in the chapter, *structurating activity theory*. The second half of the chapter reports results from a qualitative study exploring the role of contradictions in families of children with disabilities. The chapter concludes with suggestions for effective communication during crisis and coping for families of children with disabilities and professionals working with them.

Communication in Crisis

Research indicates that many parents experience initial negative reactions and shifts in family focus when a child is diagnosed with a significant disability (Fox, Vaughn, Wyatte, & Dunlap, 2002; Jackson, Traub, & Turnbull, 2008; Morison, Bromfield, & Cameron, 2003). For many families, this experience is characterized by increased stress and need for support (Jackson et al.). Accordingly, families who experience such negative reactions, shifts in family focus, increased stress, and increased needs for support are experiencing a *crisis*, which Patterson (2002) defined as "a period of significant disequilibrium and disorganization in a family" (p. 351).

The diagnosis or onset of childhood disability is an unexpected stressor on the family system. Families have reported high levels of stress in early stages of learning about or recognizing their children's disabilities (Dyson, 1993; Florian, 1989). Primary caregivers also have reported that the added time and attention required by their children with disabilities can increase stress as they also attempt to deal with other aspects of family life, such as non-disabled children and work obligations (e.g., Bower & Hayes, 1998; Todd & Jones, 2003). Dyson found that these stress levels stayed relatively stable over time, as self-reported by participants. However, other studies have demonstrated that stress, particularly for mothers, can be alleviated over time with interventions and supports, such as respite care and support from family members (Canary, 2008a).

Many parents report seeking information to learn how to resolve the crisis of initial diagnosis or recognition (Fox et al., 2002; Goldbart & Marshall, 2004; Jackson et al., 2008). Although parents might choose different sources of information (e.g., the Internet, friends, family, professionals), information seeking seems to be a common communication behavior during this crisis phase for families. Unfortunately, previous research indicates that this experience is often frustrating for parents. For example, Jackson et al. found that parents of deaf children felt inundated with information but had no tools or guidance for how to evaluate what they perceived to be biased messages about dealing with deafness in their families. Canary's (2008a) review of 10 years of research on support for families of children with disabilities revealed that one of the main parental concerns across studies is obtaining sufficient and appropriate information. These findings point to a gap between what information exists as potential resources for parents and what information parents perceive as actual resources.

The crisis phase also includes a shift in family focus (Jackson et al., 2008; Patterson, 2002). This finding is consistent with a view of crisis being a period of disorganization—a time when something must be done to "re-organize." For example, parents in the Jackson et al. study reported that when their children were identified as deaf, much of the focus of family interactions, activities, and orientations shifted to their child's disability as they re-created family structures and routines. On a less positive note, Green, Davis, Karshmer, Marsh, and Straight (2005) interviewed mothers of children with a range of disabilities and found that invisible disabilities often led to mothers being blamed for the non-normative behavior of their children. The shift for some of these mothers was to separate themselves from their previous social networks to avoid blame and stigma. Clearly, shifts in family focus can be both positive and negative. Accordingly this characteristic of the crisis phase warrants further attention.

Communication in Coping

All families experience short-term illnesses that constitute crises and with which they must cope. However, the coping continues for families of children with disabilities; it doesn't end with recovery from an injury or illness. Due to the ongoing nature of disability, much research has focused on how families respond to supports of various types across the life cycle (Canary, 2008a). Importantly, researchers consistently conclude that disability is not an individual experience, but rather a family experience. Much of this research points to the existence of contradictions in family relationships and the need to include notions of ability *and* disability as families attempt to cope with daily challenges (Canary, 2008b; Harry, Rueda, & Kayanpur, 1999; Shapiro, Monzo, & Rueda, 2004). Accordingly, each family member may become involved in coping and adjusting to the presence of disability in the family system (D'Arcy, Flynn, McCarthy, O'Conner, & Tierney, 2005; Davis & Salkin, 2008; Fox et al., 2002).

Researchers have acknowledged the family impact of disability on the family by investigating sibling relationships and communication in families of children with disabilities. Several studies document that siblings of children with disabilities engage in more caregiving than siblings of children without disabilities (e.g., Cuskelly & Gunn, 2003; Hannah & Midlarsky, 2005). A number of studies report that parents worry about how their special treatment of their children with disabilities would affect their children without disabilities (e.g., Guralnick, Neville, Connor, & Hammond, 2003; Lobato & Kao, 2002). Children often do not receive the same information about their siblings with disabilities as parents do. As a result, non-disabled siblings often remain confused about the disabilities and abilities of their family members. As Davis and Salkin (2008) conveyed, outcomes of this confusion can be both positive and negative. However, several intervention programs attempt to increase positive outcomes and decrease negative outcomes for siblings. These interventions focus on providing information about disabilities and safe forums for siblings to share their emotions about disability (D'Arcy et al., 2005; Evans, Jones, & Mansell, 2001; Lobato & Kao). In spite of progress made with previous research and intervention, there is still much to learn about sibling communication as families negotiate ability and disability in their everyday lives.

Family functioning and coping with life challenges also are strongly influenced by cultural contexts. For example, Florian (1989) investigated differences in family functioning between Israeli-Jew and Israeli-Arab families with and without children with disabilities. Results indicated that culture was a more prominent factor than the presence of disability alone in the level of family cohesion and adaptability. Research indicates an underlying assumption that collectivistic attitudes in some cultures lead to strong family support that can substitute for the lack of professional support for minority families (Gatford, 2004; Morse, 2002; Sham, 1996). However, these studies also have found the opposite process occurring in cultural minorities. Shame, cultural norms that discriminate against disability, and/or lack of knowledge about disabilities can prevent extended family members from providing practical and emotional support to parents.

An important element in family coping involves interactions between families of children with disabilities and professional support providers. For example, Morison et al. (2003) demonstrated the efficacy of a family-centered model of support for families of children with chronic illnesses or disabilities by emphasizing the non-linear and changing nature of family support needs throughout the life cycle. Families do not need support at only one or two predictable points in time. Life is more variable than that, and parents underscore the need to have quality professional support relationships for families to effectively cope with day-to-day disability issues. However, similar to the initial crisis phase, family-professional interactions are not always helpful for family coping. First, confusion exists among professionals and parents alike as to relational boundaries and types of support that should be expected or provided (Lord-Nelson, Summers, & Turnbull, 2004). Second, positive and supportive professional relationships contribute to positive child and family outcomes, whereas negative or extremely formal relationships do not provide families with support or outcomes they would like (Canary, 2008a).

In brief, understanding communication during crisis and coping is not a simple matter. Indeed, many models and theories exist to explain and predict family functioning. Structurating activity theory as described below is a theoretical framework with the requisite complexity to take into account the influence of multiple systems and the importance of attending to contradictions in crisis and coping.

Structurating Activity Theory

Structurating activity theory integrates concepts from structuration theory (Giddens, 1984) and cultural historical activity theory (CHAT) (Center for Activity Theory and Developmental Work Research, 2004) to explain connections between action and structure in social systems, such as families. Family communication scholars recently have used structuration theory to understand the co-influence of family communication and institutions (Krone, Schrodt, & Kirby, 2006). CHAT examines the ongoing activity of social systems, focusing on the mediation of activity, connections between systems, and ways that systems transform (Engeström, 1999). Structurating activity theory combines mid-level theoretical constructs from CHAT with broad constructs from structuration theory to create a framework that is both explanatory and practical.

Briefly, the theory emphasizes structuration, which means that as individuals engage in ongoing behaviors they produce, reproduce, and sometimes transform social structure such as norms, meaning, and authority (Giddens, 1984). These behaviors occur in activity systems, which are collectivities of persons, practices, and resources involved in accomplishing activity over time (Center for Activity Theory and Developmental Work Research, 2004). A family is an activity system involved in the activity of nurturing and developing its members, including family formation, economic support, education, socialization, and protection of vulnerable members (Patterson,

2002). Elements of the activity system shape, or *mediate*, actions and interactions within and between activity systems (Canary, 2010).

Because this chapter focuses on contradictions, the following discussion is limited to the theoretical construct of contradictions.

According to structurating activity theory, contradictions emerge in social activity and can serve as generative mechanisms for development within and across systems. However, contradictions must be recognized and attended to if systems are to transform. Structural contradictions are oppositional tensions that exist in entrenched social structures and are inherent in societies (Giddens, 1984). An example of a structural contradiction that affects families of children with disabilities is the tension between control and autonomy in implementing disability policies (Barrett, 2004). Parents and professionals use the structural control aspect of policy to obtain support and services, but they also rely on the autonomy of policy implementers to make provisions appropriate for particular situations. System contradictions are oppositional tensions that are specific to particular activity systems. There are four types of system contradictions: primary, secondary, tertiary, and quaternary (Center for Activity Theory and Developmental Work Research, 2004).

Primary contradictions are inherent oppositional tensions that exist within individual elements (Center for Activity Theory and Developmental Work Research, 2004). For example, ability and disability represents a primary contradiction that might exist within members of family systems. Although this primary contradiction is inherent in the nature of humans, managing the primary contradiction of ability/disability is often needed for family systems to develop effectively.

Secondary contradictions exist between activity system elements and become evident when new elements are introduced into the activity system. For example, when parents learn that their child has a disability, a contradiction between what they expected their child to be able to accomplish around the house (division of labor) might be revealed as contradictory to the nature of the child (subject). That contradiction might have existed before, but new information reveals the contradiction that had previously remained hidden.

Tertiary contradictions occur when a more advanced object or motive is introduced into the activity (Boer, 2005). In other words, a contradiction exists between the former way the system oriented toward its object and a new way that becomes necessary to orient toward the object. For example, diagnosis or realization of a disability often shifts a family's focus or orientation altogether. The shift in family focus changes (at least temporarily) the way the family orients toward the activity of "doing family," constituting a tertiary contradiction that must be managed for the family to move to the next phase of development.

Finally, *quaternary contradictions* emerge between activity systems when fulfilling the activity of one system precludes fulfilling the activity of another system (Boer, 2005). Quaternary contradictions exist because families are connected with a number of other social systems, such as schools, government agencies, and work organizations. For example, Hwa-Froelich and Westby (2003) noted a quaternary contradiction between Head Start professionals who wanted to foster independence in children and southeast Asian parents who wanted to foster dependence as a form of respect. Both systems were oriented toward the development of children with disabilities, but the ways those systems oriented to their activities were not immediately compatible.

The remainder of the chapter empirically examines contradictions and communication during crisis and coping. The study was guided by several general research questions: (1) What contradictions emerge within families and between families and professionals during the stage of initial diagnosis/recognition of disability? (2) How do family members communicatively respond to contradictions in this crisis phase? (3) What contradictions emerge within families and between families and professionals as family members cope with disability over time? (4) How do family members communicatively respond to contradictions in this coping phase?

Data Analysis

Data collected during two previous studies (Canary, 2007, 2008b) were analyzed using qualitative methods to address the research questions. Data include interview transcripts ($N = 38$) and transcripts from 14 parent-professional meetings ($N = 38$). Family participants ($N = 37$) included parents, children with and without disabilities, and extended family members. Professionals included educational administrators, teachers, psychologists, and other specialists who work with children with disabilities ($N = 39$). Participants were recruited through special education programs in two public elementary school districts in the southwestern United States. Both districts include mostly minority (non-white) student populations, with a 73.81% minority student population in District 1 and a 94% minority student population in District 2. Participants reflected the ethnic diversity of the districts, with 28 (75.7%) non-white family member participants. Of the 35 professionals who provided demographic information, 28 (80%) were white and seven (20%) were non-white.

Data were coded and analyzed using the constant comparative method (Glaser, 1978) with the aid of NVivo8 qualitative analysis software. First, participants' own words were used to create initial codes, such as "nobody is to blame." As coding continued, these *en vivo* codes were combined into larger descriptive codes, resulting in 184 codes, such as "family situation cause for disability." As coding continued, these codes were combined into a more manageable set of 86 descriptive codes. These 86 codes then were organized into 14 categories that represented major themes regarding family members, family interactions, dis/ability, and interactions with intersecting activity systems. The research questions were addressed by analyzing the coded data for both manifest (i.e., identified by participants) and latent (i.e., identified by researcher during analysis) contradictions and responses to those contradictions.

Contradictions in Crisis

All four types of system contradictions emerged for participants during the crisis stage. Children were described in both positive and negative ways, indicating that there was an inherent contradiction between what children provided to the family and what children required from the family. For example, several parents referred to their children with disabilities as "lazy" when it comes to doing chores and getting things done. On the other hand, these children also were described as "helpers" for their younger siblings. This primary contradiction of ability and disability, of requiring resources and providing resources continued into the coping period.

A secondary contradiction related to the above primary contradiction became evident in analysis. Secondary contradictions exist between elements of an activity system, such as between mediating resources, such as language, and rules, such as expectations about respectful interaction. Several participants talked about children not following expectations and not interacting appropriately. For example, siblings in one family (all four of whom have speech delays) talked about how they fight with hitting, kicking, biting, and yelling. They described each other as mean and could not recall how conflict is responded to by their parents. Their father, on the other hand, described in detail how he verbally and physically responds to sibling conflict to reinforce mutual respect. Although sibling conflict is an expected part of family life, this family experienced a secondary contradiction between the availability of language resources for children and family rules about respectful interaction in the home. Contradictions are not simple problems that can be solved with standard solutions; they require system transformations.

Consistent with previous research (Patterson, 2002), many families in this study experienced a tertiary contradiction when a professional told them that their child had, or probably had, a disability. Tertiary contradictions emerge when a new or more advanced way of orienting toward the object of activity is introduced into the system. Family members expect to encounter various stages and stresses in life as they orient around nurturance and development of the family over time. However, disability is not one of those expected challenges. This contradiction is exemplified by one mother who told me, "I didn't think that there was—you know, you never think there could be a problem there." Professionals played a key role in identifying disability for participating parents and also in recommending how parents might re-orient toward their child and family life in terms of daily interactions and future expectations.

Finally, many parents and professionals indicated that tensions between goals of family systems and goals of educational systems are quite evident in the initial crisis stage. Parents frequently recalled how required procedures and school timelines prevented them from getting the quick answers and interventions they wanted for their children. Many parents also indicated that they wanted and needed more information and support from educational organizations. It is important to note that this was not uniformly reported by parents; there were several exceptions. However, interview data, in particular, indicates that the crisis stage often included this quaternary contradiction for participants. For example, one principal explained:

> And sometimes people [parents] advocate for things that we can't do or are, you know, they are just not appropriate. I've had that. People use the law to try to get things for their children that don't make sense. And so— *educationally* they don't make sense. So we have to really work closely with them to try to present information and make our recommendations.

The contradiction between educational and family systems also persists into the coping phase.

Managing Contradictions in Crisis

There were three predominant strategies for communicatively managing contradictions in crisis. First, parents responded to contradictions by seeking information, advice, and support from professionals, friends, and extended family members. This strategy indicates the importance of intersections with other activity systems for families in crisis. For example, one mother recounted her story of seeking educational help for her daughter, "I think it was third or fourth grade where I had asked a teacher that I had noticed that she was doing homework at a slower pace, she was erasing a lot, and she was having trouble with her work." Another mother told me about how helpful her brother was in the crisis stage because he is a special education teacher, "He's given us a lot of advice, mainly about how to make sure that we're doing all we can through the schools before we try to do any outside tutoring and things like that."

The second strategy participants reported was relying on professionals to make decisions for their children. Parents and professionals noted in interviews that parents place a great deal of trust in professionals' decisions, which often led to allowing professionals to take over decisions regarding support and interventions for children. Although many parents initially sought information and professional support, the outcome of that seeking was often left to the discretion of educational professionals or specialists rather than to parents. Partici-

pants often indicated that parents are comfortable with this arrange-
ment for initial decision making during the crisis stage, as exemplified by one principal's observation:

> So I guess if you are not a teacher the expectation of education is that the
> teacher does what she needs to do and she will tell you what is right for the
> child. And I think a lot of our parents, when they accept the fact that they
> are going to put their child in special ed., just expect us to do that and do it
> correctly.

The third strategy was to ignore that there was an issue that
should be addressed within the family. Interestingly, parents who
reported using this strategy had experienced problems within their
families related to a child's disability, whether that was negative
sibling interaction behaviors, excessive school problems, negative
emotional displays, or other issues. However, these parents clearly
stated that they did not think disability was something that needed to
be talked about, or should be talked about, within the family as a
whole. For example, one child with moderate learning disabilities
reported that she gets in trouble a lot and that she is "mostly bad,"
while her siblings reported that they tease her for how slowly she
does her work and for being "in her own little world." Her mother,
on the other hand, told me, "Everybody kind of knows, but it's not
really an issue...I mean, it's not something that needs to really be
discussed so we don't discuss it."

On the most active end of the spectrum, parents diligently sought
information and help for resolving the primary contradiction of
ability versus disability, secondary contradictions such as family
expectations and children's resources for meeting those expectations,
the tertiary contradiction of a shift in family focus, and quaternary
contradictions between their family systems and intersecting systems.
A less active strategy, but still responsive to an extent, was placing
responses to disability in the hands of educational professionals and
disability specialists. The least active strategy was to ignore emergent
contradictions and not discuss disability and its effects within the
family. Not surprisingly, responses to contradictions in crisis also
carried over into the coping stage for these families, as discussed
below.

Contradictions in Coping

Some contradictions that emerged during crisis continued into the coping stage for participating families. For instance, the primary contradiction between ability and disability, or between what a child can provide the family and what a child requires from the family, remains throughout a family life cycle. Indeed, it seems part of human nature to have this inherent tension of give-and-take in social systems. Parents and educational professionals continued to recognize this contradiction through descriptions of disabled and non-disabled children, such as this mother's comments about her daughter's capabilities, "I know what she should be doing, what she should be—well, I know she's not quite capable to do the curriculum to the 'T' as it is in fifth grade, but she's not near. And that's what's frustrating to me."

Several secondary contradictions emerged between elements of family activity systems during coping. These contradictions exist between the family system's mediating resources, the community of family members, and the family's division of labor, which comports with previous research relating to family resources (Bower & Hayes, 1998; Todd & Jones, 2003). Parents indicated that they feel the pull in meeting the needs of their children with disabilities and doing everything else that is required for effective family functioning, such as staying within a family budget and giving adequate time and attention to other family functions. Decisions for children's services were often dictated by transportation resources rather than by children's needs.

The tertiary contradiction of a shift in family focus and re-orientation continued in the coping phase for some participating families. Families needed to adjust to new needs, new abilities, and new ideas for fulfilling family functions. For example, one mother related the story of how her family shifted focus when her son was diagnosed with a severe vision disability as a baby. After adjusting the family system to this disability for a few years, support specialists recommended that he have brain scans and then tests for autism. As she told me, "I never thought we would have that, rather than the eye thing, you know? And that seems to be more of a problem than the eye thing these days."

The quaternary contradiction between family systems and educational systems persisted into the coping period for many participants. One parent revealed that she questions the integrity of suggestions offered to her about her daughter's support, "but sometimes I wonder, you know, are they just brushing her off, just want to get her out of here, you know." Importantly, many participants indicated that they experienced productive and collaborative interactions with members of intersecting activity systems in coping, indicating that this contradiction does not necessarily emerge for all family systems. For instance, one mother noted that collaborative interactions with specialist systems have waxed and waned as different personalities and issues become involved, but that she is currently experiencing no tensions, "This year everybody is all together. The meetings are much more friendly. Everybody has a–the main goal and stuff."

The quaternary contradiction between family and education systems is related to two broad structural contradictions. The structural contradiction between control and autonomy was evident in meeting data. On the one hand, parents and professionals used the federal Individuals with Disabilities Education Act (IDEA) to provide structure for what decisions could and should be made for children with disabilities. On the other hand, professionals repeatedly indicated to parents that the "team" (group of adults concerned with the child) could decide how support and intervention should look for particular children. This contradiction points to a structural contradiction, not explicitly evident in these data, between what is required by statute (authoritative resources) and what is financially feasible (allocative resources).

Another structural contradiction evident is the tension between the democratic value of equal voice and the aristocratic value of privileging individuals with expert knowledge or positions of authority. When parents were asked if they thought their input was valued, most said it was. However, they could not give specific examples of when their input was used by professionals. One special education teacher noted:

> I think *we* think that the parents, especially in the initial process, are involved. I don't think they have enough knowledge - not all of them. I think that *many* of our parents do not have enough knowledge of what is expected

in education to help us write goals. Another special education teacher reinforced the privilege of expertise by stating, "any further than their child's general placement, I don't think they [parents] should be involved." Administrators at the district level identified this as a problem that often led to unilateral decisions by school-level professionals that bordered on policy noncompliance.

Managing Contradictions in Coping

Family members varied in their responses to contradictions as they engaged in the ongoing activity of being a family. Many parents developed family routines and accommodation patterns to manage the primary contradiction of ability and disability. These routines often highlighted ability while taking disability into account. For example, one mother noted, "I have to accommodate her needs. Not saying that everything goes her way or anything," and another mother generalized her approach to her non-disabled children as well, "For me, it's preventive care. Don't wait until the child gets into a situation. I feel that is a need for children whether they are in special education or not." Additionally, parents and professionals frequently mentioned ways in which children with disabilities "seem like normal" in some ways but are "different from other kids" in other ways, accepting the contradiction as integral to their uniqueness as individuals.

Several participants noted that placing their child with disabilities in a helping role in the family helped manage the tension between ability and disability and also contributed to managing the contradiction between mediating resources and the division of labor in the family. Many children were given the task of reading to younger siblings, helping with cooking and laundry, or doing other simple tasks that alleviated some of the pressures on the family to fulfill family functions with limited time and financial resources. Also, developing new family routines and individualizing responses to sibling conflicts were ways of transforming family systems to resolve contradictions between resources, rules, and the community of family members. Many children focused on ways that they have fun with their siblings and as a whole family, focusing on the positive aspects of participating in the ongoing activity of being a family.

The strategy of reframing the family situation also was used to resolve the tertiary contradiction of shift in family focus that persisted through coping. For example, one mother noted, "it's not so much [child], it's just a situation." Another mother repeatedly referenced her reframing of her family's situation in meetings and an interview. She has five children, two with invisible disabilities. She noted, "When we are in a tough situation, we learn something about how we can deal with that. Just don't give up and keep going." Many family participants talked about the positive elements of their family interactions and relationships. Importantly, participants who referenced these positive aspects referred to them as part of ongoing family life and not only as a period or phase of positivity in the family. Thus, participants indicated that both having positive attitudes and engaging in positive interactions within their families were key to family coping and development.

Many parents indicated that they worked hard to resolve the quaternary contradiction between their family systems and educational or specialist systems. One communicative strategy parents referenced frequently was taking the initiative to develop relationships with professionals who were providing support to their children. Professionals and parents saw these collaborative relationships as developing through participation in meetings over time and also through informal interactions. Several parents noted that opportunities to develop these productive relationships often occur when they drop off or pick up their children from school. Quick conversations about the child's day helped foster collaborative parent-professional relationships. Other parents noted that they resolved the contradiction by being persistent with their requests for testing and services, as one mother recounted, "you know I kept on them, we've got to test her, we've got to test her." Professionals noted that getting parent input was often difficult due to placing too much trust in professionals, language barriers, or other issues. When decisions were made without parental input, the goals and orientation of the educational activity system were privileged over those of family systems by default.

The range of strategies participants used to resolve the quaternary contradiction between family and educational systems reflect broader structural contradictions. On one end of the continuum were parents who attempted to resolve the quaternary contradiction by drawing on structures of voice and equal access through persistent and consistent efforts to develop relationships with professionals. On the other end of the continuum were parents who essentially resolved the contradiction by privileging the educational system over their family systems by allowing professionals to make all of the decisions, either explicitly or through non-participation.

Best Practices

Strategies identified above range in effectiveness, so a summary of "best practices" is warranted. First, discussing disability within the family and with others is effective for moving the family system forward into productive transformations. Families who talked about disability among their members and with key outsiders, such as specialists and extended family members, were able to garner needed support in crises and develop family routines during coping for effective family functioning. Parents who actively participated with professionals to make decisions for their children were able to bring the needs of their families into the decision making equation, resolving tensions between family and educational systems.

Families who did not discuss disability in the family were not able to effectively address issues such as sibling conflicts and tensions between family resources and family needs. Likewise, when parents did not provide input to professionals or participate in decision making meetings, the needs and goals of the family system were by default subordinated to those of the educational system. Related to this, parents often indicated that they could not understand information provided by professionals or that they were overwhelmed by the amount of information provided and simply tuned it out. Accordingly, an important strategy in this regard is providing training for parents in how to find relevant information and also training for professionals on how to put information into language or summaries that parents will understand.

A second effective communication strategy families used to resolve contradictions was incorporating all the children in the family's homework routines. For many families, this meant dividing up homework help among children or between parents, changing the family's division of labor to manage the contradictions posed by disability and lack of resources. Children with disabilities responded well to being in helping roles with younger siblings, non-disabled siblings were able to see commonalities among the needs of all the children in the family, and pressures on parents were relieved when school help was shared within the family. However, it is important to note that non-disabled siblings in families who did not talk about disability also used homework routines as a way to tease children with disabilities and focus on *in*-abilities, so effective use of this strategy seems tied to open communication about disability in the family.

Finally, participants who discursively reframed their family situations into positive learning experiences developed effective routines for family functioning. This was done by recognizing disability, and the contradictions that come with the presence of ability combined with disability, and accepting the strengths and weaknesses, challenges and opportunities, that childhood disability presents. This discursive response involves recognizing disability as one aspect of family life that provides opportunities for the entire family system to transform to benefit all members.

Conclusion

To summarize, numerous contradictions emerge in family systems when children are diagnosed with an invisible disability and as families engage in their ongoing activity of providing nurturance and support for family members. Participating families employed a wide range of communication strategies for responding to these contradictions in periods of crisis and coping. Analysis using the framework of structurating activity theory identified the role of various system and structural contradictions that both enhanced and stymied family coping and development over time. Importantly, contradictions are not viewed as problems. Rather, they are tensions that emerge in family systems that provide opportunities for transformation and development. However, results clearly indicate that contradictions need to be recognized rather than ignored for such transformation to take place. By conceptualizing the family as an activity system consisting of mediating elements, this analysis took a problem-solving approach that can be applied beyond the context of families of children with invisible disabilities. Results also indicate that entrenched structural contradictions, particularly of equal access versus expert power, influenced ways participants responded to the quaternary contradiction between family and educational systems. This is clearly not an easy issue to resolve. However, continued efforts on the part of scholars and practitioners to manage this tension holds promise for transforming future system intersections.

References

Barrett, S. M. (2004). Implementation studies: Time for a revival? Personal reflections on 20 years of implementation studies. *Public Administration, 81*, 249–262.

Boer, N. I. (2005). *Knowledge sharing within organizations: A situated and relational perspective*, ERIM PhD Series Research in Management. Rotterdam, the Netherlands: Erasmus Research Institute of Management.

Bower, A. M., & Hayes, A. (1998). Mothering in families with and without a child with disability. *International Journal of Disability, Development and Education, 45*, 313–322.

Canary, H. E. (2008a). Creating supportive connections: A decade of research on support for families of children with disabilities. *Health Communication, 23*, 413–426.

Canary, H. E. (2008b). Negotiating dis/ability in families: Constructions and contradictions. *Journal of Applied Communication Research, 36*, 437–458.

Canary, H. E. (2010). Structurating activity theory: An integrative approach to policy knowledge. *Communication Theory, 20*(1), 21–49.

Center for Activity Theory and Developmental Work Research. (2004). *The activity system*. Retrieved from http://www.edu.helsinki.fi/activity/pages/chatanddwr/activitysystem/

Cuskelly, M., & Gunn, P. (2003). Sibling relationships of children with Down syndrome: Perspectives of mothers, fathers, and siblings. *American Journal of Mental Retardation, 108*(4), 234–244.

D'Arcy, F., Flynn, J., McCarthy, Y., O'Conner, C., & Tierney, E. (2005). Sibshops: An evaluation of an interagency model. *Journal of Intellectual Disabilities, 9*, 43–57.

Davis, C. S., & Salkin, K. A. (2008). Sisters and friends: Dialogue and multivocality in a relational model of sibling disability. In L. C. Lederman (Ed.), *Beyond these walls: Readings in health communication* (pp. 235–251). New York: Oxford University Press.

Dyson, L. L. (1993). Response to the presence of a child with disabilities: Parental stress and family functioning over time. *American Journal of Mental Retardation, 2*, 207–218.

Engeström, Y. (1999). Activity theory and individual and social transformation. In Y. Engeström, R. Miettinen, & R.-L. Punamäki (Eds.), *Perspectives on activity theory* (pp. 19–38). Cambridge, UK: Cambridge University Press.

Evans, J., Jones, J., & Mansell, I. (2001). Supporting siblings: Evaluation of support groups for brothers and sisters of children with learning disabilities and challenging behavior. *Journal of Learning Disabilities, 5,* 69–78.

Florian, V. (1989). The cultural impact on the family dynamics of parents who have a child with a disability. *Journal of Comparative Family Studies, 20,* 97–111.

Fox, L., Vaughn, B. J., Wyatte, M. L., & Dunlap, G. (2002). "We can't expect other people to understand": Family perspectives on problem behavior. *Exceptional Children, 68,* 437–450.

Gatford, A. (2004). Time to go home: Putting together a package of care. *Child: Care, Health & Development, 30,* 243–246.

Giddens, A. (1984). *The constitution of society.* Berkeley: University of California Press.

Glaser, B. G. (1978). *Theoretical sensitivity.* Mill Valley, CA: Sociology Press.

Goldbart, J., & Marshall, J. (2004). "Pushes and pulls" on the parents of children who use AAC. *Augmentative and Alternative Communication, 20,* 194–208.

Green, S., Davis, C., Karshmer, E., Marsh, P., & Straight, B. (2005). Living stigma: The impact of labeling, stereotyping, separation, status loss, and discrimination in the lives of individuals with disabilities and their families. *Sociological Inquiry, 75*(2), 197–215.

Guralnick, M. J., Neville, B., Connor, R. T., & Hammond, M. A. (2003). Family factors associated with the peer social competence of young children with mild delays. *American Journal on Mental Retardation, 108,* 272–287.

Hannah, M. E., & Midlarsky, E. (2005). Helping by siblings of children with mental retardation. *American Journal of Mental Retardation, 110*(2), 87–99.

Harry, B., Rueda, R., & Kayanpur, M. (1999). Cultural reciprocity and sociocultural perspective: Adapting the normalization principle for family collaboration. *Exceptional Children, 66,* 123–136.

Hwa-Froelich, D. A., & Westby, C. E. (2003). Frameworks of education: Perspectives of southeast Asian parents and Head Start staff.
Language, Speech, and Hearing Services in Schools, 34, 299–319.

Jackson, C. W., Traub, R. J., & Turnbull, A. P. (2008). Parents' experiences with childhood deafness: Implications for family-centered
services. *Communication Disorders Quarterly, 29*(2), 82–98.

Krone, K. J., Schrodt, P., & Kirby, E. L. (2006). Structuration theory:
Promising directions for family communication research. In D. O.
Braithwaite & L. A. Baxter (Eds.), *Engaging theories in family com-
munication: Multiple perspectives* (pp. 293–308). Thousand Oaks,
CA: Sage.

Lobato, D. J., & Kao, B. T. (2002). Integrated sibling-parent group
intervention to improve sibling knowledge and adjustment to
chronic illness and disability. *Journal of Pediatric Psychology, 27,*
711–716.

Lord-Nelson, L. G., Summers, J.-A., & Turnbull, A. P. (2004). Boundaries in family-professional relationships: Implications for special
education. *Remedial and Special Education, 25,* 153–165.

Matthews, C. K., & Harrington, N. G. (2000). Invisible disability. In D.
O. Braithwaite & T. L. Thompson (Eds.), *Handbook of communication and people with disabilities: Research and application* (pp. 405–
421). Mahwah, NJ: Lawrence Erlbaum.

Morison, J. E., Bromfield, L. M., & Cameron, H. J. (2003). A therapeu-
tic model for supporting families of children with a chronic illness
or disability. *Child and Adolescent Mental Health, 8*(3), 125–130.

Morse, C. A. (2002). Keeping it in the family: Caregiving in Austra-
lian-Greek families. *Social Work in Health Care, 34,* 299–314.

Patterson, J. M. (2002). Integrating family resilience and family stress
theory. *Journal of Marriage and Family, 64,* 349–360.

Sham, S. (1996). Reaching Chinese children with learning disabilities
in greater Manchester. *British Journal of Learning Disabilities, 24,*
104–109.

Shapiro, J., Monzo, L. D., & Rueda, R. (2004). Alienated advocacy:
Perspectives of Latina mothers of young adults with developmental disabilities. *Mental Retardation, 42,* 36–54.

Todd, S., & Jones, S. (2003). "Mum's the word!" Maternal accounts of dealings with the professional world. *Journal of Applied Research in Intellectual Disabilities, 16,* 229–244.

U.S. Department of Education. (2005). *Welcome to OSEP.* Retrieved from www.ed.gov/about/offices/list/osers/osep/index.html

Chapter 8

"Linked Lives": Mother-Adult Daughter Communication after a Breast Cancer Diagnosis

Carla L. Fisher & Jon F. Nussbaum

The diagnosis of breast cancer at any age inevitably alters a woman's life. Patients do not cope with this life-changing transition alone. They seek support from loved ones, particularly kin. Families are not always given psychosocial guidance to communicatively adjust in healthy ways. To produce such knowledge, we examined how mothers and daughters change their communicative behavior to adjust to this disease. To appreciate diversity in women's experience due to age, 40 developmentally diverse women either currently or recently diagnosed with breast cancer participated in an individual in-depth interview, as did 38 of their mothers or adult daughters.

> The interpersonal communication that fuels our social world is as essential to our survival as any biological or physical process that keeps us alive. (Hummert, Nussbaum, & Wiemann, 1994, p. 3)

Family communication is especially important when encountering traumatic health changes. During such transitions, people often call on family members for support. Family, stress, and adaptation research indicates that "the way people cope is largely a function of their interaction with others" (Afifi & Nussbaum, 2006, p. 282). Thus, communication is a major factor in a family's ability to maintain well-being while adjusting to a health crisis.

A frequently experienced stressful transition that families encounter is the diagnosis and treatment of cancer. Cancer is the second leading cause of death after heart disease in the United States (Hoyert, Kung, & Smith, 2003). A plethora of research across disciplines demonstrates that a patient's family interactions are critical to his/her well-being and adjustment to cancer (Goldsmith, Miller, & Caughlin, 2007; Hagedoorn et al., 2000; Pistrang, Barker, & Rutter, 1997). Cancer patients and spouses who openly communicate cancer-

related concerns, emotions and problems exhibit better psychological
(Lichtman, Taylor, & Wood, 1987), social, and emotional adjustment
(Zemore & Shepel, 1989). Patients without positive levels of family
support often have more depressive symptoms, troubled relationships, and disease symptoms that manifest physiologically and
negatively affect health (Helgeson & Cohen, 1999). A strong family
support network can enhance patients' quality of life (Suinn &
VandenBos, 1999).

Breast cancer afflicts more than 200,000 women each year, adding
to more than 2 million women already living with the disease (Jemel
et al., 2003). Once diagnosed, they experience drastic changes including intense and complex emotional, psychological changes (see Spira
& Kenemore, 2000, for a review) and physical transformations.
Women of different ages share similar experiences, but age at diagnosis also affects women's disease concerns. Oktay and Walter (1991)
found that a woman's developmental phase in life affects which
emotional concerns are most salient to her well-being. The bulk of
scholarship on family communication following a cancer diagnosis is
based on married couples. Yet the mother-daughter relationship has
emerged as an important factor in women's adjustment to breast
cancer (Burles, 2006; Oktay & Walter, 1991; Spira & Kenemore, 2000).
The significance of this kin bond is not surprising, given that the
mother-daughter relationship is often the longest, most emotionally
connected bond a woman experiences in her lifetime (Fischer, 1986).
Mothers and daughters have been described as "linked lives" (Fischer, 1986). Their bond evolves across the life span, often becoming
closer with increasing age. Although research on this bond in a cancer
context is scarce, scholars have found that mothers and daughters
share the transition psychologically, physically, and socially (Burles,
2006; Cohen et al., 2002; Cohen & Pollack, 2005).

Although these select studies confirm that breast cancer is a
mother-daughter encounter, they do not account for how mothers
and daughters *communicatively* adjust to this turning point. Turning
points, or transitions, are exemplars of family change that scholars
examine to further understand the importance of interpersonal
communication in human survival across the life span. Turning
points are processes of change that transform a family. As Cowen

(1991) suggests, during transitions, "The individual, couple, or family must adopt new strategies, skills, and patterns of behavior to solve new problems" (p. 17).

Family communication and health are clearly connected; indeed, competent communication may be necessary for survival. Health professionals do appreciate how important cancer patients' family interactions are in their ability to adjust to cancer. Yet, families are not given much guidance in psychosocially or communicatively adjusting to changes in individual and relational life. This lack of guidance is of concern because individuals are not necessarily born with the ability to communicate competently (Nussbaum, Pecchioni, Robinson, & Thompson, 2000; Pecchioni, Wright, & Nussbaum, 2005). In fact, while women diagnosed with breast cancer characterize their mother-daughter bond as supportive, they also describe the relationship as distressful (Oktay & Walter, 1991). These divergent experiences may be tied to variance in communicative ability to adjust to the disease in a manner that maximizes their wellness. By capturing how women communicatively adjust in their family bonds, we may be able to develop interventions and services to aid families coping with cancer. Families are in need of assistance that maximizes communicative competencies related to successful coping and surviving cancer. In this chapter, we explore how developmentally diverse mothers and daughters change their communicative behavior to cope with breast cancer.

Mother-Daughter Communication and Breast Cancer

Women with breast cancer characterize the mother-daughter relationship as significant in their transitional experience (Burles, 2006; Oktay & Walter, 1991). Mothers and daughters can serve as each other's confidant, advisor, friend, and nurturer. They often become closer and more emotionally connected as their bond evolves. Though mothers and daughters struggle to understand one another and maintain their complex dynamic (Tannen, 2006), they often experience a special closeness that persists across social classes and generational differences (Fischer, 1986). Their enduring connection, especially during adulthood, undoubtedly aids them in adjusting to and emerging from strenuous transitions like a breast cancer diagnosis.

Transitions, or turning points, are important focal points in understanding human behavior across the life span (Baxter & Bullis, 1986). They are sometimes narrowly described as life-changing events that affect a family's environment or an individual alone. In actuality, turning points are long-term or multiple processes of change that can transform a family and its individual members (Cowan, 1991), leading to both individual and relational changes. Transitions alter individuals' sense of self, assumptive world, and behavior; they also can lead to relational adjustments that redefine family bonds. The communicative behavior individuals enact to adjust to these changes affects the nature of their transitional experiences.

Turning points are especially helpful in understanding mothers and daughters' unique connection and the importance of their bond as women encounter stressful changes like cancer. Turning points shape mothers' and daughters' linked lives. They lead to relational changes in boundaries, roles, behavior, and intimacy. The transitional nature of this diagnosis has been studied and demonstrates that breast cancer is both a poignant turning point in the lives of women and the mother-daughter bond. Although not focused on communication, this research illuminates the numerous changes to which mothers and daughters must communicatively adapt.

Breast Cancer: A Mother-Daughter Turning Point

Once diagnosed, women experience drastic individual changes, particularly psychological ones. Typical experienced emotions include increased anger or sadness, loss of control, feelings of helplessness, increased anxiety and depression, struggles with self-esteem and identity, as well as feelings of betrayal (Spira & Kenemore, 2000). Their age at diagnosis also results in divergent concerns. For instance, Oktay and Walter's (1991) findings showed women diagnosed in their twenties struggle with anxiety about their future (e.g., ability to have children and form intimate relationships), and women diagnosed in midlife seemed concerned with present-oriented issues like self-reliance and their children's well-being. Women's relational lives are also transformed at diagnosis. Spira and Kenemore (2000) have observed that "The closer others are to the patient, the more likely they are to feel that their life is changed" (p. 174). For example, mothers and daughters can experience a role reversal as they take on new roles and responsibilities (Burles, 2006). Daughters sometimes assume maternal responsibilities like childcare and housework and even socially support their mothers. Relational changes can be difficult, however. For instance, some diagnosed mothers perceive daughters try to take control, which can prompt a power struggle (Oktay & Walter, 1991). Their communication surely affects whether how mothers and daughters negotiate such relational changes.

Like their diagnosed mothers, many daughters ultimately live with a psychological "chronic risk" (Kenen, Ardern-Jones, & Eeles, 2003), the fear of disease reoccurrence for their mothers and fear of developing the disease themselves. This shared chronic risk can lead to negative psychological and physiological health outcomes for both mothers and daughters. For instance, Boyer et al. (2002) found that breast cancer patients can exhibit posttraumatic stress disorder (PTSD) symptoms because of their diagnosis and treatment. In such cases, their daughters do as well. Cohen et al. (2002) and Cohen and Pollack (2005) demonstrated that these effects can extend further and are linked with "chronic risk" distress. When daughters were aware of their increased disease risk, they displayed higher emotional distress, elevated levels of stress hormones, and higher psychological distress in comparison to daughters of healthy (nondiagnosed) mothers of comparable age and education level. Diagnosed mothers' psychological distress is highly correlated with daughters' psychological distress, particularly when the mother has an advanced stage of the disease. They also determined that daughters have impaired immune functions and higher levels of stress hormones. Collectively, these studies highlight the need for mothers and daughters to learn healthy ways of communicatively managing complex changes to adjust competently.

Mother-Daughter Communication and Turning Points

A plethora of research concerning the mother-daughter bond suggests that mothers and daughters communicatively shape the nature of their transitional experiences. Communication influences how mothers and daughters adjust to notable transitions like developmental changes (e.g., the daughter's adolescence or the mother's aging) and life events (e.g., marriage, divorce, death) (Fingerman, 2003; Fischer, 1986; Fisher & Miller-Day, 2006; La Sorsa & Fodor, 1990; Miller-Day, 2004). Undoubtedly, their interaction is especially critical in the face of traumatic health changes, like a cancer, and affects their ability to adjust in healthy ways.

Research Inquiry

A breast cancer diagnosis is a complicated turning point in the lives of women and their mother-daughter bond. They encounter numerous individual and relational changes. Women's developmental phase in life, in part, influences the cancer-related challenges they face. To produce knowledge helpful to mothers and, the following research question was posed:

RQ: How do developmentally diverse mothers and their adult-daughters change their communicative behavior to adjust to a breast cancer diagnosis?

Method

Sample

Sampling was purposive since predefined groups of women were needed and proportionality was not the primary concern. Following IRB approval, women were recruited in numerous ways, including postings on a large northeastern university newswire and research database of speech communication students in addition to letters, flyers, and emails distributed to rural hospitals, cancer clinics, and cancer support groups. To qualify, women had to have been diagnosed with breast cancer and received treatment (surgery, radiation, or chemotherapy) within the last 36 months. They were asked to recruit their mother or adult daughter to participate. Each woman received $25 compensation and research credit, if enrolled in the university.

Forty women diagnosed with breast cancer were recruited as well as 38 of their mothers and adult daughters. A total of 35 mother-daughter dyads (N = 70) participated. Three dyads had an additional daughter participate and five diagnosed women participated without a mother/adult daughter dyadic partner. Women diagnosed with breast cancer represented three age groups: (a) 8 young adults (*Mean* age = 34.62, *SD* = 3.34, Age Range 30-39); (b) 20 midlife adults (13 as mothers: *Mean* age = 49.42, *SD* = 2.50, Age Range 44–52; 7 as daughters: *Mean* age = 46.00, *SD* = 3.00, Age Range 42–51); and (c) 12 later life adults (*Mean* age = 61.92, *SD* = 4.48, Age Range 57–69). The remaining 38 women represented the mothers and adult daughters of diagnosed women: 25 emerging/young adults (*Mean* age = 24.74, *SD* = 6.94, Age Range 18–37), 5 midlife adults (*Mean* age = 54.00, *SD* = 2.35, Age Range 51-56), and 8 later life adults (*Mean* age = 69.86, *SD* = 7.59, Age Range 58-83). Most were Caucasian (98.7%) and from the East Coast (85.3%). Half were married and most had a college-level education.

Procedures

Upon consenting to take part, each woman independently completed a slightly modified version of the Retrospective Interview Technique (RIT) graph (Baxter & Bullis, 1986 and Huston, Surra, Fitzgerald, & Gate, 1981), to provide participants with an opportunity to reflect on mood-altering events they experienced. RIT graphs focus on experiences across time and serve to reveal how individuals adjust to changes (Metts, Sprecher, & Cupach, 1991). Women plotted the course of the disease (or its lifeline) on the RIT graph. The horizontal axis represented time and affect/emotion was represented on the vertical axis. Then, the 78 women took part in individual, in-depth, life-span interviews. The women described their mother-daughter communication experiences beginning before the diagnosis and up to the present. A modified version of two comparable interview techniques was used: Lifeline Interview Method/LIM or "flowing river of life" (Schroots & Birren, 2001), and Retrospective Interview Technique or RIT (Baxter & Bullis, 1986). The interview was semi-structured and guided by a script. Women shared how cancer affected their bond and revealed whether, when, and how communication changed to adjust. Transcriptions resulted in 2,434 single-spaced pages of data.

Analyses

Analyses were conducted using Glaser and Strauss's (1967) and Strauss and Corbin's (1998) grounded theory approach. Illuminating the participants' communicative experiences required repeated examination until saturation occurred or no new patterns were evident. Data were then analyzed via the "selective approach" (reading transcripts and coding for conceptual themes) using the qualitative management computer program ATLAS.ti.5.2 (van Manen, 1990; see also Prentice, 2008). The analytical process involved the three steps Strauss and Corbin (1998) have identified: discovery of concepts through open coding, discovery of categories via thematic salience, as well as developing and refining the categories by identifying each category's properties and dimensions. According to Owen (1984), thematic salience is reflected in recurrence, repetition, and forcefulness. When possible, category names/labels were generated *in vivo*, or from the participants' own words, to ensure trustworthiness of data. The attributes of each category were identified for thick description. In the last step, categories were reviewed again to identify similar ideas while making a note for descriptive purposes.

Results

Six themes emerged that depict communication changes mothers and daughters engage in after a breast cancer diagnosis. The themes, presented below with details about women's developmentally diverse experiences, were changes in frequency of interaction, changes in topic of talk, increased positive talk, increased affection, changes in relational connection, and altering the level of openness. Pseudonyms were used to protect women's privacy.

Changes in the Frequency of Interaction

Women often described changes in the frequency of mother-daughter interaction post-diagnosis. The frequency of communication increased in two ways: spending more time together and talking more on the phone. In contrast, some women also reported it decreasing, sometimes even drastically when mothers and daughters communicatively withdrew from one another.

Spending more time together. Diagnosed women recalled that communication increased in frequency immediately after diagnosis. They described this continuing throughout their treatment but returning to "normal" it ended. Mothers and daughters explained that this increase occurred for two reasons. First, some became the diagnosed woman's "partner" in dealing with cancer. One diagnosed daughter, Charlotte, explained this change:

> She took a very big part of being my partner. She made sure she was there with my first—you know, when we first sat down with the doctor to talk about the type of cancer I had. And she was a big part of that. And she would always drive me to my chemo treatment. She set the standard for everyone else.

Like Charlotte, some daughters described sharing more time together because their mother/daughter became their caretaker as they underwent and recovered from difficult chemotherapy treatments and surgeries. This shared time took place in the health care setting and women's homes. Mothers/daughters made more house visits to help with household duties as well as to care for adolescent children when diagnosed women were too ill. Women diagnosed in midlife seemed to especially appreciate this increase in time together, as Lara shared:

> I wanted my daughter to be taken to all of her activities and so on and so forth, and my mom made sure she did that. She also made sure that if my daughter wanted friends to come over, it was kept to a minimum, but I wanted my daughter—I didn't want her life to stop because her mom had— was down and out for a little bit. That was what she needed. So I think my mom supported me, and she supported her [my daughter] in making sure that she knew that that's what I would want, so she did it.

Many women commented that they never had to ask their mother/adult daughter to change their behavior in this way. They described it as help or support that was just automatically given.

Not all women experienced this cancer-fighting partnership with their mother/daughter. Rather they remembered an increase in time spent together simply because they had a heightened desire to be together more. Many diagnosed women reported that this change occurred because their mother/daughter would visit more often. These women recalled being invited out more (e.g., to dinner) or that their mother/daughter would stop by unexpectedly more. One woman, Victoria, recalled her daughter making this effort: "I feel we try to do as much as possible together, and it's obvious when she comes home that she likes to make sure she spends time with me, and I don't think that would happen otherwise." Daughters and mothers of diagnosed women often expressed a strong need to be with their mother/daughter as much as possible. Shared time helped them understand their mothers'/daughters' needs and brought them comfort in knowing that they were okay. Many described consciously changing their behavior, like daughter Sara:

> I [was] making it an important part of my day, making that a priority to know what's going on with her. Whereas before, even though we're really close, I may have just checked on her a couple times a week. ... It's become total priority for me to know what's going on with her at this point.

Women perceived that this increase in interaction helped them cope and adjust. Some also recognized that this need to be together may have been stimulated by a fear of losing one's mother/daughter. A diagnosed daughter recognized her aging mother coping in this way:

> I think she needs to see me more, and maybe that's just to validate that I am okay. ... I was just home recently and noticed that she was very much by me, so to speak. ... For breakfast, she'd sit right by me, and I just thought that was kind of funny. Or if I was out on the deck, she'd come out on the deck and sit there. So not that she never did that, but I just noticed it was a little bit more ... I think she thinks of me as being, how could you have something wrong with you, and I need to be with you every minute.

Time spent together may have received heightened priority given women's inevitable linkage between cancer and death. Additionally, other daughters/mothers of diagnosed women perceived this increased time together was motivated as a way to keep their mother's/daughter's mind off cancer-related distress as Maria described below:

[When] she's feeling down, I'll just get her out shopping. I'll take the kids down. They always seem to, you know, make her laugh. … We'll just go do something just to perk her up. … I take her out to lunch a lot or to the mall … just to get her thinking about other things. And usually, that does the trick … anything that's getting her out of her environment … just distracting her.

Talking more on the phone. Many women also interacted more by phone. This change seemed to occur immediately after the diagnosis was disclosed. Like women spending more time with their mothers/daughters, these women expressed that talking more on the phone was a healthy and necessary means of coping. For instance, one daughter (Carol) recalled her mother saying to her immediately after Carol was diagnosed, "I am just going to need to talk to you more…I just need to hear your voice." Many women explained this increase in communication in relation to their mothers'/daughters' heightened concern for their well-being. These women recalled their mothers/daughters frequently calling for updates, especially when they underwent cancer treatments like surgery or chemotherapy. For example, one mother, Jeanne, recalled her young-adult daughter calling to lift her spirits: "She would call me and leave me messages on my cell phone just to see how I was doing and just to encourage me." During such times, mothers/daughters admitted calling almost daily. Yet, they seemed aware that this behavior could become burdensome. As a result, many tried to not overdo it. One mother, Joanna, talked about this dilemma saying: "I might have hovered a little bit more than maybe she wanted to but she never voiced it. Sometimes you have to back off a little too." Young-adult diagnosed daughters seemed especially sensitive to this increase in interaction. Some expressed it could be overwhelming and even annoying. Angie, diagnosed in her late twenties, shared:

She was calling, calling, calling constantly. I totally understand that she was worried or whatever. It did get annoying after a while and I'm like "Mom I'm fine … I will call if I'm not fine." … It was like every day and drove me insane every single day.

Still, women connected this change with making more of an effort to stay connected. Diagnosed mothers, especially, noticed their daughters initiating talk more often. Some diagnosed women and their mothers/daughters talked about the importance of engaging in everyday conversation. Diagnosed mothers often wanted to talk about their daughters' lives because it helped them know their daughters were coping okay or, as one mother, Glenn, put it:

> I wanted to know what she was doing. ... For her to continue her life as she is, that's actually, that's comforting to me. That makes me feel the comfort I need to do what I need to do.

Women also reported that mundane talk helped them prevent cancer from taking over their lives as diagnosed daughter, Susanna, described:

> We would talk every day and talk about things and people and you know, what was going on. ... This does take your mind off of it and just keeps you more involved in everyday life you know, in getting through. So that's—I think that's good because you don't want to dwell on it too much. ... I found that if you are just home and by yourself, you would think of it [cancer] constantly.

Withdrawing. At times women described a decrease in mother-daughter interaction. In these instances, typically the women diagnosed were mothers of young-adult or late-adolescent daughters. These women recalled their daughters withdrawing sometimes completely and for extended periods of time. Often this withdrawal occurred immediately after mothers disclosed their diagnoses. Mothers recalled daughters avoiding talking to their mothers, abruptly ending conversations related to cancer, or blatantly refusing to discuss cancer at all. Most mothers attributed their daughters' behavior to protecting themselves, as Katherine shared about her daughters: "I know they really don't want to talk about it. I mean, it's too much to deal with it right now. It's overwhelming to think about." Some diagnosed women tried to alter their daughters' withdrawal as they believed it was an unhealthy response. Even so, some daughters expressed that they needed to withdraw to cope. One daughter, Clarissa, explained this saying:

> I didn't really know how to react to it so I kind of hid from it and I kind of blocked it out of my mind. ... It was easier for me at the time just to shut it out of my mind and just pretend nothing was happening. ... Once she started chemo it hit me that like, hey! I got to accept this or else it's going to keep haunting me for this entire thing.

Changes in Topic of Talk

Not surprisingly, what mothers and daughters talked about also changed. The topic of talk became more health-focused. An obvious reason for this was that women were constantly updating their mothers/daughters about their health in relation to the disease. Thus, much of this talk centered on treatment progress, how they were physically managing, appointments, and test results. Some diagnosed women also recalled their mothers/daughters giving them general information about breast cancer, even if they did not ask for it, or sharing information about other women's experiences, often in an effort to motivate them or uplift their spirits. Some women found this especially helpful in adjusting. One diagnosed mother, Cate, described this:

> She's had some experience with some of her friends who had breast cancer, and we would talk about that. She would tell me some of their experiences, and I would always ask how they were doing. So it was kind of helpful to know other people are going through this and how well they were tolerating it.

Many women also recalled discussing disease prevention quite often, especially diagnosed women with adult daughters. Oftentimes, this talk was occurring for the first time in their bond. Many mothers experienced this topic as a natural result of their diagnosis but also as a necessary step in protecting their daughters' future health. At times such interactions coincided with the diagnosed mother updating her daughter on her own breast cancer health. Diagnosed mothers reported that it was easiest to integrate these talks when cancer already was in the conversation and that this was necessary for daughters to be receptive to the information. This approach seemed especially important for women with younger daughters, as some admittedly did not want to engage in this type of talk. Yet, many young-adult daughters recognized this type of talk helped their mothers cope with the disease. They expressed that their mothers seemed comforted knowing that their daughters would do what they could to prevent their chances of developing the disease. Chris, a young-adult daughter, recalled this when her mother told her and her sisters they should get mammograms earlier than age 40:

> I don't even know if it would've been necessary for Mom to even tell us that we would have to do that because we knew we would have to do that now. I think it made her feel better knowing that we were going to do that.

Although health-focused mother-daughter interactions typically were associated with talk about breast cancer, women also recalled their mothers/daughters addressing their overall health more often in ways that were unrelated to breast cancer. Lara described this experience saying:

> There's just a lot more about my health, even not just so much surrounding my checkups but, "Are you exercising? Are you watching what you eat? Don't get so stressed out." Those types of things. And it's not that she never said it before, but it has picked up.

Increased Positive Talk

Women also described mother-daughter communication becoming more positive in nature. Many seemed to think that it was important to always have a positive outlook when discussing anything related to cancer. Some described this as a philosophy of life necessary for adjusting in a healthy manner as Patricia, a mother of a diagnosed daughter, stated: "If you had a positive attitude, you could come through a lot of things. And without one, sometimes they just didn't make it." Positive talk emerged in a variety of contexts, including when diagnosed women were in low emotional states, experiencing uncertainty or anxiety about upcoming test results, or had physical debilitation from chemotherapy treatments. A desire for positive talk also emerged in noncancer-related contexts. For instance, diagnosed women recalled avoiding their mother/daughter when they were in bad moods or talking negatively. For some women, positive communication increased and for others it was a new way of interacting. One diagnosed daughter, Mia, recalled this change as uncharacteristic of her mother's usual personality:

Like I would say "You know I talked to [the hospital]. They said this." She may say, "Oh that's great! That's good news." Or I'll get her opinion on something like, "Oh so what do you think? Do you think everything's gonna be okay?" And she's like, "Oh yeah. I don't have any bad feelings. I think things are gonna be fine." She is positive in that sense. And sometimes I'm like, "Are you just saying that?" You know? It so unusual for her! (She laughs) ... [but] sometimes I just needed to hear that.

At times, positive talk seemed to help mothers and daughters cope with cancer. Women sometimes explained it was a way to prevent negative interaction. Mothers/daughters would focus on positive things to avoid discussing negative issues that may upset the other woman. This interactive pattern was often reciprocal. For these women, positive talk seemed helpful in their adjustment. Women reported that positive talk enabled them to stay strong, maintain high spirits, prevent being pitied, and minimized excessive anxiety. However, some diagnosed women also recalled positive talk functioning as a method of censorship. As a diagnosed mother stated about her daughter, "She doesn't like me to talk about it a lot. She wants a more positive. She doesn't like me to talk in a negative; she always wants me to talk positive about it and hopeful." Abby, a mother of a diagnosed daughter reflected on this dilemma saying:

Sometimes when she was down [I was] trying to convince her that it was going to be okay, you know, it was going to get better. I think sometimes she was very, very tired and down. ... You can't go through something like that and not have the ups and downs.

Some diagnosed women viewed positive talk as not always help-ful in dealing with physical challenges, like debilitating chemother-apy treatment. For example, Cammy, a diagnosed daughter stated: "Sometimes you just want to be left alone. ... I think it was that I just didn't feel good. And it just wasn't gonna do any good at that point." Several women experienced positive talk as not helpful when it minimized their experiences, prevented them from releasing distress, or when it seemed their mother/daughter did not understand their experience.

Increased Affection

Many women talked about affectionate communication increasing verbally and nonverbally. Women recalled receiving and giving hugs more often and endearing comments like "I love you." Diagnosed women reported that their mothers/daughters were more loving and expressive, and this change was comforting. As Victoria, a diagnosed mother, stated, "She is always patting my head and thinking about giving me that extra something, just extra warmth."

For many diagnosed mothers of young-adult daughters, this behavior was rather new. These women were taken aback by this noticeable change as one mother (Diana) described:

> She never really gave me a hug or [would] kiss me or say "I love you" before this all happened. [It] completely changed. She says she loves me all the time, texts me that, gives me a hug now all the time when she sees me. That was not Gabby!

Another mother had a similar reaction and discussed how she welcomed this change:

> [She] was always a little—I don't want to say aloof like in haughty—but she didn't say "I love you" a lot or anything like that. And since all this has happened, there was one night where she just put her arms around me and said, "I love you so much, Mom. I don't want to lose you." Are you my kid? I didn't say that to her but that's what I was thinking! So she has gotten closer and taken the initiative and verbalized it so that's a good thing.

Daughters and mothers of diagnosed women seemed aware of this change in their behavior, and young-adult daughters were conscious of the "newness" of this communication in their relationship. Brandy, a daughter in her twenties, stated,

> There have been a couple of times where I kind of put my arm on her back, and I would never have done that, I think, before. I never felt the urge to do something like that. ... I knew she was having trouble. ... I remember just

looking at my mom, making eye contact with her, and putting my arm behind her.

Many women described this change having reciprocal benefits in
terms of adjusting to cancer.

Change in Relational Connection

Women described changes in their mother-daughter communication that represented a transformation in their relational connection.
Women linked this change in communication with reversing roles,
increased intuition or understanding, as well as maturity. For instance, some diagnosed women reported witnessing a role reversal in
their daughters' communication that heightened their emotional
connection. These women described their daughters engaging in
caregiving or nurturing communication for the first time. Women
stated that their daughters seemed to acquire an increased understanding of their needs, emotions and perspective. One diagnosed
mother (Patty) described this saying, "She has just shown another
side of her because now she's had to be the one that is comforting
Mom." Diagnosed women stated that this type of communication was
particularly helpful in their adjustment. For example, one mother,
Victoria, recalled struggling with severe, debilitating sadness during
chemotherapy treatment. Her daughter noticed and intervened; in a
sense, the daughter became the mother:

> I had considered stopping my treatment and told her that. She discussed the
> fact that she felt I was depressed, and I think I was, you know and she de-
> tected those signs. She talked to me before my appointment and then went
> with me to my appointment. She made a point of sitting down and talking
> with me the night before and [said] "I need to discuss this, you know...bla
> bla bla." In a very warm way, you know. So yeah it's been a very positive—
> you know it's weird to say it's a positive thing—but it is.

Other times women described an increased sense of intuition in
their communication. These women reported that their daugh-
ters/mothers had a better understanding of their needs and were
more attentive and intuitive. Several mothers described this difference in their daughter's behavior, linking it with developmental

maturity, as one mother stated: "I want to say that it was a more of a—what [word] do I use? A 'mature' support? … [She] would kind of watch me and she didn't have to ask … [She would] understand more." This change seemed particularly salient in young-adult daughters' experiences when their mothers were diagnosed. This change was helpful to both women in coping. They often discussed this behavior as a change that made them more connected. For instance, women recalled each other being less manipulative, less controlling, more tolerant, and more accepting. As one diagnosed daughter, Charlotte, put it:

> I just–I feel that she's more sensitive to my needs, and I think that—I hope—that I'm more sensitive to her needs as well. You know just in talking to each other and you know just being thoughtful of each other's feelings.

This change in connection manifested as a relational redefinition as women let go of unhealthy past issues and instead focused on strengthening their bond through communication. Sometimes this change occurred spontaneously and, in other instances, the change was communicatively negotiated, as Samantha (a young-adult daughter) described below:

> If I could really picture everything and know exactly the process and exactly what she was going through, it helps make it more real for me but in a good way. … I thanked her for protecting me but I said that's not the way I want to do this. I want to hear about everything. … She knew at that point I wanted to do this as a peer and as an adult and not to have it be like she was my mom and trying to protect me. I think that would have been way scarier for me.

Altering the Level of Openness

Women also described their level of openness changing. Some believed that they became more open, whereas others thought they monitored or disclosed less in conversations. Both changes seemed to work in positive and negative ways. Interestingly, the level of openness seemed tied to women's desire to or attempt to minimize their mother/daughter's distress. For instance, some mothers and daughters recalled sharing more. They became more open about their personal lives as they experienced an increased closeness. One diagnosed mother, Linda, described this change in her daughter: "I think she is more open and I am more accepting you know to what she has to say." Similarly, Jenny, another diagnosed mother, stated:

> I think I would get more information out of her, and she would get more information out of me as far as, you know, if she was asking me for advice or I was giving her how I felt about it. Or, you know, it's just that we could talk about more things.

Diagnosed women, particularly mothers, welcomed this, as one stated: "[We are] more open. Like she said to me she didn't want me to hide my feelings no matter how I was feeling. And I was glad." Some believed openness was necessary to prevent distress as Mary, a diagnosed mother, said: "I think they might have been concerned if I *weren't* sharing information."

Conversely, many women recalled their level of openness decreasing to minimize distress. Diagnosed women recalled not providing details to their mother/daughter to minimize their loved one's anxiety and concern about their well-being. In short, they did not include details to protect their mother/daughter. As one diagnosed mother stated, "I tend to downplay medical type things." It is also noteworthy that, typically, these women either had young-adult daughters or aging mothers. Diagnosed mothers often expressed not wanting to cause unnecessary worry. Diagnosed daughters with aging mothers explained that too much information often confused their mothers. In addition, both diagnosed mothers and their daughters recognized that certain topics were never discussed openly, namely, death, future recurrence, or negative emotions like anger or sadness. In particular, daughters of later-life diagnosed mothers stated their mothers never shared emotions. As Kacey, described:

> It was never emotional. It was always very, if I could say "clinical." It was all about the treatment. It was all about the drugs. It was about prognosis and never, never intimate [like] "How does it feel to me ..."

These daughters often expressed concern regarding their mothers' lack of disclosure regarding negative emotions as they were aware of their mothers' distress and depression. Young-adult daughters in their thirties or midlife often expressed that they wanted "all the details."

Discussion

In sum, mothers and daughters across age engage in these six communicative changes to cope with associated challenges that emerge when one has been diagnosed with breast cancer. These findings provide insight about how communication can function in both positive and negative ways in families' adjustment. While similar experiences were noted across ages, some noteworthy differences emerged that seemed tied to women's developmental place in life.

Young-adult women diagnosed with cancer (all daughters) reported more negative reactions to increased interaction. During this developmental period, daughters still struggle with the dialectic of separation-connection from their mothers (La Sorsa & Fodor, 1990). Thus, this developmental difference in women's experiences may be related to the fact that these daughters still struggle for independence from their mothers. In opposition, midlife diagnosed daughters seemed to almost always appreciate this communication change as they themselves were struggling with maintaining their house, career, and children, all while trying to beat cancer. According to Fingerman, Nussbaum, and Birditt (2004) midlife is a "juggling act" for women as they have more roles and responsibilities in comparison to other developmental periods. Therefore, it makes sense that to adjust to their new circumstances, more time with their mothers is a welcomed and needed change to help them manage their many responsibilities.

Developmental issues post adolescence likely also affected diagnosed midlife women's reaction to changes in affectionate communication. These women typically reported this communication change occurring in their daughters—women who were young adults. This period is very close to adolescence, a time in which mothers and daughters often experience more turmoil and separation in their relationship (Hershberg, 2006). Hence, receiving affection from their daughters likely seemed more unusual to them. Similarly, mothers diagnosed in mid- or later life also discussed the importance of a change allowing them to connect more intimately as daughters communicated more care and attentiveness. As many were young adults, it is likely that this change was most salient to their mothers as the role reversal was new. Studies suggest that mothers and daughters become more emotionally close when daughters see their mothers as an individual separate from their parent—a phenomenon first termed filial comprehending (Nydegger, 1991; Fisher & Miller-Day, 2006; Miller-Day, 2004). For these women, they likely experienced a similar relational redefinition that involved more equality and effort in the bond.

Clearly, women communicatively adjust to breast cancer in their mother-daughter bond and their communicative experiences are influenced by their place in the life span. Age is often an ignored factor in health communication, family research, and the social aspects of health care. Ignoring the role of development is quite surprising given that our communication competencies are influenced by age and life experiences (Pecchioni et al., 2005), and human development appears to be quite important in how women adjust to difficult changes like cancer. Hence, it will be especially important for future scholars, practitioners, and interventionists to appreciate developmental diversity to produce a complete understanding of family communication needs.

Best Practices

These findings also bring to light important practical considerations for patients and families adjusting to cancer as well as those health professionals who are assisting them with this difficult diagnosis. While most of the emergent communication changes could function in both helpful and unhelpful ways, other behaviors always seemed helpful. For example, affectionate communication appears to influence one's psychological state. Communicating love, concern, and care seemed to strengthen women's mother-daughter bonds, which aided them in coping. Moreover, on an individual level, affection helped diagnosed women feel comforted and supported and had reciprocal benefits for their mothers/daughters. Other findings demonstrate that to adjust in healthy ways, families must learn to negotiate how they will cope with cancer together. For instance, mothers and daughters had a heightened desire to spend increased time together and to interact more. Equally important was the nego-tiation of independence and privacy, while negotiating openness in their bonds. Mothers and daughters may benefit from discussing early on (and negotiating together) how much to disclose as it affects both women's coping. Finally, these findings illuminate how impor-tant it is for the health care community to recognize that breast cancer patients' families' needs are also significant. Diagnosed women seemed especially concerned about their mother/daughter's well-being and adjusted their communication in ways that reflected this. Thus, health professionals and interventionists might devise ways that attend to families' needs (not just patients') as they collectively cope with the complex changes. Doing so will be beneficial to family members' and patients' quality of life, who are appreciably just as concerned about their loved one's wellness.

Limitations

The women who shared their experiences in this study were ho-mogenous in culture. Research shows that culture and ethnicity influence mother-daughter communication (Rastogi & Wampler, 1999). Future researchers might attempt to capture ethnically diverse women's experiences with cancer. Treatment regimens, stage at diagnosis, as well as first-time diagnoses versus recurrence may influence women's communication as they adjust to the disease.

References

Afifi, T. D., & Nussbaum, J. F. (2006). Stress and adaptation theories: Families across the life span. In D. O. Braithwaite & L. A. Baxter (Eds.), *Engaging theories in family communication: Multiple perspectives* (pp. 276–292). Thousand Oaks, CA: Sage.

Baxter, L. A., & Bullis, C. (1986). Turning points in developing romantic relationships. *Human Communication Research, 12,* 469–493.

Boyer, B. A., Bubel, D., Jacobs, S. R., Knolls, M. L., Harwell, V. D., Goscicka, M., & Keegan, A. (2002). Posttraumatic stress in women with breast cancer and their daughters. *American Journal of Family Therapy, 30,* 323–338.

Burles, M. C. (2006). *Mothers and daughters' experiences of breast cancer: Family roles,responsibilities, and relationships.* Unpublished doctoral dissertation, University of Saskatchewan. Retrieved January 1, 2007, from http://library2.usask.ca/theses/available/etd-11222006-150720/

Cohen, M., Klein, E., Kuten, A., Fried, G., Zinder, O., & Pollack, S. (2002). Increased emotional distress in daughters of breast cancer patients is associated with decreased natural cytotoxic activity, elevated levels of stress hormones and decreased secretion of Th1 cytokines. *International Journal of Cancer, 100,* 347–354.

Cohen, M., & Pollack, S. (2005). Mothers with breast cancer and their adult daughters: The relationship between mothers' reaction to breast cancer and their daughters' emotional and neuroimmune status. *Psychosomatic Medicine, 67,* 64–71.

Cowan, P. A. (1991). Individual and family life transitions: A proposal for a new definition. In P. A. Cowan & E. M. Hetherington (Eds.) *Family transitions. Family Research Consortium: Advances in family research* (pp. 3–30). Hillsdale, NJ: Erlbaum.

Fingerman, K. L. (2003). *Mothers and their adult daughters: Mixed emotions, enduring bonds.* New York: Prometheus Books.

Fingerman, K. L., Nussbaum, J. F., & Birditt, K. S. (2004). Keeping all five balls in the air: Juggling family communication at midlife. In A. Vangelisti (Ed.), *Handbook of family communication* (pp. 135–152). Mahwah, NJ: Erlbaum.

Fischer, L. R. (1986). *Linked lives.* New York: Harper & Row.

Fisher, C., & Miller-Day, M. (2006). Communication over the life span: The mother-adult daughter relationship. In K. Floyd & M. T. Morman (Eds.), *Widening the family circle: New research in family communication* (pp. 3–19). Thousand Oaks, CA: Sage.

Glaser, B. G., & Strauss, A. L. (1967). *The discovery of grounded theory: Strategies for qualitative research.* New York: Aldine de Gruyter.

Goldsmith, D. J., Miller, L. E., & Caughlin, J. P. (2007). Openness and avoidance in couples communicating about cancer. In C. Beck (Ed.), *Communication yearbook 31* (pp. 62–117). New York: Routledge.

Hagedoorn, M., Kuijer, R., Buunk, B. P., DeJong, G., Wobbes, T., & Sanderman, R. (2000). Marital satisfaction in patients with cancer: Does support from intimate partners benefit those who need it most? *Health Psychology, 19,* 274–282.

Helgeson, V. S., & Cohen, S. (1999). Social support and adjustment to cancer: Reconciling descriptive, correlational, and intervention research. In R. M. Suinn & G. R. VandenBos (Eds.), *Cancer patients and their families: Readings on disease course, coping, and psychological interventions* (pp. 53–79). Washington, DC: American Psychological Association.

Hershberg, S. G. (2006). Pathways of growth in the mother-daughter relationship. *Psychoanalytic Inquiry, 26,* 56–69.

Hoyert, D. L., Kung, H. C., & Smith, B. S. (2005). *National vital statistics reports: Deaths: Preliminary data for 2003.* Washington, DC: U.S. Department of Health and Human Services, National Center for Health Statistics, Centers for Disease Control and Prevention, National Vital Statistics System.

Hummert, M. L., Nussbaum, J. F., & Wiemann, J. M. (1994). Interpersonal communication and older adulthood: An introduction. In M. L. Hummert, J. M. Wiemann, & J. F. Nussbaum (Eds.), *Interpersonal communication in older adulthood: Interdisciplinary theory and research* (pp. 1–14). Thousand Oaks, CA: Sage.

Huston, T. L., Surra, C. A., Fitzgerald, N. M., & Cate, R. M. (1981). From courtship to marriage: Mate selection as an interpersonal process. In S. W. Duck & R. Gilmour (Eds.), *Personal relationships: Developing personal relationships* (pp. 53–88). London: Academic Press.

Jemel, A., Murray, T., Samuels, A., Kaplan, A. G., Miller, J. B., Stiver, I. P., & Sorrey, J. L. (2003). Cancer statistics, 2003. *CA: A Cancer Journal for Clinicians, 53,* 5–26.

Kenen, R., Ardern-Jones, A., & Eeles, R. (2003). Living with chronic risk: Healthy women with a family history of breast/ovarian cancer. *Health, Risk & Society, 5,* 315–331.

La Sorsa, V. A., & Fodor, I. G. (1990). Adolescent daughter/midlife mother dyad: A new look at separation and self-definition. *Psychology of Women Quarterly, 14,* 593–606.

Lichtman, R. R., Taylor, S. E., & Wood, J. V. (1987). Social support and marital adjustment after breast cancer. *Journal of Psychosocial Oncology, 5(3),* 47–74.

Metts, S., Sprecher, S., & Cupach, W. R. (1991). Retrospective self-reports. In B. M. Montgomery & S. Duck (Eds.), *Studying interpersonal interaction* (pp. 162–178). London: Guilford Press.

Miller-Day, M. (2004). *Communication among grandmothers, mothers, and adult daughters: A qualitative study of maternal relationships.* Mahwah, NJ: Erlbaum.

Nussbaum, J. F., Pecchioni, L., Robinson, J. D., & Thompson, T. (2000). *Communication and aging* (2nd ed.). Mahwah, NJ: Erlbaum.

Nydegger, C. N. (1991). The development of paternal and filial maturity. In K. Pillemer (Ed.), *Parent-child relations throughout life* (pp. 93–112). Hillsdale, NJ: Erlbaum.

Oktay, J. S. (2005). *Breast cancer: Daughters' tell their stories.* New York: Routledge.

Oktay, J. S., & Walter, C. A. (1991). *Breast cancer in the life course: Women's experiences.* New York: Springer.

Owen, W. F. (1984). Interpretive themes in relational communication. *Quarterly Journal of Speech, 70,* 274–287.

Pecchioni, L. L., Wright, K., & Nussbaum, J. F. (2005). *Life-span communication.* Mahwah, NJ: Erlbaum.

Pistrang, N., Barker, C., & Rutter, C. (1997). Social support as conversation: Analyzing breast cancer patients' interactions with their partners. *Social Science and Medicine, 45,* 773–782.

Prentice, C. M. (2008). The assimilation of in-laws: The impact of newcomers on the communication routines of families. *Journal of Applied Communication Research, 36,* 74–97.

Rastogi, M., & Wampler, K. S. (1999). Adult daughters' perception of the mother-daughter relationship: A cross-cultural comparison. *Family Relations, 48*, 327–336.

Schroots, J. J. F., & Birren, J. E. (2001). The study of lives in progress: Approaches to research on life stories. In G. D. Rowles & N. E. Schoenberg (Eds.), *Qualitative gerontology: A contemporary perspective* (2nd ed., pp. 51–65). New York: Springer.

Sheehan, N. W., & Donorfio, L. M. (2002). Efforts to create meaning in the relationship between aging mothers and their caregiving daughters: A qualitative study of caregiving. *Journal of Aging Studies, 13*, 161–177.

Spira, M., & Kenemore, E. (2000). Adolescent daughters of mothers with breast cancer: Impact and implications. *Clinical Social Work Journal, 28*, 183–195.

Strauss, A., & Corbin, J. (1998). *Basics of qualitative research: Techniques and procedures for developing grounded theory.* Thousand Oaks, CA: Sage.

Suinn, R. M., & VandenBos, G. R. (1999). *Cancer patients and their families: Readings on disease course, coping, and psychological interventions.* Washington, DC: American Psychological Association.

Tannen, D. (2006). *You're wearing THAT? Understanding mothers and daughters in conversation.* New York: Random House.

Tesch, R. (1990). *Qualitative research: Analysis types and software tools.* London: Falmer.

van Manen, M. (1990). *Researching lived experience: Human science for action sensitive pedagogy.* Albany: State University of New York Press.

Zemore, R., & Shepel, L. F. (1989). Effects of breast cancer and mastectomy on emotional support and adjustment. *Social Science and Medicine, 28*, 19–27.

Chapter 9

Women Coping with Cancer: Family Communication, Conflict, and Support

Jennifer A. Samp and Tara J. Abbott

We examined the interplay of family communication patterns, conflict styles, and judgments of familial support received by female cancer patients. Forty-nine females with cancer completed a survey assessing perceptions of (a) family conversation and conformity orientations, (b) conflict styles with a primary support provider, (c) family communication about the cancer and (d) her support needs, (e) the amount and types of support received from the primary family support provider, and (f) whether the support optimally matched her expectations. Results highlighted the positive influence of family conversation orientation on the amount of communication about the cancer, the patient's expression of support needs, and her perceptions of optimal support matching. Further, when a primary support provider used a collaborative conflict styles, the cancer patient was more likely to be satisfied with the level of support she desired.

Individuals diagnosed with cancer often seek out the support of family members to cope with stressors including physical discomfort, a restricted lifestyle, and a fear of the future. Yet family members may find it problematic to provide "ideal" support as they grapple with their own uncertainty and anger about the illness, fear of losing the family member, and changes in the cancer patient since diagnosis (Sheridan, Sherman, Pierce, & Compas, 2010; Yoshida, Otani, Hirai, Ogata, Mera, Okada, & Oshima, 2010). In turn, the cancer patient may end up dissatisfied with the support provided by well-intended family members (Martire, Lustig, Schulz, Miller, & Helgeson, 2004; Zakowski, Ramati, Morton, Johnson, & Flanigan, 2004).

We examined how a cancer patient's perceptions of family communication norms are associated with judgments about the efforts of a primary support provider. To begin, we review prior research considering the interconnections of social support, optimal matching of support, family communication patterns, and conflict styles. We then describe a study examining judgments from women coping with cancer about family communication support behavior.

Social Support, Family Interactions, and Managing Cancer

Social support is a multidimensional construct describing the assistance provided to close others in coping with a variety of situations ranging from daily life events to major stressors. Support efforts may be reflective of an *emotional, tangible,* and/or *informational* focus (see Martin, Davis, Baron, Suls, & Blanchard, 1994; Sarason & Sarason, 2009). *Emotional support* involves providing love, empathy, and trust to achieve feelings of comfort or a sense of belonging. *Tangible support* reflects the provision of goods and services, such as financial assistance or help with daily chores. *Informational support* is focused on providing resources n to help solve a problem, such as providing a cancer patient with a list of oncologists in the area.

Several health-related benefits have been linked to receiving social support, including reduced distress and improved recovery from illness (see Uchino, 2009; Zakowski et al., 2004). However, social support is only effective if it comes from the right person. Not surprisingly, family members are a primary source of support during illness. Glasdam, Jensen, Madsen, and Rose (1996) reported that most married cancer patients identify a spouse as the most important source of support. For minors, parents are often the primary source of support during distress and illness (Gardner & Cutrona, 2004). However, research on *optimal matching* suggests that successful support providers, including family members, must be able to recognize the types and amount of support desired by the support-seeker and act in line with these expectations.

Optimal matching of social support

According to optimal matching theory (OMT; Cutrona & Russell, 1990), social support is most effective when the type of support needed is the type of support provided. Recognizing that social support may be reflective of emotional, informational, or tangible content, OMT posits that the relative importance of these support types as social resources depends on the controllability of an individual's stressors. When stressors are uncontrollable, such as is often the case in illness, OMT suggests that emotional support will take priority. Yet when it comes to more controllable stressors, tangible and informational support may be more important than emotional support to support seekers.

Ell (1996) argued that optimal support can only occur when there is clear, accurate communication of need by an individual and sufficient ability on the part of a support provider to meet that expressed need. Such conditions are not always present, making it difficult to determine what type of support is desired by the patient, thus causing support providers to oscillate between too little and too much support (Martire et al., 2004). Further, the degree to which family members are willing to engage in support may be influenced by the patient's ability to cope with the emotions pertaining to the illness. For example, Revenson and Stanton (2004) reported that spouses who deem a seriously ill partner as highly distressed and poor at coping may pull back their supportive efforts for fear that any additional supportive attempts will be ineffective. We argue that perceptions of effective support may in part be derived from the general patterns of communication behaviors embedded within the family of the cancer patient.

Family communication patterns and support

Fitzpatrick (see Koerner, 2007; Koerner & Fitzpatrick, 2002a) advanced that family dynamics can be defined by two sets of beliefs about communication: *conversation orientation* and *conformity orientation*. *Conversation orientation* indicates the degree to which families have an environment of unrestrained communication about a wide range of topics. For families high in conversation orientation, communication is frequent and open to a variety of topics regarding thoughts, emotions, and individual activities. In contrast, families low in conversation orientation typically spend little time interacting with one another; when they do communicate, the topics of discussion are restricted to uncontroversial, "safe" topics. *Conformity orientation* reflects how much family communication stresses shared values, attitudes, and beliefs. Families on the high end of this dimension emphasize uniformity, a hierarchical decision-making structure, and an avoidance of conflicts that highlight family discord. Further, such families frequently evaluate others based on the family's shared attitudes and perspectives (Koerner & Cvancara, 2002). Low conformity orientation families encourage independence, even at the expense of family cohesiveness (Koerner & Fitzpatrick, 2002a).

We suggest that perceptions of family conversation and conformity orientation should influence cancer patients' judgments about the support received from primary family support providers. In particular, assuming families high in conversation orientation value communication, cancer patients from such families should take comfort in using open and frequent communication as strategy by which to cope with cancer. Although a cancer diagnosis may prompt family members to make efforts to feel close to one another, families low in conversation orientation may not be accustomed to significant amounts of self-disclosure. Thus, engaging in frequent communication about feelings and concerns relating to the cancer might be uncomfortable and/or anxiety-producing. Accordingly, we advanced the following hypothesis:

H1: For cancer patients, family conversation orientation will be positively associated with the frequency of family discussion about the cancer.

It is more difficult to predict how family conformity orientation impacts the frequency of discussion about the cancer patient's illness. While a high conformity household would likely not involve the entire family in the process of making medical decisions, it is possible that even lower-ranking members may be encouraged to discuss facts and feelings geared toward the best interest of maintaining the life of the family member, without challenging normal family operations. Therefore, we posed the following research question:

RQ1: For cancer patients, what is the relationship between family conformity orientation and the frequency of family discussion about the cancer?

Considering family conversation orientation, because individuals from families high in conversation orientation expect frequent communication and high levels of self-disclosure, members of such families should expect, and be equipped to offer, emotional support to a family member diagnosed with cancer. In contrast, for cancer patients from families low in conversation orientation, the expression of emotional support may not be expected or desired. Accordingly, we posited the following hypothesis:

H2: For cancer patients, family conversation orientation will be positively associated with the amount of emotional support from a primary family support provider.

The relationship is less clear with regard to the influence of a cancer patient's family conformity orientation and the amount of support received from a primary family support provider. It is possible that because families high in conformity orientation stress family loyalty, family members should be willing and ready to be support providers. Conversely, it is also possible that the vulnerability that often comes with giving and or receiving emotional support could be viewed as threatening the balance of the established family hierarchy. Families high in conformity orientation also may have more difficulty being empathic to a cancer patient if a cancer-related decision does not adhere to family values or beliefs. Given such scenarios, it is also important to question if family conformity orientation influences family members' tendencies to provide other, less vulnerable types of support. Perhaps individuals in high conformity orientation families use tangible and informational support as a way to ensure they are protecting and being loyal to their family unit even when they do not feel comfortable providing emotional support. Thus, we proposed the following research question:

RQ2: For cancer patients, what is the relationship between family conformity orientation and the amount of emotional, informational and tangible support received from a primary family support provider?

It also seems likely that individuals from families who encourage unrestricted disclosure should be comfortable talking about what kind of support they need in coping with cancer. In contrast, patients from families lower in conversation orientation may spend less time expressing their support needs out of a concern of burdening family members with a direct expression of support needs. Therefore, we hypothesized:

H3: For cancer patients, family conversation orientation will be positively associated with the amount of time spent talking about social support needs with a primary family support provider.

With regard to the influence of family conformity orientation on a patient's disclosure about support needs, the logic for predictions is again mixed. One might suspect that the members of high conversation orientation families would encourage cancer patients to express their support needs. However, since such families have well-established family roles and a desire to maintain harmony, cancer patients may not be encouraged to introduce topics, including with own support needs, that may deviate from the status quo. Accordingly, we questioned:

RQ3: For cancer patients, what is the relationship between family conformity orientation and the amount of time spent talking about social support needs with other family members?

Because cancer patients from families high in conversation orientation should feel comfortable expressing and negotiating their desires, they could be more likely to experience optimal matching of their support needs. In contrast, since family members in low conversation orientation could be less likely to encourage open communication by and with the cancer-stricken family member, cancer patients are likely to be dissatisfied with the support from a primary support provider. In turn, we predicted:

H4: For cancer patients, family conversation orientation will be positively associated with optimal matching of support from a primary family support provider.

Thinking about the relationship between conformity orientation and optimal matching, if families from a high conformity orientation do not encourage the expression of unique needs, cancer patients may be hesitant to express the type and amount of support they desire. Further, because individuals in high conformity orientation families are not encouraged to express disapproval or disagreement with family behaviors, cancer patients also may refrain from expressing dissatisfaction with the support (or lack thereof) received from a primary family support provider. Such reticence in expressing needs could certainly circumvent receiving optimal matching of support. However, given that families high in conformity value the family unit and consider the values of the family above all else, cancer patients may view their support needs through the lens of what is best for the family. Therefore, cancer patients from high conformity families may view any support from a primary family support provider as achieving optimal support matching because is maintains the family unit. Given that family conformity orientation may have divergent implications for optimal support matching, we questioned:

RQ4: For cancer patients, what is the relationship between family conformity orientation and perceptions of optimal matching of support by a primary family support provider?

Family Conflict and Its Implications for Coping with Cancer

The additional stresses brought on by a cancer diagnosis may increase the opportunity for family conflict (Yoshida et al., 2010). Conflictual situations may not always arise from bad intentions or a person's lack of consideration for another; they can also arise from well-intentioned, but misguided or poorly executed actions (Barrera, Chassin, & Rogosch, 1993). The negative elements of conflict simply also may reflect how a family typically manages difficulties. Rahim (1983) identified five conflict management styles which vary along two dimensions of a concern for one's self and concern for the continuation of a relationship. *Competition* involves a high concern for self and a low concern for the relationship, as this style takes a "winner takes all" approach to conflict. *Collaboration* is defined by a high concern for both the self and the relationship, as the goal of conflict is for both parties work together to generate a solution that satisfies and benefits all. *Accommodation* reflects a low concern for self but a high concern for the relationship; those with this style give in to others' wishes and opinions at the expense of their own. *Compromise* reveals a moderate concern for both the self and the relationship and entails each person getting part of their needs met. Lastly, *avoidance* involves a low concern for self and the relationship and reflects efforts to shun controversy.

Research on conflictual family interactions generally focuses on a broader distinction of avoidance versus confrontation, such that those family members faced with expectations of family conformity avoid moments of conflict (e.g., Koerner & Fitzpatrick, 2002b). When avoidance is not normative to family functioning, individuals often experience increased feelings of tension, stress, and anger directed towards the family member conveying pursuing avoidance (e.g., Botta & Dumlao, 2002). Considering how family conflict orientations can impact a cancer patient's perceptions of support, it seems likely that patients who manage conflict in an avoidant manner with a primary support provider should be encouraged to distance them-selves from the support provider. As a result, cancer patients who generally practice conflict avoidance with their primary support should be less likely to voice their support needs, or their satisfaction with their current support, for fear of upsetting or insulting their support provider. Individuals with an accommodating conflict style should behave similarly to those who practice conflict avoidance when it comes to dealing with their social support concerns. Almost equally uncomfortable with conflict, accommodating individuals are accustomed to appeasing others, and thus should accept the support behaviors of their loved one with little input or suggestions for improvement, even if unsatisfied. In contrast, individuals with collaborative or compromising conflict management styles should not have these issues. Such individuals should expect to talk through concerns with their family members and should not be overly anxious about discussing sensitive issues, including cancer. The anticipated openness of collaborating and compromising individuals also should encourage discussion of support needs, and in turn a greater opportunity for optimal matching. Therefore, the following hypotheses are posited:

H5: For cancer patients, family conflict management style will be associated with optimal matching of support from a primary family support provider such that:

1. Avoidant or accommodative styles will be negatively associated with optimal matching from a primary family support provider.
2. Collaborative or compromising styles will be positively associated with optimal matching from a primary family support provider.

It is more challenging to predict the relationship between a family's competitive conflict management style and judgments of social support. Family members with a competitive conflict style have a win-lose approach to conflict. In one way, family members with such an orientation should not be hindered by the possibility of conflict, and therefore may be comfortable with any communication received by a family member. However, the intense and often hurtful behaviors utilized by those with a competitive style could cause negative feelings that may either deter a person from giving support, or prevent the cancer patient from appreciating the efforts of the support provider. Thus, we posited the following question:

RQ5: For cancer patients, what is the association with a competitive family conflict style and optimal matching of support by a primary support provider?

In short, we proposed that a cancer patient's family communication and conflict management orientations are should be associated with the frequency of communication about the cancer and support needs, as well as judgments about the type and quality of support. We now describe a study focused on female cancer patients managing a cancer diagnosis.

Method

Sample and Procedure

Forty-nine women diagnosed with cancer were recruited from several internet-based cancer discussion forums and message boards to participate in an anonymous survey about family communication and support after a cancer diagnosis. Responses were encrypted and sent via a secure 256-bit secure SSL-socket server.

Participants ranged in age from 32 to 69 years of age ($M = 47.98$, $SD = 9.08$) and were primarily Caucasian ($n = 48$; Asian $n = 1$). The majority identified themselves as both a wife and a mother in their immediate family ($n = 30$) and the remaining labeled themselves as daughters or sisters ($n = 19$). Participant cancer status ranged from newly diagnosed (less than 1 month ago) to diagnosed 10 years ago ($M = 14.82$, $SD = 9.84$ months).

Patients were asked to think about a primary family support provider while answering a series of items. These persons were on average 47.08 years old ($SD = 12.95$, range: 16-70); 37 (78%) were identified as the husband of the cancer patient. Twelve (22%) were female; of these, 8 were daughters and 4 were sisters. The average length of time the respondents had known these support providers was 26.00 years ($SD = 12.82$, range: 5–54).

Measures

Family communication patterns. A modified version of the Revised Family Communication Pattern Instrument (see Koerner & Fitzpatrick, 2000b) assessed perceptions of the cancer patient's conversation orientation and conformity orientation. The original 26-item measure was modified to exclude items about children. Items were completed on a 5-point (1 = never; 5 = frequently) scale. Eight items assessed *conversation orientation* (e.g., "We often talk as a family about things we have done during the day"; $M = 4.02$, $SD = .84$, $\alpha = .91$). Eight items measured *conformity orientation* (e.g., "My family has established rules that everyone is expected to obey"; $M = 2.15$, $SD = .84$, $\alpha = .91$).

Frequency of discussion about cancer. Out of concern about the length of the questionnaire and due to the lack of an existing measure about cancer discussion, we asked participants to estimate the frequency of family discussion about the cancer with a single item on a 5-point scale (1 = never; 5 = frequently; M = 3.32, SD = 1.06).

Types of social support. A modified version of the Revised Inventory of Socially Supportive Behaviors (Krause, 1987) assessed the type and amount of support received from primary support providers; items about a respondents' support towards others were not included, as they were not the focus of this investigation. Further, items not relevant to an immediate family situation (e.g., "Provided you with a place to stay overnight") were not included.

Participants were refer to "a family member who has provided the most support to you since your diagnosis" while answering the questionnaire items. Using a 5-point scale (1 = never; 5 = frequently), respondents completed 11 items to assess *emotional support* (e.g., Since the diagnosis, how often has this person: "Been right there with you (physically) during this stressful situation"; M = 3.97, SD = .88, α = .92). Two items assessed *tangible support* (e.g., Since the diagnosis, how often has this person: "Pitched in to help you do something that needed to get done, like household chores or yard work?"; M = 4.22, SD = 1.05, α = .79). *Informational support* was measured by six items (e.g., Since the diagnosis, how often has this person: "Suggested some action that you should take in dealing with a problem you were having related to the illness/coping with the illness?"; M = 3.51, SD = .93, α = .83).

Frequency of discussion about support needs. Using scale from 1 (never) to 5 (very often), one item asked respondents: "How often would you say you talk to your family about your support needs?"; M = 3.39, SD = 1.27).

Optimal matching of support. We created four items to measure the degree to which respondents experienced optimal support matching from their primary support providers. Items were completed on a 5-point (1 = not true; 5 = very true) scale (e.g., "I feel like I am getting the support that I need from this individual"; M = 3.89, SD = 1.17, α = .90).

Conflict styles. Perceptions of a cancer patient's conflict style with her primary family support-provider were measured with the 28-item Rahim Organizational Conflict Inventory-II (Rahim, 1983). While the original measure consists of 28 Likert-type (1 = Strongly Disagree; 5 = Strongly Agree) items to assess five conflict styles, inter-item correlations items suggested that the measure failed to capture adequately five distinct conflict styles in this context. The results of a principle components factor analysis using varimax rotation (Kaiser-Meyer-Olkin Index = .52) suggested a 4-factor measure of conflict orientation. One factor was defined by 6 items assessing *avoidance* (e.g., "I avoid open discussion of my differences with him or her"; M = 2.80, SD = 1.18, α = .92). The second factor included 3 items measuring *accommodation* (e.g., "I generally try to satisfy the needs of him or her"; M = 3.60, SD = .87, α = .74). Ten items defined a *collaboration* factor which was composed of items originally designed to capture separate dimensions of collaboration and compromise (e.g., "I propose a middle ground for breaking deadlocks"; M = 3.87, SD = .83, α = .93). The final factor was a 5-item measure of *competition* (e.g., "I use my influence to get my way"; M = 2.33, SD = .83, α = .87).

Results

Zero-order Correlations

Relationships among the variables are reported in Table 8.1. As expected, patient family conversation orientation was negatively associated with family conformity orientation, r = -.46, p < .01. Within the social support variables, there was a positive correlation between perceptions of emotional support and tangible support, r = .71, p < .001, informational support and tangible support, r = .50, p < .001, and informational support and emotional support, r = .76, p < .001. Considering the dimensions of conflict management, there was an expected negative association between avoidance and collaboration, r = -.34, p < .05, but surprisingly, conflict avoidance was positively associated with accommodation, r = .36, p < .05.

Table 8.1: *Correlations among Independent and Dependent Variables*

	1.	2.	3.	4.	5.	6.	7.
1. Conversation Orientation	—						
2. Conformity Orientation	-.46^	—					
3. Frequency of Discussion about Cancer	.66#	-.38^	—				
4. Emotional Support	.73#	-.40^	.67#	—			
5. Tangible Support	.67#	-.39^	.54#	.71#	—		
6. Informational Support	.55#	-.17	.56#	.76#	.50#	—	
7. Discussion about Support Needs	.74^	-.41^	.70#	.60#	.60#	.55#	—
8. Optimal Matching	.64#	-.24	.55#	.74#	.52#	.68#	.59#
9. Avoidance	-.47^	.53#	-.41^	-.47^	-.63#	-.38^	-.48#
10. Accommodation	-.06	.27	.18	-.03	-.15	.08	.13
11. Collaboration	.51#	-.26	.50#	.61#	.52#	.70#	.57#
12. Competition	-.17	.24	-.30*	-.39^	-.09	.15	-.21

	8.	9.	10.	11.
1. Conversation Orientation				
2. Conformity Orientation				

3. Frequency of
Discussion about
Cancer
4. Emotional
Support
5. Tangible
Support
6. Informational
Support
7. Discussion
about Support
Needs

8. Optimal Matching	___			
9. Avoidance	-.28	___		
10. Accommoda-tion	.11	.37*	___	
11. Collaboration	.61#	-.34*	.24	___
12. Competition	-.22	.21	-.05	-.26

*p < .05, two-tailed. ^ p < .01, p < .001.

One assumption underlying this project was that cancer patients from families who practice and encourage open communication should feel comfortable discussing cancer and their physical and psychological needs. In line with this expectation, perceived family conversation orientation was positively associated with both the frequency of family discussion about the cancer, $r = .66, p < .001$, and a patient's amount of talk about her support needs, $r = .74, p < .001$. Therefore, it was not surprising that family conversation orientation was positively associated with the amount of emotional, $r = .73, p < .001$, tangible, $r = .67, p < .001$, and informational support, $r = .55, p < .001$, as well as optimal matching of support, $r = .64, p < .001$ from the primary family support provider. In contrast to conversation orientation, perceived family conformity orientation was negatively associated with both a patient's frequency of family discussion about the cancer, $r = -.38, p < .01$, the frequency of discussion about the patient's support needs, $r = -.41, p < .01$, and the amount of emotional, $r = -.40, p$

< .01, and tangible support, $r = -.39$, $p < .01$. Four other patterns of significant associations highlighting the influence of communication on perceptions of support were indicated in the zero-order correlations. First, the amount of family discussion about the cancer was positively associated with all three types of social support (emotional, $r = .67$, $p < .001$; tangible, $r = .54$, $p < .001$; informational, $r = .56$, $p < .001$), as was the amount of discussion about the patient's support needs (emotional, $r = .60$, $p < .001$; tangible, $r = .60$, $p < .001$; informational, $r = .55$, $p < .001$. Also, the perceived frequency of family discussion about the cancer and a patient's amount of talk about her support needs to the family was positively associated, $r = .70$, $p < .001$. Further, the cancer patient's reported frequency of family discussion about the cancer was positively associated with her reports of optimal matching, $r = .55$, $p < .001$. These results provide preliminary support for the notion that families who engaged in more frequent communication provided more positive support. In turn, it was not surprising that perceived optimal matching was positively associated with the perceived amount emotional support, $r = .74$, $p < .001$, tangible support, $r = .52$, $p < .001$, and informational support, $r = .68$, $p < .001$.

The pattern of correlations for the conflict variables again suggested that communication is the vehicle for support. Family conversation orientation was positively associated with the collaborative conflict style, $r = .51$, $p < .001$, and negatively associated with conflict avoidance, $r = -.47$, $p < .01$. In contrast, family conformity orientation was positively associated with conflict avoidance, $r = .53$, $p < .001$. Considering the relationship between social support and conflict styles, collaborative conflict style was positively associated with a patient's perceived amount of emotional, $r = .61$, $p < .001$, tangible, $r = .52$, $p < .001$, and informational support, $r = .70$, $p < .001$. In contrast, a cancer patient's report that she engaged in conflict avoidance with her primary support provider was negatively associated with perceived emotional, $r = -.47$, $p < .01$, tangible, $r = -.63$, $p < .001$, and informational support, $r = -.38$, $p < .01$ from the primary support provider. The reported use of a competitive conflict style was also negatively associated with emotional support, $r = -.39$, $p < .01$. Given these findings, it was not surprising that the frequency of family discussion about the cancer was positively associated with the use of a collaborative conflict style, $r = .50$, $p < .001$, and negatively associated with both the conflict avoidance, $r = -.41$, $p < .01$, and competitive conflict styles, $r = -.30$, $p < .05$. Further, the reported frequency of family communication about the patient's support needs was positively associated with the collaborative conflict style, $r = .57$, $p < .001$, and negatively associated with conflict avoidance, $r = -.48$, $p < .001$.

Examinations of Hypotheses and Research Questions

Predictions and research questions were examined via hierarchical regression, where the independent variables of interest were entered on the first step and two-way interactions were entered on the second step of the analysis. Due to the restricted size of the sample, higher-level interactions were examined, but not reported here. In tests of family communication patterns, the measures of conversation and conformity orientation were entered into the same model. In analyses of conflict styles, the four conflict style measures were entered in the same analysis.

Family communication patterns and discussion about cancer

H1 predicted a positive association between a cancer patient's family conversation orientation and her perceived frequency of family discussion about the cancer, while *RQ1* asked about the relationship between family conformity orientation and the frequency of discussion about the cancer. Analyses indicated a significant main effect for conversation orientation, $R = .66$, $R^2\Delta = .44$, $\beta = .62$, $p < .0001$, but not for conformity orientation, $\beta = -.09$, n.s. on the perceived frequency of family discussion about the cancer. Thus, *H1* received support, but there was no pattern regarding *RQ1*.

Family communication patterns and support

The second hypothesis proposed that a cancer patient's perceived family conversation orientation will be positively associated with the perceived amount of emotional support provided by a primary family support provider. *RQ2* asked about the relationship between a cancer patient's level of family conformity orientation and the perceived amount of emotional, tangible and informational support from a primary support provider. Considering the influence of family communication patterns on perceptions of emotional support, there was a significant main effect for conversation orientation, $R = .73$, $R^2\Delta = .53$, $\beta = .69$, $p < .0001$, but not for conformity orientation, $\beta = -.07$, n.s. Therefore, H2 received support, but there was no evidence for any association related to RQ2 for emotional support. There was also a significant main effect for conversation orientation, $R = .67$, $R^2\Delta = .45$, $\beta = .62$, $p < .0001$, but not for conformity orientation, $\beta = -.10$ on perceptions of tangible support. For informational support, there was a significant main effect for conversation orientation, $R = .56$, $R^2\Delta = .31$, $\beta = .60$, $p < .0001$, but not for conformity orientation, $\beta = .10$. Thus, while additional support was obtained for the influence of conversation orientation on support, there was no evidence to suggest a relationship between conformity orientation and perceived social support.

Family communication patterns and frequency of communication about support needs

H3 stated that family conversation orientation would be positively associated with the amount of time that a cancer patient spends talking about social support needs and RQ3 asked about the influence of family conformity orientation on the perceived frequency of family discussions about support needs. Analyses revealed a significant main effect for conversation orientation, $R = .74$, $R^2\Delta = .55$, $\beta = .70$, $p < .0001$, but not for conformity orientation, $\beta = -.09$, n.s. on the frequency of discussion about support needs, yielding support for H3, but no evidence of the relationship queried in RQ3.

Family communication patterns and optimal support matching

H4 stated that perceived family conversation orientation will be positively associated with optimal matching of support from a primary family support provider. RQ4 asked about the relationship between a cancer patient's family conformity orientation and perceptions of optimal matching. There was a significant main effect for conversation orientation, $R = .64$, $R^2\Delta = .42$, $\beta = .67$, $p < .0001$, but not for conformity orientation, $\beta = .06$, n.s. on perceptions of optimal support matching. These results provide support for *H4*, but no evidence of the relationship queried in *RQ4*.

Conflict orientations and optimal matching

H5 proposed that the conflict management style used with a primary family support provider will be associated with perceptions of optimal matching of support, such that: (a) avoidant or accommodative styles will be negatively associated with perceived optimal matching, and (b) collaborative or compromising styles will be positively associated with perceived optimal matching. *RQ5* asked about the association between the use of the competitive conflict management style and optimal matching. Regression analyses utilizing the four factor measure of conflict management style defined by avoidance, accommodation, collaboration, and competition identified a significant main effect for the collaborative conflict management style and optimal matching, $R = .64$, $R^2\Delta = .41$, $\beta = .67$, $p < .0001$. No significant main effects for the styles of avoidance, $\beta = -.08$, n.s., accommodation, $\beta = .00$, n.s., or competition, $\beta = -.06$, n.s., on perceptions of optimal matching were found. Therefore, while *H5b* received support, *H5a* was not supported, nor what there significant evidence with regard to *RQ5*.

Discussion

Our purpose was to examine the impact of family communication patterns and conflict management styles on cancer patients' discussions about the cancer and support needs, as well as judgments about the type and quality of support provided by a primary family support provider. One of the most important themes highlighted in this investigation is that open and frequent family communication is crucial when seeking social support. In particular, patients who described their families as high in conversation orientation reportedly discussed their support needs more than those from families with lower perceived levels of conversation orientation. Further, cancer patients from high conversation orientation families reported receiving a greater quantity and diversity of support from a primary family support provider compared to cancer patients who reported lower levels of familial conversation orientation. Therefore, the results of this investigation suggest that the emphasis placed on unrestrained communication and the expression of feelings and ideas from families high in conversation orientation allows for more comfortable discussion about the cancer and about support needs, while also helping to facilitate trust and closeness among the family members. Further, the positive effects experienced by families high in conversation orientation appear to allow for an optimal support exchange with as few feelings of burden or frustration as can be expected given the circumstances.

We find the wholesale lack of significant results with regard to the influence of conformity orientation on support to be particularly intriguing. Certainly, prior research has established that family conformity orientation has implications for support and conflict-related judgments (Koerner & Cvancara, 2002). Further, an examination of the zero-order correlations suggested that a majority of the relationships between conformity orientation and the support-related variables were directly opposite of those relationships between conversation orientation and the support-related variables. Such a pattern makes sense given reports of family conversation orientation were negatively associated with judgments of family conformity orientation. However, the significant influence of conformity orientation disappeared in the regression analyses. The limited sample used in this study may have compromised the power of the analyses. Thus, the variance assumed by conversation orientation made the detection of effects for conformity orientation impossible. Additionally, because the majority of the participants in this sample were both parents and spouses, they likely identified themselves as one of the heads (if not the head) of their household. The control exerted by the head(s) of a household is particularly important to families high in conformity orientation. Therefore, an expression or expectation of support needs by a head of the household may not be a relevant process to expect from members of these families. Because heads of households often spend much time communicating, the effects of perceived conversation orientation may have overshadowed the impact of perceived conformity orientation on perceptions related to support.

Cutrona and Russell's (1990) theory of optimal matching has been relatively under explored in prior research, yet the results of this investigation suggest that the theory merits more attention in the context of family communication. One particularly insightful finding regarding OMT was the positive association between a cancer patient's perceived collaborative conflict style and optional matching from a primary support provider. This significant finding suggests that perhaps family members who are accustomed to working with family members are better attuned to have their own support needs met. Using collaborative conflict management techniques requires a heightened level of trust, patience, and self-disclosure among the family members; these characteristics should facilitate a safer and more effective environment for support. The connection between open communication practices on positive support outcomes also was revealed in positive zero-order correlations between a cancer patient's reported use of a collaborative conflict style with a primary support provider and the frequency of family discussion of the cancer, as well as the amount of talk about the patient's support needs. These findings suggest that instead of avoiding conflict, families could embrace conflict as an opportunity to become more successful communicators and social support providers. Our results imply that an existing family relationship can be enhanced by practicing conflict management that results in all family members feeling supported.

The suggestion that constructive conflict management facilitates the acquisition of the tools needed for successful support is enhanced by the positive relationship found between family conversation orientation and a cancer patient's reports of optimal matching. Given our results, it seems likely that the communication opportunities facilitated by a high conversation orientation encourages a greater awareness of a cancer patient's challenges, concerns, and support needs. Ell (1996) stated that optimal support requires a clear communication of need by the individual in need. The results of this investigation provide further evidence for this argument. Knowing that a collaborative conflict styles requires clear, encouraging, and free communication, and that we observed that reports of a collaborative conflict style and family conversation orientation were positively associated, it appears that constructive conflict management tools can be important to keeping family communication open and free, thereby providing a greater opportunity for successful support exchanges.

Although not hypothesized, the zero-order correlations indicated positive relationships between a cancer patient's perceived optimal support matching from a primary support provider and the provider's amount of emotional, tangible, and informational support. Thus, at least among our sample of female cancer patients, the more social support received, the more satisfied that patient was with her support across support types. These results suggest that in order to optimally benefit a cancer patient, the greater frequency and diversity of support, the better.

Limitations and Future Research

One of the chief limitations of this study concerns the sample. Participant recruitment occurred over 9 months and was challenging because we were bound by voluntary support with no tangible incentives. Our lack of power may account for the lack of significant main effects for conformity orientation on the support measures. Scholars (e.g., Koerner & Fitzpatrick, 2002a) frequently use median splits to divide high and low scores on both the conversation and conformity orientation measures to categorize family-related perceptions into one of four types; such a grouping was not possible due to our limited sample size. Further, our focus here was on female cancer patients' perceptions of communication and support from primary family caregivers, most of whom were male. Clearly, future research should attempt to gain a larger and more diverse sample to examine the impact of family communication patterns and conflict styles on expectations and expressions of support from family members dealing with cancer. A final limitation to this study is that we asked respondents to focus on the efforts of a primary family support provider. We acknowledge that it is likely that important support comes from other family members. Future research could consider the multiple sources of familial support to further examine how family communication patterns and conflict management styles may cause discrepancies between the support that is being provided by the family members and the support that the cancer patient perceives as being provided by their loved ones.

Conclusion: Best Practices

A cancer diagnosis is not only a life-altering event for diagnosed; the illness has broad effects on families as well. The results of this study demonstrate that the family communication patterns and conflict management styles embedded in the fabric of the cancer patient's family structure have implications for the degree to which the cancer patient shares support needs and responds to support-related efforts. The "take home" message from this study is substantial, yet simple: Share as much as you can with your family members and in times of conflict work together; if so, you will be well equipped to weather the unexpected struggles such as a critical illness. Communication instructors often spend much time training their students about the importance of effective communication in everyday life. The results of this study suggest that routine communication with loved ones can help family members deal with the often unanticipated negative events that can accompany our cherished family relationships.

This research also highlights the importance of making sure that medical staff and professionals are doing more than just treating the physical symptoms of cancer. In short, it cannot be assumed that families of cancer patients inherently possess the communication tools needed to be successful support providers during such a vulnerable time. Medical staff and professionals must, therefore, not only concern themselves with providing patients with the best possible medical treatment, but also with making sure patients' families get educated about the communication and conflict management strategies that can be used to provide the most supportive and constructive home environment. An individual's cancer diagnosis puts the well-being of every family member at risk and, therefore, steps must be taken to ensure that the environment at home is both positive and supportive.

References

Barrera, M., Chassin, L., & Rogosch, F. (1993). Effects of social support and conflict on adolescent children of alcoholic and nonalcoholic fathers. *Journal of Personality and Social Psychology, 64*, 602–612.

Botta, R., & Dumlao, R. (2002). How do conflict and communication patterns between fathers and daughters contribute to or offset eating disorders? *Health Communication, 14*, 199–219.

Cutrona, C., & Russell, D. (1990). Type of social support and specific stress: Toward a theory of optimal matching. In B. Sarason & G. Pierce (Eds.), *Social support: An interactional view* (pp. 319–366). New York: Wiley.

Ell, K. (1996). Social networks, social support and coping with serious illness: The family connection. *Social Science and Medicine, 42*, 173–183.

Gardner, K. A., & Cutrona, C. E. (2004). Social support communication in families. In A. Vangelisti (Ed.), *Handbook of family communication* (pp. 495–512). Mahwah, NJ: Erlbaum.

Glasdam, S., Jensen, A. B., Madsen, E. L., & Rose, C. (1996). Anxiety and depression in cancer patients' spouses. *Psycho-oncology, 5*, 23–29.

Krause, N. (1987). Chronic financial strain, social support, and depressive symptoms among older adults. *Psychology and Aging, 2*, 185–192.

Koerner, A. F. (2007). Social cognition and family communication: Family communication patterns theory. In D. Roskos-Ewoldsen & J. Monahan (Eds.), *Communication and social cognition: Theory and methods* (pp. 197–216). Lawrence Erlbaum Associates.

Koerner, A. F., & Cvancara, K. E. (2002). The influence of conformity orientation on communication patterns in family conversations. *Journal of Family Communication, 2*, 133–152.

Koerner, A. F., & Fitzpatrick, M. (2002a). Toward a theory of family communication. *Communication Theory, 12*, 70–91.

Koerner, A., F., & Fitzpatrick, M. A. (2002b). You never leave your family in a fight: The impact of family of origin on conflict behavior in romantic relationships. *Communication Studies, 53*, 234–251.

Martin, R., Davis, G., Baron, R., Suls, J., & Blanchard, E. (1994). Specificity in social support: Perceptions of helpful and unhelpful provider behaviors among irritable bowel syndrome, headache, and cancer patients. *Health Psychology, 13*, 432–439.

Martire, L. M., Lustig, A. P., Schulz, R., Miller, G. E., & Helgeson, V. S. (2004). Is it beneficial to involve a family member? A meta-analysis of psychosocial interventions for chronic illness. *Health Psychology, 23*, 599–611.

Rahim, M. A. (1983). A measure of styles of handling interpersonal conflict. *Academy of Management Journal, 26*, 368–376.

Revenson, T.A., & Stanton, A. (2004). Chronic illness: Psychological aspects. In N.B. Anderson (Ed.), *Encyclopedia of health and behavior* (vol. 1, pp. 179–183). Thousand Oaks, CA: Sage.

Sarason, I. G., & Sarason, B. R. (2009). Social support: Mapping the construct. *Journal of Social and Personal Relationships, 26*, 113–120.

Sheridan, M. A., Sherman, M. L., Pierce, T., & Compas, B. E. (2010). Social support, social constraint, and affect in spouses of women with breast cancer: The role of cognitive processing. *Journal of Social and Personal Relationships, 27*, 5–22.

Uchino, B. (2009). Understanding the links between social support and physical health: A life-span perspective with emphasis on the separability of perceived and received support. *Perspectives on Psychological Science, 4*, 236–255.

Yoshida, S., Otani, H., Hirai, K., Ogata, A., Mera, A., Okada, S., & Oshima, A. (2010). A qualitative study of decision-making by breast cancer patients about telling their children about their illness. *Supportive Care in Cancer, 18*, 439–447.

Zakowski, S. G., Ramati, A., Morton, C., Johnson, P., & Flanigan, R. (2004). Written emotional disclosure buffers the effects of social constraints on distress among cancer patients. *Health Psychology, 23*, 555–563.

Chapter 10

Beyond the Crisis: Communication between Parents and Children Who Survived Cancer

Kathleen M. Galvin, Lauren H. Grill, Paul H. Arntson, and Karen E. Kinahan

The purpose of the study reported here is to examine the communication practices of long term pediatric cancer survivors and their parents as they continue to interact about their cancer experiences. We wanted to know under what circumstances the family members would talk to each other about their cancer experiences, how they feel about talking to each other about those experiences, and what advice they would give to other families that are living with a child who has survived cancer.

We conducted telephone interviews with 54 pediatric cancer survivors with an average of 16 years post treatment and 43 of their parents who the survivors had nominated to also be interviewed. The survivors and their parents responded to a parallel set of closed and open ended questions in the taped telephone sessions. At the time of the study 73% of the survivors were college graduates, 79% were employed full time with 7% being unemployed, and only 25% of them lived with their parents, the others living alone, with a friend, or their spouses.

Both the survivors and the parents indicated that they only occasionally talk about cancer anymore and only about a third of the time do either of them initiate the conversation. When they did talk about their cancer experiences, current medical conditions triggered most (56%) of their cancer conversations. And less than 5% of the time did either the survivors or parents mention any negative affect accompanying the cancer conversations. Three familiar themes emerged from the advice that survivors and their parents would give families who are currently battling pediatric cancer: 1) take one day at a time, 2) talk openly about the cancer, and 3) emphasize the normal aspects of living.

Cancer is the leading cause of death by disease among U.S. children between birth and 15 years of age. In 2007, approximately 14 of every 100,000 children under the age of 14 were diagnosed with cancer (National Cancer Institute, 2010), a number which has been increasing gradually for years (American Cancer Society, 2009). When a child is diagnosed with cancer, the crisis changes the family system forever. Within the past 50 years, the survival rate among pediatric cancer patients has dramatically improved. In 1959, children had less than a 10% chance of survival (University of Minnesota Cancer Center, 2007), yet today more than 80% of children diagnosed with cancer will become long-term survivors (St. Jude Children's Research Hospital, 2007). Among 20-34 year old adults in the U.S., 1 in 570 individuals is a pediatric cancer survivor (Bhatia & Meadows, 2005). Kinahan and Nelson (2005) predict that this number will continue to grow over time.

Yet survivors may confront recurring long-term challenges. When compared to matched controls, survivors consistently report lower health-related quality of life in adolescence and adulthood (Stam, Grootenhuis, Caron, & Last, 2006). Compared to their siblings, survivors are over three times more likely to have chronic health problems and more than eight times as likely to develop at least one chronic disease (Oeffinger & Robison, 2007). With increasing survival rates, the number of survivors facing persistent health issues including reoccurrences, chronic conditions, and treatment side-effects (e.g., heart conditions, kidney disease, musculoskeletal neuropsychological development problems) also increases (Condren, Lubsch, & Vats, 2005). Additionally, clinicians also have predicted survivors' increased risk for psychological maladjustment in adulthood (Fuemmeler, Brown, Williams, & Barredo, 2003). Survivors and family members often feel uncertain about their future, which influences their perceived roles, goals, priorities, and spiritual values (Eiser, 2004). Despite declining mortality rates over the past fifteen years, survivors' capacity for psychological adjustment remains unclear (Sawyer, Antoniou, Toogood, & Rice, 1997). Such evidence calls for greater attention to survivors' long-term quality of life, both physically and psychologically (Patenaude & Kupst, 2005).

Most research focuses on pediatric cancer survivors 3–6 years post-treatment (Taieb et al., 2003), which cannot reveal long-term influences, particularly on the family. Zebrack and Chesler (2002) however, examined the health-related worries, self image, and life outlooks of survivors who averaged 11.30 years since treatment. Kupst et al. (1995) reported on a longitudinal study of coping with patients who were 10 years post-treatment. Oeffinger and Robison (2007) reported on the Childhood Cancer Survivor Study (CCSS) following a cohort of over 10,000 survivors with an average of 17 years since diagnosis. Trends in pediatric cancer survivor research reinforce the notion that more research needs to examine survivors further into remission.

Stresses Experienced by Survivors and Their Parents

Survivors often encounter some level of *stigma* due to their cancer. This stigma derives partially from norms of secrecy surrounding illness and reflects public perception of cancer as a feared disease (Fife & Wright, 2000). Many survivors experience conspicuous side-effects of treatment which may be brief and reversible (e.g., weight changes, loss of hair) or permanent (e.g., scarring, amputation, sterility), serving as reminders that they are different from others (Van Dongen-Melman & Woudstra, 1986). Pediatric cancer stigmas may be linked to survivors' interpersonal ties, social rejection, discrimination in school and the workplace, as well as to the actual diagnosis, side-effects and long-term effects (Clarke, 2005). Such experiences impact both the survivors and their families (Brown, Madan-Swain, & Lambert, 2003).

Some family members "express psychological distress as much as, if not more than, the patients" (Weihs & Politi, 2006, p. 3). Although a child's cancer experiences affect their siblings, parents carry the greatest burden of stress. Parents must struggle to understand the risks, treatment options, and prognoses inherent this diagnosis. Most parents participate in the survivor's medical decision-making and ongoing care for many years. When compared to parents of healthy children, these parents show higher levels of psychological distress, emotional strain, and anxiety (Eiser, 2004). Little is known about the concerns of parents as survivors enter adulthood, gain independence over medical follow-up decisions while facing the threat of additional health problems. Parental anxiety and distress tends to decrease in the later course of their child's illness and treatment (Sawyer et al., 1997), yet some parents suffer from post-traumatic stress disorder (PTSD) for many years (Barakat et al., 1997).

Few studies examine interpersonal interactions of parents and their children who survived cancer (Zhang & Siminoff, 2003) who may face unique communication challenges due, in part, to different coping strategies. According to Zebrack, Chesler, Penn, and Katz (2005), "Parents may want to discuss issues with their children that the children do not wish to discuss or vice versa. ... Some young people with cancer desire to protect their parents and not share their deepest worries with them, perhaps out of guilt for what their parents are going through, or perhaps just because they can see how upset their parents are" (p. 198). Mothers' worries can significantly relate to their perceptions of their child's worries, even when the cancer diagnosis occurs as much as a decade earlier (Zebrack, Chesler, Orbuch, & Parry, 2002).

Talking about Pediatric Cancer

Communication between parents and physicians has changed over the past 30 years from avoidance of communication about cancer to an emphasis on straightforward discussion of diagnoses and prognoses (Patenaude & Kupst, 2005). Van Dongen-Melman and Woudstra (1986) revealed that "The most important strategies related to positive outcomes [in family coping] were open communication and honesty... maintaining hope and the effective use of defense mechanisms, in particular denial" (p. 153). Optimal family communication exists when members share similar beliefs of their social reality and family members "communicate their individual experiences of threat so that a shared understanding of needs and appropriateness of attachment and caregiving behaviors can occur" (Weihs & Politi, 2006, p. 6).

In cases of pediatric cancer, parents establish the initial privacy rules that define how to regulate information about the illness (Petronio, 2002). Pediatric patients do not learn their diagnosis and prognosis until after their doctor and parents know the information (Helft &

Petronio, 2007). Because parents often determine when, to whom, and how much to tell others about their child's cancer, pediatric survivors may struggle when managing discussions about their illness. Many cancer treatments result in observable markers (e.g., hair loss, scarring, etc.) that trigger stigmatizing comments; therefore parents should openly discuss the illness to prepare their child to understand others' unusual reactions or responses. Although such conversations are difficult, they help the family adjust to the stress of the diagnosis and aid the child's capacity to cope (Weihs & Poiliti, 2006). As survivors mature, developing lives separate from their families, they acquire greater control over their personal health information, increasing their ability to selectively conceal such information from others. Few studies explore communication practices of long-term survivors and their parents as they interact over the life course.

Communication Privacy Management Theory (CPM)

If survivors experienced stigmatization in their youth, and were unable to regulate their own health privacy during treatment, they may be motivated to maintain stricter privacy boundaries around discussing their cancer experiences later in life. Furthermore, if appropriate coping has not occurred (e.g., they continue to feel high subjective risk in discussing cancer-related information), survivors should feel uncomfortable talking about their cancer experiences; survivors who successfully coped with their cancer experiences should feel more comfortable sharing such information. CPM thereby makes it possible to use survivors' positive or negative feelings about discussing their cancer with others, including family members, as indicators of the quality of adjustment in adulthood.

Parents of survivors may feel uncomfortable openly discussing their experiences with cancer for reasons similar to survivors'. Facing their child's potential death constitutes a traumatic experience that may be difficult to talk about, even years after remission. If their child encountered long-term negative effects following the initial cancer treatments, the topic of cancer could remain highly charged within the family. Risks of discussing their cancer experiences may depend upon how much stress and stigma that the illness caused during treatment and how many cancer-related problems currently persist for their child.

Research Questions

Because little is known about family communication after a child has survived cancer, this study examined the impact of such a severe stress on family interactions. The following research questions were posed:

RQ1: Under what circumstances do adult pediatric cancer survivors and their parents talk with each other about the survivor's cancer experiences? Most studies of families of cancer survivors capture the first three to five years after treatment, but it is important to understand the long-term stigma and stress associated with pediatric cancer, specifically, the long-range impact of cancer on the family, particularly the parent-survivor relationship.

RQ2: How do pediatric cancer survivors and their parents feel about talking to each other about their cancer experiences? Survivors' and parents' reported feelings about discussing cancer should indicate the extent to which cancer remains a stressful issue in their lives.

RQ3: To what extent do the pediatric survivors' current medical conditions and social demographic characteristics affect how the survivors and their parents report talking about their experiences? Survivors' cancer experiences may influence current life circumstances, which in turn may impact how they and their parents talk about their cancer experiences.

RQ4: What have adult survivors of pediatric cancer and their parents learned that they would tell other families living with a child who has survived cancer? The growing number of families which include a survivor of pediatric cancer could benefit from advice from other survivors' knowledge and family communication experiences and related life issues.

Method

Study Design

The current study consisted of in-depth telephone interviews with parents and survivors an average of 16 years post-treatment—who currently receive their long-term follow-up care as part of a specialized adult transition program called the STAR (Survivors Taking Action and Responsibility) Program. The information used in this study was obtained with explicit consent of participants.

Participants

With the assistance of the STAR Program, 105 eligible survivors were contacted via letter to participate in the study. Survivors were considered ineligible for this study if they had had brain tumors or received cranial radiation exceeding 2400 cGy, as these survivors sometimes experience side effects from treatment (e.g., speech disorders) which make a telephone interview too difficult for them to complete. Of the 105 eligible survivors, two survivors responded to the letter asking specifically not to be contacted. Fifty-four of the remaining 103 survivors were successfully contacted and interviewed. The following information is therefore based upon 54 survivor interviews, 43% male and 57% female. Survivors' ages when interviewed ranged from 20–45, with an average diagnosis age of 10 years old ($SD = 5.33$), and an average remission period of 16 years ($SD = 6.96$). Upon contacting each of the survivors, interviewers requested permission to contact one of the survivor's parents—ideally the parent who had "helped them the most"—for an interview. A total of 43 parents were successfully contacted and interviewed.

Previous research suggests that survivors are at high risk for maladjustment in adulthood however, the survivors we interviewed demonstrated remarkable measures of success. Seventy-three percent are college graduates, with 4% currently enrolled full-time in college. According to the U.S. Census Bureau (2007), only 71% of Americans within the age range of most of our participants (18–39 years) obtain a bachelor's degree or higher. Thus, these survivors' education rate exceeds the national average.

Furthermore, a majority of these survivors live independently from their parents; over 50% live with a roommate, partner or spouse and 18% live alone, compared to 25% who still live with parents. Seventy-nine percent were employed full-time; only 7% were unemployed when interviewed. The U.S. Department of Labor (2007) reports that only 63.3% of Americans are employed, therefore it seems that these survivors exceed average Americans in employment rates. Twenty-one percent of the survivors had been clinically depressed during some point in their remission, a number much lower than we expected given the National Institute of Mental Health (2000) reports that the likelihood for an average American becoming clinically depressed is between 20–25% for women and 10–15% for men. All of these factors suggest that these survivors have successfully overcome the stress and trauma of their cancer experiences, making them ideal candidates for discussing the effect of communication in their coping experiences.

Interviews

Procedure. Interviews were performed by 17 undergraduate student volunteers participating in a research course. All students had completed Human Subjects Training and training in standardized interviewing techniques. Upon completion of training, students received randomly assigned groups of survivors (and their respective parents) to contact via telephone. All successfully contacted survivors and parents agreed to participate. Completed interviews were audiotaped and transcribed for analysis.

Interview questions. The questionnaires for survivors and parents contained scaled and open-ended questions. The first three questions were scaled and identical between the survivor and parent questionnaire, asking: (a) how often in the past year they thought about their (or their son/daughter's) childhood cancer, (b) how often they talked with others about their (or their son/daughter's) childhood cancer, and (c) how often they talked with their parents (or their son/daughter) about their childhood cancer. Each of these three questions (on both the survivor and parent interviews) were followed with open ended questions concerning (a) the conditions or circumstances under which they talk about their cancer experiences; (b) who tends to bring the topic up when they talk about it; and (c) how does it feel to talk about cancer. Additionally, both the survivors and their parents were asked, "What is the best advice you could give a family living with a person who has survived cancer as a child?" Responses to scaled questions were recorded upon transcription of interviews; responses to open questions were analyzed to create categories, and then coded to fit the categories, as described below.

Content Analysis Procedures

Category generation. Four trained students worked with the re-searchers to create the category scheme. Each question was analyzed individually, and responses with similar themes were grouped together and assigned a category label to represent each group. Subsequently, the two senior researchers discussed these emergent categories to ensure correspondence between the categories found in the data and categories that had been established in prior research. Coding units consisted of survivors' and parents' completed re-sponses to each question, as some would change their minds about the answer while answering the question, making it difficult to code unless the entire answer was examined in full. Categories generated for the open questions used in this chapter can be found in the results section.

Coding. After development of the category schemes, a new group of trained undergraduate students coded the transcripts using the categories created through content analysis. Students' codebooks contained all category information, including rules and examples of each category and specific instructions regarding proper coding practices. Each response could be coded for multiple categories if the respondent explicitly gave multiple answers to the question. Students coded 10 sample survivor (and parent) responses to practice using each coding scheme, and their answers were compared for reliability. Once reliability was obtained (an initial 80% agreement or above), the students divided into pairs, each pair receiving a separate question to code. Eighty-percent agreement was considered appropriate to accommodate some categories that had few responses, limiting coders' capacity to disagree and still achieve an acceptable agreement rate. Coders initially coded separately and then met to review and discuss their findings and collaboratively agree upon final codes when any discrepancies arose. If agreement could not be reached, one of the researchers was the arbitrator. Coding partners switched each week when a new question was assigned, to avoid biases in dyad pairing.

Results

Answers to the four research questions were drawn from the quantitative and the qualitative responses generated by survivors and their parents:

RQ1: Survivors and their parents rated their communication about cancer on a four-point scale ranging from 1 = not at all, 2 = occasionally, 3 = fairly often, and 4 = all the time. Survivors' mean score was 2.37 (*SD* = .63). Parents' mean score was 2.30 (*SD* = .56). The survivor-parent scores were not significantly correlated (*r* = -1.00). Qualitatively, however, more interesting findings emerged. When asked *"What causes these conversations?"* most of the survivors cited medical reasons (e.g., physical health problems, checkups/medical care, etc.) (56%). Other common responses beyond medical reasons included discussions with family members (22%), anniversaries (e.g., of diagnosis date, remission date, etc.) (15%), and other people asking about it (27%). *Kappas* for these categories ranged from .92 to 1.00. When asked *"Who tends to bring it up?"* survivors reported that they initiate the conversation about 35% of the time while parents said that they bring it up about 36% of the time.

On a four-point scale (1 = not at all, 2 = occasionally, 3 = fairly often, and 4 = all the time), parents and survivors were asked to indicate how often they talked to each other about their cancer experiences. Both survivors and parents claimed they talked about cancer "occasionally" (*M* = 2.02, *SD* = .70 and *M* = 2.09, *SD* = .57, respectively); however, this correlation did not achieve significance (*r* = .23, *p* < .07). When asked *"What causes the topic to come up?"* more than half the time parents (58%) and survivors (52%) cited issues related to the survivor's health (current health problems, doctor's appointments, etc.) as the impetus for their discussion. *Kappas* for these categories ranged from .91 to 93. This finding parallels survivor and parent responses to a follow-up question asking their level of concern for their/their child's health on a four-point scale (1 = not at all, 2 = occasionally, 3 = fairly often, and 4 = all the time). Both parents and survivors were found to worry about the survivors' health a moderate amount (M = 2.70, SD =.89 and M = 2.43, SD = 1.03, respectively, t = -1.24, $p < .22$).

RQ2: When asked how it felt to talk to each other about their cancer experiences, both parents and survivors had similar, neutral responses that the conversations felt "fine" and "normal" (survivors 50.9%, parents 37.2%). Very few participants mentioned any negative affect (survivors 3.80%, parents 4.70%); yet few mentioned particularly positive feelings either (survivors 13.2%, parents 18.6%). *Kappas* for these categories ranged from .92 to 1.00.

RQ3: The following medical and social demographic conditions significantly impact how pediatric cancer survivors and their parents reported talking about their cancer experiences:

Gender was significantly related to how often survivors talked about their childhood cancer (women: M = 2.50, SD = .63; men: M = 2.14, SD = .57, t = 2.07, $p < .05$). For survivors who had experienced *depression* (less than 20%), parents reported talking to them significantly less about their cancer (M = 1.83, SD = .58) than parents talked about cancer to survivors who had not experienced depression (M = 2.20, SD = .55, t = 1.97, $p < .03$). *Living arrangements* were related significantly to how often survivors talked about their childhood cancer. Survivors living alone or with parents talked significantly less about their cancer (M = 1.92, SD = .49) than did survivors who lived with their spouses or roommates (M = 2.51, SD = .60, t = -3.10, $p < .003$). *Levels of education* were significantly related to both how the survivors reported that they talked about their cancer experiences. Survivors who graduated from college reported talking about their cancer experiences significantly more often (M = 2.49, SD =.56) than non-college graduates (M = 2.00, SD = .70, t = -2.45, $p < .01$).

RQ4: Both parents and survivors provided a wide range of advice for families currently battling pediatric cancer. Three themes emerged as important to both groups: (1) talk as healing/emotional sharing, (2) emphasize normality, and (3) take one day at a time. Additionally, four themes unique to survivors or parents were found.

Shared Themes between Parents and Survivors

Talk as healing/emotional sharing. The majority of respondents indicated the importance of openness and conversation regarding the emotional impact. Approximately one-quarter of the survivors directly suggested "Talk about it. Be open, Share" (S2). Others suggested talking with other survivors to find hope and inviting family members to talk. Parents reinforced the benefits of talking with friends and family. Some survivors reported needing times of silence. Overwhelmingly respondents depicted viewed talk as a way to face the situation and to move on.

The passage of time often normalized discussion. One survivor suggested that "It's OK to talk about it. Not to be afraid of it, because it's in the past. ... things are very different once you're a survivor. It's something they have dealt with" (S35). Talk became a way to combat ongoing issues such as managing the long-term treatment effects: "Continually communicate about it and be there when the child grows into adulthood and experiences some of the long-term side effects" (S49). Survivors viewed talk as a means to helping everyone move forward through open discussion. "You don't have to be afraid of it. But make sure the person who's involved with it is okay too. But not being afraid of it is big too. Because I know a lot of people who are like ... don't talk about it anymore" (S35). Parents supported ongoing open communication, saying: "The best survival strategy— *talk.* Talk with each other. Cry if you need to" (P21). Parents' comments focused on the emotional benefits of talking and acknowledging struggles.

Emphasize normalcy. Respondents emphasized the value of treating survivors normally and providing them with ways to move forward. "Don't treat them any differently. ... Let them pursue anything they want" (S37); "...recognize that the individual is gonna continue to lead their life as if they had not had cancer" (S21). Occasionally a parent addressed the effect of time: "You have to let the kids go and do what they need to do as human beings but it's different when they're 11 than when they're 24" (P76).

Take one day at a time. Respondents expressed the need to live in the present and cherish the good times. Survivors valued taking each day as it comes and dealing with one issue at a time. Parents also stressed this theme: "It's never going to go away. You just have to make the most of each day" (P4); "Just love each other, and appreciate each other" (P8); "You just realize that, whether it's a year, or five years or ten years, you just try to make the most of every day and just enjoy everybody and everything" (P49).

Unique Themes

Health talk as pragmatic, ongoing health maintenance. Many survivors emphasized health awareness and information-seeking. Respondents assigned all family members the responsibility for ongoing *information-seeking* talk, usually focused on researching and managing information and recognizing the survivor's limits. Comments were concrete and directive: "I guess if you're not happy with what the doctor says, always get a second opinion, but then just don't be stubborn, or don't let your child...be stubborn about getting the surgeries, the treatments. ... And ask questions, and teach yourself. Go to the library, go to the internet" (S99). Suggestions emphasized the importance of tracking advances in cancer treatments and keeping parents involved in ongoing medical consultations. Some parents noted the shift in health management responsibility: "I think he knows enough to get checkups. ... I think that he's instilled with enough something or another—*common sense*—to get a checkup" (P76).

Social support as "being there." Comments focused "being there" especially to talk. Respondents advised family members to be available and open for discussion if the survivor wanted to talk; and to recognize the survivor's need for privacy. "Be there for them if they ask for help, and just leave them alone when they don't want any help" (S57). Some survivors noted the need for family members to state their willingness to talk whenever the survivor chooses to address the subject, yet they acknowledged the competing tensions between wanting conversation as well as distance and silence. Parents were advised to be responsive to either desire

Appreciation. Whereas the survivors spoke emphasized ongoing health maintenance, parents stressed the need to appreciate everyday life and avoiding taking things for granted: "Just make sure that the child knows how much you appreciate them and that, if they ever want to talk about their fears or their future or whatever, that they're comfortable doing that" (S72).

Faith/prayers. Parents were more likely than survivors to note the importance of religion, faith, and prayer, saying, "The best advice I could give someone would be to take it to the Lord in prayer and to let their faith help them through it" (P48), and "You reach a point where you just have to say, 'He's in God's hands.' And you have to trust that it's going to be enough. That God is going to spare him" (P50).

Discussion

To put the findings of this research in context, it is important to emphasize our participants' unique circumstances relating to crises, stress, and communication practices. An average of 16 years ago these families faced extremely stressful crises, centering their communication strategies on emotional support and information-seeking so that they could make critical decisions under severe time pressures. As survivors entered remission, the risk of side-effects from treatments subsided and the threat of further cancer diminished; "normal" maturational stressors and successes became more important influences on families' communication practices. Yet cancer survivors always face a residual possibility of reoccurrence, which may explain why their parents maintain moderate concern for their health, and why they benefit from the resources provided by the STAR program. The data from this study demonstrate that this sample of survivors seems to be thriving. Education, living and employment status were all either at or above the national average. Likewise, despite research demonstrating that survivors have greater risk for depression than matched controls, depression rates among our survivors were comparable to the national average.

The majority of the survivors and parents reported that they discuss cancer because of the survivor's current health maintenance and other people's health concerns (e.g., other families coping with pediatric cancer). Most reported causes for talking about their cancer experiences were instrumental in nature—not stress related. Likewise, both survivors and parents reported primarily positive or neutral feelings when talking about their cancer experiences, suggesting that discussing cancer is not particularly difficult or stressful. Yet, consistent with CPM, survivors still seem to consider their cancer experiences personal and private, since approximately half of them indicated they would either not bring the subject up or needed to feel comfortable with another person before talking with others about their cancer. Many of the families preferred talking about cancer as an opportunity to help others with their health concerns. This finding corresponds with research suggesting people may disclose highly personal information to strangers or acquaintances when they believe they can help others struggling with a crisis (Vangelisti, Caughlin, & Timmerman, 2001).

Limitations

There were three limitations to this study that must be kept in mind. First, we sampled from a very unique population of pediatric cancer survivors. All of the survivors were members of a structured support program (STAR) which helped them to regulate their follow-up appointments and cope with any remaining issues from their cancer experiences. Second, participants were only eligible for the study if their cancer treatments had not been severe enough to limit their capacity to be interviewed over the telephone. We may have eliminated survivors from our study who were more prone to adjustment problems or depression. Third, the sample size was quite small; this both limited robust statistical analysis and generalizability. Clearly future research should expand beyond this small convenience sample and its findings.

Best Practices

Over time the impact of a child's cancer on a family moves from a crisis experience to a more nuanced sense of moving forward with some concerns, especially for parents, yet with a new appreciation of life. Ongoing communication within the family remains critical as years pass and members integrate the experience into family history. After returning to a relative sense of normalcy, family members find healing through continued conversations about the experience, "being there" for the survivor and each other, maintaining strong emotional connections to each other and truly appreciating everyday life. Many report the importance of sharing personal health news and tracking cancer-related medical advances. Some found comfort and growth through faith and prayers. Almost every respondent echoed the comment, "The best survival strategy? Talk."

References

American Cancer Society. (2009). *Cancer Facts and Figures.* Retrieved January 7, 2009, from http://www.cancer.org/lownloads/ STT/CAFF2007PWSecuredPH

Barakat, L., Kazak, A. E., Meadows, A., Casey, R., Meeske, K., & Stuber, M. (1997). Families surviving childhood cancer: A comparison of posttraumatic stress symptoms with families of healthy children. *Journal of Pediatric Psychology, 22,* 6843–6859.

Bhatia, S., & Meadows, K. A. (2005). Long-term follow-up of childhood cancer survivors: Future directions for clinical care and research. *Pediatric Blood Cancer, 46,* 143–148.

Brown, R. T., Madan-Swain, A., & Lambert, R. (2003). Post-traumatic stress syndromes in adolescent survivors of childhood cancer and their mothers. *Journal of Traumatic Stress, 16*(4), 309–318.

Clarke, J. (2005). Portrayal of childhood cancer in English language magazines in North America: 1970–2001. *Journal of Health Communication, 10,* 593–607.

Condren, M., Lubsch, L., & Vats, T. (2005). Long-term follow-up of survivors of childhood cancer. *The Indian Journal of Pediatrics, 72,* 39–43.

Eiser, C. (2004). *Children with cancer: Quality of life.* Mahwah, NJ: Erlbaum.

Fife, B. L., & Wright, E. C. (2000). The dimensionality of stigma: A comparison of its impact on the self of persons with HIV/AIDS and cancer. *Journal of Health and Social Behavior, 41,* 50–67.

Fuemmeler, B. F., Brown, R. T., Williams, L., & Barredo, J. (2003). Adjustment of children with cancer and their caregivers: Moderating influences of family functioning. *Families, Systems & Health, 21*(3), 263–276.

Helft, P. R., & Petronio, S. (2007). Communication pitfalls with cancer patients: "Hit-and-run" deliveries of bad news. *Journal of the American College of Surgeons, 205*(6), 807–811.

Kinahan, K. E., & Nelson, M. B. (2005). Issues and concerns in caring for adult survivors of childhood cancer: North American survey of needs and best practice models. *Current Problems in Pediatric and Adolescent Health Care, 35,* 203–206.

Kupst, M. J., Natta, M. B., Richardson, C. C., Shulman, J. L., Lavigne, J. V., & Das, L. (1995). Family coping with pediatric leukemia: Ten years after treatment. *Journal of Pediatric Psychology, 29,* 601–617.

National Cancer Institute. (2010). SEER Cancer Statistics Review 1975–2007. Retrieved April 15, 2010, from http://seer.cancer.gov/csr/1975_2007/index.html

National Institute of Mental Health. (2000). *Depression.* Retrieved April 16, 2007, from http://www.nimh.nih.gov/publicat/depression.cfm#ptdep1

Oeffinger, K., & Robison, L. (2007). Childhood cancer survivors, late effects, and a now model for understanding survivorship. *Journal of the American Medical Association, 297,* 2762–2764.

Patenaude, A. F., & Kupst, M. J. (2005). Psychosocial functioning in pediatric cancer. *Journal of Pediatric Psychology, 30,* 9–27.

Petronio, S. (2002). *Boundaries of private disclosure.* New York: State University of New York Press.

Sawyer, M., Antoniou, G., Toogood, I., & Rice, M. (1997). Childhood cancer: A two year prospective study of the psychological adjustment of children and parents. *Journal of the American Academy of Child and Adolescent Psychiatry, 36*(12), 1736–1743.

St. Jude Children's Hospital. (2007). *Surviving childhood cancer.* Retrieved April 13, 2007, from http://www.stjude.org/epidemiology/0,2081,864_5472_21898,00.html

Stam, H., Grootenhuis, M. A., Caron, H. N., & Last, B. F. (2006). Quality of life and current coping in young adult survivors of childhood cancer: Positive expectations about the further course of the disease where correlated with better quality of life. *Psycho-Oncology, 15*(1), 31–43.

Taieb, O., Moro, M. R., Baubet, T., Revah-Levy, A., & Flament, M. F. (2003). Posttraumatic stress symptoms after childhood cancer. *European Child & Adolescent Psychiatry, 12,* 255–264.

University of Minnesota Cancer Center. (2007). *Pediatric Cancer.* Retrieved April 13, 2007, from http://www.cancer.umn.edu/cancerinfo/ped-cancer.html

U.S. Census Bureau. (2007). *Educational Attainment in the United States: 2007.* Retrieved April 13, 2007, from http://www.census.gov/population/www/socdemo/education/ps2007.html

Van Dongen-Melman, J. E. W. M., & Sanders-Woudstra, J. A. R. (1986). Psychosocial aspects of childhood cancer: A review of the literature. *Journal of Psychology and Psychiatry, 27*(2), 145–180.

Vangelisti, A. L., Caughlin, J. P., & Timmerman, L. M. (2001). Criteria for revealing family secrets. *Communication Monographs, 68,* 1–27.

Weihs, K., & Politi, M. (2006). Family development in the face of cancer. In R. Crane & E. S. Marshall (Eds.), *Handbook of families & health: Interdisciplinary approaches* (pp. 3–18). Thousand Oaks, CA: Sage.

Zebrack, B. J., & Chesler, M. A. (2002). Quality of life in childhood cancer survivors. *Psycho-Oncology, 11,* 132–141.

Zebrack, B., Chesler, M., Orbuch, T. L., & Parry, C. (2002). Mothers of survivors of childhood cancer: Their worries and concerns. *Journal of Psychosocial Oncology, 20*(2), 1–25.

Zebrack, B. J., Chesler, M. A., Penn, A., & Katz, E. (2005). Psychosocial issues in adolescent cancer patients and survivors. *Current Problems in Pediatric and Adolescent Health Care, 35,* 195–201.

Zhang, A.Y., & Siminoff, L. A. (2003). Silence and cancer: Why do families and patients fail to communicate? *Health Communication, 15,* 415–429.

Chapter 11

Mom Is No Longer Mom: Adult Children Discuss Their Parents' Acute Health Events

Kandi L. Walker, Joy L. Hart, Lindsay J. Della, Mary Z. Ashlock, and Anita Hoag

As the U.S. population ages, more adult children are assuming the role of caregiver for their aging parents. Research suggests that caregiving is a stressful activity that may adversely affect an individual's health, financial well-being, and familial relationships. This presents difficulty when an aging parent's demands progressively increase, but when a parent suffers an acute health emergency, caregiving responsibilities increase dramatically, forcing families to adapt swiftly. This chapter reports on an exploratory qualitative study that assessed adult children's experiences caring for a later life parent during and after an acute health event. Six major themes emerged from participants' narratives: changes in the parent's personality, changes in roles and responsibilities, heightened emotions and increased tensions, selective disclosure, persuasion and guidance, and preparation for the future. The chapter reviews supporting narratives in order to authenticate each theme and discusses implications for familial communication during and after health crises. The chapter concludes by comparing acute health events with other health crises. Best practice suggestions are adapted from emergency health preparedness literature to be used as guidelines and advice for families with aging parents.

Caring for family members has a rich history and is an important component of cultures everywhere. Such caregiving includes raising children and adolescents, helping injured or ill family members, and assisting parents and relatives as they age. As the average life span in the United States increases the need for individuals who can assist an aging population also increases (Goulding, 2003; National Center for Health Statistics, 2007). Family members of the aged often call upon professional caregivers, such as elderly care, assisted living services, or nursing homes for this assistance. However, nursing home and assisted living space is scarce and expensive, and government financial assistance is limited (Centers for Medicaid and Medicare Services, 2008). Thus, it is not surprising that more and more adult children are being asked to care for their parents in later life. In fact, when the U.S. Department of Health and Human Services (Office of Disability, Aging, and Long-Term Care Policy, 1998) last conducted a prevalence study of informal caregiving, it estimated that there were seven million Americans providing informal care for an elder (defined as 60 years or older).

More recently, a study conducted by the National Alliance for Caregiving and the Center for Productive Aging (LifeCare, Inc., 2008) found that 85% of the 1,786 respondents were providing care to a parent or parent-in-law. Likewise, the Robert Wood Johnson Foundation (2002), in its survey of informal caregivers in the United States, found that 60% of its respondents, 45-years-old or older, were most likely to report providing care to individuals over the age of 65 (58%). It is therefore, important to understand the communication issues and concerns surrounding the caregiving experience as well as how caregiving affects involved individuals.

The Impact of Caregiving on the Caregiver and Family Relationships

There are many possible outcomes for the informal family caregiver (Harwood, 2007). As Garstka, McCallion, and Toseland (2001) pointed out caregiving intervention research often tries to emphasize the positive aspects of caregiving; however, negative aspects of caregiving are also apparent. One negative outcome involves the additional stresses that the caregiver may face. The Administration on Aging (2003) found that "prolonged caregiving can adversely affect one's physical and psychological health, current and future employment status and earning capability, ability to balance familial needs (both those of their older parents and younger family members), and the ability to meet personal needs" (p. 1).

Beyond these individual effects, caregiving responsibilities may also influence the relationships, with the care recipient, and with romantic partners, children, and siblings (Miller, Shoemaker, Willyard, & Addison, 2008; Willyard, Miller, Shoemaker, & Addison, 2007). Adult children and their aging parents have to adjust to changing roles and power relations. They may need to negotiate topics that may have previously been taboo or uncomfortable (e.g., the aging parent's financial status), and they may have to navigate the dialectics of independence/dependence (e.g., the aging parent's desire to continue driving). Even in the best of situations, such adjustments can be challenging. In less ideal circumstances (e.g., poor communication skills; financial problems; dementia; pressures to juggle work, the care of others, and one's personal life), the adjustments can be fraught with problems of monumental difficulty (Ilse, Feys, de Wit, Putman, & de Weerdt, 2008; Mannion, 2008).

There is substantial history of research on communication in filial and family relations in caregiving situations. Ellis, Miller, and Given (1989) looked at a conceptual model of caregiving and communication and found that increased amounts of communication can positively impact caregivers' health. Their research revealed strong relationships between the lack of social and communicative support experienced by caregivers, and increased perceptions of family abandonment and negative health outcomes. Looking more closely at filial relations, Robinson and Thurnher (1979) found that as the aging parent's health deteriorated, the adult child caregiver's perceptions of the parent and their attitude toward caregiving became increasingly negative. Mui (1995) studied gender differences in filial relationships and found that emotional strain was positively correlated with a poor child-parent relationship and employment limitations for adult caregiving daughters. In addition, Mui found that male caregivers felt greater strain when they reported less instrumental social support and when their parents exhibited disruptive behavior.

Furthermore, while some researchers have focused on filial relationships, others have looked beyond this dyad and assessed the impacts of caregiving on the entire family. In her analysis of parent care and its resulting family stress, Brody (1985) discussed how families have to adapt to changes in lifestyle, privacy, and income. She points out that caregiving situations do not exist in isolation. Instead, they occur within the "context of the individual's and family's personality and history, qualitative relationships, and coping capabilities" (Brody, 1985, p. 23). Brody found that interpersonal problems may arise between siblings as repressed rivalries are reignited.

Brody (1985) also noted that conflicts with spouses and/or children may surface as other individuals in the family compete for the caregiver's taxed attention and scarce time. Similarly, Pecchioni, Wright, and Nussbaum (2005) remarked that marital relationships encounter communication transformations due to parental caregiving. In particular, they found about lower marital satisfaction, financial and emotional costs of providing care, and decreased couple alone time to be prevalent when the parent lived in the child's (and spouse's) home. They did, however, note that decision-making communication increased within the marital dyad when in-home care for a parent was being provided.

Thus, not only does caregiving affect one's personal health, income, lifestyle, and job status, it can significantly impact one's relationships with one's parent, spouse, children, and siblings. All of these outcomes can be difficult to deal with in situations in which an aging parent's demands progressively increase. In some cases, when caregiving responsibilities arise without warning (e.g., an acute health emergency). Families cannot gradually adjust to the caregiving situation. Instead, they must adapt swiftly.

Caregiving in Acute Health Crises

Although a growing body of literature exists on caregiving and its effects on caregivers and their relationships, scant attention has been devoted to understanding caregiver responses when caregiving was prompted by an acute health crisis. A few studies have, however, assessed family communication issues in the context of an acute health crisis (Ilse et al., 2008; Lindhardt, Bolmsjo, & Hallberg, 2006). For example, Lindhardt and colleagues (2006) found that the state of filial relationships and adult child-family relationships both impact family communication and decision-making when families gather together during acute health crises. Unfortunately, very little research has examined how adult children communicate about the increasing care demands when a parent faces an acute health challenge.

Given the lack of research into caregiving surrounding parental acute health crises, we became interested in how adult children acting as caregivers experience and describe their role in providing care. To assess these experiences and role perceptions, we employed a social constructionist (Berger & Kellner, 1964) perspective. Social constructionism examines how individuals make sense of events and interactions through their communication with others. Regarding acute health crises and related subsequent events, adult children may interact with a variety of individuals, such as health care providers, family members, friends, and coworkers. In these situations, adult children's perceptions and communication will shape their interactions and impact their interpretations of the context, the interactants, and themselves. These interpretations of adult children's experiences with caregiving formed the foundation of our study. Thus, we investigated how adult children acting as primary caregivers (i.e., the designated "go-to" person in case of a crisis or emergency) described their parents' acute health events, the subsequent outcomes, and, most importantly, their own roles as caregivers. In particular, we were interested in understanding how adult children caring for family members portrayed their experiences; therefore, we posed the following broad research question: How do adult children describe caregiving and family communication during and after a parent's acute health event?

Methods

To address this research question, we employed an exploratory qualitative research design, which utilized in-depth interviews and thematic analysis to reveal embedded conceptualizations of caregiving experiences from participants' narratives. Below we detail our study sample, data collection protocol, and data analysis.

Study Sample

Recruitment. We collected data from a volunteer sample of 22 adult caregivers. To obtain participants, we employed a variety of recruitment methods, such as: 1) posting fliers around the University of Louisville campus , 2) announcing the study in graduate communication classes, 3) sending invitations to accessible local listservs (e.g., university, church, and community groups), and 4) leveraging our own interpersonal networks (e.g., book club groups and parent groups from children's schools).

Selection. Study volunteers were asked to participate if they met three qualifications. They had to be at least 25 years old, they had to be caring for a parental figure aged 65 or older and they had to have participated in within the past 2 years a parental figure's acute health crisis. For the study, we defined an "acute health crisis" as a health-related situation that required the potential respondent to make a significant medical decision (e.g., deciding on a particular cancer treatment regime) and/or redefine their parent's living situation because of the health issue. After an invitation was accepted, a time and a location were set for the interview.

Description. Of the participants ($N = 22$), the majority were women ($n = 17$). Our sample ranged in age from 33–66 years (mean age = 49) and possessed household incomes between \$20,000–\$160,000+ (mean = \$50,000). A number of life differences existed among them (see Table 11.1), which allowed us to examine a variety of experiences and viewpoints.

Table 11.1: *Breakdown of Sample Characteristics*

Characteristics	**Sample Breakdown**
Parental living situation	
	• $n = 17$; parental figure living independently
	• $n = 3$; parental figure living with them
	• $n = 2$; parental figure living in care facility
Marital/family status	
	• $n = 13$; married with children in household
	• $n = 3$; single
	• $n = 2$; married empty-nesters
Employment status	
	• $n = 18$; employed outside the home
	• $n = 5$; not employed outside the home

Ethnicity
- $n = 20$; Caucasian
- $n = 1$; Native American
- $n = 1$; African American

Educational attainment
- $n = 20$; some college
- $n = 2$; doctoral degree

Data Collection

This study was approved by the University of Louisville's Human Studies Committee. Before beginning data collection, we obtained informed consent from all participants. Additionally, participants were debriefed at the end of each interview to ensure that any lingering questions had been answered.

Most interviews were conducted in participants' homes; however, a few were conducted in the interviewers' homes, local restaurants, or participants' offices. Each interview lasted between 1 and 3 hours, which included time for the study description and fielding questions, explaining and signing the consent form, and for debriefing and answering any final questions.

Interviewing procedures. The majority of the interviews were conducted by the fourth and fifth authors ($n = 16$), and the first and second authors completed the remaining six. Each interviewer was trained in conducting qualitative interviews, used the same interview guide, and had participated in team discussions about constructing follow-up/probing questions. Beyond the primary open-ended questions about caregiving, participants also provided demographic information. All interviews were recorded in order to aid the analysis. In addition, each researcher also took detailed field notes. Immediately following each interview, the researchers documented any initial impressions and reviewed their handwritten notes, making corrections and clarifications.

Discussion topics. The interview questions were designed to uncover how participants communicate and interact with family members in order to create a perceived social reality during and after acute health crises. Additionally, our lines of questioning were intended to help reveal situation-specific artifacts of familial relationships that develop during and continue after such health crises. The interview guide contained 18 questions. These were primarily open-ended questions, which allowed the interviewee to share details, provide examples, and talk for whatever length of time they felt comfortable with. A funnel-based questioning approach prompted interviewers to ask broad initial questions and then move to more specific health and caregiving questions as the participant grew more comfortable. The interview guide included the following questions: Please tell me about your relationship with your parent or parental figure; Tell me about your parent's recent acute health event; If your parent were describing the recent health event, what would she (or he) say? If you were asked about this same event, how would you describe it? When other people ask about how your parent is doing, what is your response? How did your family talk about the health event? How did your family manage the health event? and What have you learned about yourself that you didn't know before your parent's acute health event?

Data Analysis

Upon completion of the 22 interviews, the full research team reviewed all of the interview results. This initial review helped clarify questions about the transcripts and research notes. Next, the first two authors conducted an in-depth analysis of the data using a constant comparison analytic procedure (Glaser & Strauss, 1967; Strauss & Corbin, 1998). Emergent categories were based on recurring ideas and themes that surfaced during interviewees' responses (Becker, 1998; Buzzanell & Burrell, 1997). As the analysis continued, previously coded data were compared with new examples (Lindlof, 1995). Emergent categorical groupings were then revised as more data were analyzed. In accordance with the constant comparison analysis guidelines posed by Strauss and Corbin (1998), we continued to revise our categories until we had developed a system capable of indexing new examples. Then, when no new categories or examples emerged, saturation was declared.

Results and Discussion

From our interviews, six primary themes emerged: changes in the parent's "person," changes in roles and responsibilities, emotions and tensions, selective disclosure, persuasion and guidance, and preparation. Below we examine each theme and provide examples from participant dialogues, enabling the reader to hear the story directly from the participants. Table 11.2 summarizes our findings.

Table 11.2: *Six Themes in How Adult Children Caregivers Talk about Aging Parents' Acute Health Events*

Theme	Description/Characterization
Changes in the Parent's "Person"	
	• Emotional, physical, and communicative changes
	• Turning points in relationships and relational transitions
Changes in Roles and Responsibilities	
	• Much greater role in managing, overseeing, and directing parents' care
	• Realization of more responsibility and new roles
	• Insights into how things really are
Emotions and Tensions	
	• Heightened emotions and additional pressures
	• Common emotions and emotional states: sadness, pride, aggravation, anger, happiness, disappointment, and being overwhelmed
	• Emotional tensions in navigating the health care system
	• Dialectical tensions emerge between family members

Selective Disclosure
- Masking of particular emotions to "outsiders"
- Diverting attention rather than sharing or focusing on the serious situation

Persuasion and Guidance
- Adult children shaping their parents' actions
- Strong prevalence of parents' nonverbal communication when responding
- Importance of subtle persuasion and inconspicuous guidance:
  o Adult children worry about parents feeling manipulated

Preparation
- The acute health event thrust consideration of the future into the immediate foreground

Changes in the Parent's "Person"

The first theme centered on the physical, emotional, and communicative changes that the participants' parents exhibited in the recent health crisis. One participant described the numerous changes that had occurred in her mother's condition during the health crisis and how much of her mother's vitality is now missing. When commenting on how she responded when asked about her mother, one participant indicated, "That is *not* my mother." Another participant, after a longer than average pause, tearfully remarked:

> My mom just sits and watches TV now. My mom never did that. Hell, you couldn't get her to sit down long enough to have a conversation—she had to put up dishes, fold laundry, and stuff while she talked to you. Now, she just sits there. I asked myself and my sister all the time, "Where did mom go?" She's here but she's not.

Discussions about parental changes included considerable dialogue on turning points in relationships and how relational transitions played out over time. Baxter and Bullis (1986) defined a turning point as "any event or occurrence that is associated with change in a relationship" (p. 470). For many of these participants, the acute health event fit this definition. The statement "My mom is no longer my mom," exemplifies this theme. The participant believed that her mom had changed so much that they no longer shared the same daughter-mother bond. Coming to terms with the psychological changes in their parents, along with the associated relational adjustments tests on the participants' patience. One participant captured the feelings of many by suggesting:

It's odd, and I probably can't explain it very well. This new way we interact isn't bad ... it's ok. But sometimes, I ... I just want my mom back. I want to be the kid. Now, maybe I'm too old to feel that way. Maybe I shouldn't. But I do. I want her to be the old her and I want to be the old me. But I have to be the new me because this is now her. I guess I should have known it might come to this, but who wants to think about that? Yeah, we all think we might need to help out our parents. But we don't really realize all that's associated with that, especially in cases like my mom's. When so much of who she was is gone, but sometimes I can see part of the old her. I like to think that I'm doing what's right. Doing what a good daughter would do, but sometimes I wonder if I'm doing good enough.

Another participant indicated that:

We don't talk about the things we did before. Because of her condition, the medical stuff, she's not really as in tune with what's going on with me. She doesn't ask me about my life—it's more of a self-focused thing. I want to help, but I miss those conversations. I miss her asking about me, my life. It's hard for me to get used to—because she was always so interested in hearing about my life and what was going on.

These participant quotes illustrate the process of adjusting to parental changes that prompted changes in relationship roles. Although relational transitions take place across the life span, many of these participants experienced an abrupt relational turning point due to their parent's health crisis. In several cases, these turning points forced relationships and care needs in directions that adult children felt unprepared for, and which necessitated periods of adjustment.

Changes in Roles and Responsibilities

In accord with others' findings (Keefe & Fancey, 2000; Stoller & Pugliesi, 1989; Usita, Hall, & Davis, 2004), an issue across that often arose involved changes in roles and responsibilities. Most commonly, participants mentioned that although they had been helping their parent in various ways prior to the acute health event (e.g., assisting with medical information and doctor's visits, serving as a sounding board and providing advice, helping out with household chores while visiting), after the event they were forced to take a much greater role in managing, overseeing, and directing their parents' care. Along with these shifts in tasks came a realization concerning the need to assume more responsibility. For example, one participant commented, "I'm the parent now." Another shared that the parent "looks to me for what to do, and I'm supposed to know or figure it out." In a similar vein, one participant stressed that:

> Even though as I grew up and my relationship with my parents changed, it was still clear I was their little girl. Things had started changing, but it was drastic after my mom's sudden illness. The toll was so great and the aftermath so heavy that I became the one that she looked to. I became the supporter, the advice giver, the one who organized and ran everything. It's like suddenly I was thrown into this new life—one where I was in charge and my mom was in my care. I don't mind, but I'm still kind of in shock.

Another participant put it this way:

> It's not easy to describe because clearly I'm not completely in charge. But it's like … I went from being me to being the person who runs things, who not only takes care of mom but also manages all of her stuff. … Now, I'm sort of in charge, and that's new. It's taken some getting used to. It's OK, but it's just that nothing before this in life has really prepared me for this.

These quotes illustrate that participants had to come to terms with their new roles after the health crisis occurred.

Participants also expressed that the event catapulted them into the role of "insider" in their parents' lives. As one participant commented,

> I was faced with the reality of how she really lives day-to-day after this last emergency room episode. I think I was in denial that she was as bad as she is. She needs me more than I realized. I see that now. I wasn't blind to it before just in denial.

Insight into "how things really are" was a common statement among the participants. One participant even commented,

> I talked to her on the phone and I guess I was too busy telling her about my life that I wasn't paying attention to what she was or wasn't saying. I go to her house now and I'm embarrassed that I let things get this bad for her.

Many of the participants were adapting to changes that although they might have anticipated, they had not planned or prepared for. They had moved from being a helpful adult child to primary caregiver of a parent, a role that had no script and one to which they brought no previous experience.

Emotions and Tensions

Considerable discussion focused on emotions and tensions. Milligan (2005) pointed out that there is an "embodied emotional experience" and an "affective, or emotional, entity of informal care work" (p. 2107). She further noted that caregivers have an "inner felt response to caregiving" and that caregivers undergo emotional work that involves how a caregiver "interprets and responds to the needs of the care recipient" (p. 2107). We found that, although participants acknowledged that emotion was naturally embedded in a parent's health crisis, many commented that their role after the crisis heightened their emotions and added additional emotional pressures. Heightened emotions emerged as a major theme across three key topics: caregiving responsibilities, changes in the parent-child relationship, and dealing with the health care system.

One comment came from a participant talking about the responsibility she felt for her mother. She said:

> I love my mom. I want to do right by her, my dad [he was deceased], my brothers. ... I want to set a good example for my kids. It's hard enough making decisions on what you should do with your own health in an emergency situation but now I'm responsible for mom's too. And you have all these eyes watching you, judging you, I'm even judging myself. ... Some days I just cry because I think I can't take it or do any more. And those aren't even the days when there's a health emergency. That's just because I know I'm the responsible one now.

This illustrates the participant's emotional responses to the additional pressure relating to caregiving. The emotions associated with health crises were expressed by most of the participants regardless of the question. One participant commented that she felt as though she was constantly trying to keep her emotions in check.

Sadness, pride, aggravation, anger, happiness, disappointment, and feeling overwhelmed were among the common emotions and emotional states that emerged. When participants talked about their sadness, it most often stemmed from the loss of the original parent-child relationship, of perceived upcoming loss of their parent-child relationship, and/or becoming the "matriarch" of the family. It seemed that the "matriarch" or "person in charge" was seen as the keeper of family stories, family history, and responsible for remembering past, present, and anticipate future family issues. As one participant stated, "I'm the backbone of the family where my mom used to be." Another participant put it this way "I don't want to be the mom of the whole family but that's what will happen. I'll be her. ... No one can do it like mom's done it. ... It's depressing—the reality of it all."

Strong emotional responses also emerged when discussions turned to navigating the health care system. Interactions with health care personnel included securing appointments with specialists, arranging tests, researching health information, assessing care facilities (e.g., rehabilitation centers, assisted living communities), and negotiating financial arrangements. Participants commented they had "anger," "disappointment," "frustration," and "aggravation" when arranging care for their parent. One participant said it best:

> I see why people give up. ... It's exhausting and aggravating—the hassle of it all. I think the healthcare industry is more of a test of perseverance than to make anyone better. I feel like I'm spinning my wheels most of the time. How can I help mom when I think healthcare is more interested in having the right computer code in her file than really helping her?

Throughout participant discussions of emotions, a dialectical tension (Altman, Vinsel, & Brown, 1981; Baxter, 1988, 1990; Baxter & Montgomery, 1996) emerged. This was conceptualized as an ongoing and competing contradiction (Baxter & Montgomery, 1996) that caregivers experienced. In our interviews, the emergent dialectical tension dealt with bonding versus burden communication.

Working through the parental health crisis and the time following it, some participants reported that they thought they had bonded more deeply with their parent and their siblings. Participants commented that siblings were now closer because of the parent's health crisis. They were "working together" to make sure the parent was given appropriate care. Participants also commented that siblings "took turns staying at the hospital" so that the parent was never alone and there was always "a second set of ears to hear what the doctors or nurses had to say." Other participants commented on the relational closeness they felt with their parent because of the health crisis. "We have a bond. Any gripes or complaints are just between us." Another participant summarized the thoughts of many by saying,

> We spend more time together now and we get to talk about things we never had time or never made time to do. ... I hate that he had a heart attack but it made us talk more and be more real with each other.

Participants also expressed feelings of being burdened by the caregiver role and in some cases angry that the caregiving responsibilities had been "dumped in their lap" by their parent or siblings. For example, a participant commented that "I'm the one taking care of him because I had no childhood issues with him and I have the most patience." Several participants also communicated that they were pleased to be the main caregiver but simultaneously reported that they resented their siblings for not doing enough or not volunteering to take on this responsibility. As one participant said, "I have a family too. I wish they [siblings] would just ask if I was okay. It would be nice if they would pitch in more."

Finally, participants' dialectical tensions appeared greatest under two conditions: when the parent resisted receiving care and when there wasn't a clear "go to" person already designated by the family. As one participant stated, epitomizing this theme, "when no one is in charge, everyone thinks they are in charge." Interestingly, this second condition appears, to some extent, to be modifiable.

Selective Disclosure

An additional theme within the narratives also dealt with emotions, but this one centered on decisions to selectively disclose particular emotions, such as sadness, to "outsiders." As Milligan (2005) noted, caregivers often work to "control the outward expression of his or her own feelings, performing actions that may be at odds with the inner state" (p. 2107). In the current study, we found caregivers at times resisted opportunities to let others know how they were feeling and/or to seek support. For example, many participants mentioned deflecting questions from others about their parents' condition or progress, saying "She's fine." or "Everything is going well." In short, it was easier to deflect attention away from the situation than to have to share or focus on their sadness or the gravity of the situation. One response that best captured this theme was:

> Last week my daughter asked me 'how's Gran?' I told her I had a great conversation with her and left it at that. I was so afraid she was going to ask me more direct questions. I don't want her to have to know how bad things are. She's too young. She knows that Gran is old and we've talked about death. Death seems easier to talk about than the details of how sad the situation is.

Another participant put it this way:

> It amazes me how people care but they don't really care. I know if I told my friends what was going on with mom they would listen but it's so damn depressing. ... If I told them the daily emotions, the daily calls, the daily worry, the daily crap they would find me depressing.

While hiding emotions and keeping "outsiders" pacified, the participants also commented they didn't want the complication of managing others' feelings (e.g., "I don't want them to feel sorry for me."). For example, participants would often say, "I just keep it vague." This approach helped the caregivers communicate about the socially constructed situation (e.g., "she's doing fine," or "he's a tough guy. He's okay") rather than the "real" situation (e.g., "sad," "all encompassing," or "exhausting").

In addition, participants sometimes explained their responses by describing a desire to keep the identity of their parents in the past rather than the present. One participant best exemplified this theme by stating:

> And how do you tell people what's going on with your mom? I want people to know mom but how she would want people to think and talk about her. Not that she is incontinent, depressed, and just had a stroke.

Another participant explained an interaction she had with a contractor regarding her father's roof being repaired. "I told them dad wants you [roofers] to fix it right. He was an engineer and is meticulous about details. ... I didn't want the guy [contractor] to know dad's house was a wreck and he can barely take care of himself." As these examples illustrate, participants often spoke about attempts to preserve the "dignity" of their parents while communicating with "outsiders."

Persuasion and Guidance

Issues of persuasion and guidance formed a fifth theme in our data. In that area, participants often described communication they engaged in to shape, modify, or change their parents' behavior. Now perceiving themselves as "in charge," the participants described their strategies for encouraging their parents to engage in some activities (e.g., evaluate assisted living communities) and refrain from others (e.g., driving). Several interviewees also related the difficulties in dealing with someone who was used to making decisions and not having others, especially their children, tell them what to do. For example, one participant highlighted this theme stating:

> After this last health episode, I remember talking to my brothers and sisters about dad's driving. We didn't want to have an intervention and take the keys from him. That seemed too cruel. We didn't want to embarrass him. We decided I would just tell him I wanted to spend more time with him and I would drive him where he needed to go for the next couple of weeks. He resisted a bit saying he didn't want to be a bother but I was relentless in my efforts. I told him I was coming by his house anyway and that I liked the company. I told him all kinds of exaggerations. I think he knew what I was doing.

As a common thread that tied this theme together, we noted the frequency with which participants described their parents' nonverbal communication. For example, one participant said "I can still remember the look my mom gave me when I told her I needed to look at her finances. She was pissed." Another participant commented,

> It's burned in my mind how dad looked so pitiful when we told him we needed to look at other living arrangements for him. I don't think he was going for the pitiful look. I think he meant it as mad. He even said something like "You remember Carol, I'm still your father." I don't remember much about that interaction but I do remember how I felt after he looked at me that way.

A parent's nonverbal communication seemed to increase the emotional impact of the health crisis and the necessity for subtle persuasion strategies and inconspicuous guidance. For example, rather than take a "heavy hand" in shaping parental actions, most of our participants employed less direct forms of communication to encourage particular actions. An underlying goal in such approaches always seemed to be to make the parent think the behavior was his or her own idea. An example came from a participant who was caring for her mother:

> I can't tell you why I do it. My husband doesn't understand it either. I don't want to hurt mom's feelings. What could take 2 seconds to say, "take your medicine" usually takes me 10 minutes. I'll start by commenting on the time and then move the conversation into the medicines I take and when I take them. If she doesn't get what I'm doing, and she usually doesn't, I'll move to more direct stuff like "Mom, when was the last time you took your medicine?" If she doesn't realize she needs to take it I'll make some excuse to get something to drink and say something about getting her anything while I'm up. If she still makes no move about her medicine I'll say, "Mom, I see your meds here. Do you want me to save you a trip? I can just bring them to you." It is ridiculous but I can't bring myself to be more direct. What's the real goal? The relationship or the medicine? Ridiculous what I do. It really is.

Although many of these participants were successful with subtle persuasion and guidance, emotional ramifications seemed to be attached. For instance, some participants described feeling devious—

that they were tricking, perhaps unfairly, their parents—and others remarked about the extra emotional energy required for such exchanges. For example, one participant commented, "I'm not sure what exhausts me more. Taking care of her or trying to pretend to her that I'm not taking care of her." Others worried that their parents felt manipulated or questioned their subtle guidance; this often produced feelings of guilt in the caregivers. To cope with these emotions, participants stressed that, whenever possible, they encouraged their parents to make their own decisions—"I ask her opinion all the time," "When we go to the store I make a point to let her make all kinds of decisions. The more small decisions, even about food, she gets to make the happier she seems," "Even though his clothes don't match we never say anything. It's better he makes those decisions." These small concessions seemed to assuage some of the guilt associated with telling a parent what to do.

Preparation

A final common theme was that responding to the parent's health crisis helped the interviewees to realize how unprepared they were for the crisis and the necessity of preparing for their parents' potential health events in the future. In describing how unprepared he was, a participant disclosed:

> I had no idea what hospital to take her to, what doctor to take her to, nothing. Now, I know who the best surgeon is, what hospital to take her to, I know what to expect now. The first fall she had was bad, the heart attack was worse, now I'm convinced that the next big thing is around the corner. ... I know to check on her every day. I didn't do that before.

Those participants who had since experienced additional health events talked at length about how much more smoothly things went when they were "armed with information" and knew what to expect from their family, friends, and healthcare providers. A comment that was often heard from the participants was "it's better to be prepared than to be caught off guard" when managing a parent's health. Participants commented that acute health crises took more time and energy when they weren't prepared for them. Preparation, even for minor health decisions (e.g., keeping a list of medicines the parent took in their wallets), helped the adult child from feeling "too over-whelmed" in any one moment. As one participant stated, "it's been an in-depth education" learning how to give care and "being ready for what happens next."

In a similar vein, many participants highlighted the importance of communicating about the future. In some cases, these conversations took place with the parent experiencing the health crisis. In other cases, they occurred with the parent's spouse, siblings, and/or the adult child's family (e.g., spouse). Regardless of the parties involved, the acute health event thrust consideration of the future into the immediate foreground. Even in situations where little talk or plan-ning had occurred previously, our participants were now focused on both the present (i.e., getting through the health crisis) and the future (i.e., making decisions and determining care). One particular example exemplifies the thoughts of many:

> My family doesn't talk about serious stuff. Not when it's personal. It's pretty characteristic of our family. I guess even mom's health wasn't something we [my sisters] wanted to discuss. But now we have to. It's not like she can take care of things. We need to do it for her. At first, it was just getting through the stroke. We had so much to decide in such a few short hours—hours that turned into a few days. Now, I'm deciding what's next. I should have paid better attention in Girl Scouts. I wasn't prepared for this [mom's stroke] and we paid the price. We had so much thrown on us immediately. I learned my lesson. My sisters and I have talked and we're making arrangements for mom. We won't be caught off guard for the next disaster. I shouldn't call it a disaster. I guess that gives you insight into how I feel about it all. We'll be better prepared to take care of her now. That sounds more appropriate.

By preparing for the future, participants, although frustrated at times, also saw themselves as having learned a great deal. They disclosed various means of gaining knowledge, which included word-of-mouth (e.g., talking with others), developing relationships with health personnel (e.g., getting inside information from nurses), and using technology (e.g., the Internet). Woven through their com-ments was the realization that one had to do this information gather-ing and/or negotiation on one's own—"no one will be there to guide you through it," so "you have to figure out how things work and how to get what you need." Participants also noted that behavior associated with these information gathering activities helped them cope with the emotions and cognitive ambiguities associated with managing their parent's present health crisis.

Significant Findings

Many of our findings parallel those from earlier studies on caregiving (Brody, 1985; Ilse, Feys, de Wit, Putman, & de Weerdt, 2008; Mannion, 2008; Miller et al., 2008). For example, caregiving has been noted as a very stressful activity that can result in negative physical and mental outcomes for the caregiver (Administration on Aging, 2003). Our research, however, unearthed more discussion about negative mental health outcomes than physical health outcomes. Thus, it seems that addressing the mental health of caregivers during and immediately after a parent's acute health crisis might help stave off or reduce relational difficulties and negative physical outcomes later on.

Two suggestions for addressing the mental health needs of adult child caregivers are as follows: First, our participants recounted feeling alone in the process of navigating the event, expressing sentiments such as "no one will be there to guide you through it." And while each acute health crisis will vary, caregivers' feelings of isolation could be somewhat alleviated via fairly straightforward policy changes. That is, health care providers could designate mental health staff to focus on caregivers' needs. At a minimum professionals would be trained to help caregivers traverse the basics of managing their parents' health crises while at the hospital, and might be able to help prepare them for upcoming role changes after the parent is discharged.

Second, our participants described more positive coping outcomes when they felt more prepared for a crisis. Minimal behavior such as asking friends about their experiences and researching available services on the Internet seemed to have a positive impact on our participants' stress levels. More importantly, asking friends and conducting research on the Internet do not require operations or policy-level changes within the health care system. Rather, it would simply require adult children with aging parents to engage in some up-front "leg work." To help guide adult children through this exercise, we have identified five "Best Practices" for preparing for and dealing with an aging parent's acute health crisis.

Best Practices

Because acute health crises, by nature, are difficult to predict in advance, people's reactions to these situations are similar to their reactions in other crisis contexts (e.g., natural disasters) when they are surprised, their health and/or their family's health is threatened, and they are forced to respond quickly. As such, we have drawn from key principles outlined in emergency preparedness literature to highlight a few pieces of advice for families with aging parents. Extrapolating from this literature, developing and practicing a "plan of action" ahead of time is a cornerstone of best practices (Federal Emergency Management Agency, 2004, p. 13). Thus, we recommend that families engage in the following communicative activities prior to an acute health crisis:

1. Establish a "central command" and a "chain of command." Discuss the potential of an acute health crisis with parents and siblings in advance. Determine which siblings are able/willing to take on additional responsibilities during and after such an event. Also, depending on the parent-child relationship, children may want to ask their parents who they would feel most comfortable with as a caregiver during times of poor health. And while some adult children's own family situations may allow for additional responsibilities now, backup plans should be made in case these situations are not as flexible at the time of the health event.
2. Inventory "warning signs" and "maintain threat surveillance." A parent's age may be the simplest warning sign, but other communicative signs may exist as well. The process of inventorying potential warning signs (e.g., changes in verbal/nonverbal communication with friends and family) may force adult children to step away from their own lives for a minute and look at the entirety of their parents' lives. Such a simple act may reduce the element of surprise when an acute health event does occur, which will allow faster and better decisions to be made when their parents' lives depend on them.

3. Develop a "stockpile." Like any good preparedness plan, families should think ahead about the resources/information they might need to access during the health crisis. The U.S. government stockpiles vaccines as a precautionary measure against certain viral outbreaks.

   In contrast, our participants did little to prepare for their parents' health emergencies despite the fact that they knew their parents were aging. It may be difficult to predict what kind of medical emergency will occur, but adult children can at least talk to their parents about current medications and gather their parents' health information in one central location (e.g., list of current medications, telephone numbers of physicians). Adult children should also ensure that others in the "chain of command" have access to the information as well. Then, if a crisis occurs, there is one less stressor to deal with.

4. Practice using "preparedness exercises." Adult children should spend some time discussing and role playing likely health crisis scenarios as their parents age. These discussions need to include siblings, spouses, and parents, if possible. "Preparedness exercises" involve developing strategies for handling multiple courses of events (Center for Health Policy, 2007). By having strategies in place, each member of the "crisis team" knows what to do as critical events unfold. Discussing and role playing potential acute health incidents in advance can help clarify everyone's role/role expectations during a crisis, enhance response capabilities, and minimize logistical frustrations allowing for a clearer focus on critical (perhaps life and death) decisions.

5. Identify "subject matter experts" and "support staff." Adult children, no matter how well prepared, may not be able to or may not have the ability to balance all "fronts" of a parental health crisis effectively. Thus, it is a good idea for them to identify individuals who have critical knowledge about health, the health care system, and/or the aging parents' health before a health crisis occurs. For example, adult children could introduce themselves to their parents' physicians while the parent is still in good health so that they have a better understanding of their parents' relationship with his/her physician.

Identifying and recruiting individuals who might be able to lend instrumental and emotional social support during an acute health crisis can also be an important step in preparing for an emergency situation. Social support is especially critical for coping with stressful events (Cohen & Willis, 1985), and talking with potentially supportive individuals in advance of a health crisis about the amount and type of support they feel capable of lending will help set expectations around who can be "counted on" when needed most.

Conclusions

As parents age, increased health and life assistance may stress the family system. Better understanding of the associated needs and potential stressors may ease transitions for families. One contribution of our study lies in its focus on examining experience from the adult child's perspective after a health crisis. In particular, we explored experiences in caregiving from the vantage point of the adult daughter or son caregiver. An associated contribution of the focus on the complexity of feelings and experiences enmeshed in dealing with a parent's acute health crisis is an enhanced ability to negotiate family relationships and care following the crisis. The exploratory nature of our qualitative approach allowed us to uncover participants' first-hand perspectives and may be useful in designing future research.

Despite these contributions, several limitations were present in the study. First, our sample was restricted. Additional research is needed with other more diverse samples, as perceptions and experiences may differ across geographic areas or ethnic groups. Second, although understanding the caregiver's unique perspective is important, studying family systems would allow for a broader understanding of the effects of acute health problems and caregiving needs. Our study was limited by not including other family members, such as the parent receiving care and the caregivers' siblings.

Future research efforts should build on the contributions of this study and in order to expand our findings. Additional avenues for future research include longitudinal designs that examine family systems during acute health situations and caregiving over time and/or an adult child's caregiving role over time (e.g., during a parent's health crisis, during care transitions). Future work might also explore how caregiving decisions are negotiated within family systems. For example, considerable evidence suggests that women are central in providing care and, most often, become the primary care-givers in families (Rittenour & Soliz, 2009). As such, research on caregiving often focuses on daughters' caregiving (Donorfio & Sheehan, 2001; Pecchioni & Nussbaum, 2001). Rittenour and Soliz (2009) pointed out, however, that daughters-in-law frequently play central roles here and that such relationships deserve additional research attention. Thus, future inquiry could investigate the family processes by which caregiving is negotiated and caregivers are selected.

Nevertheless, this study provides valuable insight into the experi-ence of managing an aging parent's acute health crisis. From our participants' narratives of their experiences, we were able to identify important psychological outcomes of managing health crisis situa-tions for their parents. It follows, then, that our brief suggestions for how to prepare and plan for such an event should prove beneficial in priming adult children for the unexpected.

References

Administration on Aging. (2003). *The Older Americans Act National Family Caregiver Support Program: Compassion in action.* Retrieved September 14, 2008, from http://www.aoa.gov/prof/aoaprog/caregiver/overview/docs/NFCSP_Exec_Summary_FULL_03.pdf

Altman, I., Vinsel, A., & Brown, B. B. (1981). Dialectic conceptions in social psychology: An application to social penetration and privacy regulation. In L. Berkowitz (Ed.), *Advances in experimental and social psychology* (pp. 107–160). New York: Academic Press.

Baxter, L. (1988). A dialectical perspective on communication strategies in relationship development. In S. Duck, D. Hay, S. Jobfoll, W. Ickes, & B. Montgomery (Eds.), *Handbook of personal relationships: Theory, research, and interventions* (pp. 257–274). Chichester, UK: Wiley.

Baxter, L. (1990). Dialectical contradictions in relationship development. *Journal of Personal and Social Relationships, 7,* 69–88.

Baxter, L. A., & Bullis, C. (1986). Turning points in developing romantic relationships. *Human Communication Research, 12,* 469–493.

Baxter, L., & Montgomery, B. (1996). *Relating: Dialogues and dialectics.* New York: Guilford Press.

Becker, H. S. (1998). *Tricks of the trade: How to think about your research while you're doing it.* Chicago: University of Chicago Press.

Berger, P., & Kellner, H. (1964). Marriage and the construction of reality. *Diogenes, 46,* 1–24.

Brody, E. M. (1985). Parent care as a normative family stress. *The Gerontologist, 25,* 19–29.

Buzzanell, P. M., & Burrell, N. A. (1997). Family and workplace conflict: Examining metaphorical conflict schemas and expressions across context and sex. *Human Communication Research, 24,* 109–146.

Center for Health Policy. (2007). *Public Health Emergency Exercise Toolkit.* New York: Columbia University School of Nursing. Retrieved February 28, 2009, from http://www.nycepce.org/Documents/PHEmergencyExerciseToolkit.pdf

Centers for Medicaid and Medicare Services. (2008). *Nursing homes: Paying for care.* Washington, DC: Department of Health and Human Services. Retrieved February 28, 2009, from http://www.medicare.gov/nursing/Payment.asp

Cohen, S., & Willis, T. A. (1985). Stress, social support, and the buffering hypothesis. *Psychological Bulletin, 98*, 310–357.

Donorfio, L. M., & Sheehan, N. W. (2001). Relationship dynamics between aging mothers and caregiving daughters: Filial expectations and responsibilities. *Journal of Adult Development, 8*, 39–49.

Ellis, B. H., Miller, K. I., & Given, C. W. (1989). Caregivers in home health care situations: Measurement and relations among critical concepts. *Health Communication, 1*, 207–226.

Federal Emergency Management Agency. (2004). *Are you ready? An in-depth guide to citizen preparedness.* Retrieved February, 28, 2009, from http://www.fema.gov/pdf/areyouready/areyouready_full.pdf

Garstka, T. A., McCallion, P., & Toseland, R. W. (2001). Using support groups to improve caregiver health. In M. L. Hummert & J. F. Nussbaum (Eds.), *Aging, communication, and health: Linking research and practice for successful aging* (pp. 75–98). Mahwah, NJ: Lawrence Erlbaum.

Glaser, B. G., & Strauss, A. L. (1967). *The discovery of grounded theory: Strategies for qualitative research.* Chicago: Aldine.

Goulding, M. R. (2003). Public health and aging: Trends in aging— United States and worldwide. *Morbidity & Mortality Weekly, 52(06)*, 101–106.

Harwood, J. (2007). *Understanding communication and aging: Developing knowledge and awareness.* Los Angeles, CA: Sage.

Ilse, I. B., Feys, H., de Wit, L., Putman, K., & de Weerdt, W. (2008). Stroke caregivers' strain: Prevalence and determinants in the first six months after stroke. *Disability & Rehabilitation, 30*, 523–530.

Keefe, J., & Fancey, P. (2000). The care continues: Responsibility for elderly relatives before and after admission to a long term care facility. *Family Relations, 49*, 235–244.

LifeCare, Inc. (2008). *Corporate eldercare programs: Their impact, effectiveness and the implications for employers.* Retrieved September 9, 2008, from http://www.caregiving.org/LifeCare_Study_2008.pdf

Lindhardt, T., Bolmsjo, I. A., & Hallberg, I. R. (2006). Standing guard – being a relative to a hospitalised, elderly person. *Journal of Aging Studies, 20,* 133–149.

Lindlof, T. R. (1995). *Qualitative communication research methods.* Thousand Oaks, CA: Sage.

Mannion, E. (2008). Alzheimer's disease: The psychological and physical effects of the caregiver's role. Part 1. *Nursing Older People, 20,* 27–32.

Miller, K. I., Shoemaker, M. M., Willyard, J., & Addison, P. (2008). Providing care for elderly parents: A structurational approach to family caregiver identity. *Journal of Family Communication, 8,* 19–43.

Milligan, C. (2005). From home to 'home': Situating emotions within the caregiving experience. *Environment and Planning A, 37(12),* 2105–2120.

Mui, A. C. (1995). Caring for frail elderly parents: A comparison of adult sons and daughters. *The Gerontologist, 35,* 86–93.

National Center for Health Statistics. (2007). *Health, United States, 2007: With chartbook on trends in the health of Americans.* Hyattsville, MD: U.S. Government Printing Office (DHHS publication number: 2007–1232).

Office of Disability, Aging, and Long-Term Care Policy. (1998). *Informal caregiving: Compassion in action.* Washington, DC: Department of Health and Human Services. Retrieved February 28, 2009, from http://aspe.hhs.gov/daltcp/Reports/carebro2.pdf

Pecchioni, L. L., & Nussbaum, J. F. (2001). Mother-adult daughter discussions of caregiving prior to dependency: Exploring conflicts among European-American women. *Journal of Family Communication, 1,* 133–150.

Pecchioni, L. L., Wright, K. B., & Nussbaum, J. F. (2005). *Life-span communication.* Mahwah, NJ: Lawrence Erlbaum.

Rittenour, C., & Soliz, J. (2009). Communicative and relational dimensions of shared family identity and relational intentions in mother-in-law/daughter-in-law relationships: Developing a conceptual model for mother-in-law/daughter-in-law research. *Western Journal of Communication, 73,* 67–90.

Robinson, B., & Thurnher, M. (1979). Taking care of aged parents: A family cycle transition. *The Gerontologist, 19,* 586–593.

Stoller, E. P., & Pugliesi, K. (1989). Other roles of caregivers: Competing responsibilities or supportive resources? *Journal of Gerontology, 44,* 231–238.

Strauss, A. L., & Corbin, J. (1998). *Basics of qualitative research: Techniques and procedures for developing grounded theory.* Thousand Oaks, CA: Sage.

The Robert Wood Johnson Foundation. (2002). *A portrait of informal caregivers in America, 2001.* Retrieved September 9, 2008, from http://www.rwjf.org/files/publications/other/CaregiverChartbook 2001.pdf

Usita, P. M., Hall, S. S., & Davis, J. C. (2004). Role ambiguity in family caregiving. *Journal of Applied Gerontology, 23,* 20–39.

Willyard, J., Miller, K., Shoemaker, M., & Addison, P. (2007, November). *Making sense of sibling responsibility for family caregiving: A narrative analysis.* Paper presented at the meeting of the National Communication Association, Chicago, IL.

Section Three:

Economic Crises

Chapter 12

Effective Family Communication and Job Loss: Crafting the Narrative for Family Crisis

Patrice M. Buzzanell and Lynn H. Turner

Job loss is typically described as a traumatic event in individuals' lives that requires social support, varied coping mechanisms, financial restructuring, and passage through stages of grief. Although job loss is considered stressful for individuals, the termination event and unemployment also strain families and affect family communication. In this chapter, we examine the ways that families shape narratives to craft and recraft meanings and relationships during this time of familial change. We discuss how job loss stories are stories on the margins (Jorgenson & Bochner, 2004) and how families rework stories to bring them closer to the center of family life. In the process, they recraft their identity as a family and as individuals.

Headlines in the *Wall Street Journal* and *New York Times* attest to the depth and breadth of job losses for white and blue collar workers in the United States and around the globe (Evans & Maher, 2009; Leroux & Jagger, 2009). The corporate story is fairly uniform: companies lay off workers to retain economic solvency. Layoffs arise in the context of rising energy prices, housing foreclosures, a home purchasing slump, and tightening consumer spending that affects retail and other sectors. Workers' stories, on the other hand, vary. Their narratives are cultural, moral, and personal, portraying the hopes and fears of generational, classed, and occupational cohorts and members.

Workers who perceive economic volatility and their own place in the overall economy as precarious continuously build in hedges against layoffs (Lucas, 2006). Other workers assume that they may be able to bounce back quickly in similar—if not better—jobs than they held before (Sonnenfeld, 2007), and still other workers spin a tale of betrayal, emotional labor, and identity loss who nevertheless aim toward reemployment. These latter workers resolve the loss of the old social and psychological contracts within socially constructed webs of meritocracy, commitments, and career capital (Buzzanell & Turner, 2003; Arthur, Inkson, & Pringle, 1999) through new narratives.

This research claims these new narratives as its object of study. We examine familial stories of job loss because they offer a contested site in which familial and worker roles, identities, and discourses operate in concert with material conditions, such as economic insecurities and financial resources, to create sensemaking opportunities. We also examine the individual crafting of career and work identities that occur whenever someone looks for work and must account for employment changes (see Ibarra, 2003). In doing so, we address calls for more narrative research on family (Jorgenson & Bochner, 2004; Langellier & Peterson, 2006; Turner & West, 2003) and on the meanings and meaningfulness of work (Cheney, Zorn, Planalp, & Lair, 2008). Because family members individually and collaboratively construct stories that they can tell themselves and others about their own identities and that of their individual and familial repositionings in periods of uncertainty, they offer spaces where much communicative effort to craft viable and acceptable identities, emotions, and strategies is undertaken. Following our analysis, we present recommendations for assisting individuals and families with job loss and, perhaps, other events that require narrative repositioning and behavioral changes. We believe that such research can not only contribute to the well-being and positive research undertaken in interpersonal and family communication (see Socha, 2008) but also to the ongoing exploration of resilience as a communicative construction on micro through macrolevels (see Buzzanell, 2010; Buzzanell, Shenoy, Lucas, & Remke, 2009).

Literature Review

To examine narrative craftings at individual and familial levels, we first describe how a discourse-centered lens differs from other approaches on job loss. We then present reviews of literature on narrative in interpersonal, familial, and organizational contexts.

Discourse-Centered Approach to Job Loss

Job loss is defined as a transitional process precipitated by the "trigger event" (event) of involuntary termination that occurs prior to some period of unemployment (state) (Latack, Kinicki, & Prussia, 1995). Job loss often is described as a traumatic event in people's lives that necessitates social support, coping, financial restructuring, and passage through stages of grief (Birkel, 1998; Garrett-Peters, 2009; Latack et al., 1995; Leana & Feldman, 1992; London, 1998; Strandh, 2000; Voydanoff, 1983). Although individuals experience job loss, the termination event and unemployment also affects and strains their families, sometimes prompting increased violence among family members and others, propensities toward relationship dissolution, and hopelessness among children who wonder why their parents' hard work is unrewarded (Anderson, Umberson, & Elliott, 2004; Kalleberg, 2008; Liem & Liem, 1988; National Institute of Justice, 2007; Newman, 1998, 1993; Rifkin, 1995). However, we located no previous studies that focus on the discourse of family members who are in the midst of job loss.

In a discourse-centered approach to job loss, we examine the ways individuals (re)define the meanings of work and family, (re)construct their worlds intersubjectively, and struggle against and/or are complicit with dominant discourses that privilege work over family (see Berger & Luckmann, 1967; Cheney, Lair, Ritz, & Zorn, 2010; Putnam & Fairhurst, 2001; Putnam & Boys, 2006). Although we cannot supply a moment-by-moment description of how family members' experiences with job loss influence their interactions, we can illuminate how they make sense of changes in their lives and position certain interests and identities as more important than others. We do so by examining their linguistic choices, reported changes in what they do and why, as well as the stories that they say provide insight into their decisions, emotions, and dealings with material hardship (e.g., Lucas & Buzzanell, in press; Marin, Bohanek, & Fivush, 2008). We examine how familial communication in difficult times is brought into sharp relief against the backdrop of ordinary family talk and interactions. These tensions depict a world in flux with possibilities for alternate work and family enactments in the future.

Despite extensive research on job loss, very little is known about how family members, particularly children, talk about their experiences with job loss and work-family interests. In fact, Finet (2001) reports that only indirect investigations of discourse exist in work-family research as a whole. Although there has been a dramatic increase in work-family research over the past several years (see Kirby, Golden, Medved, Jorgenson, & Buzzanell, 2003), Finet's point remains valid especially when examining work-family processes from a familial lens. We locate our study squarely in the discourse of family unlike other research that is more firmly rooted in an organizational perspective. By exploring the tensions, opportunities, and ironies within family talk following job loss, we provide insight into members' sensemaking processes and offer advice about how to resolve some of the strains that threaten to disrupt relationships when a parent or partner loses his/her job. For instance, family themes are shaped by hard economic times and the stories of resilience, strategies for saving money, and recollections of shifted resource use patterns can help families and individual members cope (e.g., Marin et al., 2008).

Narrative

Narratives provide lenses into the content and ways of expressing or making sense of life events that individuals and collectivities, such as families and communities, construct. Some narrative research describes how people craft coherent life stories—often retrospectively—and how they integrate data into these narratives (Stone, 2004). The idea is that individuals and, by extension, their families seek to understand their underlying nature and use this information to develop meaning and identity (Ochs & Capps, 1996).

Still other research portrays how individuals work toward construction of unified stories that shift in different contexts, such as when an individuals seek to recraft, brand, and provide a 30-second elevator speech about who they are and how they can add value to a company for which they seek employment (Ehrenrich, 2005; Ibarra, 2003; Lair, Sullivan, & Cheney, 2005). Yet, narratives also function as ongoing constructions in which various interests and versions jockey for control. For our work, the issues may not only be what version family members tell at any given time but also what is family and how is family enacted and performed for others (see Langellier & Peterson, 1993). Of particular importance to us is who has authorial privilege in the family, how it tends to be enacted, and in what situations authorial control takes place. In this view, the ongoing political nature of narrative may encourage the reproduction of and/or resistance to versions that mirror and/or disrupt particular familial, power, and social realities.

In this view, it is the crafting, telling, and performing of narrative that is of central concern. The content of the story is significant, but it is always subject to modification as new data are considered and negotiated among family members. We also focus on the process and content of storytelling. The performance of family storytelling is "an evolving expression of small group culture rather than a collection of stories" (Langellier & Peterson, 2004, p. 41). In job loss, older generations and family historians often have authorial privilege and rights to perform because they recall family traditions and strategies for enduring hard times. Members perform their positions in the familial social order and their generational and gendered interests (Buzzanell & Turner, 2003). They reconstitute family and, through the process of storytelling itself, transform who they are as individuals and as family members in particular circumstances (Stone, 2004). In particular contexts, different members may have authorial control (Ochs & Taylor, 1995).

In the work of constituting family and individual roles within the family, it is not simply the major stories that are important, but the ongoing, mundane events that are shaped into and shaped by family interactions. As Langellier and Peterson (2006) put it:

> equally formative of family culture is storytelling in the interrupted and intertwined conversations and habits of daily life—fragmentary, fleeting, and fluid, embedded among tasks and talk—while playing with children, doing housework and homework, reading the morning paper, preparing food, eating, and traveling to work and school. Family storytellers and listeners are multiple and dispersed, and stories may be contradictory and incoherent or simply bits of memory, speech, image. Such storytelling is so mundane that these stories may be invisible to family outsiders and even to family members themselves. (p. 110)

In job loss, changes in family patterns may be imperceptible to children (e.g., when mothers scale back on food purchases or use layaway). Changes may only be revealed when these children, now adults, wonder how their families survived economic hardship such as layoffs during deindustrialization (Lucas & Buzzanell, in press). Their storytelling as well as the narrative content portray how such changes occur in ways consistent with family values or strategies but sometimes invisible to members.

Research Question

Despite the importance of family as "the first group," meaning that family-of-origin members usually constitute the first and longest lasting set of connections of a person's life (Socha, 1999, 2009), there has not been a great deal of scholarly effort devoted toward connections of economic hardship and family storytelling and stories. How members participate in and construct their family stories has implications for their identity constructions, sensemaking about life situations, adaptability to potentially destructive circumstances, and the integrity of family itself within any given society (see Jorgenson & Bochner, 2004; Ochs & Capps, 2001). We ask: How do family members craft job loss stories to display family values and strategies during times of crisis?

Method

Participants

Twenty-three members of seven families participated in our research (for an overview of families and their members, see Table 12.1). We describe our participants in three groupings: individual who lost their jobs (n = 7), partners of these individuals (n = 7), and children over the age of six living with their parents at the time of the job loss (n = 9).

Table 12.1: Participant Demographics Listed by Family and Individual (All Pseudonyms)

Background Information	Individual Who Lost Job	Partner	Child 1*	Child 2*
Family #1	Brad	Beth	Bets	Ben

(3 months since termination)		(Wife)	(Daughter)	(Son)
Age at the time of the job loss: 39.98 yrs.		39 yrs.	15.5 yrs.	12 yrs.

Background Information	Individual Who Lost Job	Partner	Child 1*	Child 2*
Education:	Graduate Courses	Some College	High School	Middle School
Religion:	Protestant	Protestant	Protestant	Protestant
Previous Employment:	Plant Manager (14 years)	Unspecified Job	------	------
Current Employment:	Unspecified Job	Unspecified Job	-----	-----

Family #2 (5 months since termination)	Stan	Sher (Wife)	Susie (Daughter)	Young Daughter
Age at the time of the job loss: 42 yrs.		39 yrs.	9 yrs.	-----
Education:	B. A.	B. A.	-----	-----
Religion:	None Reported	Roman Catholic	-----	-----
Previous	Plant	-----	Grade	-----

Employment: Engineer   School
             (11.5 years)

Current
Employment: Part-time Job Homemaker   -----   -----

Background Information	Individual Who Lost Job	Partner	Child 1*	Child 2*
Family #3 (3 months since termination)	Trevor	Tina (Wife)	Thom (Son)	Infant Daughter
Age at the time of the job loss:	39 yrs.	39 yrs.	16 yrs.	-----
Education:	Some College	Some College	Some High School	-----
Religion:	Lutheran	Roman Catholic	-----	-----
Previous Employment:	Senior Programmer/ Analyst (7 months)	Nurse	High School	-----
Current Employment:	Unspecified Job	Homemaker	-----	-----
Family #4 (8 months since termination)	Kevin	Kim (Wife)	Kurt (Son)	Kelly (Daughter)

	Individual Who Lost Job	Partner	Child 1*	Child 2*
Age at the time of the job loss:	42 yrs.	42 yrs.	10 yrs.	6.5 yrs.
Education:	Graduate Degree	Graduate Courses	-----	-----

Background Information	Individual Who Lost Job	Partner	Child 1*	Child 2*
Religion:	Christian	Evangelical (Born Again)	-----	-----
Previous Employment:	Architect Small Business (5 ½ years)	-----	Grade school. Scoliosis	Grade school.
Current Employment:	Unemployed	Homemaker	-----	-----

Family #5 (4 months since termination)	Donald	Donna (Wife)	Dave (Son)	-----
Age at the time of the job loss:	56 yrs.	53 yrs.	26 yrs.	-----
Education:	Some College	Some College	(not specified)	-----
Religion:	Roman Catholic	Roman Catholic	-----	-----
Previous Employment:	Commissioned Officer - U.S. Army (25 years)	-----	-----	-----

Current
Employment: 3 Part-Time Jobs   Bank Teller   Misc. Jobs

Background Information	Individual Who Lost Job	Partner	Child 1*	Child 2*
Family #6 (8 months since termination)	Mark	Meg (Wife)	Max (Son)	Missy (Daughter)
Age at the time of the job loss:	33 yrs.	31 yrs.	7.5 yrs.	4 months
Education:	B. A.	B. A.	-----	-----
Religion:	Lutheran	Protestant	-----	-----
Previous Employment:	Managerial Representative Small Family Business (6 years)	----- Life Insurance Company	2nd grade; Attention Deficit Disorder	-----
Current Employment:	Small Business Owner-Sales	Homemaker	-----	-----
Family #7 (18 months since termination)	Rick	Rita (Wife)	Russ (Son)	-----
Age at the time of the job loss:	53 yrs.	51 yrs.	15 yrs.	-----
Education:	MBA	B. S.	High School	-----

| Religion: | Roman Catholic | Roman Catholic | Roman Catholic | ----- |

Background Information	Individual Who Lost Job	Partner	Child 1*	Child 2*
Previous Employment:	Managerial - Upper Administration in the Phone Company (25 years)	-----	High School	-----
Current Employment:	Partner in a smaller start-up company	Wife originally was a part-time volunteer coordinator at the parish offices, then she became a part-time employee	-----	-----

*A child must be at least 6 years of age at the time of the job loss to be interviewed for this research project.

In *Family #3*, the wife (Tina), quit her nursing job about seven months prior to our interview (or four months before her husband lost his job) because of the birth of their youngest child. In *Family #4*, there are two additional children, aged two years of age and under, who were not interviewed. The father in this family was the only individual in our data set who had lost his job prior to the current job loss. Rodney lost two jobs before the current termination. The small architectural firm for which he worked filed Chapter 11 bankruptcy. The individual who lost his job in *Family #5* knew about the termination prior to the event because of governmental mandatory age and length of service requirements at the time our data were collected. *Family # 6* has older children who were neither living at home nor in close proximity during the time of the job loss.

Individuals who lost their jobs (n = 7) were white, male, married, Christian, 44 years of age on the average at the time of the termination (with a range of 33–56 years), and had 2 children (range of 1–4 children of whom no more than two usually were eligible to participate in the research because of age constraints). Prior to the job loss, they were employed in the following jobs: plant manager, plant engineer, senior programmer and analyst, architect, U. S. Army officer, manager of a small family firm, and manager in a large public corporation. They had worked for these organizations for average for 13 years (range is 7 months to 25 years). Six individuals had never lost a job before, whereas one experienced two job losses prior to the current termination and unemployment. One knew about the termination ahead of time because of seniority rules in his work context. Their severance agreements varied from just health benefits to a half year's compensation plus health, life, medical, outplacement, and re-education benefits.

Their partners (*n* = 7) were white, female, married, Christian, 42 years of age on average at the time of the termination (range of 31–53 years). Four classified themselves as homemakers and the rest worked part- or full-time jobs such as volunteer coordinator or bank teller. Finally, the nine children whom we interviewed ranged in age from 6.5 to 26 years (average was 11 years). Three were male and six were female. With one exception, they were in elementary through high school at the time of the job loss.

Procedures

A series of advertisements requesting research volunteers were placed in a metropolitan newspaper. Our four research participation criteria were: one family wage earner must have lost his or her managerial/professional job within the past 18 months; no member of the family could know the researchers; the family must consist of two adults and at least one child aged 6 years or older; and all members had to complete interviews and surveys requesting family background and demographics. We developed these criteria to ensure that the job loss was recent enough to assume that participants would recall details accurately and that we would obtain adults' and children's versions for comparison and for details of interest to these different generations. From two series of ads to which over 25 families responded to each, only seven families met all of our criteria. These families were promised and paid $50 for their participation in our project.

Trained interviewers scheduled appointments with participants at their homes. The authors trained these interviewers by reviewing interview protocols and providing feedback on their role playing of mock interviews and their gathering of demographic information. Interviewers switched the ordering of parents and children from one session to the next then ended with written questionnaires. Each family member was interviewed separately and in private. Respondents were provided with the researchers' phone numbers for follow-up questions about the project.

Interview protocols. Two versions of the interview protocol were developed based on whether the participant was an adult or a child. Primary questions asked participants about the job loss related to: (a) its effect on family communication, (b) changes in family dynamics and routines since the termination event, (c) accounts (of and reasons for the termination, and (d) metaphors for the job loss. Prior to our actual data collection, we pretested the children's version on three children ranging from seven to 11 years of age whose father had undergone a recent job loss. We utilized their data for pretest purposes only. For our data gathering, seven families produced 23 separate interviews (that averaged from one to 1.5 hours each) which were then transcribed verbatim (including nonfluencies and pauses) by a professional transcriptionist and double-checked by the interviewers and the researchers against the original audiotapes. At this time, all names were changed to pseudonyms. The transcripts totaled 117 pages of single-spaced text.

Analyses. Our analyses focused on the themes that surfaced consistently in family members' talk about their relationships, the effects of the job loss on individual family members, and on family communication as a whole. To analyze participants' discourse, we followed Rawlins's (1992) method of living with participants' voices and with interdisciplinary sources about work-family concerns, family communication, job loss, and related issues. To live with their voices and to develop themes true to participants' meanings and life experiences, we read and reread transcripts numerous times until semantic patterns emerged through repetition of exact phrasing, recurrence of similar phrasing, and forcefulness of expression as well as other nonverbal communication (see Hoppe-Nagao & Ting-Toomey, 2002; Janesick, 1994; Owen, 1984). Consistent with family storytelling approaches, we looked at the processes, structure, and content of stories as well as how the respondents reported these shifted over time. In doing so, we formed individual family members' time lines of their emotions, account changes, material changes, revelations of what was happening and why, and day-to-day activities. We continued our individual readings and discussion until we reached agreement about the nature of the tensions as well as the character of the stories and storytelling that emerged at that point of time. We returned to our transcripts to look for evidence within and across interview transcripts to support and, perhaps, disconfirm, the patterns that were emerging in our results. We wanted to portray commonalities across families as well as the individual craftings of stories that made each of our families unique.

Results and Interpretation

We found three interrelated narrative threads that centered on how family members narrated their understandings of and strategies for managing job loss discursively and materially. First, we found that our families privileged the individual (father) who lost his job in ways that sometimes diminished others' discursive and material contributions to the family. Second, the maintenance and reworking of family rituals and mundane aspects of daily life enabled families to re-create their familial values and integrity, as well as individual identities or parts to play in family performance. Third, family communication work was most evident in metaphors and efforts toward the construction of appropriate images that underlay individuals and familial discourse. These metaphors and images operated as sense making and coping strategies for families.

Crafting Privilege: Discursive and Material Contributions to Family

First, the individuals who lost their jobs, namely the fathers in our study, had authorial control but required the performative support of other family members to accomplish family. In this, the heterosexual, middle-class American family takes center stage as generational, male, and head of household roles overshadowed current contributions to discursive, financial, and family maintenance work. Throughout, the stories displayed *individuation-connection dialectics* (Baxter & Montgomery, 1996) in the content, telling, and reordering of the timeline since job termination. Echoing prior research, family storytelling reproduced gendered hierarchies, generational power, and heterosexual partnerships privileging husband over wife (Ochs & Taylor, 1995).

For instance, Donald and his family (family #5; see Table 12.1) focused on Donald's daily experiences as their top priority. For most of his interview, Donald discussed his prior work experiences and salary; his current overqualification for jobs; his extensive job search and interviewing process; and his need to patch together part-time employment. His son, Dave, and his wife, Donna, talked primarily about Donald's emotions and activities rather than their own feelings. In contrast, Trevor's family (#3) did not engage in collaborative storytelling and a singular focus on his experiences. His family was undergoing a period of turmoil not only because of this first time that he had lost a job but also with a new baby, a wife who had just quit her job to stay home with the children, and ongoing volatility in his line of work. Trevor described his emotions—"shock," betrayal, "anger"—but stressed his need for collaborative emotion work and authoring with his wife: "When I was angry, my wife was, too." He became depressed but she was still angry: "I felt kinda like I had lost an ally so at this period I didn't feel too good." During this time (a joyless "vacation"), they fought until they got "it back in order."

To get "it back in order," Trevor wanted and needed emotional and narrative synchrony primarily with his wife. Until he could control and coordinate the job loss account and familial response, he said that he felt lost. His family worked emotionally and narratively to empathize with him and make him central in their communication as a family. His wife, Tina, regretted not being in synch with Trevor but noted that she had just given birth and quit her job. She maintained that Trevor did not change much during the job loss although she said that he stayed in his bathrobe until afternoon hours, yelled more, and seemed upset. Her feelings were raw and conflicted because of her own situation as well as that of her family. Thom, their teenaged son, supported his father's head of household status by claiming that Tina's earnings were an addition to the main source of familial income (Trevor's pay from his contract jobs).

As their stories evolved over the course of the interviews, they exerted effort to privilege Trevor's situation and his desire to have everything "in order." In doing so, they maintained traditional hierarchical pairings: husband over wife, male over female, parent over child, family unit over individual desires. The individuation-connection dialectic surfaced repeatedly as members strove to address their own needs while also considering what they could do to help family members in need and the family as a whole.

If the family did not supply the support that the individual who lost his job needed, the father would look elsewhere. In the case of family #6, Meg did not fully support Mark's version of things but, over time, her job loss account and feelings merged with his. Meg said that she "tried to be positive about his ability to go out and find more work...but it was hard." She was "questioning why did you lose your job" but "then I started realizing how unfair they [previous employers] were." However, Meg was out of synch with Mark in one key area—namely, she was skeptical about Mark's new business venture and voiced her concerns repeatedly. Mark responded by saying that he talked to his father and other business associates because they expressed "a little more interest." He maintains strict public-private, work-family, male-female divisions. In sum, Mark and the other men who lost their jobs maintained authorial privilege over how family members developed job loss stories as well as the process of telling these stories. They described how they required the support and collaboration of family members and friends before they could effectively search for work. In this respect, family members' help in crafting a viable story and situating the father as central in the story seemed essential to the fathers' and families' adaptation to termination and unemployment.

Creating Family Resilience: Maintenance and the Reworking of Family Rituals and Mundane Aspects

Second, we found that family members exerted effort to (re-)create familial integrity and values as well as individual identities and roles. In this narrative thread, all the families described how they reworked or modified mundane family interaction patterns or routines as well as rituals. This discursive strategy coincided with material efforts to lower living costs but maintain the essence of family routines. In combination, the discursive and material efforts eased feelings of crisis and of stress. For instance, Kevin (family #4) discusses the time he has been able to spend with his family as a bright spot during his unemployment. He suggests he is able to participate in family rituals and activities more as a result of his unemployment.

Their comments in this narrative thread were marked by *predictability-spontaneity dialectics*. Predictability was found in the routine patterns of conversations, daily routines, weekly rituals or events; spontaneity occurred when family members were unsure of how and where such family patterns would take place. This spontaneity was both welcomed and nerve-racking, such as when family members were delighted that they could go on their scheduled vacation but some members expressed concern and stress-related reactions up to the time that the family members left their home. As Brad's daughter, Bets (age 16 years), put it, "I still went to Florida. I wasn't sure I could still go to Florida so that was nerve racking." As Bets noted, the adherence to past promises and routines offered a sense of comfort amidst understandable deviations from predictable patterns. Sometimes families needed to continue with planned events or rituals, such as vacations (or getting new clothes at the start of an academic year; see Lucas & Buzzanell, in press) to give them a sense of normalcy. In other cases, when the unfamiliar (e.g., not going to a nice restaurant for dinner) was couched within well-recognized routines (e.g., going out to dinner), family members considered events and family interactions to be "normal." The adherence to patterns in family communication, interactions, and events seemed to reduce the stress of job loss.

This effort to maintain a semblance of normalcy amidst chaos can be aligned with family resilience or ability to bounce back and reinte-

grate after the job termination and during the period of unemployment (see Buzzanell, 2010; Buzzanell et al., 2009). In the communicative construction of resilience, our participants worked toward a
construction of a "new normalcy" in their communication, actions,
and rituals. Families reported doing a variety of things that were
atypical for them—eating food out of their freezer and only shopping
for perishables, cutting back on purchases, discussing relocations and
whether they could afford children's lessons, vacations, or family
entertainment evenings—but they maintained those interactions and
rituals that were most important to them. As Mark put it, things
"never skipped a beat" and Trevor noted that they all took things "in
stride." They still purchased clothing and took music lessons, but
they reported weighing the necessity of these expenditures, whereas
they would not have questioned them before the job loss. For the
most part, families said that they did more with less.

They also subscribed to the idea of family, particularly parents, as
protectors of the children. The children were informed about what the
parents thought they needed to know when their parents believed
they needed to know it. For instance, Thom (family #3) did not know
that the family was moving until right before their relocation. Rita
(family #7) said, "I would assure him [teenaged son, Russ] that we
were doing okay and we're not down in the food like yet and there
was no chance ... [of dire circumstances]." Despite Brad's (family #1)
irritation that his wife and daughter thought that he was still a
"bank" and that their spending patterns should not change, he did
not discuss finances with them. He apparently shielded them from his
concerns so well that they continued consumption expectations and
practices well past his termination. Brad's daughter, Bets (age 16
years), said that her father's job loss was a "bummer" because he
could no longer provide everything to which she felt entitled: "Because you couldn't do the things you used to be able to do. You
couldn't get all the things you need to."

In short, family members lessened feelings of stress by adhering
to the beliefs that things were pretty much the same as before the job
loss. These things that remained the same were the family rituals,
roles, and interactions, whereas the locations and details of their

normalcy stories may have changed drastically depending on family circumstances.

Reworking Family: Telling Metaphors and Family Images

Family members coped with job loss by making a concerted effort to construct an image that enabled them to reframe their experiences and their roles in the family. For family #6, Mark's linguistic choices portrayed his need and effort to control, refashion, diminish the negative and reassert the positive, and construct a unified family in synchronized stories, feelings, behaviors, and outlooks for the future. At different points in his interview, he commented: It wasn't like a death but it was like an illness," "It wasn't the end of the world but it was pretty serious," "my wife ... she just thought it kind of rolled off my back," "No, it was the immediate shock and absolute bomb. But it didn't remain a bomb very long. There was a lot of anger. There were a lot of unanswered questions," and "so we never skipped a beat" and we're on "same side ... united. ..." Through his linguistic choices and imagery, Mark explains the devastating ("lot of anger") nature of his own and family's job loss crisis ("death" and "bomb") and his efforts to gain (he would have had responses to his "unanswered questions") and exert (his wife thought the loss "rolled off my back" because he tried to handle everything calmly so that the family "never skipped a beat") in the rhythm of their lives.

However, other family members tell different tales and use other imagery. Mark's son, Max, commented that he could no longer play with the son of his father's former employer ("Actually it is like a war," "Hatfields and McCoys") but his allegiances where with his father, his family. In that regard, he asserted repeatedly that they were a "normal family," they act "normal," and are a "regular family." Meg contributed to the image of a regular family in control and unified toward a common cause: maintaining the family. Meg stated that although the situation was "real devastating" at first, with it seeming as though "a weight [was] being lowered on us. It just put a tremendous strain on us at the time," her son was a "real trooper" and the entire episode may have been a "blessing in disguise."

In family #7, Rita said that the whole thing was "inconvenient ... an annoyance." She continued this metaphor by elaborating: "It was frustrating. ... It was inconvenient ... it's not a death. ... It was an annoyance. It wasn't a major loss. It was an annoyance that we had to work through." Her husband, Rick, maintained the trivializing or diminishing quality of Rita's remarks when he said that "It was like a speed bump." Kurt, a 10 year old in family #4, said, "it's pretty much normal." Overall, the seven family's metaphors captured the dialectic of stability and change. They verbally acknowledged the upending changes, challenges, and dire straits that the job loss imposed on them but their metaphors for their current lives displayed adaptation and reconstruction of a new normalcy. Their lives were not stable in a static sense but had reached a dynamic equilibrium through which they could anticipate routines and maintain their families.

For most families, the initial metaphors for the termination and immediate time period afterwards were imbued with disaster, disease, and traumatic images. Stan (Family #2) discussed feelings of uncertainty at first and likened his job loss to an illness, disease, cancer, bad joke, and ironic and cruel joke. Despite attempts to control life, his actions and emotional expressions promoted uncertainty. He could not seem to acknowledge his own feelings to his family so he described the effects of his job loss on his spouse rather than on himself. He did admit that he felt as though he was drifting, unattached, pressured to find some kind of work, bored, ostracized, and ashamed. Stan claimed that the job loss was not his fault and that he did nothing to deserve. Stan's "crushing" experience and moment of "trauma" occurred one week after termination when he signed up for unemployment and found himself in "a group of losers." Unlike the other fathers who lost their jobs, Stan seemed stuck because he did not, perhaps could not, construct a story that moved from anger and betrayal to some kind of resolution. Instead, his identity was shaken as he found his new comparison group to be "a group of losers."

Stan needed his family as primary sources of support, as well as his former co-workers, to help him realize that "it wasn't something I did" that resulted in the job loss. He was beginning to feel less "ostracized" with this self-confirmation at the end of his interview. In short, over time and with considerable family effort and control, the family images changed to those of regularity and normalcy in the ordinary conduct of their lives. These images and linguistic choices depicted a new normalcy over which family members exerted control by actively crafting the rhythms and content of their lives (see Buzzanell, 2010; Buzzanell & Turner, 2003).

Discussion

Jorgenson and Bochner (2004) comment on the importance of stories when they state that "our identities hinge largely on the stories we tell about ourselves and the stories we hear and internalize that others tell about us" (p. 515). In the stories of job loss, family members' identities are shaped by their attempts to construct the overall image of a normal, regular family in which the father is still the head of household and the stories, routines, relationships, and emotions align with or are in synch with a coherent version. To craft stories in which every family member can find meaningful parts, identities, and interests is a significant accomplishment. Through synchronized communication, everyday routines and rituals, and linguistic choices, family members could construct and retain what was important about their family and maintain family itself.

Because the findings in our study are based on a relatively small and homogeneous group of families, our findings would be extended productively by replicating our study in different contexts and for larger groups of people. Moreover, for future studies, researchers might examine job loss or other periods of family trauma and chaos through diaries or other tools that can capture non-retrospective data to figure out how and when such synchronized craftings of stories begins to occur and how these stories emerge over time. In addition, it would be useful to find out the extent to which the content, structure, and process of crafting familial stories at the time of job loss were consistent across groups of people in the United States and abroad. In different family configurations of diverse race/ethnicities, class, nationalities, and sexual-social orientations, other storytelling patterns and power dynamics might emerge.

Best Practices

Based on our findings, we tentatively offer some suggestions for families in crisis and for counselors or friends trying to assist individual members and the families as a whole to bounce back and reintegrate. These recommendations include encouraging multiple story versions from individuals' vantage points so that a family story might incorporate not only the family's best interests but also some of the interests and needs of individual family members. Family members could write or tell their stories individually. These personal stories would legitimate their own feelings and versions before members engaged in collaborative storytelling of a family narrative. After an acceptable and coherent family narrative is crafted, the individual stories could be reintroduced to note both how the individuals' stories have now changed and whether there should be greater complexity and diversity to the family story. Second, families should be encouraged to consider what interaction patterns, family routines, and occasional rituals are of greatest importance to them and are most telling of who their family was and is becoming. If these interaction patterns include family dinners in which everyone voices some bright spot in their day, then that is what should continue. The issue is that each family member should have some voice in maintaining the family rituals about which they feel most strongly and positively. Maintaining the focus on positive routines would enhance the well-being (and reduce negativity during this family crisis). Finally, individuals' metaphors of the job loss or other experiences might begin with language choices expressing shock, uncertainty, surprise, and so on. Over time, individuals can be assisted in reframing these metaphors so that a coherent image of their family and where they fit within family performances can occur.

Conclusion

In closing, job loss is, by all accounts, a devastating experience not only for the individual who is unemployed but also for family members who rely on that income and feel as though their entire worlds are changing. Given the importance of the family for attachments, safety, and production of identities, any communicative attempts that can assist families in working through job loss or other potentially destructive situations should be encouraged. Our chapter begins the effort in that direction.

References

Anderson, K., Unverson, D., & Elliott, S. (2004). Violence and abuse in families. In A. Vangelisti (Ed.), *Handbook of family communication* (pp. 629–645). Mahwah, NJ: Erlbaum.

Arthur, M.B., Inkson, K., & Pringle, J.K. (1999). *The new careers: Individual action and economic change.* London: Sage.

Baxter, L., & Montgomery, B. (1996). *Relating: Dialogues and dialectics.* New York: Guilford.

Berger, P., & Luckmann, T. (1967). *The social construction of reality: A treatise in the sociology of knowledge.* New York: Anchor.

Birkel, J. (1998). *Career bounce-back: The Professionals In Transition^SM guide to recovery and reemployment.* New York: AMACOM.

Buzzanell, P.M. (2010). Resilience: Talking, resisting, and imagining new normalcies into being. *Journal of Communication, 60,* 1–14.

Buzzanell, P.M., Shenoy, S., Remke, R., & Lucas, K. (2009). Intersubjectively creating resilience: Responding to and rebounding from potentially destructive organizational experiences. In P. Lutgen-Sandvik & B. Davenport Sypher (Eds.), *The destructive side of organizational communication* (pp. 530–576). New York: Routledge.

Cheney, G. Lair, D., Ritz, D., & Kendall, B. (2010). *Just a job? Communication, ethics & professional life.* New York: Oxford University Press.

Cheney, G., Zorn, T., Planalp, S., & Lair, D. (2008). Meaningful work and personal/social well-being: Organizational communication engages the meanings of work. *Communication Yearbook, 32,* 136–185.

Evans, K., & Maher, K. (2009, January 10). Yearly job loss worst since 1945. *Wall Street Journal.* Retrieved May 9, 2010, from http://online.wsj.com/article/SB123150742539367897.html

Finet, D. (2001). Sociopolitical environments and issues. In F.M. Jablin & L.L. Putnam (Eds.), *The new handbook of organizational communication: Advances in theory, research, and methods* (pp. 270–290). Thousand Oaks, CA: Sage.

Garrett-Peters, R. (2009). "If I don't have to work anymore, who am I?": Job loss and collaborative self-concept repair. *Journal of Contemporary Ethnography, 38,* 547–583.

Hoppe-Nagao, A., & Ting-Toomey, S. (2002). Relational dialectics and management strategies in marital couples. *Southern Communication Journal, 67,* 142–159.

Ibarra, H. (2003). *Working identity: Unconventional strategies for reinventing your career.* Boston: Harvard Business School Press.

Janesick, V.J. (1994). The dance of qualitative research design: Metaphor, methodolatry, and meaning. In N.K. Denzin & Y.S. Lincoln (Eds.), *Handbook of qualitative research* (pp. 209–219). Thousand Oaks, CA: Sage.

Jorgenson, J., & Bochner, A. (2004). Imagining families through stories and rituals. In A. Vangelisti (Ed.), *Handbook of family communication* (pp. 513–540). Mahwah, NJ: Lawrence Erlbaum.

Kalleberg, A. (2008). The state of work (and workers) in America. *Work and Occupations, 35,* 243–261.

Kirby, E., Golden, A., Medved, C., Jorgenson, J., & Buzzanell, P.M. (2003). An organizational communication challenge to the discourse of work and family research: From problematics to empowerment. *Communication Yearbook, 27,* 1–44.

Lair, D., Sullivan, K., & Cheney, G. (2005). Marketization and the recasting of the professional self: The rhetoric and ethics of personal branding. *Management Communication Quarterly, 18,* 307–343.

Langellier, K.M., & Peterson, E.E. (1993). Family storytelling as a strategy of social control. In D. K. Mumby (Ed.), *Narrative and social control: Critical perspectives* (pp. 49–76). Newbury Park, CA: Sage.

Langellier, K.M., & Peterson, E.E. (2004). *Storytelling in daily life: Performing narrative.* Philadelphia: Temple University Press.

Langellier, K.M., & Peterson, E.E. (2006). Family storytelling as communication practice In L. H. Turner & R. West (Eds.), *The family communication sourcebook* (pp. 109–128). Thousand Oaks, CA: Sage.

Latack, J.C., Kinicki, A.J., & Prussia, G.E. (1995). An integrative process model of coping with job loss. *Academy of Management Review, 20,* 311–342.

Leana, C.R., & Feldman, D.C. (1992). *Coping with job loss: How individuals, organizations, and communities respond to layoffs.* New York: Lexington.

Leroux, M., & Jagger, S. (2009, January 27). Job losses mount as downturn steepens. *New York Times Online*. Retrieved May 9, 2010, from http://business.timesonline.co.uk/tol/business/economics/article5594832.ece

Liem, R., & Liem, J.H. (1988). Psychological effects of unemployment on workers and their families. *Journal of Social Issues, 44*(4), 87–105.

Lin, X., & Leung, K. (2010). Differing effects of coping strategies on mental health during prolonged unemployment: A longitudinal analysis. *Human Relations, 63,* 637–665.

London, M. (1998). *Career barriers: How people experience, overcome, and avoid failure*. Mahwah, NJ: Erlbaum.

Lucas, K. (2006). *No footsteps to follow: How blue-collar kids navigate postindustrial careers*. Unpublished dissertation, Purdue University, W. Lafayette, IN.

Lucas, K., & Buzzanell, P. M. (in press). It's the cheese: Collective memory of hard times during deindustrialization. In J. M. Cramer, C. P. Greene, & L. M. Walters (Eds.), *Food as communication: Communication as food*. New York: Peter Lang.

Marin, K., Bohanek, J., & Fivush, R. (2008). Positive effects of talking about the negative: Family narratives of negative experiences and preadolescents' perceived competence. *Journal of Research on Adolescence, 18,* 573–593.

National Institute of Justice. (2007). *Causes and consequences of intimate partner violence*. Washington, DC: U.S. Department of Justice. Retrieved May 9, 2010, from http://www.ojp.usdoj.gov/nij/topics/crime/intimate-partner-violence/causes.htm

Newman, K.S. (1988). *Falling from grace: The experience of downward mobility in the American middle class*. New York: Free Press.

Newman, K.S. (1993). *Declining fortunes: The withering of the American Dream*. New York: BasicBooks.

Ochs, E., & Capps, L. (1996). Narrating the self. *Annual Review of Anthropology, 25,* 19–43.

Ochs, E., & Capps, L. (2001). *Living narrative: Creating lives in everyday storytelling*. Cambridge, MA: Harvard University Press.

Ochs, E., & Taylor, C. (1995). The 'father knows best' dynamic in dinnertime narratives. In K. Hall & M. Bucholtz (Eds.), *Gender ar-*

ticulated: Language and the socially constructed self (pp. 97–120). New York: Routledge.

Owen, W.F. (1984). Interpretive themes in relational communication. *Quarterly Journal of Speech, 70,* 274–287.

Putnam, L.L., & Boys, S. (2006). Revisiting metaphors of organizational communication. In S. R. Clegg (Ed.), *Handbook of organization studies* (pp. 541–576). Thousand Oaks, CA: Sage.

Putnam, L.L., & Fairhurst, G.T. (2001). Discourse analysis in organizations: Issues and concerns. In F.M. Jablin & L.L. Putnam (Eds.), *The new handbook of organizational communication* (pp. 78–136). Thousand Oaks, CA: Sage.

Rawlins, W.K. (1992). *Friendship matters: Communication, dialectics, and the life course.* New York: Aldine de Gruyter.

Rifkin, J. (1995). *The end of work: The decline of the global labor force and the dawn of the post-market era.* New York: Jeremy P. Tarcher/Putnam.

Socha, T. (1999). Communication in family units: Studying the first "group." In L.R. Frey (Ed.), D.S. Gouran, & M.S. Poole (Assoc. Eds.), *The handbook of group communication theory and research* (pp. 475–492). Thousand Oaks, CA: Sage.

Socha, T. (2008, July). *Communication and the good life.* Keynote address to the NCA Institute for Faculty Development, held at Randolph-Macon College, Ashland, VA.

Socha, T. (2009). Family as agency of potential: Toward a positive ontology of applied family communication theory and research. In L. Frey & K. Cissna (Eds.), *Routledge handbook of applied communication research* (pp. 309–330). New York: Routledge.

Sonnenfeld, J. (2007). Firing back: How great leaders rebound after career disasters. *Harvard Business Review, 85*(1), 76–84.

Stone, E. (2004). *Black sheep and kissing cousins: How our family stories shape us.* Edison, NJ: Transaction Publishers.

Voydanoff, P. (1983). Unemployment: Family strategies for adaptation. In C.R. Figley & H.I. McCubbin (Eds.), *Stress and the family. Volume II: Coping with catastrophe* (pp. 90–102). New York: Brunner/Mazel.

Chapter 13

Sibling Alliances in Family Crises: Communication Surrounding Redefinitions of Family

John H. Nicholson and Steve Duck

In this exploratory study, 200 narrative accounts of sibling alliances were collected to determine how siblings create alliances to meet family-related problems. Of the 200 accounts, 100 were of successful alliances, and 100 were accounts of unsuccessful alliances. Thirty-nine accounts were identified as examples of "sibling crisis alliances." Accounts include examples in which siblings ally with one another to help their parents reconcile, avoid divorce, stop drinking, quit smoking, and respond to catastrophic injuries. Shotter's (1984) notion of "joint action" is used to explain how siblings coordinated their action. Results show that successful and unsuccessful alliance attempts can benefit the sibling relationship and the larger family. Sibling relating, rather than relatedness is highlighted. Sibling crisis alliances are shown to be potentially pivotal events in family life, and they are capable of reshaping the family in ways not recognized in earlier studies.

Families and Siblings

Dunn (1996) characterizes the sibling relationship as "The First Society" (p. 105), because a sibling relationship is often a child's first experience in a social group which extends beyond their parents. Most children grow up with siblings (over 80% of the people in the United States do so), care for or are cared for by siblings, and fight and play with siblings (Dunn, 1996) and hence experience a very broad range of social activity within this key relationship. For many individuals the sibling bond will also be their longest lasting familial bond, often extending from earliest childhood to old age (Dunn, 1996). Siblings also share a commonality of experience and shared understanding that may surpass nearly every other relationship across the lifespan (Floyd, 1996). The sibling relationship is one that is marked by change; change reflecting developmental and relational growth (Bevan & Stetzenbach, 2007; Dunn & Munn, 1986). The sibling relationship can influence the development of pro-social behavior (Dunn & Munn, 1986), cognitive development (Azmitia & Hesser, 1993), and social understanding (Dunn, Brown, Slomkowski, Tesla, & Youngblade, 1991). Despite the significant and unique contributions made by sibling relationships (Dunn et al., 1991), most research on development in children "has focused on parent-child or peer relationships, and thus...the significance of siblings remains largely uncharted" (Azmitia & Hesser, 1993, p. 431).

While largely uncharted, the relationship between siblings has recently garnered research attention in communication and in research outside the communication discipline. A substantial amount of the sibling research in developmental psychology and in related fields such as family therapy is centered on issues such as sibling rivalries, sibling sexual abuse, other manifestations of sibling aggression, sibling adjustment to disabled brothers and sisters, and the loss of a sibling to death. Whereas much research focuses on negative dimensions of sibling relationships, Dunn and her associates have done plenty in the last decade to address questions surrounding the influence and development of sibling relationships (see Dunn, 1996, and Boer & Dunn, 1992). In their research program, built around seven years of longitudinal study of siblings, Dunn and associates have begun to articulate the profound influence siblings have in each others' lives and in the life of the family. Siblings are often not only playmates, but also enemies, sources of comfort, and perhaps most importantly, resources for understanding and for relating within the family constellation. The current study seeks to continue to illuminate the profound role siblings / children play in family life.

The family communication literature is currently dominated by a view of "families" that treats them as parent-centered and marital dyads with a cast of ancillary, but second rank, players. As a result, sibling relationships have been understudied in family communication, and when studied, they often are examined from a parental perspective. When sibling relationships have been studied more extensively (as they have in developmental psychology) they are treated as rivalrous (Dunn, 1996). With the exception of Myers and Members of COM 200's (2001) study of sibling relational behaviors, and one relatively recent study of sibling communication rules by Roghaar (1995), we know practically nothing of sibling cooperation and even less of the ways in which communication is at work in sibling relationships, particularly from the perspective of the siblings themselves. Tevin, Martin, and Neupauer (1998) explore sibling relationships, but focus on verbal aggressiveness; as do Martin, Anderson, Burant, and Weber (1997). It is important that this gap in family communication literature be filled and surprising that it has not been, given the influence of systems theory upon which family communication research is overwhelmingly based. While more and more research explores marital dyads, it is not supplemented by research on siblings, and as a consequence, our understanding of the family is limited and skewed. In particular we know little of the influence of siblings on the family.

We do have recent family communication studies examining sibling relationships in greater detail. Kramer and Baron (1995) explore the relationship between parent's experiences with their siblings and its influence on how they parent their sibling children as siblings. Folwell, Chung, Nussbaum, Bethea, and Grant (1997) examined the closeness felt between adult siblings, while Kitzmann, Cohen, and Lockwood (2002) demonstrated the importance of siblings in developing pro-social skills that led to better peer relating practices. Myers (2002) study demonstrated the ongoing significance and influence of siblings across the life span among twin pairs. Myers & Members of COM 200 (2001) described the significance of relational maintenance behaviors in sibling relationships and the link between sibling liking and expressions of positivity. Bevan, Stetzenbach, Batson, and Bullo (2006) demonstrated the uniqueness of the sibling relationship on scales of partner and relational uncertainty and topic avoidance. Rittenour, Myers, and Brann (2007) revealed that closeness in the sibling relationship tends to be stable across the life span, and Myers, and Bryant (2008) identified behaviors associated with sibling commitment and satisfaction. Oetzel, Ting-Toomey, Chew-Sanchez, Harris, Wilcox, and Stumpf showed that different facework and conflict strategies were employed by participants in recalled conflicts with siblings as opposed to conflicts with parents. So, while recent work has helped develop a more developed understanding of siblings, large gaps remain.

The current study and the others in this volume will serve to give a more complete view of family communication characteristics and patterns. This study seeks to contribute to filling the gap in family communication research as it relates to siblings with a study of sibling alliances, specifically sibling crisis alliances using their own accounts. This study also includes narrative accounts from siblings rather than results from statistically based questionnaire results. We believe that narrative accounts are critical to helping us explore the details of sibling crisis alliances and their effects on siblings and their role in family life.

Alliances and Coalitions

Current research, as well as dictionaries, use and define the words "alliance" and "coalition" interchangeably. Alliances are defined as "a merging of efforts or interests by persons, families, states, or organizations. An alliance may apply to any connection entered into for mutual benefit"(*Random House Dictionary*, 1969, p. 36). The purpose of the alliance may be to accomplish some goal, and an alliance may or may not be formed against someone else, which will be called a "target" of the alliance. However, when one enters into an alliance with a target involved, one enters *with* others and *against* others simultaneously.

Researchers have explored the importance and influence of coalitions or alliances in families. Bank and Kahn (1975) first mentioned coalitions in their 1975 study. Gilbert, Christensen, and Margolin (1984) looked at alliances in non-distressed versus multi-problem families. Larson and Richards (1994) explored cross-generational coalitions. Cissna, Cox, and Bochner (1990) addressed the importance of a unified marital coalition that was "for the marital dyad" and "against the children" within blended families. Vuchinich, Wood, and Vuchinich (1995), and Vuchinich and Angelelli (1995) examined coalitions in the context of family problem solving activities. Myers (1998) specifically points to the need for research into sibling coalitions.

In family communication literature, alliances in the family are primarily discussed and researched as they concern and involve one or more of the marital partners. In Cissna et al. (1990), for example, the members of the marital dyad in a blended family are encouraged to present a united front (or coalition) to the children in the blended family. Larson and Richards (1994) discuss cross-generational alliances, most typically involving the mother and a child. Ignored by these studies and the research on alliances or coalitions are considerations of both the presence and influence of sibling alliances. Sibling alliances were not addressed in Vuchinich and Angelelli (1995) or Vuchinich et al. (1995), and they were not presented as desirable in Cissna et al. (1990). In Noller, Feeney, Peterson, and Sheehan (1995), siblings are studied, but the relationship is viewed as one which *reflects* rather than influences the conflict and interaction styles of the family (including alliances between a parent and one child). Furthermore, in Cissna et al. (1990), the parental coalition is seen as functional, as is the parental coalition (within limits) in Vuchinich and Angelelli (1995) and Vuchinich et al. (1995). Only in Gottman (1996) and Larson and Richards (1994) is an alliance involving a child presented as even moderately functional, but even then, it is less desirable than a parental alliance, and only functional as a defense mechanism against a parent. Milevsky (2005) examines emergent role of siblings in compensating for shortcomings in the amount and degree of support individuals garner from their parents and their peers. While Milevsky (2005) does examine sibling relationships, it does so from a position of secondary significance to the parental and peer relationships as it looks at how sibling relationships compensate for shortcomings in other relationships, and not vice versa.

So, in short, research presently under-represents alliances involving children and siblings, and subordinates them to parental/marital alliances. Children are shown to use sibling relationships to compensate for deficiencies in parent-child relationships, or they develop sibling relationships that reflect parent-parent and parent-child interaction patterns (Noller et al., 1995). There is no research that discusses the circumstances under which siblings will ally among themselves or for what purpose(s). This is perhaps largely attributable to the adult/parental focus of most research, which has been slow to recognize the agency of children and the ability of children to coordinate their actions against parents or in the face of other exigencies.

Siblings are often studied from a perspective that positions them almost exclusively as individuals (not as components of a *system*) and as rivals. The sibling rivalry literature presents a perspective of siblings as independent and autonomous people who frequently have other people (the other siblings) hindering their attainment of a goal. By contrast any focus on sibling alliances shifts that perspective. Siblings in the present study are conceptualized as interdependent people who are negotiating roles, responsibilities, and goals within a family system that includes other siblings, as well as parents.

Sibling alliances are the flip side of sibling rivalry. Instead of looking at times when siblings are pitted against one another, as in sibling rivalries, this study will look at times when siblings combine their efforts. Beyond looking at times when siblings combine their efforts, this study specifically seeks to explore times when siblings combine their efforts for some family related or family centered reason.

Family life, like relational life is typified by everyday experiences and punctuated by turning points, including a family crisis (Baxter, Braithwaite, & Nicholson, 1998). What counts as a family crisis can differ from one family to another, from one family member to another, and from one researcher to another. If a circumstance is called a crisis, then the responses of those involved may be understood as "crisis responses." Parents and children in a family may experience a parental fight, pending divorce or separation, or tobacco and alcohol use by a family member as a problem, situation, or as a family crisis. Family members "make" a situation a crisis by behaving as if it is a crisis. One member of a family (potentially any member) may invite other family members to confront a crisis situation using a "crisis alliance."

The purpose of this study is to explore sibling alliances in general, crisis alliances in particular, and how siblings initiate, coordinate, and execute alliances with one another. This study looks at alliances from the perspective of the siblings, rather than that of parents. The term "alliance" is preferred over "coalitions" because it connotes the insider position of the siblings in such a relationship. Coalitions connote relationships that *others* enter against one's self. This project seeks to emphasize the "insider" perspective of the sibling(s). Therefore, the term "sibling alliance" is used to refer to relationships entered by siblings with one another against other individuals, coalitions, institutions, or obstacles, with an identifiable purpose. A "sibling crisis alliance" is a special sibling alliance initiated in response to a perceived family crisis.

The following research questions were addressed:

RQ1: How are sibling alliances initiated?

RQ2: What do siblings say to one another in initiating alliance attempts?

RQ3: What types of family crisis can prompt a sibling crisis alliance?

RQ4: What do siblings say to one another concerning the goal(s) of alliance efforts?

RQ5: Communicatively, how do siblings coordinate their activities?

Methods

Participants were asked to complete a form to gather some biographical data for descriptive purposes. Open-ended questions were used in the main questionnaire to solicit accounts of one successful and one unsuccessful intra-familial sibling alliance. The larger study also included questions designed to gather information about the rules operating in alliance formation and execution, and a comparison of sibling and friendship relationships. Those data and results are not included here.

Participants

Participants were enrolled at a large midwestern university except for one, who was the parent of a student. Students were offered extra credit for their participation, and participants were asked to record their accounts electronically using a word processor. One hundred respondents composed the convenience sample. Seventy-eight subjects were female, and twenty-two were male. The average age of respondents was just under 22 years ($M = 21.99$, $SD = 4.61$) with a range of 19 years to 48 years. Ninety-six percent of all respondents were 24 years old or younger. When asked to indicate all of those people they considered to be part of their family, ninety-two subjects indicated that they had 2 parents (including natural parents, step-parents, and foster parents), (M = 2.11, SD = .40). Respondents had an average of 2.12 siblings (including natural or adopted siblings, step-siblings and foster siblings). No other demographic data were collected.

Analyses

Typologies in all categories were derived through the analytic induction method (Bulmer, 1979; Dey, 1993). Existing research and typologies served to sensitize the researcher to certain issues or potential categories in the data. However, using this method, no a priori scheme was imposed. Rather, a coding scheme was created through an iterative process between the data and the coding scheme at all stages. A secondary analysis was conducted to differentiate those alliances formed in response to a family crisis from those alliances created in response to a less critical situation or circumstance.

Results

RQ1: How are sibling alliances initiated?

How sibling alliances are initiated includes (a) the person(s) who initiated the alliance, or the "who," and (b) the manner in which the alliance is initiated, or the "how" or "why."

Not surprisingly, almost 75% of all reported alliances were initiated by one or more siblings. Responses showed that one out of five alliances began through "joint action" or they "just happened." Less than 7% of all the reported alliances were initiated by any other person or combination of persons. While it remains unclear what percentage of intra-familial alliances in families involving two or more siblings are initiated by a sibling, the overwhelming majority of alliances in this data set were initiated by one of the siblings / children in the family. This emphasizes that children (siblings) are proactive agents within their families. This point gains even more support when including the results of the remaining research questions.

Talk was found to be central in the process of initiating alliances. Over 50% of reported alliances were begun through what has been called "explicit talk," including a request by one ally to another sibling, family member, or an outsider. In many of these cases, one sibling asks for support from one or more other potential allies, and the other(s) come on board immediately. Some of the alliances started when one sibling told the other(s) about a situation, and without making a formal request, allies just joined together. This supports a belief that allying occurs with enough frequency, that an invitation from one sibling to another to join in an alliance need not be explicit. In fact, an explanation of the situation often served as enough of an "invitation" to prompt a sibling to join.

In just 8.5% of the alliances other siblings had to be begged, or vigorously persuaded to join the alliance. In such situations, allying presents the challenge of gaining the support of siblings first including balancing multiple goals, then the challenge of helping the alliance attain the goal for which the alliance was formed. Fourteen percent of all of the alliances began when siblings were talking, sometimes about a specific situation or problem, sometimes just chatting in general, and they realize or conclude that they need to do something, and the alliance begins. Responses indicated that more than 10% of the alliances "just happened."

Nine percent of the alliances began when a sibling did something which prompted an alliance and which won the support of other siblings. In one example, a respondent wrote of an alliance involving the teenage respondent and his 6 year old brother, Will who was crying:

> The alliance got started because of the fighting that would occur between my mom and [respondent's older brother] Josh, both physical and verbal. I just grabbed [Will's] arm and took him out of the room; later, however, I told him that we should stick together so that he doesn't get involved in the fighting. Will responded by saying okay. (16-S)

In this example the alliance was initiated first by the action of the one sibling removing a younger sibling from an altercation involving other family members. After the siblings were outside the immediate situation that prompted the alliance, they confirmed their alliance verbally. The threat and experience of physical violence made this a crisis alliance.

RQ2: What do siblings say to one another in initiating alliance attempts?

In the questionnaire, data were solicited seeking to establish whether siblings or allies said anything to one another in order to get others to join the alliance attempt, and if so, the form of "request" that was made. In almost 40% of the alliances, nothing was said to get others to join an alliance. These alliance instances may also be examples of joint action moments, where the simultaneous recognition of a need by both parties prompts them to ally, but the parties may feel that that the alliance, as one respondent put it, "just happened"(163-S). Theoretically, those alliances that "just happened" are particularly significant. Shotter's notion of "joint action" is used later in the discussion to make sense of these alliances (1984). In almost 30% of the alliances there was some discussion about the situation, but no direct request involved. Combined, the two largest categories account for almost 70% of all reported alliances. This seems to indicate that in those reported alliances, there was at least some mutuality in the initiation of alliances.

Twenty-two percent of the alliances began with a direct request from one ally to another. In some of these cases it is clear that one ally was unaware of the situation, and that the request served as an invitation to join in an alliance, in addition to familiarizing the prospective ally with the situation and the goals. One respondent revealed both the ease with which they could be enlisted by their sibling into an alliance and the form a request from their sibling to join in an alliance might take, saying, "I was only about 11, making Jody 18. I, of course, looked up to my big sister, and honestly, the only thing she had to say was, 'Hey, let's ...'" (89-S).

In other situations, the request serves an almost coercive function. In these situations a sibling may be made aware of the situation, but doesn't want to join, or doesn't share the same goals. The request can actually serve as a loyalty test. To ask a brother or sister, as one respondent's sibling did, "Will you help me hide this from mom and dad," is to place the sibling in a situation where two obvious alternatives are presented: "I'm with you," or "I'm not with you." One respondent indicated that although she didn't want the sibling to accomplish their goal, they felt like that had no real choice but to help the sibling. The respondent indicated that she felt some relief when the alliance failed, because she had done her "duty" and the sibling relationship was not damaged.

Allies used direct appeals to loyalty, "guilt trips," or other appeals in less than 6% of the reported cases, and in only one case was a direct threat to hurt the sibling used. This result may be evidence of the inherent undesirability of having an ally that isn't wholeheartedly committed to the alliance. Allies rely upon each other to perform critical functions, and a less than enthusiastic ally could cripple the alliance at any point. In the following situation, the only somewhat willing sibling ally did his duty, but wavered and struggled with his decision:

> I [agreed to the alliance] because I didn't think it was a big deal. Then after I thought about it, I realized he could get in a lot of trouble. But it was too late, because I promised. I couldn't back-stab my brother, I would feel bad if I got him in trouble. Also, then there would be a possibility that he would tell my parents something I wouldn't want them to know about me. He would also be expected to defend me at a later date.
>
> The way I look at it is that I was almost forced to do something that I knew was wrong, because we had this so called alliance. I felt trapped because either way I would have been betraying someone's trust. (60-S)

While this sibling did follow through and fulfill his obligation to his sibling, it seems likely that there would be times when a sibling in a similar situation would fail to do so. The data serves to support the notion that an unwilling ally may be more of a liability than an asset to the other ally/allies. When allying, especially in situations where the stakes are high, the enthusiastic or unwavering support and commitment of other allies can be critical.

RQ3: What types of family crisis can prompt a sibling crisis alliance?

Thirty-nine of the 200 accounts collected were classified as crisis alliances. Several different and surprising exigencies led to a family crisis and a subsequent sibling crisis alliance. Parental marital issues (n = 6), including heated arguments, divorces, and possible reconciliations, prompted siblings to form alliances to respond to the crisis. Multiple health related crises also motivated crisis alliances (n = 17), including alcohol abuse by a parent or sibling, tobacco use and cancer concerns, weight loss problems, catastrophic injuries to a sibling, and concerns for a lonely and a depressed parent. In the sample one sibling's coming out crisis prompted an alliance, as did parental physical abuse of a sibling, and a sibling's failing grades in school also prompted alliances. In one of the most compelling examples, the siblings tried to help their parents reconcile and avoid divorce. The kids tried to arrange a romantic evening to bring their parents together again. Once the alliance and the siblings' goal was made known, the parents confronted the alliance and the crisis in their family:

> The "romantic evening" never did take place but something even better came out of it. My parents both were present for the evening, but did not contain any dinner and romance but rather it contained a lot of talking as a family. My parents discovered what my brother and I had attempted to do and they collaborated as friends in working through this difficult situation with us. As a family we went to counseling which helped me a lot because I discovered that my anger was not really anger at all but pain and fear of losing my family. My brother too benefited from the counseling and became less anxious about the divorce. Throughout mine and my brother's childhoods and adolescence we had both our parents by our sides and although they may have not been married, they were still our parents and still are our parents forever.
>
> My brother and I are both in college now and we sometimes laugh about our little attempt to reunite our parents. In fact, our whole family often recalls this time and although it seems silly now, both my brother and I know how real our feelings and emotions were. We will always recognize the way we pulled together to work toward a common goal and I will always feel a close bond with my brother because of that time and all the times of hardships during the divorce.
>
> Although my brother and I did not achieve our goal which was to keep our parents married, we helped to keep our family's communication lines open and not confused. Through our silly plan to reunite our parents, my brother and I had each other to talk to and share our feelings with. We also communicated with our parents and did not keep our feelings inside. The

alliance with my brother and I may not have been successful in reaching our goal, but my family are all winners in the end because of that alliance. (1-S)

RQ4: What do siblings say to one another concerning the goal(s) of alliance efforts?

This question is intended to explore what siblings say, if anything, regarding, for example, the goals of the alliance, their feelings about the alliance (whether they express hope or doubt about their chances in succeeding), or particular plans for accomplishing their goals. Respondents were asked to indicate if there was specific goal talk, and then to indicate what was said or what occurred in those conversations.

In over 80% of the reported cases, respondents indicated that there was "goal talk," defined as talk about participants' goal(s), particular plans or roles to perform, and specific things to do and things to avoid doing. The previous example shows a time when the allies shared the same goals. The talk that is categorized as "goal talk" is made up of talk between allies that seeks to iron out details of the alliance that includes the goals of the alliance, but which may extend beyond the clarification of goals. More goal talk may be required if the goal is vague, or if the allies share multiple goals, and/or when siblings have different goals, or when the outcome is critical.

While the amount of planning varied greatly from one account to another, there are some details that siblings "hammer out," and times when siblings engage in conversations to confirm that they are "on the same page." One specific time when this seems to occur is when one sibling is unfamiliar with what needs to be done. This occurred in the data when a sibling ally was being introduced to the situation, when particular sibling allies were regarded as too young to understand complexities that older siblings perceive, and when the siblings were confronting a situation unlike others they previously confronted. In those situations siblings were more likely to make sure there was agreement about a plan. For example:

I was too young to understand what goals really were and all I knew was that what I was supposed to do would [achieve the goal]. My brother did keep saying that if I did what he said then we would get our way. I guess in that sense he discussed our goal. (127-S)

It would make sense that the more "conventional" the situation or goal, the more likely siblings are to understand what is needed and the smaller the need for the micro-management and micro-negotiation of details. For example:

> Nothing was talked about directly between my sister and I. I overhear the arguments because they are usually being screamed through the house. I protect my sister by voicing my opinion in a calm tone versus her, in a heated mood, she tends to have an angry tone. My sister and I have similar viewpoints because many of the battles she has with my parents, I had as well when I was younger. I see where my parents were wrong with me and I try to explain things to them through more mature eyes now.
>
> [Did you and your sibling(s) talk about each person's goals? If so, indicate what was said.]
>   No, like I said before, there is usually no discussion, I join in on the conversation on my own terms based on previous experience with my parents. (29-S)

However, the more unique the situation, the more uncertain the means of realizing the desired outcome, and the grander the scale of the alliance, the more necessary goal talk and micro-management and micro-negotiation become. More planning and direction may also be necessary if a particular sibling is performing a role that is new for them, or if a sibling is cast in a role in which they don't know how to do what is required for alliance success. But, there are times when no goal talk occurs. One respondent explained it this way: "We didn't need to talk about what our goals were. They were pretty clear to us" (26-U). If the goal is clear to the participants then there is no need for discussion among the sibling allies about the goals. It may be that goals are most clear when (a) the situation is one that has been encountered before by the siblings, and (b) when the situation is perceived to be straightforward. Such straightforward alliances may signal a unity of perspective also in keeping with Shotter's (1984) notion of "joint action." One respondent wrote, "we did this all the time, so no talk was needed" (18-U). When one sibling is beating up the other two siblings, the goal of stopping the older sibling is easily recognized (perhaps by all involved parties) for precisely the reasons articulated above. What is clear from the data, though, is that more talk surrounded the coordination of allies' actions than goals.

RQ5: Communicatively, how do siblings coordinate their activities?

In over 70% of the reported alliances, "explicit talk," or talk whose purpose was to coordinate intentions and activities, was used by the sibling allies. This result emphasizes the centrality of talk in accomplishing alliance performance. Two examples follow:

> During the planning stage of reuniting our parents, I designated my brother to invite our dad over to watch football on TV with him and I would get our mom to be home also for their "romantic evening" together. I planned to do the cooking and organizing while my brother's only part was to get our dad over and to keep his mouth shut. The conversations we had were often me telling my brother what to do and him following up with agreement. (1-S)

The reported sibling alliances varied from well-scripted performances to spontaneous, unplanned, and improvised performances. Each demands different skills from the siblings in order to be successful. Highly scripted performances worked effectively if the siblings properly predicted the responses of targets and other situational variables, constructed their plan accordingly, and then executed their assigned roles effectively. It apparently takes insight and skill to accomplish all of these tasks and to coordinate the actions of all the siblings prior to the actual events. Respondents indicated that these skills were developed through practice (rehearsal) and also over time as experience teaches the siblings (a) what they must account for in a given situation, as well as (b) how targets will respond. One respondent wrote, "We know how to play mom and get our way" (185-S). Another respondent wrote:

> We knew not to gang up on dad. If we did, he would just say no and that would be it. So, we agreed to go up to him one at a time and wear him down. It always works. I mean, we are experts at this [predicting their dad's responses]. (71-S)

Allies can also employ a different strategy. Instead of trying to account for the many possibilities and contingencies, siblings can establish goals, assign roles, and then improvise the script. This type of alliance coordination demands less skill in the planning stage, but perhaps more skill and a more intimate knowledge of one's allies in the performance. One respondent wrote, "I am sure that we talked to decide what we were going for. But, once we knew what we were going for we just went and did it" (101-S). Another respondent offered, "We know what the other is going to do, so we never plan that" (113-S).

While it is interesting to discover what occurred in the coordination talk, what may be of greater interest are those cases where explicit talk was missing. In over one-third of the reported alliances no explicit talk was reported by respondents. In 21.5%, respondents reported "playing it by ear," or just determining and doing what needed to be done, as it needed to be done. In a previously cited example, a respondent indicated that an alliance was spontaneously initiated when "...we both kind of just attacked him at the same time." In that example, when asked how the allies worked out who was going to do what, the respondent indicated, "We didn't" (16-S).

This manner of conducting an alliance would seem to demand greater confidence among allies than one where the details are planned out in advance. The source of that confidence is unclear. Data were not collected to explore this particular issue. When siblings had previously confronted a similar situation they coordinated their activities based upon that prior alliance. One respondent indicated that he and his sisters had established the roles or actions each sibling was to enact. Another respondent indicated that she and her sister knew each other so well, that each can anticipate the actions of the other and respond appropriately. This strategy also allows greater latitude for adaptation and improvisation should circumstances change or targets respond in some unexpected manner. One respondent wrote, "We just know what the other is going to do, and go with the flow. I can't really explain it, we just do it" (54-S).

In 15% of the alliances, respondents indicated that some conversation took place to coordinate their actions, and some things were explicitly left to be worked out as things happened. In 12% of the alliances respondents remarked that there was no coordination talk because none was needed; that is, everyone knew what to do. One respondent says as much when describing an alliance, "There really wasn't much to be talked about. We all knew what we had to do" (2-S). It would be incorrect to say that there was no need for coordination, however. The coordination had, in fact, already taken place in previous alliance episodes. This might be similar to a basketball team running a pick and roll play. No words would be needed because the play had been run and perfected in practice, and everyone understood their role in the performance. Shotter might say that such "rehearsals" could help generate the prerequisites for "joint action." Beyond knowing how it should be run ideally, experienced and well practiced siblings might also better understand how they should respond in situations calling for adaptation or improvisation.

The desirability of improvisation may be mitigated or minimized by several factors including the significance of the goal to one or more of the allies; where the greater the rewards of accomplishment and/or the consequences of failure may make improvisation too risky. One respondent wrote, "This was too big a deal for me to let her [younger sister] screw it up [like she had done before] so we spent a lot of time talking about what we would all do" (40-S).

When siblings are very small children, it seems most likely that almost all sibling alliances that are coordinated would be so coordinated face to face. This may of course include nonverbal as well as verbal codes. However, as siblings age the phone, e-mail, text messaging and even letters become more convenient and practical communication channels for many siblings. In fact, as siblings leave their family of origin, the use of alternative channels may be necessary in order to coordinate alliances.

In almost all of the reported alliances, face to face coordination is primary. In most of the cases reported, the telephone was used when face to face was impractical or impossible due to distances that separated allies. While alliances of this sort were not the most frequently reported type, they were also not rare.

Discussion

When seeking to understand alliances, communication is central. Other disciplines, such as psychology and sociology may look to psychological measures and institutional factors affecting alliance development and coordination. However, for the respondents in the reported study, how someone thinks and feels about an alliance (what a psychologist might study) has been shown to become significant in alliance accounts only when those feelings are made manifest in what they (sibling allies and targets) did behaviorally and communicatively. Knowing the institutional and structural limits and pressures placed upon siblings (what a sociologist might study) was also less important than how alliance participants responded to those forces. Those responses were and are communicative responses. Our understanding of sibling alliances in practice must be an understanding that extends from our understanding of the communication that creates the social world in which alliances occur.

The goals of the alliances evident in the data ranged from the mundane, "trying to get out of doing daily chores," to the critical, "trying to help a family member in a medical emergency." Because the seriousness and urgency of the alliances varies so dramatically, one should be cautious when trying to characterize all sibling alliances or alliance attempts. Clearly, they vary as much as the families and relationships they touch. However, some useful insights are generated by, or are verified through, these data.

The sibling alliances reported in the data were most likely to include only 2 siblings as allies, and to therefore be initiated by a sibling. Most alliances were initiated through explicit talk, but indirectly, rather than through an explicit request. In most of the alliances siblings engaged in goal talk where they would establish and clarify the goals of the alliance and where specific plans would be established. Alliances were more likely to be worked out in multiple talk episodes than they were likely to be discussed only once or worked out exclusively "in the flow" of events. Alliance failure and alliance success were most commonly evaluated based upon the alliance achieving or failing to achieve the established goals of the alliance. Alliance success or failure was found to be linked to 3 key factors: (1) siblings' ability to properly understand the situation and predict the responses of targets; (2) siblings' ability to perform their roles and their executing them properly; and (3) the siblings' attitude toward the alliance and commitment to the alliance and their allies.

The targets of the alliance were just as likely to respond positively to an alliance attempt as they were likely to respond negatively. When outsiders were aware of alliances, they were more likely to be pleased or otherwise respond positively. Alliance attempts were almost as likely to affect the relationships among the sibling allies as to not affect them. However, when there was an effect on those relationships, it was much more likely to be positive. Most of the alliances had no effect on the relationships between targets and the sibling allies. However, when there was a change in those relationships as a result of an alliance, it was about as likely to be negative as it was likely to be positive.

Centrality of Sibling Alliances

While not every sibling crisis alliance (SCA) will have a profound effect on the family, some SCA's change the family forever. In one poignant example siblings ally to confront a parental marriage crisis, including spousal physical abuse after each child individually had unsuccessfully tried to change the situation. The respondent wrote:

> The goals were simple: the first was to stick together no matter what occurred; the second was to make it known to them how we felt after each time that they fought, and try to make them realize that they were hurting more than each other.

> Basically I told Will [six year old brother] that we needed to show them that we are not invisible in this situation, and then I remember him saying "yeah 'cause sometimes I'll scream and they won't even look at me. They'll just keep fighting." I told my brother that it was okay to speak up, and assured him that they wouldn't get mad at us for telling them how we felt. He was afraid, and gave me an uncertain "O.K.!?" I knew that if he would have spoken up that it was all we needed to get through to them, so I continued to build his confidence, and let him know that I was going to lead and support him.

> After one of their fist fights, Will and I went in to the kitchen while they were still making up. I started by telling them that they need to "for once stop this fucking hugging bullshit if they were ever going to hit each other again." I continued by saying, "We both need to talk to you and expect your full attention." I then started by telling them how hard it is to watch your family fight and then Will started crying. He said it all with every tear that

ran down his cheeks, and then screamed "I hate it!" That was all that got said. I proceeded to go cry in my room as my mom and Dad realized the pain they were causing everyone. Thankfully it worked, and although we had planned it a bit smoother, it was just fine.

We didn't talk about it for quite a while because it was such a powerful moment of change that we kind of blocked out the bad times so that we could relish the good. It took us about four years to really talk about it. Then we would just laugh about it in front of my mom and Dad, mocking how they acted and how ridiculous they looked. A few months ago I confronted my parents with the seriousness of that at dinner. I told them that the fighting really affected me in the way that I grew up my making me more self-reliant because I couldn't talk to anyone I felt. That's all that was really said though, my mom cried and apologized, and that was as far as it went.

Why did you consider the alliance successful?

Because of the fact that together we accomplished something that had been looked over when we approached the situation alone. (16-S, Note: all names have been changed.)

Joint Action

Many of the alliances in the data demonstrate what Shotter calls "joint action" (1984; 1993). In joint actions participants coordinate without any prior intention or goal to create a given outcome. In joint action moments the participants coordinate to create a single voice of two parts, or a single message with two composers, or (seemingly) no composer. Communicatively, the two parties work like one, but "the outcome of joint action is thus essentially independent of any particular individual's wishes or intentions" (Shotter, 1984, p. 144). Shotter goes on to extend his position beyond those moments outside interacting parties' intentionality by recasting individual intentionality:

People must interlace what they do in with the actions of others. We remain ignorant of quite what it is we do, not because the "plans" or "scripts", etc., supposedly in us somewhere informing our conduct are too deeply buried to bring out easily into the light of day, but because its informative influences are not wholly there within us to be brought out. The actions of others determine our conduct just as much as anything within ourselves. In such circumstances, the overall outcome of the exchange is simply not up to us; in fact, it cannot be traced back to the intentions of any individuals. Thus rather than being experienced as a product of those actually producing it, it is experienced as an event which *just happens*. (1984, p. 100) (Italics added.)

Theoretically, among the most interesting accounts are those instances when things "just happened." Shotter's (1984) idea of "joint action" has been used to explain alliance events that in their entirety "just happened" as well as events or moments within the alliance that "just happened." Joint action allows us to understand the emergent and highly fluid nature of interactions, as well as the role that all of the interacting parties play in constructing/creating the events as they occur. While people do plan and anticipate (and siblings are not exceptions) the spontaneous and the unpredictable nature of some interactions cannot be adequately accounted for theoretically when only considering plans and strategies. Joint action accomplishes this by allowing for planning and accounting for the unpredictable.

The critical ingredient for a joint action moment or event, is an intersection or correspondence of the *Umwelten* of two or more social beings (Shotter, 1984). Put simply (or as simply as it can be put), the concept of *Umwelten* can be thought of as a worldview, or way of seeing, understanding, and engaging the world and the social creatures that inhabit that world; complete with responsibilities, patterns of relating, and norms of interaction. Joint action moments occur when the interacting parties view and engage the situation they are in (and that they are constructing) from or using the same *Umwelten*. That way of seeing the world is so powerful that it can be perceived by the interacting parties as a force outside them, acting upon them, and making the situation or conversation move outside the boundaries of their intentions, "scripts," or control. At those moments, however, the interacting parties and their *Umwelten are* constructing the situation, even as their *Umwelten* is constructed by the situation and the interacting parties. Further examples from the data will bring the concept of *Umwelten,* and the issue of scripts and performance, into clearer focus. It is the conclusion of this study that it is through relating that the shared vision that generates joint actions that "just happen" with siblings. It is not a product of their relatedness as siblings, rather it is a result of their relating as siblings.

The importance of sibling alliances for siblings

Siblings are defined as such in relation to one another. Simultaneously, they are children of their parents. As young children, they are reliant upon their parents for many things. This "disempowered" position makes it necessary for children to rely upon the kindness, generosity and goodwill of their parents. It also encourages children to develop their skill at getting things from their parents. Parents make rules, grant permission, are a source of necessary resources and funding for siblings/children. Parents may be the only agents capable of changing rules, granting necessary permission, or supplying required monetary or other resources. Thus, siblings benefit from being proficient at lobbying for rule changes, for permission, and for support (financial or otherwise). Children/siblings may, in a very real sense, enjoy tremendous benefits as a result of being expert manipulators of their parents.

In many of the non-crisis accounts in the data, the penalties for unsuccessful efforts are often slight when compared to the benefits that may be enjoyed if successful. Often, the penalties for being "caught" manipulating, or "scheming" as one participant put it, against parents may be limited to angering the parents. Given that, many siblings seem to treat those alliances where they are specifically trying to get a rule changed, or to get their parent(s) to buy a car for them, or install a swimming pool, as situations where they have nothing to lose. In a previously cited example, the respondent indicated that she and her sister decided to try to get their parents to include them on a vacation the parents were going to take to Europe. Although they had little hope for success, they proceeded anyway with the respondent explaining, "the worse they [the parents] could do was say no" (40-U).

In several cases, respondents indicated that their parents (when they were the targets) would say, "Nice try, kids" (65-U). The parent(s) would confirm that they were aware of the alliance, and sometimes they would even acknowledge that the kids devised and implemented a good plan. Some respondents would indicate that the alliances had no effect on their relationship with their parents because, "[their parents] know that we do this all the time." Sibling alliances of that type and in those families are obviously a normal part of everyday life. But, a crisis is different. A divorce in a family is a crisis for the children/siblings still living with the parents and the consequences of the divorce have a measureable negative impact on male children and their peer relationships (Lindsey, Colwell, Frabutt, & MacKinnon-Lewis, 2006). Sibling crisis alliances may serve to mitigate that negative effect and to thwart divorce. Particular responses in the data tell of some siblings successfully allying to intervene in a parental marital crisis. It is critical that the transformative power of sibling crisis alliances be noted and accounted for in theories and research on marital relationships. Children in a family system are not just influenced by the quality of the parental marriage, they can transform the marriage or the post-divorce relationship the parents create.

Why siblings form alliances

Simply put, siblings form alliances to accomplish goals that they could not accomplish on their own. This is consistent with much of the small group literature that posits that we do some things together because we could not do them alone (Johnson & Johnson, 1997). This study did not explore when siblings would individually engage in activities similar to those pursued using alliances. Such information would allow for useful comparisons to distinguish which goals and activities are pursued more frequently, or exclusively, through alliances, and which goals or activities are not considered appropriate for alliances.

Changes over time

The developmental nature of sibling relationships is well established (Dunn & Munn, 1986). While little communication literature addresses this issue, Roghaar's 1995 study does identify rules and rule changes that come about as a result of changes in sibling relationships over time. Roghaar notes that as siblings mature into adulthood they often grow to appreciate their sibling more, become closer to them, and fight less (1995). Her study further notes that interaction rules among siblings also change over time.

The age of siblings also influences the roles they are capable of performing. The age of a sibling or siblings and the relationships between siblings and targets can also influence the roles siblings will play. One respondent wrote:

> Since James was the youngest, and mom's "favorite" he got to do the talking and convincing with her. I got father duties due to our close relationship, and Jon was the go between, meaning that whomever was struggling at that particular time would get Jon to throw in his two cents. It was almost implied who would talk to who based on our knowledge of the relationships that we had with our parents as well as our ages at the time. (128-U)

Each sibling is unique, and each sibling brings particular characteristics and abilities that affect their performance potential in an alliance. In the example above, the respondent points to the relationship a particular sibling has with a particular parent (target) as one determining factor for the siblings in assigning or determining the role a sibling will occupy. These relationships, and the abilities of each sibling, will also likely change over time.

Patterns of allying

It seems likely that patterns of allying develop in families, just as patterns of antagonism (called rivalry between siblings) develop (Roghaar, 1995). A greater understanding of the patterns of allying could give insight into the complex dynamics within the family, and the constantly developing and changing relationships between siblings and between siblings and parents. Patterns of allying may also illuminate the reasons for which siblings will ally, and the reasons for which siblings frequently form alliances. It may also reveal "standing alliances." A standing alliance would be the result of an ongoing commitment between two or more family members (including siblings) to stick together, despite the circumstance. In those cases, which are hinted at in some of the accounts in this data set, an alliance would be presumed by the allies. Roghaar (1995) identified a sibling rule that stated that siblings should "stick up for each other" (in an alliance) against their parents. In situations such as those where a standing alliance may be operating, the need for explicit communication may diminish, and the possibility of sophisticated cues and codes among the allies become more likely.

Best Practices

When confronted by what *they perceive* as a crisis, siblings will sometimes join their efforts in alliances. Siblings coordinate to try to stop parents from fighting with one another, to stop violence against other family members, to address a health crisis such as alcoholism or tobacco addiction, and to provide support after an incapacitating health event. Divorce necessarily locates the marital dyad at the center of the crisis, but we must recognize that siblings are sometimes actively working to reduce the likelihood of divorce, to get separated parents back together, and to make real their sense of the proper family dynamic. Parents, counselors and researchers would do well to fully embrace the intersecting, parallel and sometimes alternate family experience of the siblings/children of the family system.

Siblings are not ancillary characters or part of a supporting cast in their own family experience. Siblings represent a critical family constellation in both the everyday experiences of siblings, and particularly at critical times in a family's journey. Family members and those working with them should encourage the recognition of the significance of siblings in shaping one another's experiences, and in fostering the health and wellness of the larger family system.

A child is ushered into sibling *relatedness* with the birth or adoption of another child, and children become stepsiblings with the blending of families. But sibling *relating* is more important than sibling relatedness. Earlier research has conceptualized and represented the sibling bond as involuntary and permanent, and while this is a commonly shared perspective, it is nevertheless off the mark. The fact that 2 people are called brothers, sisters, or siblings does not define their relationship, it merely labels it. The best practice is to remember that siblings make, remake and change their relationship as they relate. Sibling relating is at the true heart of sibling relationships. Therefore emphasizing the significance of how siblings interact and relate is more important than the fact that they are siblings.

Limitations

Clearly, communication between siblings in the process of doing an alliance would be ideal, but was impractical for the limited scope

of this study and the time constraints within which it is being produced. Because it is a "first look" at the domain, we believe that our
efforts in gathering data were maximized by compiling accounts
using questionnaires, instead of completing a much smaller number
of in-depth interviews. Still, this could be considered a limitation.

The design of this project, using questionnaires, was quite successful at generating details of what happened in alliance events. It
was, however, only moderately successful at identifying the particular communicative activities that contributed to those outcomes.
Future studies, using an interview design, or direct observation of
alliances would serve better in that capacity.

References

Azmitia, M., & Hesser, J. (1993). Why siblings are important agents of cognitive development: A comparison of siblings and peers. *Child Development, 64*, 430–444.

Bank, S., & Kahn, M. (1975). Sisterhood-brotherhood is powerful: Sibling subsystems and family therapy. *Family Process, 14*, 311–337.

Baxter, L., Braithwaite, D., & Nicholson, J. (1999). Turning points in the development of blended families. *Journal of Social and Personal Relationships, 16*, 291–313.

Bevan, J., & Stetzenbach, K. (2007). Jealousy expression and communication satisfaction in adult sibling relationships. *Communication Research Reports, 24*(1), 71–77.

Boer, F., & Dunn, J. (Eds.). (1992). *Children's sibling relationships: Developmental and clinical issues.* Hillsdale, NJ: Erlbaum.

Bulmer, M. (1979). Concepts in the analysis of qualitative data. *Sociological Review, 27*, 651–677.

Cissna, K., Cox, D., & Bochner, A. (1990). The dialectic of marital and parental relationships within the stepfamily. *Communication Monographs, 57*, 44–61.

Dey, I. (1993). *Qualitative data analysis: A user-friendly guide for social scientists.* London: Routledge.

Dunn, J. (1996). Siblings: The first society. In N. Vanzetti & S. Duck (Eds.), *A lifetime of relationships* (pp. 105–124). Pacific Grove, CA: Brooks/Cole.

Dunn, J., Brown, J., Slomkowski, C., Tesla, C., & Youngblade, L. (1991). Young children's understanding of other people's feelings and beliefs: Individual differences and their antecedents. *Child Development, 62*, 1352–1366.

Dunn, J., & Munn, P. (1986). Siblings and the development of prosocial behavior. *International Journal of Behavioral Development, 9*, 265–284.

Floyd, K. (1996). Communicating closeness among siblings: An application of the gendered closeness perspective. *Communication Research Reports, 13*(1), 27–34.

Folwell, A., Chung, L., Nussbaum, J., Bethea, L., & Grant, J. (1997). Differential accounts of closeness in older adult sibling relationships. *Journal of Social and Personal Relationships, 14*(6), 843–849.

Gilbert, R., Christensen, A., & Margolin, G. (1984). Patterns of alliances in non-distressed and multi-problem families. *Family Process, 23,* 75–87.

Gottman, J. M. (1994). *What predicts divorce: The relationship between marital processes and marital outcomes.* Hillsdale, NJ: Erlbaum.

Johnson, D., & Johnson, F. (1997). *Joining together: Group theory and group skills.* Boston: Allyn & Bacon.

Kitzmann, K., Cohen, R., & Lockwood, R. (2002). Are only children missing out? *Journal of Social and Personal Relationships, 19*(3), 299–316.

Kramer, L., & Baron, L. (1995). Intergenerational linkages: How experiences with siblings relate to the parenting of siblings. *Journal of Social and Personal Relationships, 12*(1), 67–87.

Larson, R., & Richards, M. H. (1994). *Divergent realities: The emotional lives of mothers, fathers, and adolescents.* New York: Basic Books.

Lindsey, E., Coldwell, M., Frabutt, J., & MacKinnon-Lewis, J. (2006). Family conflict in divorced and non-divorced families: Potential consequences for boys' friendship status and friendship quality. *Journal of Social and Personal Relationships, 23*(1), 45–63.

Martin, M. M., Anderson, C. M., Burant, P. A., & Weber, K. (1997). Verbal aggression in sibling relationships. *Communication Quarterly, 45,* 304–317.

Milevsky, A. (2005). Compensatory patterns of sibling support in emerging adulthood: Variations in loneliness, self-esteem, depression and life satisfaction. *Journal of Social and Personal Relationships, 22*(6), 743–755.

Myers, S. A., & Members of COM 200. (2001). Relational maintenance behaviors in the sibling relationship. *Communication Quarterly, 49*(1), 19–34.

Neyer, F. (2002). Twin relationships in old age: A developmental perspective. *Journal of Social and Personal Relationships, 19*(2), 155–177.

Noller, P., Feeney, J., Peterson, C., & Sheehan, G. (1995). Learning conflict patterns in the family: Links between marital, parental, and sibling relationships. In T. J. Socha & G. H. Stamp (Eds.), *Parents, children, and communication: Frontiers of theory and research* (pp. 273–298). Mahwah, N J: Erlbaum.

Random House Dictionary of the English Language, Laurence Urdang, editor in chief, Staurt Berg Flexner, managing editor. (1969). New York: Random House.

Roghaar, L. A. (1995). Talking about rules in young adult sibling conversations: An exploration of everyday interaction rules and thematic content. Unpublished doctoral dissertation, The University of Texas at Austin.

Shotter, J. (1984). *Social accountability and selfhood.* New York: Basil Blackwell.

Shotter, J. (1993). *Conversational realities. Constructing life through language.* Thousand Oaks, CA: Sage.

Tevon, J. J., Martin, M. M., & Neupauer, N. C. (1998). Sibling relationships: Verbally aggressive messages and their effect on relational satisfaction. *Communication Reports, 11,* 179–186.

Vuchinich, S., & Angelelli, J. (1995). Family interaction during problem solving. In M. A. Fitzpatrick & A. L. Vangelisti (Eds.), *Explaining family interactions* (pp. 177–205). Thousand Oaks, CA: Sage.

Vuchinich, S., Wood, B., & Vuchinich, R. (1995). Coalitions and family problem solving with preadolescents in referred, at-risk, and comparison families. *Family Process, 33,* 409–424.

Chapter 14

Communication Challenges of Parenting in Homeless Families

Fran C. Dickson, Justin P. Borowsky, Kathryn Tiffani Baldwin,
Jennifer Kelly Corti, Daniel Johnson, Lucie Lawrence,
and Joseph Velasco

This study examines the communication challenges associated with parenting among homeless families. Following semi-structured interviews with forty-four homeless parents, thematic analysis (Owens, 1984) identified five major parenting challenges: maintaining privacy, surrogate parenting, managing health issues, managing legal issues, and maintaining stability. In addition, the analysis revealed three communication strategies homeless parents employed in talking about the family's homelessness to their children: concealment (reframing reality and avoidance); reassurance (emphasizing togetherness and faith); and openness (open discussion of the family's present living situation).

This study examines the communication challenges associated with parenting among homeless families. According to the Urban Institute (2000) approximately 3.5 million people in the United States experience homelessness, and an estimated 25% of homeless individuals are under the age of 17 (U.S. Department of Housing and Urban Development, 2007). Approximately 29% of emergency shelter users are families (U.S. Department of Housing and Urban Development, 2007). While it is difficult to estimate the number of homeless families on the streets today, the recent mortgage crisis may significantly increase the number of homeless families. As parents lose their homes, the need for parenting their children remains constant. As a result, the purpose of this study was to examine the parenting strategies that homeless families employ when talking to kinds of conversations homeless parents have with their children about their homelessness.

In the 2008 Annual Homeless Assessment (AHA), the U.S. Department of Housing and Urban Development estimated that there were as many as 759,000 sheltered and unsheltered homeless people in America. This number can fluctuate greatly depending on the season, for example, January 2006 saw as many as 205,000 families residing in shelters. Perhaps the most disturbing statistic concerning homelessness is the rising number of homeless families. Recognition of the rise in the homeless family population has stimulated research concerning the characteristics of homeless family members (McChesney, 1990, 1995) and the effects of homelessness on mothers and their children (Anooshian, 2003; Cosgrove & Flynn, 2005; Wadsworth, Raviv, Reinhard, Wolff, Santiago, & Einhorn, 2008). Few (e.g., Lindsey, 1998) have addressed how homelessness has affected communication dynamics in the family. Therefore, the current study seeks to contribute to the knowledge of homeless families by observing family communication, focusing on messages about and meanings of family life for homeless families.

Defining Homelessness

Given the often constant fluctuations in the homeless population, estimating the exact number of homeless people in America is a difficult task. Homelessness is a multi-layered construct that is difficult to define. To begin to explain the homeless experience, it is important to illuminate who the homeless are and what characterizes their homeless experiences. The Annual Homeless Assessment Report to Congress (2007) makes distinctions among the homeless population based on the types of homeless spells that are experienced. Those who are homeless for a short period of time are considered to experience *crisis* homelessness, those who are homeless for a long period of time are *chronic,* and those who experience it off and on are considered *episodic.*

The Annual Homeless Assessment Report to Congress (2008) reported that 1,150,000 people used shelters or transitional housing during a six month period in 2006; just over a quarter were families with children. Women represent 83% of the adults entering shelters with their children. Many of those women are single mothers (The Second Annual Homeless Assessment Report to Congress, 2008). Well over half (61%) are African American, and 40% of these families consist of four or more people (The Second Annual Homeless Assessment Report to Congress, 2008). In addition, families tend to stay predominantly longer in shelters and transitional housing than do unaccompanied men and women. The median length of stay for families was 37 days in emergency shelters and 135 days in transitional housing (The Annual Homeless Assessment Report to Congress, 2008).

Further, because the nature of the homelessness often changes, defining homelessness can also be challenging. For the purposes of this study, we defined *homelessness* as not having a stable residence for which one assumes primary responsibility. In this case, a mother and her daughter living in a friend or relative's house would be considered homeless even though they are not living in a shelter or on the streets. The statistics reported in the AHA represent those families who are physically homeless, meaning they are living on the streets or in a shelter, and would describe the mother and daughter living at a friend or relative's house not as homeless, but rather as "precariously housed." This population is often seen as being at imminent risk for homelessness and indeed faces many of the same challenges encountered by the physically homeless family. For this reason, this study includes both the physically homeless and the precariously housed.

Homeless Families and Parenting

Research concerning the effects of homelessness on the health and well-being of homeless families reports increased stress levels for all family members (McArthur, Zubrzycki, Rochester, & Thomson, 2006; Russell, Harris, & Gockel, 2008; Sobolewski & Amato, 2005; Wadsworth et al., 2008) as well as for relatives of homeless families (Polgar, Pollio, & North, 2006). Past and current research rarely examines communication within homeless families as is the focus of this study. Drawing on multidisciplinary research the following sections review what is known about homeless families, homeless family members, and the social interaction within the homeless family members.

Parenting. While attention has focused on demographics and resource struggles of the homeless and homeless families, a lack of attention has been paid to the family relationships of homeless families as embodied and constructed through family communication. Nonetheless, the existing literature does offer insight into parenting and parent-child relationships by addressing how parenting behaviors may be affected by homelessness, including how homeless parents view their parenting and its effects on their children.

Researchers have documented a strong association between child competency and parenting qualities including warmth (i.e., positive affect displays), contingent responsiveness, inductive discipline, and encouragement of autonomy (Dornbusch, Ritter, Leiderman, Roberts, & Fraleigh, 1987; Putallaz & Heflin, 1990). Parents faced with poverty and homelessness may experience tensions between providing for basic survival needs and enacting effective parenting qualities, such as the behaviors listed above. Obviously, stressors associated with homelessness (e.g., lack of social support and compromised physical and mental health of parents) may hinder parents from providing for all of their children's needs. Specifically, recent research sheds light on the complexity of parenting under the stressors of poverty, revealing that parents experiencing poverty may feel negatively about their parenting skills and ability to provide for their children (Russell, Harris, & Gockel, 2008); in addition, other research has indicted that social support does not predict negative nor positive parenting, and that mental health is not a significant mediator of negative parenting (Torquati, 2002). As a result, these research findings challenge our current understanding of parenting and provide a warrant for further research that examines homeless families and the parenting challenges that homeless parents face.

Mothers and Children. Although being homeless is associated with many problems, it may also strengthen family ties. According to Lindsey (1998), homeless mothers experienced increases in emotional closeness as well as the quality and quantity of their interactions with their children. In addition, Boxil and Beaty (1990) revealed that older children with younger siblings took on parental responsibilities in an attempt to comfort their mothers as they struggled within the constraints of shelter rules. Despite reports of homeless mothers and their children becoming closer through their homelessness, other studies (e.g., Molnar, Rath, & Klein, 1990) also report a high degree of ambivalence in homeless preschoolers' relationships with their mothers and a high prevalence of depression among homeless mothers.

With the majority of homeless families headed by single mothers (Kondratas, 1991), caretaking is an issue for many mothers. Many homeless mothers have little contact with friends or relatives and can count on few people in times of need (Letiecq, Anderson, & Koblinsky, 1999, 1998). Therefore, as a result, homeless mothers may receive less help from their families than housed mothers.

Fathers and Children. There have been few studies on homeless fathers, perhaps due to the sheer numbers of homeless families that are headed by single mothers. Although little is known about homeless fathers and their experiences, available research suggests that homeless fathers face unique challenges such as developing parenting skills as well as receiving emotional and material support (Schindler & Coley, 2007). For many men who become custodial parents, their parental role and responsibilities experience a sudden shift often associated with their homelessness (i.e., divorce, loss of employment), resulting in anxiety and frustration about not knowing how to care properly for their children.

Men often find that they do not have the emotional and material support they need to help them build parenting skills. For example, many men are not able to stay with their children in shelters due to rules prohibiting men from staying at family shelters. Such rules confound the problem that few services are available to homeless fathers and their children.

Rationale and Research Questions

The goal of this study was to identify the special challenges and communication strategies that are associated with being a homeless family. The value of studies such as this extends beyond the generation of scholarly knowledge to address a very practical need. Recent downturns in the U.S. economy—as illustrated by the increase of bankruptcies and foreclosures, as well as record-setting crude oil prices and the unprecedented implementation of an economic stimulus package—underscore the need to further explore understudied family interactions that occur in the homeless or precariously housed family. To further explicate the challenges and strategies associated with living in homeless conditions, we identify parenting challenges experienced by parents who are homeless and identify the strategies that homeless parents utilize in talking about their homelessness to their children. To this end, we explored the following two research questions:

RQ 1: What are the communication challenges associated with parenting while homeless?

RQ 2: What are the parenting strategies that homeless parents utilize in talking about their homelessness?

Method

Design and Procedure

Upon gaining approval from the institutional review board and event directors, parents in homeless families were recruited during their participation at a one-day urban outreach event for the homeless hosted at a midsized western university. Flyers describing the project were distributed to potential participants via the welcome packets given to each homeless attendee upon registration at the event. After receiving the provided services associated with the outreach event, interested parents were escorted by event volunteers to research team members, who were easily identifiable in event-approved black research team T-shirts. Upon meeting potential participants, research team members secured a quiet location on the event grounds to complete the 15–40 minute, face-to-face tape-recorded interviews. Participants were initially asked several basic demographic questions regarding age, ethnicity, education, marital status, duration of homelessness, living arrangements, employment, pets, and children's demographics (age, gender, and schooling). Participants then engaged in semi-structured, focused interviews led by individual and paired research team members, who had received sensitivity training on working with at-risk research populations. A total of fourteen questions were asked. Specifically, the first eight questions were designed to allow participants to share and discuss their communicative experiences as parents in homeless families. The final six questions were added at the request of the event directors to obtain specific insights from the participants on helpful ways to prevent homelessness and were not relevant to this study. In appreciation of their participation, participants were given a twenty-five dollar gift certificate to a local grocery store after completion of each interview.

Participants. We conducted 47 interviews with homeless parents including 14 males and 33 females with an average age of 34.89 (*SD* = 8.92) years. The sample contained 15 (31.9%) Caucasians, 15 (31.9%) African Americans, 9 (19.1%) Latino/a, 5 (10.6%) multi-racial, 1 (2.1%) Native American, and two participants did not identify their ethnicity. The marital status of the sample was as follows: 18 (38.3%) were married, 16 (34%) were single, ten (21.3%) were divorced, and three (6.4%) were separated. The average number of children per family was 2.42 (*SD* = 1.79) and the average age of the children was 10.63 (*SD* = 7.43) years. The average number of pets was .34 (*SD* = .71).

The average duration of the families' homelessness was 15.48 months (*SD* = 27.78). Twenty (42.6%) families currently lived in shelters, twelve (25.5%) lived with family members, seven (14.9%) lived in rental units, three (6.3%) lived with friends, two lived in hotels, and two lived outside. Eighteen (37.5%) individuals were employed, and 30 (62.5%) were not. Of those who were employed, 14 worked full-time and four worked part-time. The education level of the participants was as follows: 15 participants had some high school education, eight had graduated from high school, eight had their GED, one had a vocational degree, 13 had some college, one participant had graduated from college, and one participant did not disclose their educational level.

Analysis and Verification. The interview data was analyzed using Owen's (1984) thematic analysis. Analysts coded for specific themes that emerged from data based on recurrence (same thread of meaning), repetition (same word or phrase), and forcefulness (paralanguage). Research team members listened to the recorded interviews multiple times, transcribed the interviews, and read over the transcripts several times before they began the coding process. During the initial phase of coding, research team members individually underlined key words and phrases in seven transcripts (approximately 18 percent of the data) that emerged given their recurrence, repetition, and forcefulness. As key ideas started to appear and reappear in the transcripts, research team members began to identify emerging themes from the interview data. Team members wrote analytic memos and detailed notes throughout the coding process to describe these potential themes. Following their individual analyzes research team members met and reviewed their memos, notes, and ideas concerning emerging themes and to discuss similar findings and resolve any discrepancies. The team members reached consensus on an initial set of themes that were then used as a coding guide by team members to analyze the remaining interviews, with the possibility that additional themes might emerge during this second wave of coding. Upon completion of the second phase of coding, team members then met jointly for a second data analysis meeting. They reached consensus regarding the final list of themes through discussion (Table 14.1).

Table 14.1. *Themes*

Parenting Challenges
    Maintaining Privacy
    Surrogate Parenting
            Support
            Institutional Undermining
    Managing Health Issues
            Maintaining Cleanliness
            Physical and Mental Health
            Problems with Drugs and Alcohol
    Managing Legal Issues
    Maintaining Stability

Strategies for Talking about Homelessness to Children
    Concealment
            Reframing Reality
            Avoidance
    Reassurance
            Maintaining Togetherness
            Having Faith
    Openness

Results and Interpretations

The first major analysis identified five themes associated with the parenting challenges experienced by homeless parents: maintaining privacy, surrogate parenting (including the categories of support and institutional undermining), managing health issues (including the categories of maintaining cleanliness, physical and mental health, problems with drugs and alcohol), managing legal issues, and maintaining stability. In addition, we identified three major themes associated with the communication strategies homeless parents utilized in talking about the family's homelessness to their children: concealment (including the categories of reframing reality and avoidance), reassurance (including categories of maintaining togetherness and having faith), and openness (including open discussion of the family's present living situation).

Parenting Challenges

Maintaining Privacy. The theme of privacy indicated that homeless parents struggled with the need for personal and parental privacy. For example, parents reported it was hard to simply be alone with their family. Specifically, homeless parents struggled with the need to have personal privacy when they were interacting with their children in temporary housing. For example, a 46-year-old Hispanic mother of a teenage daughter, who has been living in a shelter for two weeks, discussed the public nature of parenting in a shelter:

> Because everybody, everybody is there. Everybody can see. There really is no privacy actually, you know I mean in order for me to talk to my child I have to be, we have to be just in our room and then there is still other people in the room, so we are never alone, ever. And everybody always listening, always, always. ... Nobody minds their own nose. Everybody is all up in our business, you know. (Interview 40, lines 146–153)

In another example, an African American couple, who have lived in shelters for two months, discuss the difficulties of parenting their son in the public area of a shelter. The wife stated:

> We're in front of other people. [You] try to be on your best behavior as a parent. Make sure you don't lose control ... because you know there's negativity in that. (Interview 2, 133–143)

In addition, a 19-year-old Latino father with a toddler son, homeless for two years and now living in a shelter, stated:

> I just don't like *putting him* (referring to his son) on the spot. *I don't like* being like told what to do in front of other people, so I kind of just pull him away. To me I think it is more respectful. That is why *I don't like* parenting in public. If you have something to say to him, I'll just pull him aside or hold him or something. (Interview 37, lines 137–140)

These examples illustrate the lack of privacy that parents reported when communicating with their children. Homeless parents experience their parenting as more public than they prefer and thus under scrutiny. They are expected to adhere to the rules of the shelter or household in which they are living; rules that may undermine or contradict their own family rules. The lack of privacy and subsequent modifications in parenting behaviors may also negatively impact their own parenting authority with their children.

Surrogate Parenting. This theme emerged from statements that parents made about other adult family members who watched their children when the parents were busy and/or institutional services that provided support for the parents. Two categories emerged within this theme.

Support. Parents described other adult family members, such as mothers and grandmothers, as helping the parent during their homelessness. Such support providers always had a previous relationship with the homeless parent. Children often stayed with grandparents or grandparents babysat while the parent looked for a job and housing. One 20-year-old Caucasian father of a toddler daughter, who had been homeless for two years, discussed the kinds of support he received from his daughter's maternal grandparents, who assumed the primary responsibility for raising his daughter.

> I will be there, but just kind of. We have mutual respect; they are always helping me a lot with me life. You know, they are supporting me. (Interview 1, lines 137–139)

In another example, a 52-year-old homeless African American grandmother described caring for her seven grandchildren while her two adult daughters are not able to be with the children. Her oldest daughter (age 33) is a single mother who works full-time, and the younger daughter (age 30) has a pattern of experiencing both homelessness and incarceration. The grandmother acknowledges that her homelessness affected her relationship with her younger daughter.

> Basically, I've had her children off and on while she's been in and out of jails or living here and there. And that's mostly another reason why I do stay with my other daughter is for the sake of my grandchildren. Because she's 30 and acted like, "Well you can take care of yourself." I just can't see her

dragging my grandkids around from place to place. It wouldn't be fair. My kids were grown when I lost my place with my job and went homeless. (Interview 8, lines 190–195)

These examples reveal how homeless parents seek out and receive help from relatives such as grandparents, who help prevent their homeless sons and daughters from needlessly taking their children from one temporary home to another. As a result, surrogate parenting can provide support to homeless parents.

Institutional undermining. Our participants reported experiencing that the institutions that provided support for them, such as shelters, undermined their parental authority. For example, one 47-year-old Caucasian mother with one child, who has been homeless for two weeks, discussed her difficulty coping with shelter rules. She states:

They are not allowed to go outside back in the backyard and play by themselves. Somebody's always got to be there so they can monitor them. ... Well they are just boys, they are outside playing they are not really hurting anything and she goes well they are not supposed to be out back, that's the rule, so see then the rules step in. (Interview 25, lines 174–176, 181–183)

In another narrative a 50-year-old African American female living in a shelter for two months discussed how residing in a shelter provides too much structure for her family.

We have chores. We have house meetings. Umm, we eat dinner. And get ready for the next day because we have a curfew. And the lights have to be out at a certain time so we try to cram everything we need to do within those last two hours. It's really hard, but that's the rules of the shelter. So if were going to be there we have to follow the rules. (Interview 2, lines 75–80)

While rules and routine can benefit a child's mental and physical growth, it can be difficult to parent under institutional policies and timelines. Specifically, it can be very difficult for homeless parents to have to adjust their parenting strategies into mandatory organizational requirements. As a result, residential mandates can institutionally undermine a homeless parent's ability to independently raise their children.

Managing Health Issues

Parents consistently reported struggling with health-related issues when parenting their children. This theme has been divided into three categories: Maintaining Cleanliness, Physical and Mental Health, as well as Problems with Drugs and Alcohol.

Maintaining cleanliness. Parents reported that it is very difficult to maintain cleanliness while living in a shelter or with other family members. For example, a 19-year-old Caucasian father of a toddler son living with a relative discusses challenges associated with being a homeless parent:

> *Being clean* I guess. Trying to stay *clean,* that really sucks. I don't like being dirty, so that is probably the most difficult part about it. (Interview 42, lines 157–159)

In another example, a 19-year-old married African American mother living in a shelter discussed personal hygiene as an issue:

> People are like, they're nasty, they don't clean up after themselves. Like me and my husband have had to clean up after plenty of people because either we don't want our child sitting on the toilet. ... Everybody in there is older than us and they're really nasty. They don't act adult like, they act like children. (Interview 26, lines 124–129)

Physical and mental health. Our participants reported that their own physical and mental health issues impacted their parenting while they are homeless. For example, a 35-year-old African American father of a toddler son had been had homeless for about four and half months before moving into a shelter. He reported:

> He [the son] is young, you know. He can look at me and he will be like, are you *sick*? You are losing weight, you know, are you sick? What is going on? He asks little small questions. (Interview 36, lines 124–125)

In this example, the father is struggling with his health, yet the child is too young to recognize that his father's illness may be related to the family's homelessness.

In another example, a 52-year-old, homeless African American mother discussed how her adult daughter talks to her about her homelessness and how her health has made it impossible for her to work.

> Uh, yeah. My oldest daughter she's like, "Mom, why do you choose to be. …" You know, but it's not that I 'choose to be' it's just that I did a disability and the price of rent is way beyond what I can afford. … But, you know, it's not that I choose to be like that; it's just a situation that sometimes can't be helped. (Interview 8, lines 166–171)

Many of the homeless parents also reported suffering from mental and emotional stress. Some parents reported that they were severely depressed and found it difficult to parent their children. For example, a 39-year-old African American mother of two sons, who has been homeless for three years and living in a rescue mission, discussed her depression:

> Not knowing where food is going to come from, or *where* are you going to sleep. *How* are you going to be able look for a job, or *have the money* to go look for a job, or umm, it's the not knowing. It's truly the not knowing, and then you feel as a parent, when you are in that position that you are a bad parent. You feel worthless. You know, you wonder what your kid is thinking of you. So, it is a lot of different emotions, and unless you have *gone* through it you don't understand it. (Interview 41, lines 184–188)

Problems with drugs and alcohol. Some parents reported that they had issues with drugs and alcohol that made it difficult for them to parent their children. Some reported that they lost custody of their children due to problems with drugs and alcohol. For example, one 43-year-old, divorced, Hispanic father of two teenage children, who had been homeless for about 13 years, discussed how his children "grew up quickly" because he was a drug addict.

> They know about it [his addiction]. They grew up real fast because me and their mother. We were drug addicts so they had to grow up real, you know. So I know they want a change and they're hoping right now that they get some stability and they have a place like they've never had like their own bedroom. (Interview 15, lines 177–180)

A 19-year-old Caucasian male, with a toddler daughter, who had been homeless for seven months, explained that drugs contributed to their homelessness.

> Yeah, if I wasn't dealing drugs, cause that is what started it all. If I would have made better choices, and just kept a job, instead of trying to make money the easy way, I would probably be in my house still. (Interview 42, lines 164–166)

In sum, health-related concerns can be a very prominent issue in the life of a homeless family. Maintaining cleanliness and physical and mental health issues can be challenging for a family without a stable residence; however, they can become extremely difficult while residing in settings like homeless shelters, which often share communal spaces that would normally be personal spaces if the family were traditionally housed. Furthermore, drug and alcohol addiction can be a direct cause for a family's lack of shelter.

Managing Legal Issues

Many of our participants reported that legal issues contributed to their homelessness. For example, a 47-year-old Caucasian mother of one, who had been homeless for two weeks, reported that her homelessness was caused by an ex-husband not paying child support. In this example case, the issue revolves around the lack of enforcement of a legal order (to pay child support),

> What happened is if he would have been paying his child support like he needed to, when 'cause ya' know he hasn't taken Samuel in almost two years. (Interview 25, lines 207–209)

In another example, a 34-year-old African American mother of a disabled son, who had been homeless for four months, reported that social and legal restrictions make obtaining housing difficult:

> I've been to a whole lot of places to seek houses and they deny me. I'm an ex-felon. But they know I'm trying to find my own place. (Interview 44, lines 134–135)

In these cases, we also find examples of a theme mentioned elsewhere in this paper: Social structures may have an undermining effect on the parenting efforts of homeless family members.

Maintaining Stability

In this theme, the parents discuss how their families need stability but that it is very difficult to provide that for them. For example, a 39-year-old African American mother of two sons, who had been homeless for three years and is now living in a rescue mission, discussed her struggles. She said:

> Making sure they have food, some place stable, some place to live. Umm, really just, just trying to keep them the *same*, have nothing affect them. Trying to keep them protected from all that, from as much as I can, but they are there, so I mean … from umm, just the thoughts of homelessness. I mean this, we have some place now, but we were homeless for quite a while. Lived in motels, wherever we could, you know. Just really just keep them focused on what they need to do as kids and *stay kids*. (Interview, 41, lines 98–106)

In another example, a 31-year-old African American female living in a shelter, who had been homeless for four months, discussed how the lack of stability affected her daughter.

> I've never been homeless before, so having to shuttle her around back and forth not knowing if they'll give us a place here or there. It's not conducive to the life of a 3-year-old. She meets a lot of different people and that's what I'm concerned about. Because she'll get attached to maybe this little girl over here and then we have to leave. You know what I mean? (Interview 7, lines 40–47)

Overall, these narratives candidly reveal that families desire stability, yet can be severely handicapped by the transitory patterns that challenge homeless families.

Strategies for Discussing Homelessness with Children

The second research objective of this study was to identify the strategies that homeless parents reported using when discussing their homelessness with their children. Three themes emerged:

concealment (with subcategories of reframing reality and avoidance), reassurance (with subcategories of togetherness and faith), and openness.

Concealment. The theme of concealment represented a number of ways that parents reported concealing their homelessness from their children. Two subcategories emerged: reframing reality and avoidance.

Reframing reality. This category represents the way parents talk about their homelessness to their children. Parents reported creating stories about their living situation that masked the truth. For example, a 31-year-old African-American mother, who has been homeless for four months and lived in a shelter, described explaining homelessness to her young daughter:

> I think she thinks she's on a little adventure right now. I just tell her that, like, maybe she'll get upset because she didn't see her friend because we had to leave. So I'll tell her we're moving towards something better. She'll have her own room again. She'll have her toys again. And umm, I tell her that were on a little vacation. (Interview 7, lines 58–64)

In the next example, a 35-year-old father and a 23-year-old Hispanic mother with two pre-school children, who have been homeless off and on for approximately five months, reported that they have received hotel vouchers from the city and that they are living in a motel. The father stated:

> We never stayed in a motel with the kids so we tell them we are on vacation. They play with their [inaudible] and watch TV in bed. They think this is fun. (Interview 43a, lines 256–258)

The previous examples illustrate that some homeless parents reported to choose to fictionally and positively reframe their homelessness in the eyes of their younger children.

Avoidance. Conversely, parents reported not talking to their children about their living situation. For example, a 55-year-old African American mother living in a shelter discussed how her son does not ask her about their living situation, and she does not explain it to him. She stated:

> He doesn't ask. You can just see it in his face. In his expression and his demeanor. So why bring it to him? It's not so much giving him an explanation; it's more or less telling him that life is not perfect. (Interview 2, lines 115–119)

A 19-year-old Caucasian single mother also reported choosing to avoid the topic of homelessness when she responds to questions from her child about their homelessness.

> I kind of steer it away 'cause I don't like answering it straight on. 'Cause I don't think she's old enough. 'Cause my mom went through the same situation with me and didn't actually describe it to me until I had my daughter. I feel uncomfortable sometimes trying to describe it to her so I try to steer it off and distract her. (Interview 27, lines 89–97)

As seen in the previous narratives, some homeless parents reported using discussion avoidance as a parental strategy to possibly help protect their children from unnecessary anxiety.

Reassurance. Most of the parents in this sample described methods of reassuring their children about their present living situations. There were two categories embedded in this theme: maintaining togetherness and faith

Maintaining togetherness. Parents reported discussing the importance and desire of having a normal family life together even in the face of their homelessness. For example, a 39-year-old African American mother of two sons, who had been homeless for three years and now lives in a rescue mission, stated:

> We [the parents and children] interact a lot to have fun. Whatever we can do together. Like I said we play board games a lot, card games, checkers, Sorry, crazy eights—of course, umm, and we go to the park, just simple, simple things that they will remember. I am trying to give them memories, and not spending a lot of money because we cannot afford that. (Interview 41, lines 88–92)

A married couple (the wife is 41 and the husband is 36), who had been homeless for the past four months and temporarily left their children with her parents, described the importance of the family needing to be together. The wife stated:

I mean we actually have to stop and think about paying attention to the simple needs instead of it just coming naturally. Umm, still more attention to their feelings and their being comfortable. It's just actually they get more attention that way. They don't have their own room to go play in all day or something. We have to be together. We've already gotten to know them a lot better. (Interview 5, lines 70–85)

These examples demonstrate that homeless parents express an invaluable need and benefit for their family to stay and be together.

Having faith. Many of the homeless parents felt that their present situation was out of their hands, as a divine force was intervening. For example, a 23-year-old African-American mother with three young children who had been homeless for three weeks, discussed the belief that she and her family were meant to be in this situation. She stated:

If it was meant for that job to go through it would have gone though so I don't feel that and this is just my religion talking, that God intended me, for us to be here cause things are working out the way they are. … It is not as hard as some people make it to be. Ya know, I can't really say 'cause this is all God, honestly. I have nothing to do with it. As long as I sit back and allow God to do his work. (Interview 24, lines 263–265, 298–300)

In another example, a 50-year-old African-American female living in a shelter for two months discussed how faith has helped her during this difficult time.

We pray a lot. We read the Bible. And we keep each other encouraged and show as much love as we can. … I would like to say that I'm a Christian and I have faith in God. And I know that He is in charge. And I know that. He's going to make a way out. And that gives me hope and endurance and perseverance. (Interview 2, lines 185–188)

In these narratives, faith emerges as a guiding force helping some homeless families to persevere over their challenging circumstances.

Openness. The openness theme represents the degree to which parents openly discuss their present living situation with their children and recommend that their children do the same with others. For example, a 39-year-old African-American mother of two sons, who has been homeless for three years and was living in a rescue mission, explained that she used an open approach when her children ask her about their present living situation. She reported:

> *Really be open*, and don't be embarrassed. *Not to be embarrassed* that is something I had to fight, but not to be embarrassed, and to get help wherever you can. If it is offered take it, don't be too proud to take it. (Interview 41, lines 135–138)

In another example, a 39-year-old Caucasian mother, who has been homeless for one month with five children, explained that she openly discussed the situation with her kids. In this situation, she is being open and honest about their need for money.

> They want to know when we are gonna get our own place. … I told them that when we can get the money together. (Interview 38, line 95)

From these examples, honesty and openness surface as direct and practical strategies that homeless parents use when discussing their current living situation with their children.

Discussion and Conclusions

This unique study provides a window into the parenting struggles and strategies utilized by parents who are homeless. In their own words, parents described their day-to-day experiences and the strategies they use to talk to their children about their homelessness. The study identified five major parenting challenges associated with being a homeless family: maintaining privacy, managing surrogate parents (both relational and institutional), coping with health concerns (such as issues of cleanliness, physical and mental health problems, and problems with drugs and alcohol), managing legal issues, and maintaining stability for their family. Though parenting is difficult in normal situations, these parents highlighted the additional stress added to the parenting experience while being homeless. Their narratives present evidence that homeless parents attempt to maintain consistency and parental authority but also realize that being homeless makes these goals difficult to achieve.

These reports identified aspects of normal family life, such as privacy and cleanliness, that are everyday struggles for homeless parents. Particularly surprising were parental reports that they did not experience privacy to talk to their children or have a clean toilet seat for their son or daughter to use.

These parents also were very open to accepting parenting support from others—either family members or institutions–even if it undermined their parental role. We found this trend in the data pronounced and concerning. Some parents felt it was better to leave their child with someone else than have their sons or daughters experience the stress of homelessness. However, they did not express concern for their children feeling abandoned. Furthermore, these themes highlight how services that are provided for homeless families fulfill only the basic physical needs of the family, while failing to address the psychosocial needs of the parents or family units.

The study also examined the communication strategies that parents reported using when discussing their homelessness with their children. Parents with young children reported concealing the fact that they were homeless by reframing the reality of their situation. For example, some parents said that their children thought they were on a vacation and not homeless. Other parents just avoided the topic. In both cases, it was evident that the parents were ashamed of their present situation and tried to hide it from their children. Another frequently reported strategy was to offer children reassurance by acknowledging that they were having hard times, but stressing that they were together, and that they needed to maintain their faith and things would work out. These parents were optimistic about their future and tried to remain positive. Parents reported employing a final strategy, openness, where the parents openly discussed their homelessness with their children and did not reassure the children or hide their homelessness from them. It was as if they were stating, "This is a fact of life; hard times will always come."

These themes highlight the difficulty homeless parents have attempting to keep their family together and safe. While parents were very clear about the challenges they experienced and how they talked to their children about their homelessness, there were also subtexts of shame and failure embedded in their narratives. Many parents attempted to justify and explain their homelessness, while also struggling with the effects of it on their sense of worth. Although these issues were not directly addressed in this study, exploring how feelings of shame and failure impact the homeless family-experience would be a fruitful area for future research.

Overall, this study acknowledges the importance of providing shelter to homeless families and reveals the need to acknowledge the social struggles associated with homelessness as well. Fulfillment of basic needs is important for this population. However, the emergent themes from the personal narratives of the homeless parents in this study reveal that assistance could be provided to parents in ways that support their parenting role.

References

Anooshian, L. J. (2003). Social isolation and rejection of homeless children. *Journal of Children & Poverty, 9*(2), 115–134.

Boxil, N. A., & Beaty, A. L. (1990). Mother/child interaction among homeless women and their children in a public night shelter in Atlanta, Georgia. *Child and Youth Services, 14*(1), 49–64.

Cosgrove, L., & Flynn, C. (2005). Marginalized mothers: Parenting without a home. *Analyses of Social Issues and Public Policy, 5*(1), 127–143.

Dornbusch, S. M., Ritter, P. L., Leiderman, P. H., Roberts, D. F., & Fraleigh, M. J. (1987). The relation of parenting style to adolescent school performance. *Child Development, 58,* 1244–1257.

Kondratas, S. A. (1991). Ending homelessness: Policy challenges. *American Psychologist, 46,* 1226–1231.

Letiecq, B. L., Anderson, E. A., & Kroblinsky, S. A. (1996). Social support of homeless and permanently housed low-income mothers with young children. *Family Relations, 45,* 265–272.

Letiecq, B. L., Anderson, E. A., & Kroblinsky, S. A. (1998). Social support of homeless and housed mothers: A comparison of temporary and permanent housing arrangements. *Family Relations, 47,* 415–421.

Lindsey, E. W. (1998). The impact of homelessness and shelter life on family relationships. *Family Relations, 47,* 243–252.

McArthur, M., Zubrzycki, J., Rochester, A., & Thomson, L. (2006). "Dad, where are we going to live now?" Exploring fathers' experiences of homelessness. *Australian Social Work, 59*(3), 288–300.

McChesney, K. Y. (1990). Family homelessness: A systemic problem. *Journal of Social Issues, 46*(4), 191–205.

McChesney, K. Y. (1995). A review of the empirical literature on contemporary urban homeless families. *Social Service Review, 69*(3), 429–460.

Molnar, J. M., Rath, W. R., & Klein, T. P. (1990). Constantly compromised: The impact of homelessness on children. *Journal of Social Issues, 46*(4), 109–124.

Owen, W. F. (1984). Interpretive themes in relational communication. *Quarterly Journal of Speech, 70,* 274–287.

Polgar, M., Pollio, D., & North, C. (2006). Stress and coping among members of families with homeless relatives. Paper submitted to the American Psychological Association Annual Meeting, Montreal, Canada.

Putallaz, M., & Heflin, A. H. (1990). Parent-child interaction. In S. R. Asher & J. Coie (Eds.), *Peer rejection in childhood* (pp. 189–216). New York: Cambridge University Press.

Russell, M., Harris, B., & Gockel, A. (2008). Parenting in poverty: Perspectives of high-risk parents. *Journal of Children and Poverty*, 14(1), 83–98.

Schindler, H. S., & Coley, R. L. (2007). A qualitative study of homeless fathers: Exploring parenting and gender role transitions. *Family Relations*, 56, 40–51.

Sobolewski, J. M., & Amato, P. R. (2005). Economic hardship in the family of origin and children's psychological well-being in adulthood. *Journal of Marriage and Family*, 67, 141–156.

Torquati, J. C. (2002). Personal and social resources as predictors of parenting in homeless families. *Journal of Family Issues*, 23(4), 463–485.

U.S. Department of Housing and Urban Development Office of Community Planning and Development (2007). *The Annual Homeless Assessment Report to Congress.* Retrieved from http://www.huduser.org/Publications/pdf/ahar.pdf

U.S. Department of Housing and Urban Development, Office of Community Planning and Development March (2008). *The Second Annual Homeless Assessment Report to Congress.* Retrieved from http://www.hudhre.info/documents/2ndHomelessAssessmentReport.pdf

Wadsworth, M. E., Raviv, T., Reinhard, C., Wolff, B., Santiago, C. D., & Einhorn, L. (2008). An indirect effects model of the association between poverty and child functioning: The role of children's poverty-related stress. *Journal of Loss and Trauma*, 13, 156–185.

Chapter 15

Family Communication Surrounding Emotional Trauma: The Aftermath of Hurricanes

James M. Honeycutt and Christopher M. Mapp

One of the great calamities affecting any family is the loss of home and property through a natural disaster such as a flood. Massive floods affected numerous families in June 2008 in Iowa, Illinois, and Missouri along the upper Mississippi River. For example, the University of Iowa had to evacuate 16 buildings on its campus when the Iowa River overflowed its banks. Moreover, this flood was less severe in terms of the number of flooded properties and displaced families compared to the Gulf Coast and New Orleans flooding in 2005. Hurricanes Katrina and Rita in August and September of 2005 were the deadliest and most traumatic storms to strike the Gulf Coast since the 1927 Mississippi River flood, which displaced over 700,000 people (Barry, 2002).

The immediate period following a traumatic event is a crucial time in a family's recovery. During this time, the family creates a trauma narrative that assists survivors with the cognitive processing of the etiology of the traumatic events (Tuval-Mashiach et al., 2004). Based on narrative descriptions, Honeycutt, Nasser, Banner, Mapp, and DuPont (2008) found that displaced students at a number of Gulf Coast universities—people isolated with cell phone and internet problems, those with poor social networks, as well as those expressing negative emotional valence—were more likely to report a high level of trauma anxiety. Basic expressed emotions that indicated trauma anxiety were fear, anger, sadness, and guilt.

Overview

In this chapter, we discuss in-depth interviews with individuals representing different families' coping strategies with traumatic events. With hurricanes chosen as a major calamity and stressor point, we discuss trauma, family stress models, and the emotional aftermath of dealing with lost homes, businesses, and property on the Gulf Coast. We examine trauma, effective patterns of communication, and coping in the aftermath of the storms.

Trauma in Families

According to Brewin et al. (1999), most attempts at coping occurs in the first weeks and months following a traumatic event. Shalev (2002) asserts that coping requires a complex process involving emotional, biological/ hormonal, social and cognitive levels of interaction and healing. By its very nature, trauma breaks the continuity and smooth flow of daily life. Trauma is typically experienced in two forms: incidental trauma or enduring trauma. Incidental trauma is defined as chaotic events such as a death of a close family member, or loss of property through fire/flood. The event in and of itself, is momentary with lingering effects. The National Council on Family Relations (2008) states that in terms of incidental trauma, the majority of families in crisis are not pathologically ill, nor will they manifest symptoms of long-term mental illness. Most people experiencing a traumatic situation are relatively healthy, functional, and resilient and are merely experiencing the effects of incidential trauma.

Foa et al. (1992) have established that perceived control is a key to the emergence of post-traumatic stress disorder (PTSD) and other trauma-related disorders. The diagnosis of PTSD first emerged following the Vietnam War and is used to describe the long-term psychological effects of battle trauma (Groome & Soureti, 2004). The main symptoms of PTSD are intrusive, painful memories, avoidance of stimuli associated with the trauma and increased physiological arousal (Horowitz, 1976). An example of PTSD comes from the follow-up story of Jennifer (see accounts that follow). Jennifer communicated with her mother, who lived three hours away. Being the only daughter in the family, her mother worried excessively. Both mother and daughter were unable to use cell phones for two weeks after the storm.

Data reported by Honeycutt and his associates (2008) in the Gulf South on individual differences in dealing with emotions, PTSD, and trauma anxiety after Hurricanes Katrina and Rita reveal that negative emotions lingered well after the hurricanes, even though media coverage faded. Further analysis of trauma anxiety reveal that stress was positively correlated with emotional valence and imagined interaction catharsis, and negatively with social network size. Basic emotions that predicted trauma anxiety after the hurricanes are fear, anger, sadness, and guilt

Catharsis is a function of imagined interactions with missing family members and friends allowing the individual to release tension and anxiety. For example, a person may feel better "venting" at his brother/sister about how other family members showed favoritism when providing electrical generators during the storm. Individuals in the Honeycutt et al. (2008) study reported numerous instances of imagined interactions (see Honeycutt, 2003; 2008; 2010) with missing family members and friends. Furthermore, larger social networks are considered better sources of social support because of the presence of more people to provide support for the respondent. Honeycutt and his associates (2008) found that mixed emotions of sadness and joy predicted catharsis.

Additional findings revealed that women reported more catharsis than males. People who had fewer problems with cell phone connections reported better catharsis. A possible explanation for this finding is that individuals who were able to contact their family members and friends through the use of cell phones had more positive, which may have provided catharsis by alleviating stress.

Social Networks and Support

Support from social networks focuses on the benefits that social networks may provide during stressful situations. Honeycutt and his colleagues (2008) found that students transferring from universities damaged by Hurricane Katrina and Rita to another large Southeastern university reported having less social network members than non-transfer students. Naturally, transfer students were more likely cut off from their friends and/or family from affected regions. Similarly, all the people in the ensuing case reports were temporarily cut off from communication with various family members, some for as long as three weeks.

However, all of them report using the compensation function of imagined interactions. Imagined interactions are used to substitute for the absence of real communication (Honeycutt, 2003; 2010). Moreover, during physical separation, the imaginary conversations serve a relational maintenance function. Family members think about the well-being of others; absence makes the heart grow fonder due to worry and rumination associated with the uncertainty of how parents, siblings, or children are coping with the aftermath of the storms. One of our case studies consists of a mother and daughter who provided numerous examples of the relational maintenance function of imagined interactions. Other respondents comment how they periodically thought about distant family members while separated during the storm. As shown below, Dale G., is a 41-year-son who was the caregiver of his mother. While carrying out his duties as a university public relations consultant, he constantly worries about his mother's health. He indicates that he had many imagined interactions while working at the university following the storm.

Basic Emotions

Studying emotions in disasters is important because it helps explain how victims cope with the emotional strains they are likely to endure (Honeycutt et al., 2008). Kessler, Galea, Jones, and Parker (2006) found serious mental health problems among 11.3% of the sample, compared with 6.1% in a similar sample surveyed before Hurricane Katrina. However, there is evidence that enduring these painful emotions can have positive benefits. For example, 69.5% of the survey respondents reported having discovered new inner strength because of their experiences after Katrina and 75% reported having found a deeper sense of meaning or purpose in life. (Kessler et al., 2006).

Many social scientists claim that certain emotions are more basic than others. For example, Ekman's (1999) classic work on facial expressions in different cultures reveals happiness, sadness, fear, surprise, anger, and disgust. The following are definitions of the basic emotions used for this study. Fear is apprehension, distress, dread, or alarm expressed through an identifiable stimulus in the presence of anticipation of danger. Fear is differentiated from anxiety, which has no easily identifiable stimulus (LeDoux, 1996). Happiness is a feeling or show of pleasure, contentment, or joy. Surprise is a feeling of sudden amazement caused by the unexpected. Anger is a feeling of extreme annoyance. Sadness is a feeling of grief or sorrow. Disgust/contempt is a feeling of horrified, sickened distaste for something (Stedman, 2006). Some scholars claim that defining *emotion* is a delicate proposition because instead of knowing it when you see it, you feel an emotion (Guerrero, Andersen, & Trost, 1998).

Finally, we examine anticipation as a type of emotion. While not technically being an emotion, it is important due to the research in terms of the grief cycle of Kubler-Ross & Kessler, 2007). They discuss stages of shock, denial, anger, bargaining, depression, and positive acceptance. Acceptance is important in forging ahead after trauma. Michael H. hoped to be a pediatrician and worked in the National Guard as a medic after the hurricanes. He was angry at missing his pre-med classes while helping people who were unappreciative of his assistance. Yet, he concluded his interview (see Michael's report later in this chapter) by commenting how his negative experience prepared him for a future career as a physician. He had accepted the adversity of his experience and reframed it as a positive event.

Catastrophes like hurricanes Katrina and Gustav create a groundswell of feelings beyond the basic emotions. For instance, people experience guilt for having survived the storm when others did not. With hurricane survivors, there may be variations on this theme since survivors may wish to change places with the person who died, while also experiencing guilt. Sometimes this guilt happens as the result of a person's having done something to ensure his or her survival. Such actions include avoiding others' needs, making decisions that resulted in other people's deaths, or seeking refuge when others remained threatened or suffering. After the hurricanes, people's responses escalated into mixed feelings of having survived and of remorse for loved ones who did not.

Methodology

Participants, five in all, were mostly recruited based on snowball sampling, with different participants recruiting additional hurricane survivors based on their willingness to share their experiences. Semistructured interviews were conducted both in person and by telephone. Participants also rank-ordered a list of basic emotions reportedly experienced during the trauma.

Case Studies of Family Members

Interviews were conducted among survivors who recounted their families' survival experiences (four individuals survived Hurricane Katrina in August 2005 and one survived Hurricane Gustav in August 2008). Two of the interviewees were married, Matthew B. and Janet B., and were interviewed together. Table 15.1 contains a list of emotions ranked by the participants, including fear, grief (sadness), anger, surprise, guilt, acceptance, disgust, anticipation, happiness and (no emotions at all). The names of the family members have been changed to protect their anonymity. Following is a brief report of each family member's reactions to the storms.

Table 15.1: *Emotions Associated with Hurricanes Katrina and Gustav**

Emotion	Matt 38 yrs	Janet 37 yrs	Jennifer 28 yrs	Mike 21 yrs	Dale 41 yrs	Jan 46 yrs	Ann 21 yrs
Fear	10	1	1	8	9	2	1
Anticipation	5	2	4	1	2	1	3
Surprise	1	3	2	3	1	3	2
Disgust	4	8	6	4	5	6	6
Acceptance	3	4	3	5	4	7	4
Happiness	2	5	9	9	3	9	7
Anger	6	9	5	2	6	5	8
Grief	7	6	7	6	7	4	5
Guilt	8	7	7	7	8	8	9
No Emotion	9	10	10	10	10	10	10

*Emotions ranked in intensity/frequency from 1-10, with 1 being the most intense or frequent and 10 being the least.

Table 15.1 reveals that the husband and father, Matthew B. ranked surprise as his most intense emotion while Janet, his wife ranked it number three. Yet, she ranked "fear" as the most intense emotion she experienced during and after the storm, while it was not felt by Matthew; who ranked it number 10. Indeed, the argument can be made that he appears to be calm in the face of storm adversity while she is more uncertain and fearful. She commented that sometimes it is better to be lucky than good. Her husband, Matthew B., remembered his days in the Boy Scouts, whose motto is "Be prepared." Reflecting on their tribulations following the worst hurricane in American history, the parents of three young children marveled at how lucky they were compared to others who lost lives and fortunes and how fortunate they were for taking the measures they did to ensure their survival.

Matthew, B., 38, and Janet B., 37, of Hattiesburg, MS; Have 3 kids ages 10, 7, & 3 (computer animator & homemaker).

Like most people in the storm's path, Matthew and Janet watched nervously as Katrina approached with gathering strength. A tad dismissive, the pair remained cautiously optimistic that it would turn slightly, careening to a neighboring state as so many hurricanes had done before. But the storm not only kept coming, it kept growing. With just one day to decide whether or not to evacuate, Matthew and Janet decided to hunker down, get supplies and ride the storm out rather than join the mad rush to unknown destinations. After deciding to buy the last generator and one of the few remaining chainsaws at Wal-Mart the day before landfall, Matthew and Janet hoped for the best. "We were laughing about it because we thought we'd just write it off as a business expense. We stopped laughing the next morning when the first tree fell on our front porch," Janet said.

Stretching 500 miles across, Hurricane Katrina took more than 1800 lives and caused billions of dollars of damage to the Gulf Coast. It made landfall in the early morning of August 29, a day Janet will never forget. "When we saw how big it was, I got very worried about my parents. They're older and they didn't want the hassle of leaving their stuff, so they stayed put." Janet was on the phone with her mother, an hour from the coastline, as multiple tornadoes touched down on her property. "I heard my mother screaming. The eye-wall was coming straight through them. She said trees were snapping like twigs and twisters were everywhere. Then we lost our signal."

The next several days were an emotional rollercoaster, to say the least. Unable to reestablish contact with her parents, Janet, Matthew and their three children, ages 7, 3 and 9 months, piled into the family van and made their way south toward her parents. They didn't know what they'd find. What was normally a one-hour trip on the interstate took four hours because of the downed trees, signs and other debris. When they finally arrived, they found her parents, alive but bedraggled. "My mother started crying like a baby. My dad said seeing us was like seeing the cavalry coming. We were a sight for sore eyes."

After setting Janet's parents up with supplies, cash and gasoline, which was unavailable in their hometown of Picayune and nonexistent in the neighboring town of Waveland, which was utterly destroyed by the storm surge, they made their way back to Hattiesburg. The destruction there was unbelievable, Matthew said. "The eye of the storm really went straight up the coast, through here, and all the way up the state of Mississippi. They even lost power in Oxford, which is 30 minutes from Memphis. That's how far-reaching this storm was," he said.

When they got back, they returned to a scene reminiscent of a post-Apocalyptic B-movie, Matthew said. A Red Cross distribution center set up down the street from his house, outside of which throngs of angry citizens demanded supplies, cash and debit cards issued by the government for food and other supplies. "We had National Guard soldiers and a HUMVEE in my front yard. They were there to control the crowds, which got very loud and aggressive. We brought the soldiers some water. It was madness," Matthew said.

Few in town had gasoline. Some had ice. The lucky ones who bought generators at a couple thousand bucks a pop had electricity. Those who found themselves at the top of the social totem pole, with others ingratiating themselves daily. But most frustratingly, no one, even the most well-prepared, had electronic communications. The hurricane had seen to that, leveling cell towers throughout south Mississippi. "It was literally like someone had dropped an atom bomb," Matthew said. "Just nothing. That was really hard, not being able to find out how family was doing or to let them know we were OK."

As the only family with power on their block, Matthew's house soon became the hub of civilization. In the two weeks following the storm when electricity was still unavailable, Matthew ran five different lines to surrounding houses, feeding his neighbors with precious energy used to cook food, cool ice and power fans. Considering the storm knocked out power in August, possibly the most stultifying summer month in the Deep South, tempers ran high for those without power as temperatures outside soared.

Janet said: "We heard news through people around the neighborhood, you know, hearsay, of shootings and lootings and stuff like that. It was hard to separate fact from fiction. But with young children, we didn't take many chances. We kept our doors locked. The kids didn't have any fear–for them, it was like a big camping adventure. But I get nervous in situations like those, so I made Matthew take every precaution, even keep a gun with him while he was working in the yard."

Two weeks into the ordeal, Matthew and Janet's division of labor became routine: he cut trees, hauled lumber and kept the neighborhood juiced with electricity from his generator, and she washed clothes, cooked meals, and tended the children. Janet said their primitive living arrangements reminded her of one of her favorite childhood shows, "Little House on the Prairie." "I thought, 'It's no fun being Laura Ingalls.'" But while that show's story arcs and conflicts were fictitious, Matthew and Janet's were becoming increasingly real.

"As supplies started to dwindle, I got a little panicky, but fortunately we made it through and we got our power back. Slowly life got back to normal," Janet said. As long as the two had a common goal—conducting the day-to-day chores and keeping the family safe—all was fine between Janet and her husband. But to this day, when the weather gets bad, the two start to argue reflecting anxiety.

"Matthew is very laid back and 'take-it-as-it-comes.' He believes if you're prepared, everything will work out fine. But Katrina put the fear into me. It changed me. Now, when it gets bad out I want to leave immediately." Janet even convinced Matthew to buy a used mobile home for family trips. But she thinks there's a more practical use on the horizon. "When the next Katrina comes, and it will come, we're heading to the mountains in Tennessee. And this time, we're taking the whole family, my mom and dad and Matthew's included. I don't care if we have to tie them up. They're going. We're all going," she said with a laugh.

Matthew and Janet's case highlight the importance of discussing common goals and plans in family communication. Both credit their survival during Katrina to their mutual preparedness and understanding, specifically their clearly defined domestic roles. With each occupying different jobs, the family was able to weather the storm together and reduce the traumatic potential of its aftermath. While Janet did express feelings of fear—both then and now when thinking of the possibility of future storms—she said those feelings were mitigated by preparedness and communicating with her family members. Still, the experience was traumatic enough to still cause interpersonal conflict when bad weather threatens. This highlights the distinction between the sexes, with more women reporting experiencing fear as opposed to men, who likely feel "tested" by their ability to brave the storm, both figuratively and literally.

Jennifer S., 28, Columbia, MS, master's student in education

A single brunette just out of college, Jennifer S. never worried about her safety. After all, the self-proclaimed "survivalist" had taken judo in college and packed a taser, pepper spray and other sundry weapons into her Dooney & Burke handbag. However, Jennifer had never witnessed the kind desperation that commonly follow in the wake of tragedies like the one she went through in August, 2005, the kind of desperation that makes otherwise good people steal food, gas, and supplies or that makes seemingly gentile people explode in fits of heat-induced rage. In short, Jennifer had never been through something like Hurricane Katrina.

"My mother always used to joke with me that any man who was foolish enough to mess with me was going to wish he hadn't," Jennifer said. "But after the things I saw during Katrina, I had to question how tough I really was. I don't know if I could do some of things I saw people do to survive."

Being alone and living in an apartment surrounded by strangers wasn't easy on Jennifer, or her mother. Living about three hours from her daughter, Jennifer's mom lost touch with her for at least a full week after the storm devastated the college town of Hattiesburg, MS. Jennifer describes the week of debauchery in unflinching terms, but decided to not give her mother all the terrible details of the events that unfolded. She appeared more concerned with her mother's well-being than her own safety. "Mom worries about me a lot. I'm her only daughter, and here I am living in the city during this storm. And she can't reach me, or talk to me. And she's hearing all these horrible things about rapes and murders going on two hours away in New Orleans. Of course, she's imagining I'm dead."

But Jennifer wasn't dead. After a close call with a man whose intentions she's still not fully sure of, she rendezvoused with a couple of male friends who happened to work in law enforcement. "This creepy guy came to my house after the storm and asked to use the phone. I told him nothing was working, and he asked if he could come in. I closed the door and got really scared. I got my pepper spray out and watched him through the window. He went around to my back door and was looking around, and I got really freaked out. I screamed that I had a gun—I really didn't—and he wandered off. After that, I knew I had to get out of there."

Jennifer stayed with friends for a while before returning home to make sure her property was still intact. Thankfully, it was, she said. "I wasn't that concerned with my stuff. I had a cat, which was OK. I knew I could replace all my stuff if it got stolen, but I can't replace me," Jennifer said. Coming from a close-knit family, Jennifer said she and her mother fought about her independent streak in the months after Katrina. While her mother urged her to check in more regularly and inform her of Jennifer's whereabouts, Jennifer still tries to maintain her privacy and personal boundaries. "Moms worry. That's what they do. But I tell her I've got to live my life, and she's got to live hers. But it makes me feel good, I guess, that she worries about me. I'm sure I'll worry the same about my daughter one day, if I have one."

Maintaining the relational dialectic of openness and closedness is difficult for families to do when tragedy strikes, as Jennifer's story illustrates. Her ability to maintain her independence was tempered with her mother's need to know that her daughter—grown-up or not—was safe from harm's way. As is often the case during traumatic events, navigating personal boundaries between family members is tricky, as this report suggests.

Dale G., 41, Hattiesburg, MS; public relations manager (single with no children; primary care giver for mother)

In times of crisis, people have questions. And in times of crisis, it's Dale G.'s job to have answers. Needless to say, keeping your head while everyone else around you is losing theirs is easier said than done. As a public relations practitioner at a university in Hurricane Katrina's direct path, Dale was back at work immediately after the storm hit, working 15-hour days. There, he helped shovel out information to thousands of people— all of whom seemed to have thousands of questions. On top of this, Dale was also managing the care of his elderly, disabled mother, who lived with him. In the weeks prior to the storm, Dale's mother had undergone surgery that left her incapacitated and reliant on Dale for most of her most needs. Torn between the overwhelming demands of his job and caring for his ailing mother, Dale felt like he was coming apart at the seams.

"It was a mess. A real mess," Dale recalled. "There were days when I thought I was going to lose my mind. I often imagined talking to my mother about her convalescence following her surgery. The imagined interactions made me psychologically feel closer to her and relieved anxiety when I couldn't be with her. Sometimes, I wanted to escape and just wanted to get in my car and start driving away. I didn't care where. I just wanted to get away. Only problem was you couldn't get anywhere because the roads were all blocked."

So there he was, trapped, spending his days at the university in semi-primitive conditions, fielding questions and providing information to those in need. Whenever he could, he would get in his car and make the five-mile trip home to care for his mother, who was left in a house with no electricity, no air conditioning, and no ice. But with gas-rationing in effect, Dale had to time his trips just right. He didn't have the luxury of wasted time or of wasted travel. "That was very hard on mom. She didn't understand that I had a job to do, and I would get frustrated because I couldn't check on her since the phones were out."

When he was at home, Dale said, it wasn't long before the two were at each other's throats. He said he remembers the stifling heat, and how his mother would just sob for what seemed like hours, cursing and "asking God why he was punishing her like this."

There were days when he looked for excuses to get out of the house early. To be working was far preferable to bickering with his mother, he said. But guilt would soon set in and he would be looking for time to break away from work and go home and check on her.

"Sometimes I didn't know if I was coming or going, literally," he said, with a laugh that comes easy now. But at the time of the tragedy, these were not laughing matters. And his experiences he won't soon forget. Since then, he's seen other storms come and go, but the memories of Katrina will linger forever. "It was a once-in-a-lifetime thing. I hope we never have to go through anything like that again. Ever."

Dale said he struggles with how he handled himself at times during Katrina, losing his temper amidst the chaos, the uncertainty and that dreaded, awful heat. With his sister living in the vicinity but unable to help attend to his mother's demanding needs, Dale felt a simmering resentment that he tried to suppress. But he said he'd be lying if he said he wasn't angry that the burden of caring for his mother fell on his shoulders at a time when he was needed in so many other places.

"Me and my mom fight like old sisters sometimes. I guess living together will do that. But she needs me. She's always been there for me. I owe her that, and I love her. Even if she can get on my last nerve," Dale said.

Dale's experience reveals the fragility of people's coping mechanisms under the duress of a natural disaster. Absent much, if any, help from his sibling when it came to caring for his sick mother, Dale began to feel overwhelmed by the demands of his job and her constant care. It is not surprising that he admitted to intense feelings of anger and despair, both of which were certainly compounded by the forces over which he had no control, like his inability to travel at will or even having basic electricity. Still, in the end, Dale communicated that his role as loving son is the most important and rewarding one he has.

Michael H., 21, Baton Rouge, LA, pre-med student; medic in National Guard

Thousands of students in the Gulf South region experienced Hurricane Gustav in August 2008. Few, if any, experienced it like Michael H. For two weeks following the Category 4 storm, Michael worked in the rural areas of southern Louisiana, where he administered intravenous drips, gave shots, bandaged wounds and dispensed medicines to the needy citizens of his state. Part of a medical unit called the 756

ASMC, Michael assisted National Guard soldiers called out by the state's governor in response to the crisis that left millions without power, fresh water and other much-needed supplies. Whether sleeping in tents in mosquito-infested fields or in abandoned buildings that got hotter than saunas, Michael and his fellow soldiers did whatever was necessary to help the state get back on its feet and he was glad to do it.

But as a college student in Baton Rouge, his hometown, each passing day after the storm represented a different kind of challenge for the pre-med major. "I was desperate to get back in school," Michael said. "The semester had just started and every class I had to miss because of work meant I fell further and further behind. It caused a lot of anxiety for me because I couldn't communicate my situation [back home]." Moreover, Michael's job kept him away from home, where his family struggled to regain their own footing after the storm. His homestead had been hit hard by Gustav, with trees uprooted and other property damage causing water damage to the interior of his parents' house. Tension built back home, as his father labored to return things to normal., A day before the storm hit, Michael's mother loaded her twin pre-teen daughters into the family van and headed to a fishing camp the family owns in north Louisiana. But Michael's 15-year old brother stayed behind to help his father protect and repair the house, a decision which ended up causing as much grief as it did gratitude.

"My brother, let's just say he's an inside-kind-of-kid. He's kind of soft, a momma's boy. My father never really taught him how to use a chainsaw like he did me and my older brother, so he wasn't really any help after the storm hit. He got in the way, mostly, and my dad and him got in arguments. So my brother stayed inside while my dad did most of the work. There was a lot of tension there for a while. I felt really guilty knowing that my dad needed my help fixing up the house and stuff and that I couldn't be there to help. Plus it made me mad at my little brother for wimping out on my dad when he needed him most," Michael said.

Fortunately for Michael's father, the storm allowed him to patch up an old rift with a neighbor. With a common cause, Michael's father and the neighbor united to accomplish the task of cleaning up the neighborhood and getting its occupants going again. "That was good," Michael said, chuckling. "They're friends again now, but I think my dad still hates our neighbor's dogs."

And Michael's dad wasn't the only one experiencing a range of emotions. There was plenty of that for Michael, too. Although he enjoyed serving the needs of the residents of south Louisiana who were hit hard by Gustav, he felt a slow, burning resentment build with each passing day. After nine days without the ability to communicate with family, friends or professors back at school, Michael was starting to feel cut off from his regular life. And as the unit's medical mission became less necessary as weeks went by, Michael wondered if he'd ever get the call to head back home and resume his own life.

"I was pissed, I'll be honest," Michael said. "I was upset with the chain-of-command because nobody knew anything and I kept waiting for the word, which never came. Other people who weren't in school were getting to go back home before me, and that made me mad as hell. I wasn't angry because I had to be there, but I was angry because I was in classes, pre-med classes, that I needed to do well in, and I'm missing all this class time."

Meanwhile, when his unit wasn't busy working in the communities surrounding the National Guard headquarters in Houma, La., it busied itself in an abandoned Fruit-of-the-Loom warehouse, where they at least had some modern amenities. "We watched some football, and played cards. But I couldn't enjoy it because all I could think about was getting back home to my family, my girlfriend, and to my classes," he said.

The mission itself was an intense learning experience for Michael. A specialist who has trained at the nation's leading burn center in Houston, Texas, Michael particularly enjoyed helping children after the storm. While most people that he and his associates helped were extremely grateful, many were not. "We had people spit at us, call us names. When people didn't get the stuff they wanted fast enough or when the government wasn't there to help like they thought they should, some got real nasty. I couldn't believe that. We were just there trying to help them. We didn't have to be," he said.

In the end, Michael said his experience has prepared him abundantly for a future career in medicine. "Most people," he said, "haven't seen the things I've seen in the field. Especially, not at my age. I don't think there's much you could throw at me at this point that I haven't handled already. So in a way, it was a good experience. But man, I don't think I'd want to ever go through that again."

As Michael's story illustrates, dealing with other people's problems effectively is difficult when one has similar problems of his or her own. In Michael's case, his inability to help his father repair their home after the storm, coupled with his anger at his younger brother for letting down the family, stretched his patience as he attended to the medical needs of hurricane survivors. Anxiety about the welfare of his mother and sisters also weighed heavily on the young man's mind, all while he wondered if he'd ever get to go back to college or be stuck "in the field" forever.

Families undergoing traumatic experiences like natural disasters struggle with many issues and a range of emotions, making communication difficult at best and impossible at worst. As our interviews revealed, sometimes technology fails family members, creating an information void that prevents communication altogether. This can create increased anxiety, fear, confusion, loneliness and the use of imagined interactions to cope with the unknown. Other times, the situational specifics of a family's travails create incendiary scenes that produce anger, resentment or other conflict. But true to each case, the individuals involved acknowledged an increased understanding and appreciation for their loved ones, despite the respective hardships that each endured.

Best Practices

The interviews with our families revealed a combination of emotions. The men reported surprise as their most intense and frequent emotion while women reported fear. Perhaps these men thought it was not masculine to show fear. Other research has revealed that boys compared to girls are not socially reinforced for communicating fear while girls are allowed to communicate a greater variety of emotions (e.g., Gottman, Gottman, & DeClaire, 2006). It can also be said that at least for two of the male participants, Matt B. and Mike H., the storm—while it did produce ample anxiety—also provided a real-life survival scenario that allowed the two to "test their mettle." Each expressed a certain amount of satisfaction in knowing that they could not only take care of themselves during the crisis, but also to help others in their time of need, which gave them a sense of purpose and served to minimize their own personal trauma.

Each participant, male and female, also ranked anticipation as a prevalent emotion felt during the hours preceding landfall. For those who heeded experts' warnings and prepared adequately, gathering supplies and making last minute communication with loved ones and family members, anxiety was reduced. While a family can never fully prepare for all of the contingencies that occur during the unpredictable aftermath of a natural disaster, at least taking some precautions seems to lessen the impact on interpersonal communication within the family structure. Hence, we advise families to openly communicate a variety of positive and negative emotions and to have imagined interactions with absent family members. A variety of studies clearly reveal the benefits of thinking about loved ones while outside of their physical presence (review Honeycutt, 2003; 2008).

References

Barry, J. M. (2002, October). The 1927 Mississippi River flood and its impact on U.S. society and flood management strategy. Paper presented at the Geological Society of American annual convention, Denver, CO.

Ekman, P. (1999). Basic emotions. In T. Dalgleish & T. Power (Eds.), *The handbook of cognition and emotion*, pp. 45–60. New York: John Wiley & Sons.

Foa, E., Zinburg, R., & Rothbaum, B. (1992). Uncontrollability and unpredictability in post-traumatic stress disorder: An animal model. *Psychological Bulletin*, 112, 218–238.

Gottman, J. M., Gottman, J. S., & DeClaire, J. (2006). *Ten lessons to transform your marriage.* New York: Crown.

Groome, D., & Soureti, A. (2004). Post-traumatic stress disorder and anxiety symptoms in children exposed to the 1999 Greek earthquake. *British Journal of Psychology, 95,* 387–397.

Guerrero, L., Andersen, P., & Trost, M. (1998). Communication and emotion: Basic concepts and approaches. In *Handbook of communication and emotion: Research, theory, applications, and contexts* (pp. 1–29). San Diego: Academic Press.

Honeycutt, J. M. (2003). *Imagined interactions: Daydreaming about communication.* Cresskill, NJ: Hampton.

Honeycutt, J. M. (2008). Imagined interaction theory. In D. O. Braithwaite & L. A. Baxter (Eds.), *Engaging theories of interpersonal communication,* pp. 77–87. Thousand Oaks, CA: Sage.

Honeycutt, J. M. (2010). Introduction. In J. M. Honeycutt (Ed.), *Imagine that: Studies in imagined interaction,* pp. 1–14. Cresskill, NJ: Hampton.

Honeycutt, J. M., Nasser, K. A., Banner, J. M., Mapp, C. M., & DuPont, B. W. (2008). Individual differences in catharsis, emotional valence, trauma anxiety, and social networks among Hurricane Katrina and Rita victims. *Southern Communication Journal, 73,* 1–14.

Horowitz, M.J. (1976). *Stress response syndromes.* Oxford, UK: Jason Aronson.

Kessler, R.C., Galea, S., Jones, R. T., & Parker, H. A. (2006). Mental illness and suicidality after Hurricane Katrina. *Bulletin of the World Health Organization, 84,* 921–1000.

Kubler-Ross, E., & Kessler, D. (2007). *On grief and grieving: Finding the meaning of grieving through the five stages of loss.* New York: Simon & Schuster.

LeDoux, J. C. (1996). *The emotional brain.* New York: Touchstone.

Shalev, A. Y. (2002). Acute stress reactions in adults. *Biological Psychiatry, 51,* 532–543.

Tuval-Machiach, R., Freedman, S., Bargai, N., Boker, R., Hadar, H., & Shalev, A. (2004). Coping with trauma: Narrative and cognitive perspectives. *Psychiatry, 6,* 280–295.

Authors' Academic Biographies

Tara J. Abbott (MA, University of Georgia, 2008) is a Research Associate at the Medical College of South Carolina.

Patricia Amason (PhD, Purdue University, 1993) is an Associate Professor and Associate Chair, Department of Communication, University of Arkansas. Her research examines provision of social support in interpersonal relationships and the communication surrounding sexual issues between romantic partners. Her research appears in *Journal of Applied Communication Research, Communication Studies, Communication Yearbook 10, Southern Communication Journal, Sex Roles, Health Communication,* and *Journal of Family Communication.*

Christine Aramburu Alegría (PhD, University of Nevada Reno, 2008) is Assistant Professor at the Orvis School of Nursing at the University of Nevada Reno. Her work appears in the *Journal of Psychiatric and Mental Health Nursing, Journal of the American Academy of Nurse Practitioners,* and the *Encyclopedia of Family Health* (Vol. 1). Her research focuses primarily on health promotion and identity in vulnerable and marginalized populations.

Paul Arntson (PhD, University of Wisconsin) is on the faculty of the Asset Based Community Development Institute and a Fellow at the Center for Communication and Medicine, Northwestern University. Current research includes understanding how pediatric cancer survivors and their parents communicate about their cancer experiences, how to improve communication between primary care providers and deaf patients, how community based organizations contribute to the well-being of their neighborhoods, and how families can make informed decisions concerning fertility options when their daughters are diagnosed with having cancer.

Mary Z. Ashlock (PhD, Florida State University, 1989) is an Assistant Professor in the Department of Communication at the University of Louisville. Her extensive background in business adds to her expertise in her research on organizational communication, gender, and health communication.

K. Tiffani Baldwin (PhD candidate, University of Denver) is a fourth year Fellow, University of Denver, who is currently completing her dissertation on aging and masculinity. She teaches courses in gender, culture, and interpersonal communication.

Deborah S. Ballard-Reisch (PhD, Bowling Green State University, 1983) is the Kansas Health Foundation Distinguished Chair in Strategic Communication, Professor, Elliott School of Communication, Wichita State University. Her work appears in *The Family Communication Sourcebook* and *Computer Mediated Communication in Personal Relationships.* She has published articles in *Personal Relationships, Women and Language, Journal of Family Communication, Public Health Reports, Journal of Social and Personal Relationships, Patient Education and Counseling, Family and Consumer Sciences Research Journal, Family Relations,* and the *Journal of Family Issues* among others. Her scholarship focuses on relationship maintenance, commitment and satisfaction in romantic relationships, family communication, health, and community-based change initiatives.

Justin P. Borowsky is an Assistant Professor of Speech Communication at Central Oregon Community College. Justin's areas of interest include conflict, conflict resolution, mediation, and hostage/crisis negotiation. His most recent work examines the use of persuasive strategies in hostage negotiation events. Justin's work has been published in the *Journal of Police Crisis Negotiation.* He holds a master's degree in Communication and Information Studies from Rutgers University and is a Ph.D. candidate at the University of Denver.

Patrice M. Buzzanell (PhD, Purdue University) is Professor and 2008-2010 W. Charles and Ann Redding Faculty Fellow in the Department of Communication at Purdue University. Her research centers on leadership, work-life issues, and gendered careers associated with science, technology, engineering, and math (STEM). Buzzanell has edited *Rethinking Organizational and Managerial Communication From Feminist Perspectives* (2000), *Gender in Applied Communication Contexts* (2004, with H. Sterk and L. Turner), and *Distinctive Qualities in Communication Research* (2010, with D. Carbaugh). Author of 100 articles, chapters, and reviews, she also has edited *Management Communication Quarterly* and has served as President of the International Communication Association (ICA).

Heather E. Canary (PhD, Arizona State University, 2007) is Assistant Professor in the Department of Communication at the University of Utah. Her work appears in *The International Encyclopedia of Communication* as well as *Communication and Organizational Knowledge: Contemporary Issues for Theory and Practice.* She has published articles in the *American Journal of Public Health, Communication Education, Communication Monographs, Communication Quarterly, Communication Theory, Health Communication, Journal of Applied Communication Research, Journal of Business Ethics,* and *Management Communication Quarterly.* Her research focuses on organizational and family processes, particularly processes that co-influence each other in contexts of disability, health, and public policies.

Jennifer Kellie Corti (PhD, University of Denver, 2009) is an Assistant Professor, Azusa Pacific University. She has presented her work on sibling relationships at annual meetings of the National Communication Association. Her research focuses on communication in sibling relationships during the young adult years.

Lindsay J. Della (PhD, University of Georgia, 2006) is an Assistant Professor in the Department of Communication at the University of Louisville. She holds a doctorate in public health and conducts health communication research.

Fran C. Dickson (PhD, Bowling Green State University, 1983) is Professor and Department Chair of Communication Studies, Chapman University. She previously served as a tenured faculty member at the University of Denver. Her work appears in *Handbook of Marriage and the Family* (2nd ed.), *Engaging Theories in Family Communication: Multiple Perspectives,* and *The Family Communication Sourcebook.* She has published articles in the *Southern Communication Journal, Qualitative Research Reports in Communication, The Journal of Applied Communication Research, Journal of Social and Personal Relationships,* and *Journal of Family Communication.* Her research focuses primarily on later-life adults' communication in personal and family relationships.

Steve Duck (PhD, University of Sheffield, UK, 1971) is the Daniel and Amy Starch Distinguished Research Professor at the University of Iowa, where he is Chair of the Rhetoric Department. He has written or edited 50 books on relationships. He founded and served for 15 years as editor of the *Journal of Social and Personal Relationships.* He is the 2010 Distinguished Scholar for the National Communication Association. His 1994 book, *Meaningful Relationships: Talking, Sense, and Relating* won the G.R. Miller Book Award from the Interpersonal Communication Division of the National Communication Association.

Carla L. Fisher (PhD, Pennsylvania State University, 2008) is an Assistant Professor at George Mason University. She is a former Pre-doctoral Fellow with the National Institute on Aging and received advanced post-doctoral training in health behavior theory co-sponsored by the National Cancer Institute. Her research uses a life-span perspective and focuses on the centrality of family communication to health. Her research has appeared in *Health Communication* and *Journal of Applied Communication Research.* She is currently expanding her research on mothers and daughters coping with breast cancer in a collaborative study with Mayo Clinic and a forthcoming book on the subject.

Kathleen Galvin (PhD, Northwestern University) is a Professor of Communication Studies at Northwestern University. She is the author, co-author, or editor of eight books and numerous articles and book chapters in family communication and relational communication. She is the senior author of *Family Communication: Cohesion and Change*, now in its eighth edition. Currently Professor Galvin is involved in two lines of research: these are (1) family interaction regarding issues of health as well as genetics and (2) the role of discourse in the creation and dissolution of family identity.

Lauren Grill (PhD, Northwestern University) is a Visiting Lecturer in the Department of Communication at the University of Illinois Urbana-Champaign. She is also the program coordinator and academic advisor for the Health Communication Online Master's Program. She is the co-author of "Opening Up the Conversation on Genetics and Genomics in Families" in *Communication Yearbook* (2009) and "Expressing Affection: A Vocabulary of Loving Messages" in *Making Connections: Readings in Relational Communication*.

Joy L. Hart (PhD, University of Kentucky, 1988) is Professor in the Department of Communication at the University of Louisville. Her research focuses on health and organizational communication. She is particularly interested in language and sense-making processes.

Anita Hoag (MA, University of Louisville) conducts research on communication in close relationships. She is specifically interested in family communication and adolescent friendships.

James M. Honeycutt (PhD, University of Illinois, Urbana-Champaign) is Professor of Communication Studies at the Louisiana State University and co-editor of *Imagination, Cognition, and Personality*. The winner of numerous scholarly awards, he has published books dealing with relational and intrapersonal communication as well as more than 75 articles and chapters. His research focuses on relationship scripts and imagined interactions.

Daniel Johnson (PhD candidate, University of Denver) reports primary research interests in family and interpersonal communication, with a dissertation focus on the development of the parental role in higher education evolving from the triadic relationship between students, parents, and university personnel. He received his master's degree in speech communication from the University of Southern Illinois Edwardsville.

Kayla B. Johnson (MA, University of Arkansas, 2008) serves as Executive Director of The Zoe Foundation Inc. (http://www.zoe-foundation.org), a not-for-profit organization that provides financial and emotional support to families who have experienced the loss of an infant due to miscarriage, stillbirth, SIDS, and chromosomal disorders. Her research has been published in the *Journal of Family Communication* and presented at annual meetings of the National Communication Association, the American Communication Association, and the Western States Communication Association.

Karen E. Kinahan (MS, RN, PCNS-BC) is a Clinical Nurse Specialist at Robert H. Lurie Comprehensive Cancer Center of Northwestern University in Chicago, Illinois. She has spent her entire 24 year nursing career in pediatric oncology, and has spent the last 16 years working with survivors of childhood cancer exclusively. In 2001, with the support of the Lurie Cancer Center she started a comprehensive follow-up program for adult survivors of childhood cancer called the STAR Program (Survivors Taking Action & Responsibility). Karen is recognized as a nursing pioneer in the field of childhood cancer survivorship, and adult transition. She has made numerous presentations at both national and international nursing meetings.

Lucie P. Lawrence (PhD, University of Denver, 2011) conducts research on family communication, health communication, and disability studies. Her work appears in the *Journal of Loss and Trauma* and the *Journal of Marriage and Family*. Her dissertation uses narratives to examine the lived experiences of mothers raising children with and without disabilities

Katheryn Maguire (PhD, University of Texas at Austin, 2001) is an Assistant Professor in the Department of Communication at Wayne State University. Her work has been published in books including *Computer-Mediated Communication in Personal Relationships* and *Current Advances in Anti- & Pro-Social Communication: An Examination of Theories, Methods, and Applications,* as well as journals, including *Communication Monographs, Journal of Applied Communication Research, Communication Education,* and *Communication Quarterly.* Her research centers on how individuals use communication to maintain relationships and cope with stressful situations in challenging contexts, such as military deployments, long distance romances, and hurtful family environments.

Christopher Mapp (PhD candidate, Louisiana State University) is an Assistant Professor of Mass Communication at the University of Louisiana at Monroe. In addition to teaching journalism and quantitative methods, he is the Director of Student Publications, including the student newspaper, yearbook, and a literary magazine. Mapp's research interests include imagined interactions, forgiveness, verbal aggressiveness, revenge, long-distance relationships, social media, parasocial relationships and loneliness.

John Nicholson (PhD, University of Iowa, 1998) is an Assistant Professor of Communication Studies at Mississippi State University. He previously served as a tenured Associate Professor at Angelo State University. His research focuses primarily on family communication. He examines the intersection of rhetorical and the interpersonal in research on nicknames and sibling alliances. He has published in the *Journal of Family Communication, Journal of Social and Personal Relationships,* and multiple edited volumes.

Jon F. Nussbaum (PhD, Purdue University) is a Professor of Communication Arts & Sciences and Human Development & Family Studies at Pennsylvania State University. An International Communication Association Fellow, Fellow within the Adult Development and Aging Division of American Psychological

Association, and 2008 International Communication Associa-
tion/National Communication Association Health Communication Scholar of the Year, he is considered a leading international
researcher in life-span, health, and aging communication. He has
published extensively about communication across the life span,
including 11 books and more than 70 articles and chapters.

Jennifer A. Samp (PhD, University of Wisconsin, Madison, 1999) is
Associate Professor in the Department of Communication Studies
at the University of Georgia. Her work examines how people
translate and communicate their thoughts about relational problems to others, with a focus on how people manage conflict,
stress, and difficulties in their close romantic relationships.

Erin Sahlstein (PhD, University of Iowa, 2000) is an Associate Professor of Communication Studies, University of Nevada, Las Vegas.
Her work appears in *Relating Difficulty: The Processes of Constructing and Managing Difficult Interaction, Maintenance Enhancement,
Interpersonal communication: Advances through Meta-Analysis, Handbook of Language and Social Behavior,* and *Balancing Disclosure, Privacy, and Secrecy.* She has published articles in *Journal of Applied
Communication Research, Journal of Social and Personal Relationships,
Communication Monographs, Western Journal of Communication,* and
Qualitative Research Reports in Communication. Her research focuses
primarily on communication within geographically separated relationships such as military families and long-distance dating
couples.

Allison R. Thorson (PhD, University of Nebraska) is an Assistant
Professor in the Communication Studies Department at the University of San Francisco. Her primary area of research is the communication surrounding unanticipated and hurtful family and
relationship events, with a particular focus on the communication
surrounding infidelity.

Lynn H. Turner (PhD, Northwestern University, 1989) is Professor of
Communication Studies at Marquette University in the Diederich

College of Communication. Her articles have appeared in *Management Communication Quarterly, Journal of Applied Communication Research, Women and Language, Journal of Family Communication,* and *Western Journal of Communication.* Her books include *From the Margins to the Center: Contemporary Women and Political Communication* (with Patricia Sullivan), *Gender in Applied Communication Contexts* (with Patrice Buzzanell and Helen Sterk), *Introducing Communication Theory, 4th ed., Perspectives on Family Communication, 3rd ed.,* and *The Family Communication Sourcebook* (all with Richard West). Her areas of research include interpersonal, gendered, and family communication.

Joseph G. Velasco (PhD candidate, University of Denver) is a Lecturer of Communication at Sul Ross State University. His research focuses on the communication of emotion within family contexts and other personal relationships, as well as the cognitive bases of relationships and their influence on interpersonal communication.

Kandi L. Walker (PhD, University of Denver, 1999) is an Associate Professor in the University of Louisville's Department of Communication. She conducts research in interpersonal, health, and family communication. She is especially interested in communication, families, and aging.

Lynne M. Webb (PhD, University of Oregon, 1980) is Professor in Communication, University of Arkansas. She previously served as a tenured faculty member at the Universities of Florida and Memphis. Her work appears in *Motherhood Online: How On-Line Communities Shape Modern Motherhood, Computer Mediated Communication in Personal Relationships, Applied Health Communication: A Sourcebook,* and *Communication in Later Life.* She has published articles in multiple journals including *Journal of Family Communication, Journal of Applied Communication Research, Health Communication, Computers in Human Behavior,* and the *International Journal of Social Research and Methodology.* Her research focuses primarily on young adults' interpersonal communication in romantic and family contexts.

Megan L. Wilson (MA, University of Arkansas, 2009) is a doctoral student at the University of Kentucky. Her work appears in the edited volume *Social Media: Usage and Impact* and has been presented at annual meetings of the Southern States Communication Association and the National Communication Association. Her research focuses on the communication of social support within family contexts and other personal relationships.

Index